ESSAYS IN ENGLISH LITERATURE FROM THE RENAISSANCE TO THE VICTORIAN AGE PRESENTED TO A. S. P. WOODHOUSE

Essays in English Literature from the Renaissance to the Victorian Age

PRESENTED TO

A. S. P. WOODHOUSE

1964

Edited by Millar MacLure
and F. W. Watt

UNIVERSITY OF TORONTO PRESS

Reprinted 1965 in U.S.A.

Reprinted in 2018
ISBN 978-1-4875-7723-0 (paper)

Introduction

IN ONE VERY IMPORTANT SENSE Professor Woodhouse is the "onlie begetter" of this collection of essays in his honour. For the contributors are representative of his professional colleagues in this University and elsewhere, and of his former students, and these essays range over the interests which for forty years he has made his wide province: Spenser and Milton, the imaginative and ideological writings of the seventeenth century, the origins of romanticism and the history of ideas in the eighteenth century, the main traditions and revolutions of nineteenth-century thought. This book is a token of associations entered upon in goodwill and sustained by many happy occasions, academic and personal.

The essay by Douglas Bush places A. S. P. Woodhouse's work in its larger context of international scholarship. It remains for us to refer briefly to associations which are of a more local character, though no less significant on that account. Not the least of these is Professor Woodhouse's connection with the *University of Toronto Quarterly*, continuous almost since its founding in the mid-1930's; he has been associate editor, co-editor, chief editor, chairman of the editorial committee, and chairman of the advisory board, and some of his most important articles and reviews have appeared in its pages. It is scarcely too much to say that the *Quarterly* has been the focus of all his manifold concerns, so that it seems appropriate that this volume should appear under its auspices, arranged by its present editors.

The allusion in "onlie begetter" is in another sense highly incongruous. No one could be less anonymous. All of us whose names are in this book, and hundreds of others in the academic community, whether in Toronto, across Canada, in many American universities, or in the common rooms of older foundations overseas, have felt the influence of a unique and powerful personality, by turns genial and stern, diplomatic and intransigent, a treasurer of uproarious academic anecdotes, an expositor of uncommon lucidity, and a formidable disputant. His role as academic statesman has had, like his scholarly publication, a strongly centrifugal movement. At the centre has always been his vigilant faith in the honours course at the University of Toronto, a tradition whose continuance was assured for English studies largely through his own work (in close collaboration with E. K. Brown) of renovation and reformation. From exemplar and defender of the honours system, then director and apologist for the graduate program in English, he has extended his influence to the executive of the Modern Languages Association and the International Association of Professors of English, and in another direction to the editorial boards of the Yale Edition of Milton's Prose and the Columbia Variorum commentary on Milton's poetical works.

But here it is his contribution to the advancement of learning in Canada which deserves the greatest emphasis. When in 1943 the humane disciplines were near to extinction in this country, and the Royal Society of Canada (to which he had just been elected and was later to give guidance as an executive officer) began its counter-attack through the formation of the Humanities Research Council of Canada, he was among those who laid the groundwork for the programs of assistance to scholarship, the surveys of traditions and needs (epitomized in *The Humanities in Canada*, written, compiled and edited by him and Watson Kirkconnell), and the unabashed scrounging for funds from the Rockefeller Foundation and elsewhere, which until the creation of the Canada Council made possible the continuance and development of research and teaching in the humanities in Canadian universities. There was a time, during which he was either an influential member or chairman of the Humanities Research Council, besides holding his position as head of the only fully established graduate department of English in the country, when he created careers as his daily work: he taught the students in honours and graduate courses, he supervised theses and the supervisors of theses, he found the funds for research and recommended grants in aid of publication of research, and he recommended his men for academic positions. His office in University College was an imperial secretariat, from which proconsuls departed to Canadian universities from coast to coast, and to universities outside Canada.

We write as if this had ceased: it has not, but with the proliferation of universities, and the growing influence of those whose influence he created, it has become part of a very complex system; the empire has not dissolved but has been transformed. If a single occasion had to be chosen to signify that transformation it might well be that June day in 1957 when he presided in Ottawa over the formal creation of the Association of Canadian University Teachers of English, now a flourishing institution. If we could only collect his correspondence over these years, and the "academic exercises" (appraisals of theses, memorials, reports) to go with it, we should have an invaluable record of English studies in Canada during their most important period of development and expansion. If we could assemble his letters of recommendation during the same period we who have been his protégés would appear as heroic figures prepared to dare the provincial philistines, if not in "the armour of a Christian man" (though that too in some cases, we suspect), at least in the humanist equipment which he and his trusted colleagues had done their best to provide.

We return to the centre, to the discipline of letters, which all these actions of policy have served, and to the relations between persons which that discipline in turn serves, and without which it is sterile. We do not expect Professor Woodhouse to agree with all the versions of literary history exhibited in this collection, or to find congenial all the critical strategies employed. He may, however, discover much here to support his faith in "productive scholarship" as he once defined it: the kind of scholarship that helps bridge the chasm between "research" and "education," and that produces men as well as books. We hope that he will take pleasure in reading these essays, and that retirement from the multiple responsibilities he has borne for so long will afford him for many years to come the busy leisure of the scholar.

M.M.
F.W.W.

Contents

ESSAYS IN ENGLISH LITERATURE FROM THE RENAISSANCE TO THE VICTORIAN AGE

PRESENTED TO A. S. P. WOODHOUSE

"Spenserus"[1]

ROSEMOND TUVE

ON THE LAST PAGE of a Bodleian manuscript of Gower's *Confessio Amantis* written in a clear early fifteenth-century hand, and bearing the signature of a dedicatee of Spenser's, we encounter the following Ovidian album-sentiment, written in an Italian hand too ordinary to identify as Spenser's or not Spenser's:

Tempore foelici
multi numerantur amici
Cum fortuna perit
nullus amicus erit
} Spenserus

This is not likely as a mistaken attribution; Spenser nowhere translates, quotes, or puts forward as his own the two lines from Ovid's *Tristia* (I.ix.5) which are the proper form of the tag. The closest it ever came to the Spenser canon—and this is interesting enough—is that it is the "Theame out of Ovid" which Harvey says he set as an exercise, and of which he gives all three English versions alleged to be done by his brother John, in one of the *Three Proper and Wittie Familiar Letters* printed in 1580 as having been exchanged between Harvey and Spenser.

What other "Spenserus" would inscribe sentiments in Lady Warwick's Gower, or rather the Russell Gower in which she wrote while she was still a Russell? And sentiments, moreover, which arose out of the famous Ovidian punishment for having written what Spenser was reproved for, too-amorous love poems? For we remember that the dedication to Lady Warwick (jointly with her sister) was the one to the *Fowre Hymnes* wherein we learn about that reproof. Though Ovid's exile was far harsher than anything which happened to make Spenser feel the cold wind of loss of support when one wrote the wrong thing, we recall that the snub may have been quite noticeably discouraging in an age of patronage, when "one of you two most excellent Ladies," either Lady Warwick or her sister, actually urged the calling-in of two hymns in praise of Love and Beauty, because they overmuch pleased young readers "vehemently caried with that kind of affection." Ovid's *Ars Amatoria* of course *was* called in (expelled from libraries), and the quoted bit comes from that poem, the *Tristia*, in which he makes the same several excuses for it that Spenser was to make when he addressed to the two ladies a "retractation" for *his* unfortunate love poems.

But this puzzling dedication is not the only token of Spenser's connections with the family whose Gower volume was inscribed by "Spenserus" and by "Anne Russell." Anne, Lady Warwick, shares with her sister Margaret Russell Clifford, Lady Cumberland, the dedication of the *Hymnes*, is the Theana of *Colin Clouts Come Home Againe*, and is addressed throughout several stanzas of the *Ruines of Time*; her father the second Earl of Bedford and his grandson and heir Edward are praised in the same poem; Anne was sister to a Lord Deputy of Ireland (1594–7; Sir William Russell) whom Spenser mentions in the *Veue* and could not but know; she was step-sister to Lord Grey's wife; she was married in 1565 to Leicester's brother Ambrose Dudley, Earl of Warwick, and was thus Leicester's and Lady Sidney's sister-in-law; she was a member by birth of one, by marriage of another, of two great houses (closely and continuously associated) who outstandingly represented the Protestant faction to which Spenser gave lifelong allegiance, and he had early connections with both.

This *Confessio Amantis* in MS. Bodl. 902, its easy Middle English as legible as blackletter, at least had enough sixteenth-century attention to be inscribed several times, but it belonged to a very bookish family. On f.80^{v} we find in a sixteenth-century hand "Be me Anne Russell."[1] The Anne Russell who became Lady Warwick and Spenser's friend and dedicatee did not break off her Bedford connec-

1. No description remarks upon the Latin "Spenserus" note. See the otherwise full description in Macaulay's edition of Gower, II, cxxxix, mentioning Anne Russell's signature and identifying d'Annebaut's. If we may suppose Macaulay's description correct, two errors may be amended in that of the *Summary Catalogue* (no. 27573)—Anne Russell's name and that of the donor: Gilbert *Dolben*, grand-nephew of Archbishop Sheldon.

tions when she married into the allied and congenial Dudley-Sidney connection; her husband died in 1589/90 but she herself continued to be an influential court figure until 1604. She was eldest daughter to Sir Francis Russell, second Earl. The family was an important one in the annals of Protestant statesmanship and literary patronage in England.[2] Her grandfather John, the great first Earl of Bedford (d. 1555) was Lord Privy Seal and Lord High Admiral, after decades of varied services, was an important official in the West, an "encourager of literature" and author of two Latin treatises (Wiffen, I, 395). Her father (?1527–1585) was an important Protestant servant of the state; imprisoned for his religious opinions and (evidently largely by his own choice) forming ties with the group of reformers in Switzerland during Mary's reign, he was one of Elizabeth's first Privy Council, helped to remodel the religious establishment, was sent on important missions to France and Scotland, was associated continuously with the Sidneys and the Leicester group (*v.* Wiffen, I, 397 ff.), and was the owner of one of the most extensive Elizabethan libraries of whose contents we have record.[3] In fact, the recent discovery of the importance among Elizabethan patrons of this family, to whose various members Spenser gives such repeated attention, calls for some new observation of relations, and "a Bedford book" or "a Bedford copy of a mediaeval author" becomes something more interesting than it was. The outstanding collector, the second Earl, lost his son on the day before his own death in July, 1585, and the heir and young grandson Edward was the ward of his influential aunt, Anne—a relation on which Spenser comments in the *Ruines of Time* passage (1591). Of Anne's sister and co-dedicatee, Margaret Lady Cumberland (Spenser's Marian, also), and of their brother Lord William Russell of Thornhaugh, the Lord Deputy mentioned in the *Veue*, we may speak more particularly later.

2. Biographical facts on the Bedfords are taken from the *DNB* articles and from Jeremiah Wiffen, *Historical Memoirs of the House of Russell* (London, 1833); corrections and additions are made from G. Scott Thomson, *Two Centuries of Family History* (London, 1930).

3. See M. Byrne and G. Scott Thomson, "My Lord's Books," *RES*, VII (1931), 385–405, for a contemporary list of the printed books in this library, with identifications, dedications, and other useful materials. The reference to the uncatalogued earlier MSS. is at 385; some may have been kept in his house in the West. The patronage and interest in "reformer" authors is noteworthy. Some information above (e.g. on Francis Bedford's religious opinions) is to be found in Scott Thomson, *Two Centuries*, 204–11.

Did Spenser read some of the medieval books he knew, in manuscript? What we know about the attitudes of Elizabethans toward manuscript books is likely to be confined to the great collectors—the Arundels and the Archbishop Parkers and the Dr. Dees. I should say at once that in this case it makes very little practical difference, for Gower's famous poem could be read by men of Spenser's time—when it had very much more prestige than now—in three editions. Caxton printed it in 1483, Berthelet provided two editions, 1532 and 1554. Still it would be pleasant to envisage Spenser as having access to the Bedford books, including "all my auncient written englishe bookes..." not in the list of 1584, and reading or turning over this Gower with its miniature of the old poet, and writing his name (as did another visitor) on a flyleaf at the end. There are several obstructions to be removed before one would dare enjoy this pleasant picture even as conjecture.

To previous describers of the MS., the signature on f.80ᵛ was simply that of any sixteenth-century "Anne Russell," and at first there seemed to be nothing to connect the book indisputably with the Bedford Russells. But on f.184ᵛ there appears several times in an early sixteenth-century hand the name "John Browghton"—and Sir John Bedford, later first Earl, married in 1526 Anne Sapcote the widow of Sir John Broughton. So this was undeniably a Bedford book. It probably came to them with the manor of Chenies, a Broughton property that became the Russell family's chief seat and was a favoured residence of Lady Warwick; she was buried there.[4] Here then is an earlier "Anne Russell" if one thinks the signature thus early, but one is more interested in the fact that we may surely connect this volume with this family.

In addition, however: Bodleian MS. Ballard 43 contains (f.133) a letter from Anne Lady Warwick, 1579. A mild complication occurred here in Ballard's appended (eighteenth-century) identification of its writer with Anne *Seymour*, Lady Warwick; but this lady had been mad for twenty-three years. Moreover, a scrap of endorsement proves the letter to be written to the wife of Sir Nicholas Malbie in Ireland—

4. See Wiffen, I, 272, 396 n.; II, 61; the book probably passed to the Bedfords, like Chenies or with it, in consequence of the death of Lady Bedford's son "young Mr. Broughton"; Sir John Bedford became Baron Russell of Chenies (1538) and passed on the Broughton properties, to his son the second earl, Lady Warwick's father.

formerly secretary to Ambrose Dudley—and its contents fit in with our Lady Warwick's importance at court as favour-dispenser for Elizabeth, and her friendship with the correspondent, a previous dependent.[5] These facts are another tie between Spenser and this whole set of people, especially perhaps Lady Warwick; he too evidently knew Malbie.[6] It is safe to assume that Spenser's friend Anne Russell wrote this letter; though a signature is too little for proof, the similarities between this one and that in the Gower MS.[7] are persuasive enough, added to the rest of the circumstances, to convince us that at least one learned lady whom Spenser knew did not leave a Gower in manuscript untouched on her father's shelves. It must have been got out to show to interested visitors—a not unfamiliar habit of bookish men in their libraries—if we are to explain another sixteenth-century inscription on the same leaf as the little squib labelled "Spenserus" (f.184^{r}). For down the side we read "Anniballis·Admiralis·dominicalis" in a sixteenth-century hand, and this can hardly be any other than Claude d'Annebaut; the Broughton connection puts ownership by him out of the question, and the signature or inscription must belong to Sir John Bedford's time.[8] Or it may have been written in later for some reason we could not now hope to guess.

5. Lady Warwick's letter thanks Lady Nicholas Malbie for a gift of linen, praises Sir Nicholas' services in Ireland, and protests willingness to further their prospects if she can. The Bodleian *Summary Cat.* (no. 10829) identification depends solely upon Ballard's note, I am told, but his statement is a far from likely one; Anne Seymour married John Dudley (Earl of Warwick 1552, who died in 1554 when the title became extinct); his lady remarried, and became insane 1556 (G.E.C., *Complete Peerage*). None of this fits the letter's date and contents.

6. Malbie or Malby belonged to the Leicester faction, had Sir Henry Sidney's approval, came to Grey's aid at Glenmalure (Spenser was there, 1580), was interested in "undertaking," and as President of Connaught was criticized much as was Grey for too free use of the sword. See an account of a 1581 consultation at which Spenser was present (*View*, ed. Renwick [London, 1934], 240). On all these Irish matters I use the apparatus to the *Var. Sp.* prose volume, but also very frequently the articles of R. Jenkins based on letters in Spenser's hand (as here the one touching on Spenser and Connaught, in *PLMA*, LII [1937], 338–53, "Spenser with Lord Grey in Ireland"). Judson's *Life* in the *Var. Sp.* is the source of some connections and dates.

7. In the capital *A*, in the *n* penstroke; allowance made for the difference in the writer's age and for that between writing on the margin of a large parchment book and on a sheet of letter-paper.

8. Claude d'Annebaut or d'Hanybal, Admiral of France, after his inept expedition against England in 1545, came over to sign the peace of June 7, 1546 (Ch. de la Roncière, *Histoire de la marine française* [Paris, 1906], III, 417–31). The Earl of Bedford would no longer officially represent England for he had ceased to be Lord High Admiral in 1542, but he had taken an active part in the affair as

The importance of the Bedford family as possible patrons for a poet and civil servant like Spenser to look to, despite their lack of male scions who could stay alive, was not apparent until the discovery of his 1584 book-list revealed Sir Francis the second Earl as an outstanding support to letters. Even if the twenty-three dedications discovered by editors of the book-list were his total, no one approaches him but that famous dedicatee Leicester. They discovered also ten dedications to members of the Earl's immediate family; and of the other most famous patrons, Hatton, Walsingham, Sidney, Lord Oxford, three (with Leicester) must be accounted as attached to this interrelated and congenial group of families. The web of relationships is of course especially pertinent for Spenser, with his early tie to Leicester, particularly if Ambrose Dudley's wife Anne Russell had connections with the poet for some time before the late dedication to her (1596). Several books in the list were dedicated to the Earl's son-in-law Lord Warwick, some jointly to him and his wife Anne.[9] The size and solidity of the Earl's book-list (162 separate mostly "current" books, 221 with duplicates), the continued close interest in religious and theological affairs shown in patronage and in ownership, the cultivated variety (given this date), remind us of the owner's distinguished past services and his firm connection, like this whole knot of families, with the Protestant faction we think of most as Sidney's and Leicester's. For the Earl had been an important court figure. Aside from the businesses with which she entrusted him, Elizabeth evidently maintained cordial relations with the family: she visited him (with her court, for several days) at Chenies, at Woburn,[10] quartered her foreign guests upon

President of the four southwest counties (see Wiffen, I, 336, 347, and letter in W. L. Clowes, *Royal Navy* [London, 1897], I, 465), was Privy Councillor 1546–7 and Lord Privy Seal 1542 till his death; Clowes describes a state visit of d'Annebaut to England August 24, 1547 (I, 466).

9. See numbers 11, 18, 48, 103, 113, 115 in the article referred to in n. 3; discussions of the character of the books and of some of the Earl's interests and patronage may be found especially at 391, 388–9. *Leicester Patron of Letters* has been thoroughly studied by E. Rosenberg (New York, 1955), extending vastly the number of known works dedicated to him (from the 22 known to the earlier scholars, to a list of 94). Also noticed and clarified are the relations with the reforming Protestant party of this group of patrons—Bedford, Warwick, Walsingham, Huntingdon (another brother-in-law of Anne Russell's), etc.; see Index, or, for example, 22–3, 229.

10. There Elizabeth was entertained with great liberality and the usual reluctance; see letters to Burleigh in Wiffen, I, 474, 479; for description of following events see *ibid.*, I, 426 ff., II, 13, I, 502.

him, stayed with his daughter-in-law; she attended her maid of honour Anne Russell's wedding, in state, to see Leicester give the bride away and view the two days of jousting and tourneys; she was godmother to Lady Warwick's niece by Lady Warwick her deputy.

Yet for all their marks of worldly success and the unassailable prestige of their connections, the Bedfords remained a family which stood for learning and for militant but dignified piety. The hope of poetry, to Spenser's eye, lay in such families. Lady Warwick was an exponent par excellence of the combination, and it is what Spenser stresses in his many praises. She had power and court prestige as her family had had before her. She was reputed Queen Elizabeth's chief feminine favourite (Wiffen, I, 430), having remained in attendance since the time when she was maid of honour, before her marriage in 1565. She had lived at court over a long period of years; the famous diary of her niece Lady Anne Clifford contains many references to her influential court connections. She evidently had the ear of the Queen. She acted, for example, as go-between for Essex, advising him to take lodgings in Greenwich while she would apprise him of the Queen's good moods that he might board her to his advantage (Wiffen, II, 56). There is often an accent of surprise in conveying the fact that it was Anne Clifford who put up the belated monument to Spenser in Westminster. But this is the Anne Clifford who tells of going up to court to festivities when she was 14 or thereabouts, and being lodged on a pallet in her aunt Warwick's chamber, for she is the daughter of Anne Russell's favourite younger sister Margaret (not married until 1577), and great shoals of her aunts and uncles dead and alive had had connections with the poet. No mere half-forgotten dedication to mother and aunt is behind this act of *pietas*, and it would be strange if Anne as a girl had never met Spenser, say at some such time as when he dates his letter from Greenwich where the court lay, and mentions the "great graces and honourable favours" which her aunt and mother "*dayly* shew" unto him.

Recent years have seen vigorous and badly needed correction of the old ideas about the appointment under Lord Grey, when it was thought correct to talk much about "exile" and "disappointment." We have been brought to realize that things may not have looked thus at all, especially to anyone who had been for a year or more in close contact with the Dudley circle; also, a sharper look at the Bedford connections with Grey shows us some other attitudes and possibilities, while Anne Russell, married to a Dudley, typifies the way these tight family groups, congenial in politics, pulled things together. Even long before, at Lady Warwick's wedding, Grey had been one of the knights chosen to "answer the challenge" (Wiffen, I, 426); he resided many years—from 1562 through the 1570's—at Whaddon, in the same county as Chenies (about twenty-five miles as the crow flies), where the Bedfords then chiefly resided. But whichever house they were living in, Grey probably came to court his wife in it, for she was Jane Sibylla Morison and her mother had become Lady Bedford in 1566 (after the death of her husband Sir Richard Morison, and the death in 1561 of the mother of the numerous Russell children). Moreover Jane Morison had gone from being step-sister to Anne, Margaret, William and the others, to being their sister-in-law, for her first marriage was to Edward Lord Russell their brother, probably about 1572; he must have died soon after 1573, since the marriage to Grey took place *ca.* 1574–75. Grey was at Whaddon; and his son and heir was born there *ca.* 1575–6.[11] It must be remembered that this twice-related Lady Grey was soon, beyond doubt, known well by Spenser; for the closeness with which Spenser worked with his chief has been very much illuminated by the discovered letters, and Ireland (and danger) drew men together. We need not question Judson's idea (71) that the Sidneys had much to do with Spenser's being recommended to Grey, but we begin to see that there is little need to wonder how well these various benefactors and friends knew each other.

In fact, a family contribution to the struggle in Ireland was made practically at the same time as Spenser in his different capacity was attached to Grey, for William Russell, the Earl's fourth and youngest son, just down from Oxford and back from the grand tour, went to Ireland in 1580—but in October, not August—and was knighted by Grey the next September. He was later to be Lord Deputy of Ireland (1594) and be mentioned in the *Veue* as "the honorable gentleman that nowe governethe theare," but there was an interlude in the Netherlands, with Leicester; he evidently had been intimate with Sidney, who had bequeathed him his best gilt armour and before as governor of Flushing had supported Leicester in his quarrel with the

11. He was 17 in 1592/93 (G.E.C. *Complete Peerage*). See *DNB*, and Wiffen, I, 430–80, on these marriages.

estates. He was to become Baron Russell of Thornhaugh, but it would be hard to believe that the two young men of 1580 remained strangers to each other, considering what ties there were between those interested in their futures, and considering what the older of the two had done and was doing. And to persons familiar with the milieu we have been delineating, an appointment in Ireland under Lord Grey would not seem either like losing touch with the civilized world or like burying the talents with which one had meant to serve one's country.

Spenser's esteem for the Russell family is most circumstantially evidenced by the long passages in *The Ruines of Time*. The context is important. Anne Russell, Lady Warwick, is addressed with praise and trust in several stanzas (240 ff.), in the voice of the woman who figures the destroyed, dead, forgotten Roman city of Verulam, once so proud and strong. This direct address is drawn in quite properly by the lament for Ambrose Dudley's death, which follows naturally the lament for his brother Leicester who so deserved the gratitude of poets, and of this poet; and thereafter follow references to Anne's father Lord Bedford, her nephew Edward the heir, Lady Sidney sister of the two Dudleys, dead before them, in the same year as her husband, and her son their nephew Sir Philip, who is lamented in the climax to this sad heap, that only makes one ask

> What booteth it to have beene rich alive?
> What to be great? what to be gracious? . . .
>
> How manie great ones may remembred be,
> Which in their daies most famouslie did florish;
> Of whom no word we heare. . . .

The direct address and eulogy of Anne Russell has all one burden, and with it comes the consolatory turn we expect in this pastoral elegy. She will defeat the death of her own Lord, of his brother, of his sister, of her father Lord Bedford; she will teach the sole "bud" yet spared, the "Brave Impe of *Bedford*" her nephew, the one way to defy the ruins of time. The turn from mortality and its sad proofs to the hope and trust of immortality comes in a motif as conventional as the visions of heaven that we find instead in a *Lycidas* or a "November." There is only one everlasting monument: frail words. It is interesting that Spenser's poem addresses Lady Warwick in order to make one thing of the devotion and love of the living and the famed power of poetry to immortalize the dead—rehearsing their "worthie praise," keeping their vertues from ever dying *though* death do soul from body sever (255). "So whilst that thou . . . Dost live, by thee thy Lord shall never die"; and the very personification of vanished greatness, wasted "through spoyle of time"—Verulam—cries "Thy Lord shall never die, the whiles this verse Shall live . . ."; "Ne shall his sister, ne thy father die."

This may be a platitude but Spenser believed it. To wisdom, learning, poetry, he granted immortality; all his poetry says so time and again, and nowhere says otherwise. It is as a protector of learning and godly wisdom that Lord Bedford is praised—and we have lately seen the support brought by other facts to Spenser's choice here when he ignores the many dramatic and pious actions that had filled Russell's busy life as servant of the state, and chooses to eternize rather this man within that public figure, who collected books and patronized authors. He was a "noble Patrone of weake povertie" (261); quite particular "steps of his" are to be followed by his grandson. Spenser knows whose ward Edward is; it is "under the shadow of" Anne Russell's countenance (272) that he

> Now ginnes to shoote up fast, and flourish fayre
> In learned artes and goodlie governaunce, . . .
> Brave Impe of *Bedford*, grow apace in bountie,
> *And count of wisedome more than of thy Countie.*

One is at a loss to see why there has been so much complaint about the lack of unity of this poem, and its disjointed organization. "O trustlesse state of miserable men." Its theme, which is single, is just what its title declares, the ruins of time, and the one single remedy (in time) which man has found for this universal destruction and oblivion—the celebration of greatness in letters. Nothing could be more germane to the subject as it is here seen than the praise of Camden (169); indeed it is startlingly relevant, supplying that one little thin frail thread upon which a remembrance of busy living Verulam, as she once was, so tenuously hangs—just as the greatness and goodness of all the long list of the dead depends for remembrance on the breath of friends, a breath which can crystallize into poetry and so outwit time. Commentators have asked for more connection between Verulam and Leicester; he has the supreme connection with her (all but identity) which we shall all have: dead, under ground, "and all his glorie gone, And all his greatnes vapoured to nought."

All these are the one subject of Spenser's poem; there runs as a uniting thread through all the sections of the poem, so often pulled apart and scorned as ill-planned and disunified, not only the lament but the answering confidence in man's recording and celebration of greatness and goodness. The poet whom Spenser looks to see aided by young Bedford's "bountie" will be just what Camden was, a "lanterne unto late succeeding age," to see the truth (170), to undo what Time does—bury and re-bury in ruins, obscure all monuments, raze even memories. Of the early patriotic antiquarian authors who tried to hold their lights up to the buried and recovered face of old Britain and distinguish what she had been, Camden is of course the rightly chosen type. It is idle to remark that Spenser is "more indebted to Harrison and Holinshed";[12] they would do, but Camden includes them, in standing for something which had Spenser's ardent faith in a way we cannot but catch: the power of learning and letters to hold truth safe as in a vial.

The early antiquarians and later chroniclers of whom Camden is the type—the Saxonists, the manuscript collectors, Bale, Leland, Parker, Lambarde[13]—found their special justification in this attempt which Spenser praises: to uncover and show by their lanterns an earlier "simple veritie," become obscured by time's defacements and by frivolous false evaluations. And *The Ruines of Time* finds its prototype not only in the *Musophilus* kind of literature in-defence-of-poetry but in the harangues of a John Bale calling on the noble families of England to preserve her antiquities, safeguard her primitive religious purity, listen to the words of her ancient writers.[14] It is

12. These comments and others later are made against the background of the collected commentary easily to hand in *Var. Sp.*, Minor Poems II. This quotation is a reference to 291 (Osgood); of course the error of thinking that the poet has been caught out is based on the error "Spenser is praising Camden as the only worthy commentator of Verulam." Camden meant a good deal more to Spenser than that, and does to us; he is not a bibliographical item but the epitome of faith in that one way of defeating time which is the hope of this poem: to record the very truth of the life that was once so fair, and so cheat the mortality that awaits it. Camden's life, motives, and works declare this as no others could; the parallel with the poet's tasks was apparent to any reader of *The Faerie Queene.*

13. The last man Spenser possibly knew, besides his books; see *View*, ed. Renwick, 297; also *Var. Sp.* edition *passim*, and 411.

14. Some such typical adjurations as that in Bale's *Laboryouse Journey*, and other such defences showing motives for the new "Modern" learning of antiquarian research, are given or cited in R. Tuve, "Ancients, Moderns, and Saxons," *ELH*, VI (1939), 165–90. The didactic Protestant patriotism which motivated the early

entirely natural that Spenser's plea for poetry, and faithful naming over of those who will live on because they supported her, should have this patriotic and archaizing cast, for his greatest poem shows that this power of ancient truth, wisdom, and beauty to defy mutability is all of a piece to him with the perennial argument that poets confer immortality. If he ever read any of his favoured words of ancient English writers, his charmed archaisms, in Lady Warwick's Gower, all the more natural that he should speak of "bountie" to the now owner of it, and consider whether some might come from the Bedford treasuries of power, to give such a plea strength in a world occupied with the ephemeral, forgetful of goodness as soon as the vital thread was cut, and destined to the oblivion of silence. But no such neat little connection is necessary to recall that the author of *The Faerie Queene*, with his sense of the extreme significance of British history, linked all the three together as actors in the discovery and keeping-alive of truth: poets, and patrons, and restorers of antiquities.

This not only unmistakably unified *The Ruines of Time* but it is one reason why hopefulness predominated in the sections given to the Dudley-Russell-Sidney families. There is a firm and proper coherence as we enter upon the Philip Sidney passage proper (280), which has no longer the heavy bitterness of the laments over transience but carries the mood of its later line, "So thou both here and there immortall art" (342). The transition seems to me careful and poetical, not awkward, disconnected, pedestrian or any of the other hard things said of it. At line 260 Lady Sidney and Lord Bedford enter, the former properly following her brothers as a third Dudley just dead, the Earl as the first (1585) of that pitiful tally of deaths among these patrons that were all close connections of the addressee here, Anne Russell. Then in the reverse order which befits their dates he treats in relation to his theme the ruins of time, first Lord Bedford and his services as patron, and his heir, and then Lady Sidney and her far greater service —she bore the poet-patron-knight who is the apotheosis of all these praised foes of decay and mortality. Thereupon the dedicatee Mary Sidney, niece of the Dudleys, and Anne Russell, closest literary heir of her brother, come to the fore. And with that last most recent death of

students of Gothic antiquities and especially of early English stands in amusing contrast to the nostalgic romanticism which we tend to fasten indiscriminately upon all "revival of the medieval."

Walsingham (Sidney's father-in-law, proverbially generous to him), already celebrated in poetry (435) and not depending on the vanity of pyramids and brass pillars (410), the figure who as Verulam usually speaks of this vanity which was her own case, states it piteously once more (465) and with her warning vanishes.

We do well to notice that Spenser believes his "consolation."[15] It is common to think ill of this poem, "mainly official verse, melodious and uninspired," and see a spark only when Sidney is mentioned, though its most careful editorial commentator went far to readjust the balance. It is true that the visions, even with Renwick's help on the "double structure," seem singular as poetic method for this date. But it is a different *genre* of poem from those lyrics we are likeliest to think of as characterizing the nineties; and even much later in that rapidly moving decade, not all poems were created as direct presentations of psychological experiences. The poem's first section presents a large and important subject with more passion than is given to any single human being who enters into it; it is sobering and salutary to realize that, sniff and cry humph as we may at the notion of an immortality in letters for virtue, Spenser really believed that

> . . . deeds doe die, how ever noblie donne,
> And thoughts of men do as themselves decay,
> But wise wordes taught in numbers for to runne,
> Recorded by the Muses, *live for ay*; . . .
> *Nor age, nor envie, shall them ever waste.* (400–6)

15. So engrained is the idea that the only consolation of a Christian is the final heavenly harping that this traditional division has been located in the few lines picturing Sidney in heaven (332–42; see *Var. Sp.*, 522, from Erskine). Of course much more of the poem treats the consolatory ideas, and all the instances of mortality, including that of Verulam, are set in opposition to the suggested hopes of immortality. The medieval commonplace reappearing in Pegasus as carrying "a good fame" (426) is discussed with extreme acumen in M. Lascelles, "The Rider on the Winged Horse," in *Elizabethan and Jacobean Studies Presented to F. P. Wilson* (Oxford, 1959).

Probably more should be made here of the fact that Vision 5 is most likely another form of this image (625, to be connected with Renwick's larger significances of the vision-images; see, e.g., *Var. Sp.*, 309); the interpretation was fairly widespread which read *the soul* as she whom Perseus delivered to eternal life, mounted on his virtuous steed (uses in Christine de Pisan and others will be described in a forthcoming book by the writer). The difference in tone and point of the suggested Ariosto source remains no matter how often we read Harington on the "senses" of Perseus (ed. Gregory Smith, *Elizabethan Critical Essays*, II, 202; referred to by Renwick). For a similar reason one may refrain from bringing in Rosalind's friend, whom she is asserted to have christened "her Segnior Pegaso" (Oxford *Spenser*, ed. de Selincourt, 625).

If we can disabuse ourselves of accepted modern assumptions long enough to follow sympathetically in each of its steps the long argument which Spenser states and re-states, claiming that letters, truth, learning, poetry are among things indestructible, we see the nobility of this lengthy and passionate protestation of faith. It sheds a new light on his series of eulogized noble persons, so often denigrated.

He holds this hard faith in the teeth of a stubborn set of painful facts, and so did those he addressed. When Spenser came to England for the visit that began in 1589/90, Lord Bedford's death was a fact of four years since; though a great and hopeful patron he was not young (in his late fifties), was an ill man, and left an heir, though one too young to help any current poet. But in 1586 came the death which Spenser says cut off his young Muses' "hope of anie further fruit"; in October Sidney died, of the wound received a month after his mother died in August 1586. His father Sir Henry had died three months before her; three deaths shockingly clustered in the summer of 1586. In 1588 Leicester died. In February of 1589/90 his brother Ambrose died. In April 1590 Walsingham died. Two of these deaths came after Spenser arrived in England; the last is ironic in the face of the dedicatory sonnet to the still living man. In an era when patronage was not only a plain fact but the idealized fact Spenser presents to us, the women who still remained of this great three-or-four-family fortress of active defenders of virtue and truth, and the Bedford youth, still a ward, must have seemed a pitiful remainder of once solid hopes.

Not only the fact of his Muses' blossoms being "nipped and quite dead," but the other narrated events of the dedication to *The Ruines of Time* may be quite simply true. Though we have no need to guess who the "friends" were, the Russells, Anne especially, obviously suit particularly well:

Yet sithens my late cumming into England, some frends of mine (which might much prevaile with me, and indeede commaund me) knowing with how straight bandes of duetie I was tied to him: as *also bound unto that noble house*, (of which the chiefe hope then rested in him) *have sought to revive them* [the blossoms and the hope of further fruit] *by upbraiding me*: for that I have not shewed anie thankefull remembrance towards *him or any of them*; but suffer their names to sleep in silence and forgetfulnesse. Whome chiefly to satisfie, or els to avoide that fowle blot of unthankefulnesse, I have conceived this small Poeme . . . speciallie intended to the renowming of that noble race, from which both you and he sprong, and to the eternizing of *some of the chiefe of them late deceased*. . . .

Spenser's connection with Lady Pembroke is obviously bound up with the web of connections he writes about, and since Sidney's death is climactic she is a fitting choice.

It is proper to the ideas we have outlined that wisdom and support of learning are stressed in Spenser's praises of each successive member of the group so cruelly decimated in these years, when he was becoming a poet whose patron would be important—an unforeseen "ruin" of time which endangered the cause he had at heart, surely alarmingly and discouragingly. Each utterance on Lady Warwick stresses this zeal for things of the mind rather than her beauty or more generalized virtue. Comparison of the *Colin Clout* passage on her with the praises of the other nymphs would point the contrast. The widow Theana is introduced (492) as one who is "Ne lesse praise worthie" than Urania, Lady Pembroke, "In whose brave mynd" as in a coffer all gifts and riches are locked; she in turn is herself praised as "the well of bountie and brave mynd." Excelling in "glorie and great light," her advancement at court is the just reward of "her great worth and noble governance," for she is one who has power—but virtue with it:

> She is the ornament of womankind,
> And Courts chief garlond with all vertues dight.
> Therefore great Cynthia her *in chiefest grace*
> Doth hold, and *next unto her selfe advance*,
> Well worthie of so honourable place. . . .

It will be remembered that in this poem Spenser plays very heavily on his old theme of the false values of courts, the "enormities" he saw there that sent him back (650 ff.) to the "barrein soyle" and penury and "rude fields" and sheep of his adopted island; any honest shepherd's life is better than the climbing over others, the filed tongues and wits applied only to pleasing, of the court where "each mans worth is measured by his weed" and gain motivates all (despite Cynthia's attempt to support "sciences" and learned arts). Then comes the famous section ironically describing false love, "and love, and love my deare," and the opposing of it to "loves perfection" that created the world, which is so much more fully delineated in the *Hymnes*.

This theme of gain not virtue as the spring of action in the world of the powerful is also the theme of much of the earlier letter of

Harvey to Immerito, which had dictated his use of the cynical remark from Ovid which we noticed. Harvey gives an edge to a similar mood of ironic disillusionment by quoting the idea in four (rather than two) lines from Ovid, and in the form as found in the Ovidian text, a little different from our first quotation:

> Dum fueris foelix, multos numerabis Amicos,
> Tempora si fuerint nubila, solus eris. . . .[16]

This and the three verse variations in English follow upon the exasperated and biting satire of the court in the *Speculum Tuscanismi*, giving an opportunity for some three pages of ironic comment on the "Theame out of Ovid" and much ironical advice to young Immerito. He will probably learn, as Harvey has, to employ his "travayle, and tyme wholly or chiefely on those studies and practizes, that carrie as they saye, meate in their mouth." Of course "Master *Collin Cloute* is not every body," and albeit his old companions may lose favour with Mistress Poetrie, "yet he peradventure, by the meanes of hir special favour, and some personall priviledge, may happely live by *dying Pellicanes*, and purchase great landes, and Lordshippes" by what his *Calendar* and *Dreames* bring in. We cannot conjecture all that these remarks implied, in the days of 1580, with friends all still alive and *The Faerie Queene* under way (this is the famous letter discussing it). But it must have read ironically when in such different circumstances, not a lifetime later but some eleven years, the printer of *The Ruines of Time* is hunting for copies of *The Dying Pellican* and other odd-ments to publish, and *The Faerie Queene* is well launched, but Spenser's poems lament such long lists of those he had not guessed would never read it.

But Spenser's harsh words are not all kept for impersonal Death. There is an element that we did not notice in our first description, in the complaint against the ruins which time assists. Not all mutability and oblivion and impermanence comes of the irrational working of forces men cannot control; for also "*Spite* bites the dead." The "painted faces" that flatter, the "courting masker"—"*All is but fained*"

16. This is in Letter V, published in App. I of the *Prose Works* (*Var. Spenser*, at 468), and supposed to be an answer to Spenser's Letter III; in the Oxford *Spenser*, the passages described are at 626–8. My attention was first called to this reference by Dr. Mary Parmenter. The variant *felix* comes from good MSS. and is common in Renaissance quotations.

(204). This satirical tone and acrid disillusionment are most apparent when the bitter generalization that "after death all friendship doth decaie" is applied to Leicester:

> . . . the Foxe is crept
> Into the hole, the which the Badger swept.
>
> He now is dead, and all his glorie gone,
> And all his greatness vapoured to nought, . . .
> His name is worne alreadie out of thought,
> Ne anie Poet seekes him to revive;
> Yet manie Poets honourd him alive.

The little squib from Ovid about how many our friends are, *tempore foelici*, and how in bad times not one remains, was evidently in the later Middle Ages a common *sentence*, or conventional tag for indicating two states of mind. One, that just exemplified, is especially clear in the embittered English verses Harvey's letter quotes. The venomous sarcasm is as vehement in a two-stanza poem in the *Paradise of Dainty Devises* which is given the title, "Donec eris Felix multos numerabis amicos. . . ." It begins with an image: "Even as the Raven, the Crowe, and greedie Kite" swarm about carrion, tear the carcass to and fro, then go on to more—so where gold grows friends resort full thick, but when mischance changes wealth to want, "They packe them thence, to place of ritcher haunt."[17] The other less bitter notion is indicated in the phrase to which this and two other poems are assigned in the *Paradise*. All are signed, "My Luck is losse."

I would only call attention to the pertinence of these evidently almost proverbial meanings of the tag from Ovid to the whole history of Spenser's relations with the noble houses whose members he makes Anne Russell typify and represent. Especially the latter sad sense, the turn of events so that good fortune and hope become nothing but a flat record of pure loss, fits what had happened in the half-decade while *The Faerie Queene* was being seriously got ready, and it is no special addition to the train of mishaps that the *Stemmata Dudleiana* was lost too. The living scions were barren in their graves; why take great care of the withering stalk? Meanwhile it is at least a nice little

17. See H. Rollins' edition (Cambridge, 1927). This is no. 44; the notes at p. 213 add information. The title appears also in the *Gorgious Gallery of Gallant Inventions*, where (100) the proper next line follows as in Ovid; the *Paradise* title gets its second line by skipping five lines to *nullus* . . . (*Tristia*, I, ix. 5, 10). Elyot in Bk. ii ch. 12 of *The Governour* translates seven lines from "sweet Ovid," beginning with our two but in the form they show in *Tristia* texts.

morsel that somebody called "Spenserus" either wrote in, or was felt to be obviously connected with, the Ovidian tag which signified "my Luck is losse"—on a page of a Russell manuscript, one even signed by the particular almost last active Russell he did finally dedicate something to; it did appear in 1596 at last, and it was his "retractation," pretending at least that he like more famous authors before him is apologizing for something indiscreet written in the greener times of his youth. Though it scarcely lost him all his friends, still whatever did happen must have seemed one more case of "my Luck is losse."

Questions have always arisen regarding the dedication to the *Fowre Hymnes*. Perhaps it came as late as 1596, despite the early ties, for the simple reason that time's ruins left few alive of this once large group, to receive dedications or help poets. We may put aside immediately the fact that it unaccountably calls Lady Warwick "Marie," acknowledged by everyone to be an inexplicable slip and not due to distance or formality in the relation. The dedication jointly to the two sisters (the other Margaret, Lady Cumberland, Anne Clifford's mother), signalizes a friendship between them that is apparently typical of the close relationship most members of these families seem to have kept up with each other;[18] hence as everyone is aware we shall never know which one of "you two most excellent Ladies" moved Spenser to call in his first two hymns. Yet he is very exact. It was but one. The stress has been on Lady Warwick in earlier poems, but Lady Cumberland was the more famous for serious-minded piety. Spenser's wording implies that it is not quite to be laid at the author's door that readers "do rather sucke out poyson to their strong passion, then hony to their honest delight"; yet he claims to have attempted calling in his copies, is willing to admit some need for an excuse by assigning them to "greener times," and resolves "at least to amend, and by way of retractation to reforme them" by adding the two final Hymnes.

Much is made of the fact that having admitted this he nevertheless publishes the four, and slurs are also sometimes cast upon ladies, surely only prigs, who could take exception to the two first hymns we

18. *Diary of Lady Anne Clifford, passim,* and Wiffen—see, e.g., I, 509–10. Both these also support the character of Lady Cumberland presently mentioned, well known through other poets too; see Lady Anne on her mother's own writings, 84, 90, or dedicated books such as Christopher Shutt's *Sermon* (no. 141 of Lord Bedford's library).

have. But it is typical of the retractation (and Spenser surely knew Dante's, Chaucer's, Sidney's) that it does not answer an accusation of lasciviousness by repairing phrases, but answers an objection of misplaced Love by substituting Heavenly Love for earthly love idolized. It would be quite possible, where a literary convention is so usual, for all these to be largely made-up situations and phrases; however, the author's publication of all the four, and the Lady's request that human and natural love should not usurp Love's title, seem to me to indicate neither lip-service and pretence on the one side nor priggish piety on the other. A true retractation is the more effective if what is retracted remains extant; we possess it in all the famous cases. We need not make the whole matter too solemn; if some hesitation or reproof intervened, there may have been just enough bite in what happened to bring home the truth of "Cum fortuna perit, nullus amicus erit." Similarly, there must have been something of the feeling of "my Luck is losse" in the fact that one's patrons no sooner lent support than they fell from favour—Ralegh was out of favour, Grey was out of favour. Nothing lasts, friends least of all, and one false step is enough.

Far more seriously, this is the actual situation responsible for Ovid's poem whence the tag is drawn. The famous and pathetic exile, or rather *relegatio*, to the rigours of Tomis among the barbaric Getes on the shores of the Black Sea, was Ovid's punishment for a truly erotic poem, the *Ars Amatoria*, teaching not merely describing these arts; he lost all hope of favour with Augustus, and the book was expelled from public libraries. He did not live in Rome again, and the *Tristia* are written to discuss his misfortune, his defences, his virtuous present ideas on the matters where youthful indiscretion had caused a fault. They show with pitiful seriousness what may be mostly pose and allusion in the later writer, that is, the love poet declaring his basic innocency though admitting enough guilt to make a form of retractation. When the *Tristia* are not taken up with Ovid's lamenting his misfortune in that his conceptions of love have been misread, he is apologizing for such "songs of his youth" ("id quoque, quod viridi quondam male lusit in aevo").[19] Ovid makes these defences in the

19. The text used (and translation when quoted) is that in the Loeb Classics, ed. A. L. Wheeler (London, 1924). The extracted or adapted lines are at I.ix.5, 6, quotations in the text above from the rest of that section, or II.339, or III.i.7.

very section, written to a "steadfast friend," whence come the two lines that we have seen plucked out often; the context must have been familiar to every Latin reader, for the *Tristia* were thoroughly popular and their moving quality much appreciated.

The bitter sentiment about loss of friends by those who have lost credit, which fits Ovid's case so well and became a tag phrase for that situation, fits only with the obliqueness of most literary allusion an author who has lost friend after friend through death, in the quarter where he thought them surest, only to feel finally the smart of some disapproval where it was not deserved. Spenser had written pieces and passages certain to be unpalatable to those in authority, often enough to have tasted the truth of Ovid's cynical observation. But any subterranean connection such as we now speak of is of a different order, and much less serious. For there is no question of a real similarity between the poems of Spenser and Ovid asserted to be *lusus iuveni,* as there is none between what the two poets paid, in losses; the recognized reference would merely make a delightful, and pointed, highly educated joke out of such a proverbial sentiment inscribed at the close of a benefactress's book titled *Confessio amantis*. Someone wrote it there.

If the joke we are looking at was never made, one hopes there was another as good. For showing the conspiratorial obligingness that facts often show when there is some hypothesis in the offing toward which they can bend themselves, there is also the fact that the close of Gower's *Confessio* is a recantation of earthly love in favour of heavenly love. Presenting his book to the king, this writer on love takes his "fynal leve" of earthly love,—"but *thilke* love," that other which "stant of charite confermed," charges no man's conscience; God grant us *that* "love and alle pes" and bring us to heaven where it is enjoyed.[20] Gower too excuses his writing, begun earlier, in that though tending to "lust and game," seen another way "It mai be wisdom to the wise." The contents of this framework-poem-on-love, organized around the virtues, are of no great importance to our present concerns, however, since one would think anyhow that Spenser read Gower. He was printed; he and Chaucer and Lydgate make up the commonly mentioned trio of medieval poets; Harvey read him; so must anyone have

20. *Works*, ed. Macaulay, III, vv. 3088* ff., 3061*; MS. Bodl. 902 is a very good manuscript of the first-recension-revised text (see introd., clxx).

done who had a large interest in Chaucer. I append nevertheless, to be tidy, a note on some of Spenser's preoccupations which would be enforced by greater attention to the *Confessio*.[21] The most interesting, the attachment to a virtues-framework, using not the four-plus-three (cardinal and theological) but the "other virtues" usually opposed to the sins, with their suggestive connections with Spenser's alterations, is part of a much larger medieval inheritance and is being treated elsewhere.

There is another little oddity about actual medieval use of this tag, in ways which explain its appearance as a commonplace in the Renaissance. We may chance to read that romance of the 1450's, Antoine de la Sale's *Le Petit Jehan de Saintré*, with its many chapters of instructions to the squire by "My Lady" who is enamoured of him. In chapter 16, when the story promotes some discourse on largesse, Fortune, and friends, the squire is told never to forget that "Tempore felici multi numerantur amici . . ." and so on. Our curiosity is especially wide awake because we notice that instead of the strictly Ovidian form of all the other Renaissance references, we meet here Spenserus's exact wording. Our curiosity is not likely to be satisfied, though the only other example I know of precisely this wording is the citation in Richard Hill's Commonplace Book; this is in a Balliol MS., about 1520, but these bunches of "Latin proverbs" represent earlier forms and popularity. Without a word about Ovid, here too sits "Tempore felici . . . ," ending "Cum fortuna perit, nullus amicus erit" like the other "medieval" citation.[22] In the *Petit*

21. It has always been necessary to be more chary about Lowes's suggestions touching "Spenser and the *Miroir de l'Omme*" (*PMLA*, XXIX)—unprinted and in a single MS.—though connections would be more attractive; on large debts to widespread virtues-materials see forthcoming articles in *JWCI*, and book. The *Confessio* has a long discourse on Justice as the important *princely* virtue, in a section on the education of kings (vii, 2695 ff.). And a Renaissance reader would have noticed in the Prologue (hence not engulfed in the long text; such attention-factors are important in MS.-reading) the comparison of earlier times with the stony present (Prol. 100 *et al.*, with the usual contrasts as in *FQ*, V, Prol.); there are numerous treatments of the law of continuous change which all things obey (e.g., Prol. 930, seas, seasons, etc.), treatments as expected of Envie and Detraccioun (beg. Bk. II), the world weighing with deceit in his balance and countered with the firm blandness of platitudes (Prol. 540), visions of Venus, of Cupid with his meynee (Bk. VIII). It is always sensible to note how long some things for which we seek sources have been commonplaces. All these are commonplaces.

22. Not having the Champion-Desonay edition of *Le Petit Jehan* to hand, I use I. Gray's translation based on it (London, 1931; see 103). The romance customarily uses Latin *sententiae* to bolster advices in these instructional chapters,

Jehan we are directed to a properly medieval source for its popularity, for the squire is not to forget that which *Alanus* says in *Anti-Claudiano* . . . and the quotation follows. But Alanus does not say it. The reference is to 7.351–55, where the chief idea of the Ovidian tag is put into similar phrases, and the editor duly cites *Tristia.*[23] So we are left with our mystery, and are likely to be, and as with the many other loose ends in this set of observations, it is of no importance that we cannot find out reasons for these variants and these implications and private allusions that only mattered to those who made them. The small things about periods and connections and groups and "common" knowledge which we *are* reliably led to perceive are no less interesting.

No doubt it would be pleasing to sew the whole trifle up with bright thread by identifying the hand beyond question; then a paragraph would be forthcoming on Spenser's hours among the medieval MSS. of Lord Bedford's library, with some speculations perhaps on a handsome *Fall of Princes* MS. owned by Lady Cumberland's husband George Clifford,[24] or his sister Lady Strange's MSS.[25] (mother of Spenser's Amyntas, mother-in-law of his Amaryllis, claimed as kinswoman). Unfortunately we are not sure of Spenser's Italian hand. Scraps like that on the back of Grey's letter of July 10, 1581, are too small for certainty; there are definite resemblances to the Italian

---

which significantly follow, partially, the pattern set for pious virtues-treatises by thirteenth-century ecclesiastical constitutions (7 sins with 7 corresponding virtues, 10 commandments, etc.); other similar mixtures of idealized profane love with courtly etiquette and moral advice remind us that courtier literature did not begin with Castiglione. The variant *evit-erit* is likely in any hand (not in the French texts I know). Hill's Commonplace Book is edited in *EETS* extra ser. 101 (1907) by R. Dyboski; see 133 and introd. 27 (5th proverb). It is described by H. A. Mason, *Humanism and Poetry in the Early Tudor Period* (London, 1959), 145–55.

23. By an error referring to *Tr.* III.ix instead of I.ix (Alain de Lille, *Anticlaudianus,* ed. Bossuat [Paris, 1955], 167). The passage does not appear to be in the Ellebaut O.F. thirteenth-century *Anticlaudien* (ed. Creighton [Washington, 1944]).

24. B.Mus. MS. Royal 18 D iv; this former ward of Lord Bedford owned the illustrated Latin book of prayers Vienna cod. 1840, and MS. Bodl. 3 (Summary Cat. 1843) of the *Pore Caitif.*

25. This other Margaret Clifford, Lady Strange, apparently owned two Gower *Confessio* MSS. (Royal 18 C xxii and Camb. Mm. 2. 21); especially interesting is the strange copy of Hardyng's Chronicle, Bodl. MS. Arch. Selden B. 10, with a provocative illustration and set of verses on "The palais of Pluto," beginning "Blak be thy bankes and thy Ripes also" (f.185^r). The four black streams of hell ebb and flow and blow misrule *thurgh Scotland.* This connection between Scotland and Pluto's "palais of *pride,*" *his daughter,* in one of Spenser's chronicle sources, is not in the printed copies (the material would occur at f.234^r).

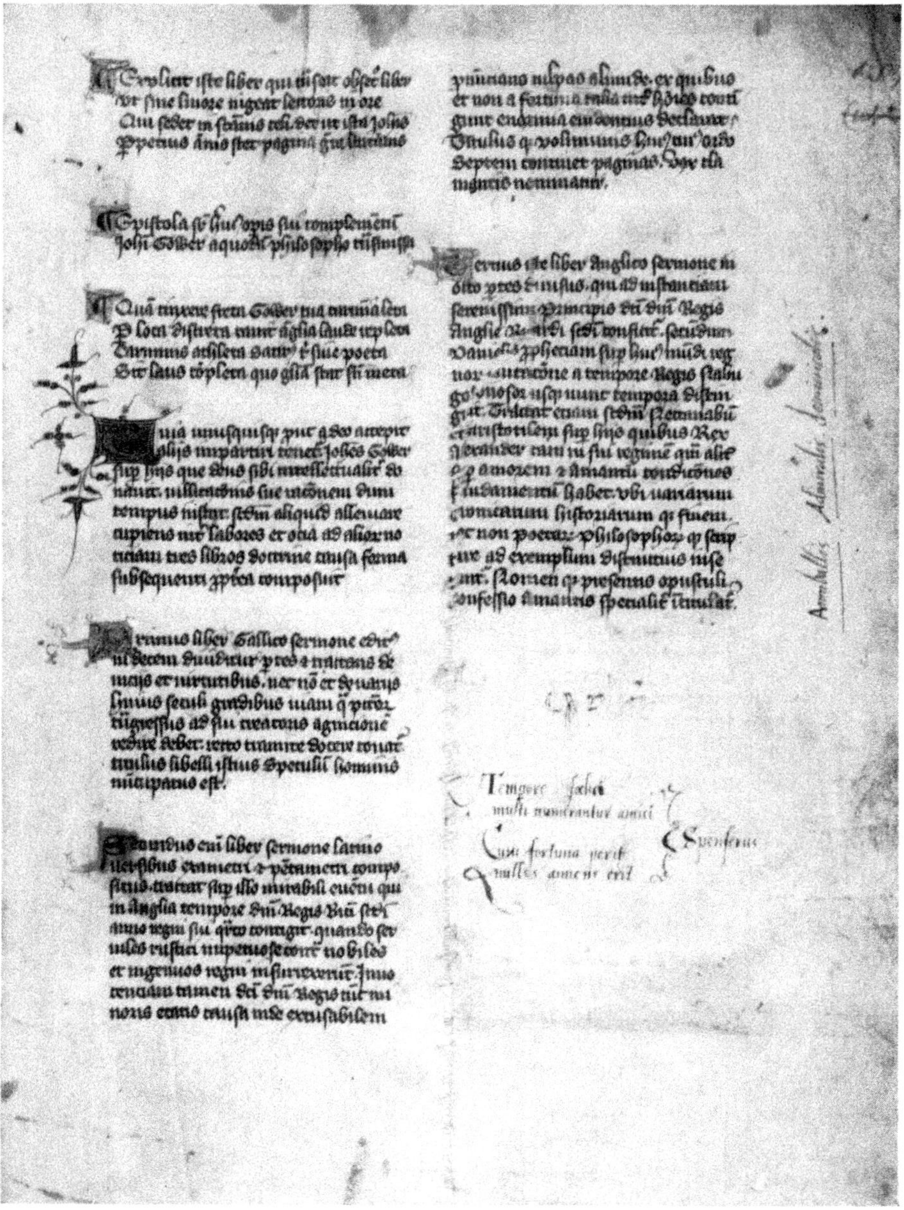

MS. Bodl. 902, Gower's *Confessio Amantis*, early fifteenth century, f.184r.

hand of *State Papers* 78:29, said by Renwick to be Spenser's. One *can* say definitely that the Spenserus passage could with great probability have been written by the same hand which wrote the scraps we know are Spenser's.[26] But certainty on this point would not explain for us other and more teasing puzzles of where this sixteenth-century annotator got the "medieval" wording, whether its proverbial status came of its being perhaps elsewhere in Alanus, whether we are helped to more knowledge of the *Fowre Hymnes*' earlier history.[27] Though the whole curious little set of connected facts helps us to remarkably little provable knowledge, we see as much as we were meant to, at that, of our betters' allusions and feelings and ironies, and think chiefly how lost are the implications which make facts important, in the ruins of time, while ideas and persons the poet did set out to "eternize" still shine brightly as he promised, if we look. His volume too was one written to honour and extol, but by a series of sad interferences his grateful reasons for celebration of those he honours were never permitted to have the reality of ours.

26. See H. R. Plomer, "Edmund Spenser's Handwriting," *MP*, XXI (1923–4), 201–7, and R. Jenkins, "Spenser with Lord Grey in Ireland," *PMLA*, LII (1937), 338–53, particularly the notes to the latter. Dr. Jenkins has seen a rotograph of the Spenserus inscription and agrees with my statement about the quite possible identity of the hands. If the letter from Grey to Elizabeth, from Smerwick, in *State Papers* 78 no. 29 is in Spenser's cursive Italian hand, as Renwick says in his edition of the *View*, similarities include: the long-tailed *s* and *f* (as in his secretary hand), the straight upstanding capital *T*, the slender narrow oval *o*, the shape of the *e*, the *m*, *r*, *l*, *a*, *s*. If the letter in *State Papers* 87 : 29 is also in Spenser's hand, as is possible, there occur in it similar capital *S* and *p*.

27. Though there is some possible implication of these discussions with old puzzles such as the matter of date (two "earlier" hymns, early relations with Russells and Dudleys, etc.), the points are not capable enough of being fixed. Meanwhile arguments are cogent for late dates based on Spenser's not using more "technical" Platonism in pieces of earlier date (as in Ellrodt, *Neoplatonism in the Poetry of Spenser* [Geneva, 1960]), and in general I think the half-knowable facts of the present article are more valuable if we use them for suggestions, not proofs.

Spenser's Mutabilitie

WILLIAM BLISSETT

FIRST, AN ASSUMPTION, not subject to proof on the evidence at our disposal. Edmund Spenser's "Two Cantos of Mutabilitie"[1] may in fact be, as they appeared to his printer after the poet's death, "both for Forme and Matter . . . parcell of some following Booke of the Faerie Queene, under the Legend of Constancie"; or they may be material left over from an earlier version of *The Faerie Queene*; but I regard them as being now most patient of interpretation as a detached retrospective commentary on the poem as a whole, forming as they do a satisfactory conclusion to a foreshortened draft, a stopping place at which, after a seriatim reading, can be made a pleasing analysis of all. Indeed, from the high ground of Arlo Hill perhaps more of Spenser's total work can be held in conspectus than from any other vantage point. He rounds out his poetical life with a pageant of times and seasons as he had entered upon it with eclogues proportionable to the twelve months; in one of their aspects the cantos are "complaints and meditations of the worlds vanitie; verie graue and profitable"; with the *Daphnaida* volume they share the figure of Cynthia and a summer day in Ireland; the relations with *The Faerie Queene* in everything but narrative are apparent; and it is only a little too fanciful to see in the outcome of the story of Faunus and Molanna an account of the present state of Ireland, cloudily enwrapped in allegorical devices.

Second, a few summary assertions, to be supported in the ensuing

1. All quotations from Spenser are taken from the Variorum edition edited by Edwin Greenlaw and others (Baltimore, 1932–57). Evidence for the date of the "Cantos" and their relation to *The Faerie Queene* may be found in *Variorum* VI, 433 ff. See also Northrop Frye, "The Structure of Imagery in *The Faerie Queene*," *UTQ*, XXX (1961), 111–112.

pages. "Mutabilitie" has been variously explained[2] by reference to Lucretius, to Empedocles, to Bruno. More convincingly, it has been proved to derive from certain passages in Ovid's *Metamorphoses*, and to be related to the tradition of Boethius. It has also been linked speculatively with the poet's own life story. I shall treat the poem as of intrinsic, not just documentary interest; moreover, I shall argue that it is not confused, not lugubrious, not defeatist, not pietistic. Instead, it is the product of an unusually subtle poetic intelligence, handling with great skill and verve combinations of ideas and modulations of feeling ranging from what the Elizabethans called satire, through mythological romance and masque-like pageantry, to end, equally to our surprise and satisfaction, in prayer. So original is it that it may be termed (with what reservations we shall see) that rare phenomenon in Renaissance literature, a poem without analogues. And it is not a mere virtuoso piece, of purely technical interest, for it has at its centre the permanent problem, or paradox, or mystery, of the alienated consciousness, *l'homme révolté*. Spenser has been said to be no ironist and of all poets to stand furthest from existentialism;[3] it is true—until he makes this final bold foray.

The poem opens in the tone of Elizabethan melancholy: in the same dark voice that Hamlet is to use in considering how a king may go a progress through the guts of a beggar, Spenser promises to tell of Mutabilitie's cruel sports and briefly identifies her (VII, vi, 5–6) as a Titaness, sister of Hecate and Bellona, who now aspires to heavenly honours along with them:

For, she the face of earthly things so changed,
That all which Nature had establisht first
In good estate, and in meet order ranged,
She did pervert, and all their statutes burst:
And all the worlds faire frame (which none yet durst
Of Gods or men to alter or misguide)
She alter'd quite, and made them all accurst
That God had blest; and did at first prouide
In that still happy state for euer to abide.

2. To the commentators in the *Variorum* should be added Kathleen Williams, "Eterne in Mutabilitie," *ELH*, XIX (1952), 115–130; Judah L. Stampfer, "The Cantos of Mutabilitie: Spenser's Last Testament of Faith," *UTQ*, XXI (1952), 140–6; and Sherman Hawkins, "Mutabilitie and the Cycle of the Months," in William Nelson, ed., *Form and Convention in the Poetry of Edmund Spenser* (New York, 1961), 76–102.

3. C. S. Lewis, *English Literature in the Sixteenth Century* (Oxford, 1954), 392.

Ne shee the lawes of Nature onely brake,
But eke of Iustice, and of Policie;
And wrong of right, and bad of good did make,
And death for life exchanged foolishlie:
Since which, all liuing wights haue learn'd to die,
And all this world is woxen daily worse.
O pittious worke of MVTABILITIE!
By which, we all are subiect to that curse,
And death in stead of life haue sucked from our Nurse.

If satire is made from our quarrel with the present and complaint from our quarrel with time, the poem thus far promises certainly to be a complaint, probably to be a satire.

Here should be supplied the sort of allegorical note—moral, historical or political, and physical—that would spring to mind in Spenser's day. For Dante's particular kind of divine poem the four levels of scriptural exegesis are appropriate; modern allegorical works are related in elaborate and idiosyncratic ways to various psychological, theosophical, and metapolitical systems; but allegorists of the tradition ending with Spenser regularly arranged their interpretations in three rather simple categories—*morale, historice, physice.*[4]

In moral allegory, as a state of soul, Mutabilitie embodies vain ambition and presumption, restless titanism, the unhappy consciousness. In political allegory, this state of soul, the temper of the malcontent, expresses itself as a force of restless innovation, a Marlovian "overreacher," daring the gods out of heaven and raising the standard of revolt against constituted authority. And in physical allegory, as a state of the world, Mutabilitie embodies destructive change, *vicissitudo rerum* as a cosmic principle, the "vanity" to which the creature is made subject at the fall, in Pauline phrase. It will be observed that all three allegories[5] conspire to present a dangerous, demonic figure whom any

4. Jean Seznec, *The Survival of the Pagan Gods,* tr. Barbara F. Sessions (New York, 1953), pt. I.

5. For the morality and politics of the "malcontent" type, see Lawrence Babb, *The Elizabethan Malady* (University of Michigan Press, 1951), ch. IV and bibliography; for the background of the suggested physical allegory, see Victor Harris, *All Coherence Gone* (Chicago, 1949), esp. 86–128, and bibliography. Hyperbole and bold presumption combine in the Elizabethan word chosen by Harry Levin as title for his book on Marlowe, *The Overreacher* (Cambridge, Mass., 1952). The quotation from St. Paul is central to C. S. Lewis's discussion of the "Cantos" in *The Allegory of Love* (Oxford, 1936), 353–7. John Norden in *Vicissitudo Rerum* (1600; facsimile, Oxford, 1931) teaches the physical lesson of mutability without fable—or poetry. Albert Camus seems to have regarded the period before 1789 as pre-history; but

reader of *The Faerie Queene* will expect to be required to condemn unequivocally, as he has condemned Duessa and Acrasia and other enemies of Gloriana. But we shall soon learn from Mutabilitie's own mistaken haste not to presume too much or to get ahead of ourselves.

From the beginning, this Mutabilitie is a formidable figure: "were he liefe or sory," she passes through the celestial gates guarded by Time—Time the (Aristotelian) measurer of motion, not Time the (Ovidian) devourer of all things, for she herself has taken over that second function. As she sweeps onward, men on earth fear the return of chaos, and Jove calls to mind other cases of presumption in the earth-born, and their punishment.[6] But when she embarks on the stupendous exploit of forcing the gates of heaven and evicting its occupants, the violence and hubris of the Titaness become, surprisingly, not more but less obnoxious. Whatever the ethical judgment may tell us, we cannot help admiring her audacity, her resolution, her *virtù*; and it is a law of fiction that a reader or spectator always desires to see an action well begun completed—witness our implication in the designs of Tamburlaine and our anxiety lest the murder of Duncan in *Macbeth* be interrupted.

Storming into the palace of Cynthia, the bold intruder orders the goddess to give up her throne, to the amazement of the witnessing stars. The scene is brisk and violent, especially so for Spenser, and if the modern reader is stimulated by it, how much more shocked would be the reader for whom the poet wrote, for whom the prime and unmistakable reference of Cynthia must be none other than the Queen-goddess of England at present reigning. Let us pause a moment to attune our ears to an "Ode of *Cynthia*" sung on May Day, 1600, "before her sacred Maiestie at a shew on horsebacke. . . ."[7]

> Th'Ancient Readers of Heuens Booke,
> Which with curious eyes did looke
>   Into Natures story;
> All things under *Cynthia* tooke
>   To bee transitory.

---

much of what he says about "metaphysical rebellion" applies in our context of thought. See *L'homme révolté* (Paris: Gallimard, 1951), pt. 2.

6. The reader will recall the Giant in F.Q., V, ii, 30 ff., whom Artegall is allowed to out-argue easily and punish with capital severity. Jove and the Giants appear in *Ruines of Rome*, ll. 4, 11, and 12. Jove himself, however, is accused of "doome unjust" and favouritism in *Teares of the Muses*, ll. 69–70.

7. E. C. Wilson, *England's Eliza* (Cambridge, Mass., 1939), 317–18; for other references to the Queen's constancy in the face of time, see 46, 258, 355, 408 n. 16.

This the learned only knew,
But now all men finde it true,
    Cynthia is descended;
With bright beames and heuenly hew,
    And lesser starres attended.

Landes and Seas shee rules below,
Where things change, and ebbe and flowe,
    Spring, waxe olde, and perish;
Only Time which all doth mowe,
    Her alone doth cherish.

Times yong howres attend her still,
And her Eyes and Cheekes do fill
    With fresh youth and beautie:
All her louers olde do grow,
But their heartes, they do not so
    In their Loue and duty.

Who is this Titaness that dares grapple with one who "reigns in everlasting glory" and in the style and metre of *The Faerie Queene* lifts her hand against a type of Gloriana herself? No vulgar upstart, surely, but a figure darkly grand, burning with sullen intelligence: if Dürer's Melancholia, impelled after long immobility by *furor melancholicus*, were to bestir herself to action, she would resemble Mutabilitie.[8] Very early (VII, vi, 2) the poet finds it

fittest to vnfold
Her antique race and linage ancient,
As I haue found it registred of old
In *Faery* Land mongst records permanent.

And Mutabilitie herself later on will recount its details. But where have we heard something like that before, indeed almost the very phrases? Where but in the proem to the second book, in which Spenser promises to present to the "fayrest Princesse under sky" the

8. Erwin Panofsky, *Albrecht Dürer* (Princeton, 1948), I, 156–71. Babb, 77, quotes the earliest English reference to the picture (Burton's *Anatomy*, ed. Shillitoe, I, 451): the malcontent is "not affable in speech, dull, sad, austere, cogitabundi still, very intent, and, as *Albertus Durer* paints Melancholy like a sad woman leaning on her arm with fixed looks, neglect habit, &c. held therefore by some proud, soft, sottish, or half mad . . . and yet of a deep reach, excellent apprehension, judicious, wise, & witty." Melancholia and Mutabilitie strikingly figure the related opposites of resentment and rebellion as discussed by Camus (following Scheler) and of *acedia* and furious activity as discussed by Josef Pieper, *Leisure the Basis of Culture* (London, 1952), 49.

"antique image of [her] great auncestrie." I do not mean to suggest that Mutabilitie and Gloriana are identical, just that they are of comparable stature and allegorical weight. The stanza about Mutabilitie's sisters bears out this interpretation. Hecate may be said to personify the sinister side of things lunar and hence to balance Diana—and the Virgin Queen of the lunar land. Bellona may by the same token be called a sort of violent step-sister of Britomart—and of her Tudor descendant. This is in direct line with the conception of the Titans throughout Western literature and thought:[9] they always possess a certain god-like grandeur, and if in their arrogance they want nothing as a gift, this is balanced by a sense of justice in demanding their rights.

Pride and reaching for power are the reverse side of Glory, and demonic presumption goes with greatness. The balancing of Gloriana and Mutabilitie is not a simple opposition such as we find in Una and Duessa or in the true and the false Florimell: there is nothing of Duessa in Una, and the false Florimell vanishes in the presence of the true. We have been told incidentally that Argante, the lustful giantess, is a daughter of Titans, but not a word do we hear of her in the grander context of Mutabilitie. Indeed, as the poem develops, Mutabilitie is seen to have little to do with ordinary moral evil, but rather, in moral and political allegory, to represent the taint of evil, or presumption, in even the highest natural good, the pursuit of rightful glory; and in the physical, the subjection to destructive time of all earthly things, including the woman whom a conspiracy of song had feigned to be divine and immortal.

Elizabethan poets, and Spenser foremost among them, had invested heavily in Elizabeth's golden and perpetual youth, exempt from all

9. "Titan" for Spenser, as for Shakespeare, is normally metonymy for the sun. "Titans" are mentioned (III, vii, 47) as parents of Argante, elsewhere a "giantesse," and (V, i, 9) as adversaries of Jove subdued by Artegall's sword. The word "titaness" is reserved for Mutabilitie, who is only once (VII, vi, 13) called a "giantess." H. G. Lotspeich points out that Spenser, following classical precedent, conflates the Titans, who are gods supplanted by the superior force or guile of the Olympians, with the Giants, who are in a sense a second appearance of the Titans but are earthborn and in rebellion against established authority. See *Classical Mythology in the Poetry of Edmund Spenser* (Princeton, 1932) under *Giants, Titans,* and *Mutabilitie.* Nevertheless, in our context, much of the original distinction survives, for Mutabilitie is no crude heaper-up of mountains, but a skilled pleader, and belongs by birthright in the company of Atlas and Prometheus and whatever is nobly titanic from Milton to Beethoven.

variableness and shadow of turning. In this connection a passage from Thomas Dekker is apposite as showing the working of a lesser imagination, strongly influenced by Spenser. *Old Fortunatus* was probably played at court in December, 1599—that is, after Spenser's death but before the posthumous publication of the "Cantos of Mutabilitie." In the prologue two old men speak of their Queen, Eliza: "Some call her *Pandora*: some *Gloriana*, some *Cynthia*: some *Belphoebe*, some *Astraea*: all by seuerall names to expresse seuerall loues." And one of them sings her conquest of time:

> I weepe for ioy, to see so many heads
> Of prudent Ladies, clothed in the liuerie
> Of siluer-handed age, for seruing you,
> Whilst in your eyes youthes glory doth renue:
> I weepe for ioy to see the Sunne looke old,
> To see the Moone mad at her often change.
> To see the Starres onely by night to shine,
> Whilst you are still bright, still one, still diuine:
> I weepe for ioy to see the world decay,
> Yet see *Eliza* flourishing like May. . . .[10]

Could he have alluded so confidently to Spenser's many types of Queen Elizabeth if he had known what lay unpublished with the dead man's papers? When Elizabeth Tudor made her first progress through London as Queen, she saw a pageant erected at the Little Conduit in Cheap, in which a young woman, the Word of Truth, was represented as the daughter of Time. "*Time?*" said the young Queen, "and Time hath brought me hither."[11] But as her reign wore on, it was not the happy moment or process of time but her timelessness that became the theme of poets, the more when the problem of the succession as she declined in years became the unspoken preoccupation of the graver sort. How Spenser and his friends were privately thinking and feeling on the subject is perhaps best illuminated by a

10. Thomas Dekker, *Dramatic Works*, ed. Fredson Bowers (Cambridge, 1953), I, 113–14. Gloriana and Belphoebe are clear allusions to types of Queen Elizabeth in *The Faerie Queene*, and Astraea is a possible further Spenserian allusion. Following Ralegh, Spenser speaks of the Queen under the name of Cynthia in *Colin Clout*, and in *The Teares of the Muses* (578–80) he exclaims:

> The true *Pandora* of all heauenly graces,
> Divine *Elisa*, sacred Emperesse:
> Live she for ever. . . .

11. John Nichols, *The Progresses and Public Processions of Queen Elizabeth* (London, 1823), I, 48.

phrase used by Sir Walter Ralegh at his trial in 1603, when he referred to his late sovereign mistress as "a lady whom time had surprised."[12] The phrase would apply to the well-known portrait (necessarily posthumous) of Queen Elizabeth with Time and Death.[13] It would likewise apply to his friend Spenser's Mutabilitie in the palace of his own Cynthia.

In the encounter, though Cynthia retains some dignity, the attention and sympathy of the reader are entirely diverted from her. I am suggesting no more, but no less, than that we are jolted when "Time strong, a checklesse Queene"[14] enters her precincts and touches her person, that we feel a secret sympathy with the aggressor because she acts while her victim merely possesses, that we undergo with the poet a tacit abandonment of homage to a figure who (like Oriane de Guermantes) had exacted too long a sacrifice.

The irony of the poem becomes patent in the encounter of Mutabilitie with Jove (VII, vi, 23), which follows hot upon the indecisive clash with Cynthia:

So, forth she rose, and through the purest sky
To Ioues high Palace straight cast to ascend,
To prosecute her plot; Good on-set boads good end.

Jove's stern aspect takes her momentarily aback, but she rallies her spirits and boldly claims legitimate rule through Titan, elder brother of Jove's father, Saturn. Against this, Jove can only appeal to right of conquest. A disturbing thought must cross every reader's mind, that Jove is not the Law but merely nine points of the Law. Mutabilitie is quick to draw the perfectly valid conclusion that he is no equal judge in his own cause, and so she appeals to the higher authority of Nature. Jove's grudging allowance of this appeal is a clear admission of moral defeat for him and victory for her.

If Mutabilitie had less dignity than Cynthia, she has more dignity than Jove and her arguments carry more weight than his. A woman orator, impudent, paradoxical, surprisingly cogent in confounding the right-thinking, persistent and imaginative in her claim to universal sway, Mutabilitie now begins to resemble no one so much as the

12. Willard M. Wallace, *Sir Walter Raleigh* (Princeton, 1959), 206: we are reminded that the day of Ralegh's trial in 1603, November 17, was Queen Elizabeth's accession day, now for the first time in over forty years not kept as a holiday.

13. Roy C. Strong, *Portraits of Queen Elizabeth I* (Oxford, 1963), 153–4.

14. John Norden, *Vicissitudo Rerum*, stanza 157.

Folly of Erasmus.[15] An Erasmian ironic tone is pervasive, sharpening here into satire, and we enjoy the discomfiture of Mutabilitie's victims as we enjoy the discomfiture of Hamlet's victims, or Malevole's, or even Vindice's. And yet there is something inherently unstable about an alliance of the reader or spectator with the satirist: it can last only while the moral ambiguity of the satirist's own position is obscured by the patent hypocrisy of his opponents. At the moment, however, Mutabilitie shows herself not inconstant but constant in demanding her rights, and Jove is revealed (or stripped and whipped and anatomized) as an embodiment not of constancy but of mere self-satisfaction in moral allegory, the status quo in political, and in physical of a cosmological worldliness that is pleased to regard the outward governance of the universe as ultimate. The argument of the poem and its tone of feeling are themselves proving mutable; our sage and serious poet is also a chameleon poet.

At this point Mutabilitie and Jove occupy a position in our esteem comparable to Satan and God the Father in the more shamefaced of the Satanists' misreading of Milton. But Milton opens his poem by presenting Satan at his most heroic and humanly appealing and then contrives to make the figure shrivel, whereas Spenser presents Mutabilitie initially as menacing and demonic and then goes on to admit the cogency of her argument and, what is just as important for him, the beauty of her person. The reader fresh from *The Faerie Queene* will recall other women who combine a natural beauty with an element of the sinister. The beauty of Duessa and Lucifera, of Philotime and the False Florimell is unnatural, and that of Acrasia merely seductive; leave them aside. Radegund is the closest parallel, and it is worthy of note that she disarms her masculine antagonist by her loveliness and can be vanquished only by a female figure. For the present no woman except the hapless Cynthia appears within the purview of Mutabilitie, and her appeal is to the "god of Nature," who can only be presumed another Jove. And at the moment, if Mutabilitie is abashed by the majesty of Jove, Jove in turn is struck by her beauty: though they both rapidly recover themselves, the poem never quite reverts to the grinding grimness of some of the early stanzas.

15. H. H. Hudson, ed. and tr., *The Praise of Folly* (Princeton, 1941), esp. 14, 39, 51, passages in which Folly exposes the pretentions of Stoic apathy as Mutabilitie is to expose those of Stoic constancy. Spenser's figure is closer to Erasmus's than to any of the varieties of fool described by Enid Welsford, *The Fool* (London, 1935).

To effect a transition Spenser allows himself a mythological digression, a traditional feature of the *epyllion,* or little epic, of which genre the "Cantos of Mutabilitie" may perhaps be regarded as an example.[16] This is the story of foolish Faunus, who bribes Diana's attendant, the nymph Molanna, to conceal him while the goddess is bathing, and then so enjoys his treat that he laughs aloud, to the alarm and indignation of Diana and her ladies. The story purports to explain the reason for the present desolation of Arlo Hill, and so it has a narrative and a thematic connection with the poem as a whole—narrative as supplying a description of the place where Mutabilitie and Jove are to plead before Nature, thematic in being an account of destructive change, a story of over-reaching and misdemeanour, of punishment not only of the culprit but of the scene, the world, of the crime. But "crime" surely is too strong a word. Like Cynthia in the main story, Diana in the digression loses only a little of her dignity, her sacrosanctity. Actually, the final effect is one of pleasantness and delight: in contrast to the rushing dark satire of the earlier stanzas, the digression dreamily delights in its own narrative, spreading out to fill the time between the appeal and the hearing with the true plenitude of romance.

Even the outcome of this subordinate action is not too stern. Arlo Hill is spoiled, but Molanna is united with her lover as Faunus promised her, and Faunus himself escapes serious punishment. One of the vindictive virgins advocates gelding him, but this is vetoed on the ground that the woodgods' breed must still endure; and here too the digression moves in the same direction as the poem as a whole: in effect, nature intervenes to limit the consequences of the fall to suffering and discomfort, not annihilation.

After this relaxation of tension, the main action resumes in the presence of Nature; and with the decision to use the feminine pronoun the poet arouses a curious new feeling of expectation, awe, and repose. The figure of Nature in the "Cantos of Mutabilitie"[17] has long been

16. Compare the digression in Marlowe's *Hero and Leander*. See M. Marjorie Crump, *The Epyllion from Theocritus to Ovid* (Oxford, 1931), 23; see also 228–9 for a discussion of the set speech of formal appeal as a convention of the epyllion.

17. The figure of Nature is most fully discussed in a series of articles by E. C. Knowlton: "The Goddess Natura in Early Periods," *JEGP*, XIX (1920), 224–253; "Nature in Middle English," *JEGP*, XX (1921), 186–207; "Nature in Old French," *MP*, XX (1923), 309–329; "Spenser and Nature," *JEGP*, XXXIV (1935), 366–376. See also E. R. Curtius, *European Literature and the Latin Middle Ages*, tr. Willard

recognized as related to the goddess in Spenser's Garden of Adonis and Temple of Venus, and as belonging to a long literary and philosophical tradition including Chaucer's *Parlement of Foules* and Alain de Lille's *Complaint of Nature,* to both of which the poet alludes. Of two points we may remind ourselves. The first, common to Alain, Chaucer, and Spenser, is that Nature is altogether numinous, not at all secular, *natura naturans,* not *natura naturata;* and, as sage Heraclitus long before observed (fragment 123), "Nature likes to hide." The second, common to Spenser and his English master, is that Nature herself does not complain but rather embodies a serene and just power to which high and low, the satisfied and the disaffected, may present their case.

As all living things gather round Nature on Arlo Hill, finding their centre in her, we have a sense, as before in the Garden of Adonis, of being at the still point of the turning world.[18] In the palace of Cynthia, Mutabilitie was an intruder, but not here. By this juncture in the development of the poem we recognize in her a creaturely goodness, as her just appeal has proved and her beauty symbolized. Mutabilitie cannot simply represent sin if she humbles herself before Nature and if Nature in turn can call her "daughter." Perhaps this makes too much of a word of kindness; but there is a family resemblance between the two, for Mutabilitie is presented as a restless tomboy—aggressive as a man and passionate as a woman, and Nature is presented as possessing and rising above the limitations of both sexes. An Italian motto (a favourite saying of Queen Elizabeth) applies to both and joins them: *per molto variare la natura è bella.*

When all is quiet, Mutabilitie begins her case by arguing that the four elements—earth, water, air, and fire—are all subject to her and not to the gods, and then goes on to call the times and seasons of the year in procession so that Nature may either "demand in generall" or "judge her selfe, by verdit of her eye." Nature assents and commands Order to marshal them, and the pageant of Mutabilitie, the procession of the four seasons, the twelve months, Night and Day, Life and

R. Trask (New York, 1953), ch. 6; J. A. W. Bennett, *The Parlement of Foules* (Oxford, 1957), 108, 112; Edgar Wind, *Pagan Mysteries in the Renaissance* (London, 1958), ch. 14.

18. This is more than the *locus amoenus* described by Curtius, 195 ff.: it is also the "centre" as understood by Mircea Eliade in *The Myth of the Eternal Return* (New York, 1955), 12 ff.

Death, files past. It is not a ragged and shambling shuffle such as might have befitted a spectacle of the decay of the world; neither is it the headlong rush that the Titaness in her earlier mood might have devised. Instead, in its festive ease it cancels, or compensates for, all earlier statements of the idea of destructive time in the *Complaints* or in *The Faerie Queene*, much as (for instance) the marriage of the Thames and the Medway had righted any imbalance of feeling caused by the presentation of the watery part of the world as teeming with monsters and hostile to life. Mutabilitie herself is a keen competitor, but here in her pageant she presents no *agon* of winter and summer, no *hubris* of the year-daemon demanding a reversal of situation:[19] the figures in the pageant, the spectators on Arlo Hill, the poet and the reader from beginning to end accept the totality of the vision and each of the elements comprising it.

If Mutabilitie intended her argument to be a treatise of reformation without tarrying for any, what actually has emerged, in the presence of Nature, is a ritual procession full of decency and order. The rebel has become for the moment Mistress of the Revels.[20] The unruly rout, satiric or comic, strident or grotesque, of the opening of the poem and the digression, has been succeeded by a pageant, an antimasque by a masque, *discordia* by *concors*.[21] Spenser does not labour the paradox, but it is unmistakable: the more successfully Mutabilitie pleads her case against Jove, the more she depends on a constant order implicit in the created world. Here she anticipates the experience of alienation

19. The prime literary source is Book XV of Ovid's *Metamorphoses*, as was demonstrated by William P. Cumming, *SP*, XXVII (1931), 241–256. The passage (ll. 75–478) is elevated and emphatic: it is a description (not a pageant) of change working in all things, its argument being *omnia mutantur, nihil interit* (165); but the speaker uses his arts in the interest of mild government and vegetarianism, and his voice is less living and urgent than Mutabilitie's.

20. The *O.E.D.* traces the development in Old French of "revel" through the senses of rebellion, tumult, disturbance, noisy mirth before its appearance in English. See Enid Welsford, *The Court Masque* (London, 1927), 359. The double senses of "rout" as tumult and as succession, order, retinue; and of "brawl" (separately derived) as noisy turbulent quarrel and pace or movement in dance—both current in sixteenth-century England—likewise provide corroboration in the details of language for the psychological phenomenon of which *Mutabilitie* is an expression.

21. Cf. Enid Welsford, *The Court Masque*, 304, who likens the pageant to a masque; C. S. Lewis, *The Allegory of Love*, 356, who speaks of the "grotesque antimasque of Faunus"; Sherman Hawkins (see n. 2), who observes (88): "The entrance of the months and seasons resembles the climax of a masque: we have had the allegorical *débat* and the comic antimasque; now in glorious procession the masquers march before us."

characteristic of intellectuals in politics and the arts throughout modern times. What have we to show today for Elizabethan melancholy and Gothic melancholy, for the "spleen" in England and France, for *Weltschmerz* and *mal du siècle*, for the lost generation and the beat generation, but the happy works of the unhappy consciousness?[22]

The enthralling pageant comes to an end; while the spell is still upon us, Jove in a single prosy stanza (VII, vii, 48) states his case:

> Right true it is, that these
> And all things else that vnder heauen dwell
> Are chaung'd of *Time*, who doth them all disseise
> Of being: But, who is it (to me tell)
> That *Time* himselfe doth moue and still compell
> To keepe his course? Is not that namely wee
> Which poure that vertue from our heauenly cell,
> That moues them all, and makes them changed be?
> So then we gods doe rule, and in them also thee.

But Mutabilitie will have none of this. Spenser does not intend his shrew to be easily tamed. Reverting to her earlier, scolding tone, and breaking the spell of the pageant altogether, she expresses a rough scepticism of things that cannot be seen and of secret influence, and goes on to argue (but not, as in the pageant, to show) that the planets are mutable and their gods of earthly origin like herself.[23] And then in superb self-confidence she calls on Nature—"O thou greatest goddesse trewe!"—for judgment.

The following stanza (VII, vii, 57) is beautifully placed and beautifully modulated:

> So hauing ended, silence long ensewed,
> Ne *Nature* to or fro spake for a space,
> But with firme eyes affixt, the ground still viewed.
> Meane while, all creatures, looking in her face,
> Expecting th'end of this so doubtfull case,

22. There is a fine passage in Janet Spens, *Spenser's Faerie Queene* (London, 1934), 47: "All the figures in the masque—the Seasons, Months, Hours, Night and Day and Life—are, like Death itself, mere creations of our minds. The details of the pictures—winter's breath frozen on his beard, October 'tottie of the must'—are concretely vivid, but the seasons and months themselves are abstractions—ideas or names round which our constructive thought groups these pungent but fleeting impressions and by this grouping gives them 'a local habitation and a name.' "

23. Mutabilitie's euhemerism is her own, but her astronomy resembles that of the proem to Book V. In both passages, I am convinced, the physical decay of the cosmos is essentially a metaphor of the Fall. See Millar MacLure, "Nature and Art in *The Faerie Queene*," *ELH*, XXVIII (1961), 17.

Did hang in long suspence what would ensew,
To whether side should fall the soueraigne place:
At length, she looking vp with chearefull view,
The silence brake, and gaue her doome in speeches few.

A long silence, for an emphasis awful and apocalyptic. A great expectation and doubt, because the gods and creatures at the parley know as well as we that Mutabilitie has made the better case, but all must fear that she would make the worse ruler. And then, so important for the interpretation of the tone of feeling of the poem, Nature looks up cheerfully.[24] Cheerfulness breaks in as never in Alain de

24. See E. C. Knowlton, "Spenser and Nature," 370. Compare also the figure of Nature at the beginning and the end of John Lyly's *The Woman in the Moon* (registered 1595, published 1597), in *Complete Works*, ed. R. Warwick Bond (Oxford, 1902), III. The play opens thus:

NATURE

Nature descends from farre aboue the spheeres,
To frolicke heere in fayre Vtopia,
Where my chiefe workes do florish in their prime,
And wanton in their first simplicitie. . . .
But what meanes *Discord* so to knit the browes,
With sorrowes clowde ecclipsing our delights?

DISCORD

It grieues my hart, that still in euery worke
My fellow *Concorde* frustrates my desire,
When I to perfect vp some wondrous deed,
Do bring forth good and bad, or light and darke
Pleasant and sad, moouing and fixed things,
Fraile and immortall, or like contraries:
She with her hand vnites them all in one,
And so makes voide the end of mine attempt.

NATURE

I tell thee *Discord* while you twaine attend
On *Natures* traine, your worke must prooue but one:
And in your selues though you be different,
Yet in my seruice must you well agree.
For *Nature* workes her will from contraries,—
But see where our Vtopian Shepheardes come.

The Utopian Shepherds come to beg Pandora of Nature, and from that request arises the action of the play, the inconstancy and folly of Pandora being preyed upon by the envious gods. At the end Pandora makes this speech of submission to Nature as judge:

Fayre *Nature* let thy hand mayd dwell with her,
For know that change is my felicity,
And fickleness *Pandoraes* proper forme.
Thou madst me sullen first, and then *Ioue*, proud;
Thou bloody minded; he a Puritan:
Thou *Venus* madst me loue all that I saw,
And *Hermes* to deceiue all that I loue;
But *Cynthia* made me idle, mutable,
Forgetfull, foolish, fickle, franticke, madde;
These be the humors that content me best,
And therefore I will stay with *Cynthia*.

Lille, as never in Spenser's own *Complaints*. The very absence of anxiety and strain is a judgment against Mutabilitie: before she says a word, Nature tells the unhappy consciousness what it most needs and most fears to hear: rejoice. And this cheerfulness if we reflect for a moment should come as no surprise to us or to Mutabilitie, for the impresario must have inwardly rejoiced with all the other spectators at the success of her show. Spenser has a little modified, and greatly deepened, the insight of his friend Gabriel Harvey—"Nature herself is changeable and most of all delighted with vanitye; and art, after a sort her ape, conformeth herself to the like mutabilitye."[25]

This is the long-awaited doom of Nature (VII, vii, 58–59):

> I well consider all that ye haue sayd,
> And find that all things stedfastnes doe hate
> And changed be: yet being rightly wayd
> They are not changed from their first estate;
> But by their change their being doe dilate:
> And turning to themselues at length againe,
> Doe worke their owne perfection so by fate:
> Then ouer them Change doth not rule and raigne;
> But they raigne ouer change, and doe their states maintaine.

Like all other creatures, Mutabilitie seeks her own perfection. This is promised in the beauty of her person, it is performed in her masque. But her own perfection is not to have absolute sway:

> Cease therefore daughter further to aspire,
> And thee content thus to be rul'd by me:
> For thy decay thou seekst by thy desire;
> But time shall come that all shall changed bee,
> And from thenceforth, none no more change shall see.

Nature's judgment is perhaps not far different from Jove's plea—with the important difference that it issues from Nature, not from Jove, who if "confirmed in his imperial see," is seen to hold power not in his own right but by Nature's delegation. As for Mutabilitie, we realize now (if we follow out the implications of the argument)[26] that in claiming all the works and manifestations of nature as her own, she

25. Gabriel Harvey, *Letter Book*, ed. E. J. L. Scott (Camden Society, 1884), 87.

26. Milton Miller, "Nature in the *Faerie Queene*," *ELH*, XVIII (1951), 199: "She tries to prove that the heavens are, in fact, mutable, and yet is attempting to extend her sway over them. But obviously if the heavens are mutable, she does already reign in them; if they are not, she is merely overreaching herself, as both Jove and Nature maintain."

has also illogically claimed both to be Nature and to be judged by her —to be judge, that is, in her own cause, the very injustice she would not allow to Jove. *La femme révoltée* is "quite put down and whist," with many of her arguments allowed provisionally, all disallowed ultimately, and one refuted on the spot—for Mutabilitie, who had appealed to Nature, argued against the power and the very existence of the unseen, and yet, when judgment is delivered, "Natures selfe did vanish, whither no man wist." What we have seen in the "Two Cantos" is Mutabilitie dilating her being, first in strident aggression born of frustration and resentment, then in imaginative order springing from joy of creation, and finally at the word of Nature returning to herself again.

Attached to the two cantos are two stanzas, perhaps as the cantos themselves are attached to *The Faerie Queene*:

When I bethink me on that speech whyleare,
Of *Mutability*, and well it way:
Me seemes, that though she all vnworthy were
Of Heav'ns Rule; yet very sooth to say,
In all things else she beares the greatest sway.
Which makes me loath this state of life so tickle,
And loue of things so vaine to cast away;
Whose flowring pride, so fading and so fickle,
Short *Time* shall soone cut downe with his consuming sickle.

Then gin I thinke on that which Nature sayd,
Of that same time when no more *Change* shall be,
But stedfast rest of all things firmely stayd
Vpon the pillours of Eternity,
That is contrayr to *Mutabilitie*:
For, all that moueth, doth in *Change* delight:
But thence-forth all shall rest eternally
With Him that is the God of Sabbaoth hight:
O! that great Sabbaoth God, grant me that Sabaoths sight.

The last line is a full stop, both to the "Cantos" and to *The Faerie Queene*: to read it is really to be "in at the death of the Blatant Beast" —nothing more can happen. Again, it is a return, in its explicit Christianity, after much dilation in the order of nature, to the order of grace,[27] and so links the end of the poem as we have it with the beginning, the omega with the alpha.

27. See A. S. P. Woodhouse, "Nature and Grace in *The Faerie Queene*," *ELH*, XVI (1949), 194–228.

The stanzas have something of the quality of a medieval "retractation"—in glorified Renaissance version.[28] They recall the prayer with which Chaucer brings his long secular poem *Troilus and Criseyde* to a close; they recall too the direction and goal of Petrarch's *Trionfi*, in which Chastity triumphs over Love, Death over Chastity, Fame over Death, Time over Fame, and Eternity over Time. "Thou my mind, aspire to higher things," Spenser is in effect saying—"And death once dead, there's no more dying then."

If this is a retractation, what does the poet retract? The presumptuous and demonic in Ann Boleyn's daughter, in Gloriana, in *The Faerie Queene*. This is done in no fit of pietism or religious melancholia. The "Cantos of Mutabilitie" is not a lugubrious poem: quite apart from the promise of eternity, Nature and the poet's Muse look upon the mutable world itself with calmness and joy. Spenser and his poem and his land of faerie desire ultimately to vanish with Nature, or turn their view as Nature does from the world to God, but this longing, which in another context might be called escapism or a failure of nerve, is expressed—and only expressed—in the last stanza of a poem printed at the end of an immense unfinished epic, a lifework dealing with every conceivable contingency, both private and public, in the secular world. But simply because the epic, with the exception of the Legend of Holiness, is secular, time-ridden, written under the inspiration of Clio, Spenser may, indeed must, round it out by leaving it behind, give significance to the milling crowd of contingencies by asserting the one ultimate:

> These things have served their purpose: let them be.
> So with your own, and pray they be forgiven
> By others, as I pray you to forgive
> Both bad and good.—[29]

Both Mutabilitie and Gloriana.

28. For medieval retractations (or retractions) see F. N. Robinson's note in his *Complete Works of Geoffrey Chaucer* (Cambridge, Mass., 1933), 880–1. Sidney speaks of "certaine verses, which . . . she would haue adioyned as a retraction to the other"; *Arcadia*, ed. A. Feuillerat (Cambridge, 1912), 173. This is the word; "leave me, o love" is the thing.

29. T. S. Eliot, *Four Quartets* (London, 1944), 39.

Ben Jonson's Poems:
Notes on the Ordered Society

❁

HUGH MACLEAN

"THE REPUTATION OF JONSON," Mr. Eliot once remarked, "has been of the most deadly kind that can be compelled upon the memory of a great poet. To be universally accepted; to be damned by the praise that quenches all desire to read the book; to be afflicted by the imputation of virtues which excite the least pleasure; and to be read only by historians and antiquaries—this is the most perfect conspiracy of approval."[1] Perhaps the prospect is not quite so gloomy now: "Jonson criticism has at last commenced to grow green," Jonas Barish observes, and the articles he has recently collected indicate, over a variety of critical approaches, some avenues that may be profitably explored.[2] But it is striking that no essay in his collection bears directly on the lyric and occasional verse. If the lawn of Jonson criticism is newly green, brown patches are still perceptible.[3] That is not very surprising, of course, for *Timber* invites attention to the comedies:

The *Poet* is the neerest Borderer upon the Orator, and expresseth all his vertues, though he be tyed more to numbers; is his equall in ornament, and

1. T. S. Eliot, "Ben Jonson," *Selected Essays, 1913–1932* (New York, 1932), 147.
2. *Ben Jonson: A Collection of Critical Essays*, ed. J. A. Barish (Spectrum Books, 1963), 10.
3. R. M. Adams's admirable estimate, in *The Norton Anthology of English Literature*, ed. M. H. Abrams *et al.* (New York, 1962), I, 750, may be cited to indicate the elements in Jonson's poetry most often stressed by his critics: " . . . Ben Jonson and his followers produced verse which had the special Latin quality of being 'lapidary.' At its best their poetry gave the impression of being written to be carved in marble. Restrained in feeling, deliberately limited in its subject matter, intellectually thin but meticulously clear and incisive in expression, the poems of Jonson are models of this style."

above him in his strengths. And, (of the kind) the *Comicke* comes neerest: Because, in moving the minds of men, and stirring of affections (in which Oratory shewes, and especially approves her eminence) hee chiefly excells.[4]

Given this remark, and the elaborations that follow, to say nothing of the triumphant Jonsonian comedies themselves, later critics could hardly be expected to spare the poems more than an appreciative glance before passing to the main course of comedy. It has often been the fate of the poems to be praised chiefly (sometimes exclusively) for their formal virtues, while the best criticism of the comedies, more than ever since L. C. Knights's *Drama and Society in the Age of Jonson*, has kept steadily in view Jonson's comment that "the Study of [Poesy] (if wee will trust *Aristotle*) offers to mankinde a certaine rule, and Patterne of living well, and happily; disposing us to all Civill offices of Society."[5]

That is rather curious, too. The comedies, by their nature, present this "certaine rule, and Patterne" indirectly, appealing (as Knights says) to the "sardonic contemplation" of an audience characterized by "a lively sense of human limitations."[6] The epigrams, as a rule, repeat that method; but a significant number of the poems, particularly in *The Forrest*, deal explicitly and directly with "high and noble matter," with "the mysteries of manners, armes, and arts." Geoffrey Walton, following Leavis, remarks on Jonson's regular attention, in the poems, to "serious moral matters in a social context."[7] I suggest that, while the plays deal principally in the satiric recognition and description of the factors that contribute to social disorder, we find in the poems (with the *Discoveries* behind, as theory to practice), not an explicit and detailed outline of the social order Jonson admired, but rather "notes"

4. *Ben Jonson*, ed. C. H. Herford and P. Simpson (11 vols.; Oxford, 1925–52), VIII, 640. All references to Jonson's poetry and prose are made to this edition, hereafter cited as *H&S*. I have normalized i, j, u, v, and have reduced capitals to conform with modern usage.

5. *H&S*, VIII, 636. Critical works that attend to the "total achievement" of Jonson's poems include G. B. Johnston, *Ben Jonson: Poet* (New York, 1945); W. Trimpi, *Ben Jonson's Poems: A Study of the Plain Style* (Stanford, 1962), and the articles by G. R. Hibbard, Paul Cubeta, and Geoffrey Walton referred to in this essay (notes 7, 45). I am particularly indebted to the studies by Johnston and Trimpi and to Hibbard's article.

6. L. C. Knights, *Drama and Society in the Age of Jonson* (London, 1937), 208, 198.

7. Geoffrey Walton, "The Tone of Ben Jonson's Poetry," in *Seventeenth Century English Poetry*, ed. W. R. Keast (New York, 1962), 197.

on particular elements that ought to mark a society properly ordered, as well as suggestions for conduct in the midst of a disordered one. The negative strictures of the comedies, accordingly, are supplemented and completed by positive advices in the poetry and the *Discoveries*.

One must be careful not to claim too much: no integrated grand design for society emerges from the "lesser theatre" of these poems, so often committed to compliment. But the recurrence of three related themes is striking. In brief, the poems lay stress on the virtue of friendship between good men, who are receptive by nature to the free exchange of opinion and counsel, and on the strong resource such friendships constitute for the ordered society and the secure state. They reflect also Jonson's views on the relationship that ought ideally to obtain between prince and poet, in the interest of the people at large. Finally, they indicate the social attitudes and actions befitting a "ruling class" which thoroughly understands the nature of its responsibilities and desires to make them effective. It is relevant to observe here also that, when Jonson speaks to this third question, he is apt to select the verse-epistle as a vehicle peculiarly suited to the poet who outlines, for the benefit of those in high place, "holy lawes / Of nature, and societie." In this, as in much else, "there must be a Harmonie, and concent of parts."[8]

A dominant and recurring theme in the *Discoveries* is the humanistic insistence on man's power, in spite of his own nature and the vicissitudes of time, to maintain ethical standards, not in a spirit of reactionary opposition to change, but in large measure by adapting classical precepts to contemporary circumstance. "Rules," Jonson noted, "are ever of lesse force, and valew, then experiments"; men find truth by following "the *Ancients* . . . but as Guides, not Commanders."[9] Still, Jonson never pretended that this would be easy. He knew all about the shortcomings of human nature; when the character of mankind is in question, a note of disenchantment is often heard. "*Envy* is no new thing, nor was it borne onely in our times. The Ages past have brought it forth, and the comming Ages will. So long as there are men fit for it . . . it will never be wanting." "*Natures* that are hardned to *evill*, you shall sooner breake, then make straight; they are like poles that are crooked, and dry: there is no attempting them." Human nature "oft-times dies of a *Melancholy*, that it cannot be

8. *H&S*, VIII, 617.

9. *H&S*, VIII, 617, 567.

vitious enough."[10] It is clear too that Jonson recognized the threat of vice not merely to individuals but to the community much more.

When too much desire, and greedinesse of vice, hath made the body unfit, or unprofitable; it is yet gladded with the sight, and spectacle of it in others: and for want of ability to be an Actor; is content to be a Witnesse. It enjoyes the pleasure of sinning, in beholding others sinne; as in Dicing, Drinking, Drabbing, &c.

Indeed, "A native, if hee be vitious, deserves to bee a stranger, and cast out of the Common-wealth, as an Alien."[11] It goes without saying that Jonson would never abandon the effort to improve matters by any available means. He gathers up, for instance, Quintilian's gentle suggestions about the best ways in education and in criticism.[12] But in the final analysis, he depends on a continuing supply of naturally "*Good men* . . . the Stars, the Planets of the Ages wherein they live, [who] illustrate the times."[13] The well-known observation, "Men are decay'd, and *studies*: Shee [Nature] is not," needs to be compared with less familiar passages in the poet's commonplace book: "They are ever good men, that must make good the times: if the men be naught, the times will be such." "A good life," for Jonson, "is a maine Argument."[14]

It is in the light of these attitudes that we should read those poems in which Jonson turns his attention to friendship. Geoffrey Walton touches on this matter but does not come closely to grips with it, beyond an approving glance at a few of the poems addressed to friends in various walks of life; and while it is true that in these pieces "one can observe . . . [Jonson's] feeling for civilized personal relationships,"[15] there is more to be said. For Jonson, friendship is the bond enabling those good men who illustrate their times to group together and, by means of their collected virtue, cast out or resist vice. So they serve each other; but they help to safeguard the state as well.

These views are, of course, not original with Jonson, who might have been influenced by any of a number of authorities. But while it is not very feasible to suggest particular sources for his poetical comments on friendship (given their relatively orthodox detail, together with the wide range of his reading), it should at least be

10. *H&S*, VIII, 571, 564, 608.
11. *H&S*, VIII, 608–9; see also 597, ll. 1083–90.
12. *H&S*, VIII, 614, 617–18.
13. *H&S*, VIII, 597.
14. *H&S*, VIII, 567, 571, 566.
15. Walton, 200.

observed that Jonson, unlike Spenser, is not much interested in the conception of friendship "as a harmonizing and unifying principle of cosmic love operating in the realm of man to promote concord."[16] As usual with him, metaphysical theory takes second place to, or is eclipsed by, moral and social considerations. Friendship matters to Jonson because it is a moral virtue and because it contributes to social stability. His position recalls, in particular, that of Aristotle's dissertation on friendship (*Ethics*, VIII–IX), which contains some passages that must certainly have called out Jonson's approval, whether or not they directly influenced his poetry.[17] Having classified the three categories of friendship in terms of its object ("what is good, pleasurable, or useful"), Aristotle shows that friendships based on utility and pleasure must soon dissolve; he concludes that the only "perfect Friendship" subsists

> between those who are good and whose similarity consists in their goodness: for these men wish one another's good in similar ways; in so far as they are good (and good they are in themselves); and those are specially friends who wish good to their friends for their sakes, because they feel thus towards them on their own account and not as a mere matter of result; so the Friendship between these men continues to subsist so long as they are good; and goodness, we know, has in it a principle of permanence.[18]

"Some go so far as to hold that 'good man' and 'friend' are terms synonomous," he remarks in the same place, pointing out that "requital of Friendship is attended with moral choice which proceeds from a moral state." Relevant also is Aristotle's distinction between friendships moral and legal, and between elements within a "legal" friendship: "The Legal is upon specified conditions . . . the obligation is clear and admits of no dispute, the friendly element is the delay in requiring its discharge."

All this is reflected in Jonson's poems, which often repudiate, as in "An Epistle answering to one that asked to be Sealed of the Tribe of Ben" (9–15, 25–7), friendships based on utility or pleasure.

> Let those that meerely talke, and never thinke,
> That live in the wild Anarchie of Drinke,

16. C. G. Smith, *Spenser's Theory of Friendship* (Baltimore, 1935), 25.
17. The text referred to here is that edited by J. A. Smith: *The Ethics of Aristotle* (London, 1911).
18. This passage and those in the remainder of the paragraph are taken from *Ethics* (*ed. cit.*), 186–7, 183, 191, 205.

Subject to quarrell only; or else such
As make it their proficiencie, how much
They'ave glutted in, and letcher'd out that weeke,
That never yet did friend, or friendship seeke
But for a Sealing . . .

. . . . . .

Let these men have their wayes, and take their times
To vent their Libels, and to issue rimes,
I have no portion in them. . . .[19]

Flattery, the extreme of that "friendship whose motive is utility," Jonson condemns in a thoughtful phrase: "To flatter my good Lord" is "To lose the formes, and dignities of men" (*Under-Wood* XV, 146–7). The view that "those are specially friends who wish good to their friends for their sakes, because they feel thus towards them on their own account and not as a mere matter of result," informs poems as various as "Inviting a friend to supper" or the ode to a "high-spirited friend" (*Und.* XXVI); notable too is the "Epistle to a friend" (*Und.* XXXVII),[20] where the quality of "friendship which no chance but love did chuse" is heightened by contrast (7–9) with that of

Your Countrie-neighbours, that commit
Their vice of loving for a Christmasse fit;
Which is indeed but friendship of the spit. . . .[21]

These and other poems repeatedly emphasize certain qualities of friendship: moderation, candour, generosity, mutual esteem. The opening lines of the "Epigram: To a Friend, and Sonne" (*Und.* LXIX), perhaps to Lucius Cary, summarize those qualities with terse dignity:

Sonne, and my Friend, I had not call'd you so
To mee; or beene the same to you; if show,
Profit, or Chance had made us: But I know
What, by that name, wee each to other owe,
Freedome, and Truth; with love from those begot:
Wise-crafts, on which the flatterer ventures not.

That friendship is "attended with moral choice" is asserted by Jonson

19. See also "An Epistle to a Friend, to perswade him to the Warres" (*Und.* XV), 11–18, in *H&S*, VIII, 162.

20. See also *Ungathered Verse* XLIX, in *H&S*, VIII, 421.

21. Compare *H&S*, VIII, 597 ("*Livery-friends*, friends of the dish, and of the *Spit*, that waite their turnes, as my Lord has his feasts, and guests"); and see also "An Epistle to Master Arth: Squib" (*Und.* XLV), 7–8, in *H&S*, VIII, 216.

less emphatically than one might expect. Still, membership in the Tribe evidently involved selective distinction between suitable candidates and those who sought friendship "but for a Sealing"; and the poet seems to assume that his "high-spirited friend" cannot after all "mis-apply" the "wholsome Physick for the mind" prescribed by Jonson, but will in fact choose to accept the honest counsel of a friend. Another kind of moral choice emerges in *Under-Wood* XXXVII (25–30):

> It is an Act of tyrannie, not love,
> In practiz'd friendship wholly to reprove,
> As flatt'ry with friends humours still to move.
>
> From each of which I labour to be free,
> Yet if with eithers vice I teynted be,
> Forgive it, as my frailtie, and not me.

Friendship, in short, confers (or should confer) a capacity to recognize and accept some frailties in human nature, and so to overlook minor vices that may otherwise obscure or even destroy a relationship essentially virtuous: to resist vice, therefore, by a moral decision. One is struck by Jonson's recurring use of the term "free": true friends may fearlessly exchange ideas, give an opinion, advise, censure even. Men come to know liberty through friendship; or again, to be a friend is to free both oneself and one's friend. The term itself does not appear in yet another "Epistle to a Friend" (*Und.* XVII), on the distinction between legal and moral friendships, but the poem deals with the right use of that freedom which only friends can know (1–6, 11–16):

> They are not, Sir, worst Owers, that doe pay
> Debts when they can: good men may breake their day,
> And yet the noble Nature never grudge;
> 'Tis then a crime, when the Usurer is Judge.
> And he is not in friendship. Nothing there
> Is done for gaine: If't be, 'tis not sincere. . . .
>
> . . . he that takes
> Simply my Band, his trust in me forsakes,
> And lookes unto the forfeit. If you be
> Now so much friend, as you would trust in me,
> Venter a longer time, and willingly:
> All is not barren land, doth fallow lie.

The associations of friendship with moral virtue, however, are no less important for Jonson than the role of friendship in its social context. Aristotle had said that "Friendship seems to be the bond of Social Communities," and also that, if some forms of "Communion"

> are thought to be formed for pleasure's sake, those, for instance, of bacchanals or club-fellows, which are with a view to Sacrifice or merely company . . . [yet] all these seem to be ranged under the great Social one, inasmuch as the aim of this is, not merely the expediency of the moment but, for life and at all times. . . . So then it appears that all the instances of Communion are parts of the great Social one: and corresponding Friendships will follow upon such Communions.[22]

In "An Epistle answering to one that asked to be Sealed of the Tribe of Ben" (*Und.* XLVII), Jonson draws his view of friendship between individuals together with a statement on the obligations of friends to the body politic. The poem suggests that Jonson regarded the Tribe, his own band of brothers, not at all as an association "formed for pleasure's sake . . . or merely company," but as a dependable nucleus of virtuous companions, secure in self-knowledge and the wit to eschew triviality, upon whom the state might rely in all honourable causes. No doubt, too, while he would endorse all friendly connections established between virtuous men, he was bound to pay particular respect to any such group including a majority of poets, whose art is that "*Philosophy*, which leades on, and guides us by the hand to Action. . . ."[23] The title, with its scriptural allusion, and the lines glancing at heaven's purposes decorously reinforce the note of high seriousness recurrently dominant in this poem. While the "Epistle" is not precisely balanced in its structure, it seems to be true that Jonson deals at first (1–30) with the distinguishing features of men unfit for friendship, and in conclusion (51–78) with the characteristics of true friends. The intervening passage, for the greater part a contemptuous catalogue of trivia dear to gossiping courtiers, contains also (37–42, at the poem's centre, as it happens) a concise and plain-spoken affirmation of the good citizen's obligation to act as a member of the larger community.

> I wish all well, and pray high heaven conspire
> My Princes safetie, and my Kings desire,
> But if, for honour, we must draw the Sword,

22. *Ethics*, 182–3, 198.
23. *H&S*, VIII, 636.

And force back that, which will not be restor'd,
I have a body, yet, that spirit drawes
To live, or fall a Carkasse in the cause.

Fops chatter, men act. But the passage throws into high relief a more significant contrast. The wastrels described in the opening section of the poem may be "received for the Covey of Witts," but in fact no "ignorance is more then theirs." Their crass concerns mark them as slaves to passion. Knowing nothing of friendship, each cares for himself alone. Jonson's statement of personal principle that opens the concluding section (56–62) seems at first to assert merely another kind of self-centred aloofness. But the poet at once draws into his circle all men with whom "square, wel-tagde, and permanent" friendship is possible, men (that is) of Jonson's own stamp:

. . . all so cleare, and led by reasons flame,
As but to stumble in her sight were shame;
These I will honour, love, embrace, and serve:
And free it from all question to preserve.
So short you read my Character, and theirs
I would call mine. . . . (69–74)

Such men, devoted to principle not appetite, serve each other and the community; and on such men the state can rely when it is time to "draw the Sword." Through friendship, then, good men who understand the rights and duties of the freedom they enjoy, and who are prepared to act in defence of virtuous principles, form a reliable sub-stratum upon which the state and society at large may depend for health and survival.[24]

To match what may be called this broad "horizontal" principle of friendship among men of active virtue, one means of preserving a

24. This "Epistle" by Jonson should be compared with the following passage from Aristotle's *Ethics* (225): "The good man . . . must be specially Self-loving, in a kind other than that which is reproached, and as far superior to it as living in accordance with Reason is to living at the beck and call of passion, and aiming at the truly noble to aiming at apparent advantage. Now all approve and commend those who are eminently earnest about honourable actions, and if all would vie with one another in respect of the καλὸν, and be intent upon doing what is most truly noble and honourable, society at large would have all that is proper while each individual in particular would have the greatest of goods, Virtue being assumed to be such. . . . the good man does what he ought to do, because all Intellect chooses what is best for itself and the good man puts himself under the direction of Intellect.
Of the good man it is true likewise that he does many things for the sake of his friends and his country, even to the extent of dying for them, if need be. . . ."

desirable social order, Jonson was impressed also (as the *Discoveries* chiefly show) by the need for a "vertical" king-post of order: the healthy relationship of king and people. Details of mutual rights and duties, however, interested him less than the establishment of conditions that would be likely to ensure good government. Critics have often noticed that *dispositio*, arrangement, in plays or poems, receives Jonson's particular attention; the *Discoveries* everywhere reflect this concern.[25] In the state also, it is vital that administration be properly arranged, especially that the good prince shall be attended by good advisers; "for though the *Prince* himselfe be of most prompt inclination to all vertue: Yet the best *Pilots* have need of *Mariners*, beside Sayles, Anchor, and other Tackle," and "the good Counsellors to Princes are the best instruments of a good Age." "The best Counsellors," Jonson noted from Lipsius, "are books"; but the proposition implicit throughout the *Discoveries* is that, in fact, the best counsellor of all is the poet.[26]

Most of the Renaissance commonplaces about the relations of king and people are present in the *Discoveries*. "*The vulgar* . . . commonly ill-natur'd; and alwayes grudging against their *Governours*," are like a many-headed beast; the good prince "is the Pastor of the people . . . the *soule* of the Commonwealth; and ought to cherish it, as his owne body"; "*After God*, nothing is to be lov'd of man like the Prince." Jonson is orthodox on rebellion too: "Let no man therefore murmure at the Actions of the Prince, who is plac'd so farre above him. If hee offend, he hath his Discoverer. *God* hath a height beyond him."[27] For these views and others like them, there was plenty of authority in Seneca, Erasmus, Lipsius, and "the great *Doctor of State, Macchiavell*," on whom he draws directly for a mordant passage about advisers to the prince. Yet if he recognizes Machiavellian wisdom in some things, Jonson does not give way to cynicism. "The *Princes* Prudence" (as he notes from Farnese) may well be "his chiefe Art, and safety"; but it is "the mercifull *Prince* . . . safe in love, not in feare," whom Jonson admires. "A *good King* is a publike Servant," by no means "(as it is in the Fable) a crowned Lyon." He can agree that "*the strength* of Empire is in Religion. . . . Nothing more commends the

25. See, for example, *H&S*, VIII, 645 (Jonson's discussion of "*the magnitude, and compasse of any Fable*"), and even 569–70 (on the "*tedious* person").
26. *H&S*, VIII, 601–2.
27. *H&S*, VIII, 593, 602, 594, 600.

Soveraigne to the Subject, then it," but then his own voice breaks in, "For hee that is religious, must be mercifull and just necessarily. . . . Justice is the vertue, that *Innocence* rejoyceth in."[28] The prudence that adjusts flexibly to change and circumstance, and yet serves virtue still, he thought an essential element of administration, that princely art. "*Wise*, is rather the attribute of a Prince, then *learned*, or *good*"; but the governor who is truly wise must in the nature of things be a good man too.[29]

Well enough; yet, "*Princes* are easie to be deceiv'd . . . what wisdome can escape it; where so many Court-*Arts* are studied?" One answer recalls that of Lipsius: "A *Prince* without Letters, is a Pilot without eyes." But a more effective response is to choose the right sort of counsellor: "Soveraignty needs counsell." Jonson knew from Vives what to look for:

In being able to counsell others, a Man must be furnish'd with an universall store in himselfe, to the knowledge of all *Nature*: That is the matter, and seed-plot; There are the seats of all Argument, and Invention. But especially, you must be cunning in the nature of Man: There is the variety of things, which are as the *Elements*, and *Letters*, which his art and wisdome must ranke, and order to the present occasion. For wee see not all letters in single words; nor all places in particular discourses. . . . The two chiefe things that give a man reputation in counsell, are the opinion of his *Honesty*; and the opinion of his *Wisdome*. . . . *Wisedome* without *Honesty* is meere craft, and coosinage. And therefore the reputation of *Honesty* must first be gotten; which cannot be, but by living well.

And of all such persons, the poet is most clearly qualified:

I could never thinke the study of *Wisdome* confin'd only to the Philosopher: or of *Piety* to the *Divine*: or of *State* to the *Politicke*. But that he which can faine a *Common-wealth* (which is the *Poet*) can governe it with *Counsels*, strengthen it with *Lawes*, correct it with *Judgements*, informe it with *Religion*, and *Morals*; is all these. Wee doe not require in him meere *Elocution*; or an excellent faculty in verse; but the exact knowledge of all vertues, and their Contraries; with ability to render the one lov'd, the other hated, by his proper embattaling them.[30]

The prince is the apex, so to speak, of society's pyramid, but he needs the special insight of the poet, who combines "goodnes of natural wit" with the capacity ("as by a divine Instinct") to utter "somewhat above

28. *H&S*, VIII, 599, 594, 600–1.
29. *H&S*, VIII, 594.
30. *H&S*, VIII, 603, 601, 565–6, 595.

a mortall mouth." When the prince attends to the counsel of his best adviser, the learned poet (who ought also to be his truest friend), he serves his people as ideal example, almost in the fashion Jonson noted from Euripides: "Where the *Prince* is good . . . *God is a Guest in a humane body*." Philosopher-kings and poet-princes are rare: for the rest, "no man is so wise, but may easily erre, if hee will take no others counsell, but his owne."[31]

Jonson was ready and willing to advise the monarch: he said to Drummond, "so he might have favour to make one Sermon to the King, he careth not what yrafter sould befall him, for he would not flatter though he saw Death."[32] This was, perhaps, bravado, although the notes for a disquisition on kingship lay at hand in the *Discoveries*, and this poet, at least, enjoyed high favour, amounting almost to friendship, with James I. But Jonson was quite aware that the "free" exchange of advice and counsel natural to friends could scarcely be duplicated in these circumstances. He had read Vives on the problems of counselling kings, "especially in affaires of *State*." And of course his own encounters with officialdom, notably in connection with *Sejanus* in 1603, when Northampton accused him "both of popperie & treason," must sufficiently have impressed even the poet who "never esteemed of a man for the name of a Lord."[33] In any event, although one could compose verse-epistles or odes to advise one's high-spirited friends, even, by judicious indirection, counsel a whole class of society, it was difficult to extend these methods to the monarch. A few pieces, however, are relevant to Jonson's prose observations on the conduct appropriate for the good prince; and these bear also on the poems to and about his patrons.

Most of the poems addressed by Jonson to royalty are "occasional" in a narrow sense;[34] one or two others repeat the commonplace that a poet ensures fame or notoriety for his subjects. "The lesse-*Poetique* boyes" may expect "a Snake"; but "in the *Genius* of a *Poets* Verse, The Kings fame lives" (*Und.* LXXVI, LXVIII). "The humble

31. *H&S*, VIII, 637, 600, 563. 32. *H&S*, I, 141.

33. *H&S*, VIII, 566; I, 141. A letter of 1605 requesting support from a sponsor now unknown acknowledges that "there is no subject hath so safe an Innocence, but may rejoyce to stand justified in sight of his Soveraignes mercie. To which we must humblie submytt our selves, our lives and fortunes" (*H&S*, I, 197).

34. Epigram LI, "To King James, upon the happy false rumour of his death," many of the birthday poems in *The Under-Wood*, and the "Song of Welcome to King Charles" (*Ungathered Verse* XLIV), exemplify the range of these pieces.

Petition of poore Ben: To . . . King Charles" (*Und.* LXXVI), however, primarily a request for more money, takes care to stress the rationale of the poet's position (3–7):

> . . . your royall *Father*,
> James *the blessed*, pleas'd the rather,
> Of his speciall grace to *Letters*,
> To make all the Muses debters,
> To his bountie. . . .

That Jonson claims his due "for goodnesse sake" is apt enough, since the best princes know that poetry is "neerest of kin to Vertue." Another "Epigram: To K. Charles . . . 1629" (*Und.* LXII) varies the same theme:

> Great Charles, among the holy gifts of grace
> Annexed to thy Person, and thy place,
> 'Tis not enough (thy pietie is such)
> To cure the call'd *Kings Evill* with thy touch;
> But thou wilt yet a Kinglier mastrie trie,
> To cure the *Poets Evill*, Povertie. . . .

This poem, too, concludes on a note of nearly explicit advice:

> What can the *Poet* wish his *King* may doe,
> But, that he cure the Peoples Evill too?

Jonson, however, does not as a rule presume to counsel the prince in these poems even thus indirectly. He prefers to draw attention to the fact (illustrated, fortunately, in both James and Charles) that the character and actions of a prince should be exemplary and therefore instructive, and to indicate some suggestive parallels between king and poet. An "Epigram: To . . . K. Charles" of 1629 (*Und.* LXIV) makes the first point, in somewhat fulsome tones:

> Indeed, when had great *Britaine* greater cause
> Then now, to love the Soveraigne, and the Lawes?
> When you that raigne, are her Example growne,
> And what are bounds to her, you make your owne?
> When your assiduous practise doth secure
> That Faith, which she professeth to be pure?
> When all your life's a president of dayes,
> And murmure cannot quarrell at your wayes?[35]

35. "A Parallell of the Prince to the King" (*Poems Ascribed to Jonson*, II), *H&S*, VIII, 429, rejected by Herford and Simpson as not Jonson's, nevertheless is reproduced in *Poems of Ben Jonson*, ed. G. B. Johnston (London, 1954), 301–2. On this

More striking are two of the *Epigrams*. "To King James" (IV) all but proclaims the monarch that ideal "poet-prince" who needs no other counsel.

> How, best of Kings, do'st thou a scepter beare!
> How, best of *Poets*, do'st thou laurell weare!
> But two things, rare, the Fates had in their store,
> And gave thee both, to shew they could no more.
> For such a *Poet*, while thy dayes were greene,
> Thou wert, as chiefe of them are said t'have beene.
> And such a Prince thou art, wee daily see,
> As chiefe of those still promise they will bee.
> Whom should my *Muse* then flie to, but the best
> Of Kings for grace; of *Poets* for my test?

A second poem (XXXV) with the same title enlarges on the principle of rule.

> Who would not be thy subject, James, t'obay
> A Prince, that rules by'example, more than sway?
> Whose manners draw, more than thy powers constraine.
> And in this short time of thy happiest raigne,
> Hast purg'd thy realmes, as we have now no cause
> Left us of feare, but first our crimes, then lawes.
> Like aydes 'gainst treasons who hath found before?
> And than in them, how could we know god more?

The prince, then (who is the better ruler for a youthful poetic bent), governs, as the poet teaches, by persuasion and example; and at length, through the laws that reflect his wisdom, the subjects discover for themselves that here indeed, "God is a guest in a human body."

That these poems are few in number was to be expected: even if wisdom had not checked the impulse to counsel a king, Jonson was not the man to lavish his talents on this particular variety of panegyric. But an attractive alternative remained. One could, if one were reasonably decorous, address a ruling class instead. Those members of aristocratic families who extended their patronage and support to Jonson, especially those with whom the poet could consider himself to

---

hint, it is worth mentioning that the poem, likening Charles to Achilles, includes the passage, "His all his time, but one Patroclus findes, But this of ours a world of faithfull friends," and also, "His had his Phoenix, ours no teacher needs, But the example of thy Life and Deeds."

be on terms at least relatively informal, must in any event be honoured in the poet's verse. While he could not ordinarily expect to be as candid (or blunt) as with his own colleagues, he could claim with some justice to have attained something like friendship with a number of highly placed individuals. Relatively free, therefore, from the limitations imposed where princes were in question, yet still addressing or chiefly complimenting persons regularly concerned, in various spheres, with the maintenance of order in social and political life, Jonson could counsel while appearing chiefly to praise. For young Sir William Sidney, the poet might assume an oracular tone; with others, the note of approbation or reminder would often be more fitting. Particularly in *The Forrest*, but elsewhere too, he incorporates in gracefully complimentary verse those principles of social responsibility which the actions of a ruling class ought in his view to reflect. The poet, in short, transfers his advisory function (properly directed to a prince) to that class from which, as a rule, the monarch will draw his counsellors; and he can address some of them, at least, in a manner formal and "easy" at once.

Jonson's attitude to his patrons is conditioned primarily by three factors. He needed their support, of course, but that is in some ways the least important of the three: poems that openly request or acknowledge financial support appear only in the last years, when the poet's fortunes were palled. As a rule, Jonson chose to ignore the subject, or to make it the occasion for a lecture on the art of giving and receiving, as in the "Epistle to . . . Sacvile" (*Und.* XIII), which strikes a characteristic note.

> You . . . whose will not only, but desire
> To succour my necessities, tooke fire,
> Not at my prayers, but your sense; which laid
> The way to meet, what others would upbraid;
> And in the Act did so my blush prevent,
> As I did feele it done, as soone as meant:
> You cannot doubt, but I, who freely know
> This Good from you, as freely will it owe;
> And though my fortune humble me, to take
> The smallest courtesies with thankes, I make
> Yet choyce from whom I take them. . . . (7–17)

The lines reflect a cast of mind also apparent in Aubrey's allusion to

"Mr. Benjamin Johnson (who ever scorned an unworthy patrone)."[36] No doubt unworthiness might consist in the refusal to honour a promise of support, as Epigram LXV ("To my Muse") may indicate. But the poem hints at deeper causes of scorn; and Epigram X ("To my lord Ignorant") is perhaps relevant:

> Thou call'st me *Poet*, as a terme of shame:
> But I have my revenge made, in thy name.

While the episode at Salisbury's table is familiar, there were others of the sort:

> Ben one day being at table with my Lady Rutland [Drummond writes], her husband comming in, accused her that she keept table to poets, of which she wrott a letter to him which he answered My Lord intercepted the letter, but never chalenged him.[37]

A patron may be "unworthy" on several counts, but his failure to acknowledge the poet's right to a privileged place in society is particularly reprehensible. Finally, Jonson expected the patron and his class to exemplify virtuous conduct, and so to persuade a society and secure a state. The *Epigrams* are dedicated to Pembroke, "Great Example of Honor and Vertue"; and whatever Jonson thought of the man described by Clarendon as "immoderately given up to women," Epigram CII illustrates the poet's ideal.

> . . . thou, whose noblesse keeps one stature still,
> And one true posture, though besieg'd with ill
> Of what ambition, faction, pride can raise;
> Whose life, ev'n they, that envie it, must praise;
> That art so reverenc'd, as thy comming in,
> But in the view, doth interrupt their sinne;
> Thou must draw more: and they, that hope to see
> The common-wealth still safe, must studie thee.

More specifically (as the poems reveal), Jonson expected a patron to pay more than lip-service to the ideal of fraternity; to illustrate in thought and action the continuing virtue of ancient traditions; to renew in each age, by the wise application of inherited talent, the life and force of those traditions. When hard circumstance closed every other avenue, there remained an obligation to exemplify (if

36. John Aubrey, *Brief Lives*, ed. A. Powell (London, 1949), 371.
37. *H&S*, I, 142.

need be, "farre from the maze of custome, error, strife") the ideal of virtuous life appropriate to one's station.

Jonson, accordingly, looked for a good deal more than financial support from the highly placed persons who could sponsor him. And he "counselled" his patrons, directly and indirectly, in a good many genres, from the epigram to the ode. The verse-epistle in particular he found well suited to his personality and his purposes. As Trimpi shows,[38] the genre by Jonson's time combined regard for a continuing stylistic tradition with an attitude toward the range of matter proper to the verse-epistle considerably more liberal than that of classical practice. Cicero's observations on the characteristics of the plain style in oratory, and the view of Demetrius that, in genres suited to the plain style (i.e., comedy, satire, epigram, epistle), "the diction throughout [will be] current and familiar," particularly that the epistle should "obey the laws of friendship, which demand that we should 'call a spade a spade,' as the proverb has it," contributed to a tradition of epistolary style endorsed by Lipsius, Vives, and John Hoskyns.[39] On the other hand, Demetrius' opinion that "there are epistolary topics, as well as an epistolary style," and that "in the case of the plain style, we can no doubt point to subject matter which is homely and appropriate to the style itself," had gradually given way to the view that the range of topics proper to the epistle may extend to "all public, private, and domestic concerns."[40]

A verse form at once traditional and evolving in this way suited Jonson very well. The manner of any one epistle will certainly vary with the occasion; one does not address a noble lord as one might ask a friend to dinner. Nor are we to expect advice directly given so much as the counsel implicit in the poet's approbation of the action and character he describes; for "it . . . behooves the giver of counsell to be circumspect."[41] Still, the humanist who allowed Aristotle his due while insisting on the right to "make further Discoveries of truth and fitnesse," and who thought rules less forceful than experiments, recognized the suitability of the verse-epistle for precepts turning on the principle, "Newnesse of Sense, Antiquitie of voyce!"[42] Again, it was an appropriate medium for the poet concerned to remind society and

38. Trimpi, *Poems*, 60–75.
39. *Ibid.*, 6–9.
40. *Ibid.*, 68, 70.
41. *H&S*, VIII, 566.
42. "An Epistle to Master John Selden" (*Und.* XIV), 60: *H&S*, VIII, 160.

its leaders of the dangerous temptation to "rest / On what's deceast": rather (*Und.* XIII, 131–4),

> 'Tis by degrees that men arrive at glad
> Profit in ought; each day some little adde,
> In time 'twill be a heape; This is not true
> Alone in money, but in manners too.

And, of course, for one whose sense of injur'd merit lay always ready to hand, the relatively plain-spoken style of the verse-epistle might usefully reinforce expressions hinting at an equality of merit, or even at actual friendship, between poet and the highly placed person addressed.[43]

Evidently Jonson employs forms other than the verse-epistle proper to endorse or counsel the social actions of his patrons. It may be observed, however, that while XII and XIII in *The Forrest* are explicitly termed "epistles," III ("To Sir Robert Wroth") is surely one also. The "Ode: To Sir William Sydney" gives advice as directly as does the "Epistle to a Friend, to perswade him to the Warres" (*Und.* XV), or even the "Epistle to . . . Sacvile." And the *Epigrams* (among which appears "Inviting a friend to supper") include several pieces not obviously representative of Jonson's taut standards for the epigram. Jonson was fond of mingling literary kinds, and in any event he had good classical precedents for the practice.[44] That various formal labels attached to these poems should not obscure the fact that they all reflect his conviction that the poet has a clear right, a duty even, to speak out to his patron in a manly fashion. Perhaps one may risk the suggestion that Jonson found the verse-epistle especially congenial and that something of its character and tone often echoes in poems not formally so described. If he employs the verse-epistle to remind a ruling group of the constant standard it must uphold and of the continual adjustment to circumstance this will require, and to insist besides on the essential fraternity of a healthy society, poems called "odes" or "epigrams" reflect those elements too.

"To Penshurst," formally both ode and "country-house poem," has been rather thoroughly examined by G. R. Hibbard (and others),[45]

43. In this connection, see J. A. Levine, "The Status of the Verse Epistle before Pope," *SP*, LIX (1962), 658–84, esp. 675–6. 44. See Trimpi, *Poems*, 159–60.

45. G. R. Hibbard, "The Country House Poem of the Seventeenth Century," *Journal of the Warburg and Courtauld Institute*, XIX (1956), 159 ff.; and see Paul Cubeta, "A Jonsonian Ideal: 'To Penshurst,' " *PQ*, XLII (1963), 14–24.

but since Jonson here explicitly considers the role of an aristocratic dynasty (in terms of one with which he felt particular sympathy), one or two points need emphasis. Penshurst, apt symbol of the Sidney line, instructively illustrates Jonson's social ideal in one aspect at least: the contrast with those more magnificent ancestral piles that betray pride and ambition points up Penshurst's vitality and their lack of it. But we are not regularly made aware of "the world outside" Penshurst in this poem, although opening and conclusion remind us of that world's existence: Jonson's emphasis falls deliberately on the positive ideal exemplified at Penshurst. That nature is everywhere compliant, even eager to serve man, effectively supplements the fraternal atmosphere prevailing in this household, where all classes are as welcome as the poet (45–50, 61–4):

> . . . though thy walls be of the countrey stone,
> They'are rear'd with no mans ruine, no mans grone,
> There's none, that dwell about them, wish them downe;
> But all come in, the farmer, and the clowne:
> And no one empty-handed, to salute
> Thy lord, and lady, though they have no sute. . . .
> [There] comes no guest, but is allow'd to eate,
> Without his feare, and of thy lords owne meate:
> Where the same beere, and bread, and self-same wine,
> That is his Lordships, shall be also mine.

And while the family that acknowledges its social responsibilities spreads genial influence on all sides, so too it prepares for its successors, those aristocratic patrons of the next age, by properly educating and directing offspring who (96–8) may

> every day,
> Reade, in their vertuous parents noble parts,
> The mysteries of manners, armes, and arts.[46]

If this is how a great family ought to act, Jonson remarks also on the conduct appropriate to individual members of that family. Of the various poems addressed to members of the clan, the "Ode: To Sir William Sydney, on his Birth-day" is of special interest; since the person addressed is at the point of transition from youth to manhood, his responsibilities to a noble line and to society at large are emphasized in conjunction. Jonson thought that "no perfect Discovery can bee

46. See also "An Epigram on . . . Burleigh" (*Und.* XXX), 13–19.

made upon a flat or a levell"; also that "to many things a man should owe but a temporary beliefe, and a suspension of his owne Judgement, not an absolute resignation of himselfe, or a perpetuall captivity."[47] These principles underlie his advice to the young Sidney (27–50):

> . . . he doth lacke
> Of going backe
> Little, whose will
> Doth urge him to runne wrong, or to stand still.
> Nor can a little of the common store,
> Of nobles vertue, shew in you;
> Your blood
> So good
> And great, must seeke for new,
> And studie more:
> Not weary, rest
> On what's deceast.
> For they, that swell
> With dust of ancestors, in graves but dwell.
> 'T will be exacted of your name, whose sonne,
> Whose nephew, whose grand-child you are;
> And men
> Will, then,
> Say you have follow'd farre,
> When well begunne:
> Which must be now,
> They teach you, how.
> And he that stayes
> To live until to morrow' hath lost two dayes.

These poems clearly reflect important elements in Jonson's "theory of social order": they are guide-lines for a ruling class that collectively and individually cares about its responsibilities. But they lack a dimension. The bright perfection of a Sidney-world obscures the sombre social backdrop that requires to be regulated by Sidneys and those like them. Leaders cannot forever prevent the incursions of vice, after all, by exemplifying virtue at a cool remove; they must often descend into the arena and actively wrestle with the enemy. Perhaps Jonson felt some reluctance, for reasons of decorum, to present Sidneys in postures other than serene: one recalls the "Epode" (*Forrest,* XI):

> Not to know vice at all, and keepe true state,
> Is vertue, and not *Fate:*

47. *H&S,* VIII, 627–8.

Next, to that vertue, is to know vice well,
And her blacke spight expell. (1–4)

In any case, other poems not addressed to members of the Sidney clan complement and amplify the views approved in "Penshurst" and counselled in the "Ode." And each presumes a context appropriate to the second couplet of the "Epode."

Epigram LXXVI ("On Lucy Countesse of Bedford") has often attracted the admiration of critics: "How to be" may be suggested as the theme of this poem, which wittily translates ideal into fact. Less often noticed, but more significant here, is Epigram XCIV ("To Lucy, Countesse of Bedford, with Mr. Donnes Satyres"), an equally polished piece, with the theme, "How to act."

Lucy, you brightnesse of our spheare, who are
Life of the *Muses* day, their morning-starre!
If workes (not th'authors) their owne grace should looke,
Whose poemes would not wish to be your booke?
But these, desir'd by you, the makers ends
Crowne with their owne. Rare poemes aske rare friends.
Yet, *Satyres*, since the most of mankind bee
Their un-avoided subject, fewest see:
For none ere tooke that pleasure in sinnes sense,
But, when they heard it tax'd, tooke more offence.
They, then, that living where the matter is bred,
Dare for these poemes, yet, both aske, and read,
And like them too; must needfully, though few,
Be of the best: and 'mongst these, best are you.
Lucy, you brightnesse of our spheare, who are
The *Muses* evening, as their morning-starre.

Here is a poem decorously circular in design, turning on the role appropriate to patrons and exemplified by Lucy, who is not simply "Life of the *Muses* day," but who has the wit to discern and distinguish: to be, in fact, one of those "rare friends" that "rare poems" demand, patrons who, by extending favour to the poet, acknowledge the quality of the poetry—one might say, pay court to it. Far from assuming an attitude of aloofness and hauteur, his patroness, who deliberately seeks out satirical poems for their "matter," is concerned with the moral character of all levels of society, not merely her own. As true aristocrat, the Countess of Bedford justifies her place in the social order by gaining knowledge, through the mirror held up to nature by the poet, of social conditions upon which she may then (Jonson seems to imply) bring her beneficent influence to bear. But even if she does not act in that way, her refusal to turn away from unpleasant or disturbing aspects of society, her insistence on a full view, indicate the completeness of her own nature, one fit to be described as evening and morning star both: a "full constant light," in fact, perfectly exemplifying the recognition that ancient privilege never exempts from present responsibility.

"To Sir Robert Wroth" (*The Forrest*, III) parallels "To Penshurst" in its emphasis on the acquiescence of external nature in the pursuits of man ("A serpent river leades / To some coole, courteous shade"), and on the mingling in this household, when occasion arises, of all classes (53–8):

> The rout of rurall folke come thronging in,
>   (Their rudenesse then is thought no sinne)
> Thy noblest spouse affords them welcome grace;
>   And the great *Heroes*, of her race,
> Sit mixt with losse of state, or reverence.
>   Freedome doth with degree dispense.

However, unlike the other, this poem continually reminds the reader of threatening and vicious forces at court and in the world environing Wroth's home; the "thousands" who (85–8)

> . . . goe flatter vice, and winne,
>   By being organes to great sinne,
> Get place, and honor, and be glad to keepe
>   The secrets, that shall breake their sleepe. . . .

The natural surroundings of Durrants provide, not a permanent haven, but merely a "securer rest," to which Wroth may intermittently retreat for spiritual refreshment and moral strength, before returning to the task Jonson considers appropriate to every leader: "To doe thy countrey service, thy selfe right." Further, while divine power and natural influences may direct Wroth and his highly placed fellows to peace of mind, and enable them to meet the temptations of city and court with equanimity, still (93–4)

> . . . when man's state is well,
>   'Tis better, if he there can dwell.

These tentative expressions point to the fact that the life even of the good man is one of continual and rigorous struggle, to shore up or regulate social order, and also, through self-examination, to guard against the "subtle traines" (as the "Epode" has it) by which "severall passions invade the minde, / And strike our reason blinde."

The "Epistle to . . . Sacvile" (*Und.* XIII), in which social vice and disorder are once again extensively detailed, with special attention to "hunters of false fame," adds a final note of counsel to the active leader. It is not enough merely to hold at bay the forces making for disorder in society and in oneself. The point of struggle is to secure virtue or to alter a vicious situation: to make something happen. At the very least, one may demonstrate in one's own person what others may also achieve (135–44). ("They are ever good men, that must make good the times").

> . . . we must more then move still, or goe on,
> We must accomplish; 'Tis the last Key-stone
> That makes the Arch. The rest that there were put
> Are nothing till that comes to bind and shut.
> Then stands it a triumphall marke! then Men
> Observe the strength, the height, the why, and when,
> It was erected; and still walking under
> Meet some new matter to looke up and wonder!
> Such Notes are vertuous men! they live as fast
> As they are high; are rooted and will last.

All these poems counsel or approve social actions befitting persons responsible for the maintenance and direction of social order. But what if society, hardened in bad moulds, too toughly resists the efforts of dedicated leaders to re-direct its course? For Jonson had read his Seneca: "Wee will rather excuse [a vice], then be rid of it. That wee cannot, is pretended; but that wee will not, is the true reason. . . . It was impossible to reforme these natures; they were dry'd, and hardned in their ill."[48] The "Epistle: To Katherine, Lady Aubigny" (*The Forrest*, XIII) gives counsel for just such a situation. Not surprisingly, Jonson advises his patroness to profit by the poet's example: fortitude in adversity and confidence to endure in the midst of trial will both be required. The poem opens with a warning:

> 'Tis growne almost a danger to speake true
> Of any good minde, now: There are so few.

48. *H&S*, VIII, 580.

> The bad, by number, are so fortified,
> As what th'have lost t'expect, they dare deride.
> So both the prais'd, and praisers suffer. . . .

But the poet, "at fewd / With sinne and vice, though with a throne endew'd," does not recoil. "Though forsooke / Of *Fortune*," Jonson proudly claims (15–20)

> [I] have not alter'd yet my looke,
> Or so my selfe abandon'd, as because
> Men are not just, or keepe no holy lawes
> Of nature, and societie, I should faint. . . .

The character of Lady Aubigny, "perfect, proper, pure and naturall" (for so her "beauties of the mind" are shown in the poet's mirror), enables her to take a stand analogous to that of the beleagured poet. Even friendship may fail (53–58); but the individual's responsibility to virtue remains constant (51–2):

> 'Tis onely that can time, and chance defeat:
> For he, that once is good, is ever great.

In an unregenerate world that "cannot see / Right, the right way," the virtuous individual may continue to influence others merely by being true to herself, as Jonson reminds Lady Aubigny (110–12),

> . . . since you are truly that rare wife,
> Other great wives may blush at: when they see
> What your try'd manners are, what theirs should bee.

But this, he knew, was rather to be wished than expected; and since even a poet might sing, in fierce adversity, "high, and aloofe," the key passage of the poem (59–63; 121–4) advocates the pursuit of virtue in a larger context. When the times defy moral redemption, and friends fall off,

> This makes, that wisely you decline your life,
> Farre from the maze of custome, error, strife,
> And keepe an even, and unalter'd gaite;
> Not looking by, or backe (like those, that waite
> Times, and occasions, to start forth, and seeme) . . .
>
> Live that one, still; and as long yeeres doe passe,
> *Madame*, be bold to use this truest glasse:
> Wherein, your forme, you still the same shall finde;
> Because nor it can change, nor such a minde.

Exemplary action, therefore, may now and again be matched by an exemplary endurance that conquers time and circumstance.

The "Epistle to Elizabeth Countesse of Rutland" (*The Forrest*, XII), to conclude, draws together a number of views already noted, now with special reference to the poet's central role. The epistle touches on the "credentials" of the poet-counsellor and on the conditions most favourable for the exercise of his gifts. As Hercules, Helen, gods and men owed their lives beyond life "onely [to] *Poets*, rapt with rage divine," so Jonson's poetry (89–91) will undertake

> . . . high, and noble matter, such as flies
> From braines entranc'd, and fill'd with extasies;
> Moodes, which the god-like Sydney oft did prove. . . .

In an age when

> . . . almightie gold . . .
> Solders crackt friendship; makes love last a day;
> Or perhaps lesse,

Sidney's daughter can be trusted to

> . . . let this drosse carry what price it will
> With noble ignorants, and let them still,
> Turne, upon scorned verse, their quarter-face:
> With you, I know, my offring will find grace.
> For what a sinne 'gainst your great fathers spirit,
> Were it to thinke, that you should not inherit
> His love unto the *Muses*, when his skill
> Almost you have, or may have, when you will?

But the poem intends more than this: by spelling out the nature of that fame awaiting patrons fortunate enough to hold a place in Jonson's verse, it establishes the claim of the poet to a seat among the highest ranks of the social community. Jonson can promise "strange *poems*, which, as yet, / Had not their forme touch'd by an English wit"; poems, however, that also recall and confirm the powers of Orphic song. Ancient truth will live again in modes newly suited to contemporary conditions and taste. This poet can, of course, assure the worthy patron of earthly fame, "like a rich, and golden *pyramede*, / Borne up by statues." But Jonson's commitment is more explicit (86–7): to

> . . . show, how, to the life, my soule presents
> Your forme imprest there. . . .

The exemplary form of virtue embodied in the Countess of Rutland while she lived will not merely be remembered through Jonson's verse, but truly re-created in it; as "god-like Sidney" had given the mark of the right poet to be his capacity so to create another nature. "To flatter my good Lord," we recall, is "To lose the formes, and dignities of men." False friendship destroys life; but the poet, like a true friend, preserves the "formes" of the men and women he addresses in his poems. The true poet gives life, in fact, as kings can "create new men" (*Ungathered Verse*, XVI). And only such poets, whose art "hath a Stomacke to concoct, divide, and turne all into nourishment,"[49] are thoroughly qualified to counsel the princes and patrons whose art is the ordering of society and the state. The structure of society severely limits the extension of friendship proper, on the pattern of the Tribe; that is a pity; but community of interest among good men may serve instead. And Jonson's poems record his constant care for that harmonious ideal.

49. *H&S*, VIII, 638.

Historical Doubts Respecting Walton's Life of Donne

R. C. BALD

SIR THOMAS MORE'S *History of King Richard the Third* is a classic. It can be read with pleasure more than once, and one's interest in the presentation of the figure of Richard is independent of the fact that for over two hundred years doubts have been cast on More's veracity. The book, it has been alleged, is a piece of political propaganda designed to aid the cause of a conqueror by utterly discrediting the line he had overthrown. More's literary art, however, has made it almost irrelevant to ask whether his historical facts are true or false. Some of the same things can be said of Walton's *Life of Donne*. It too has the gift of conferring repeated pleasure, and that pleasure is independent of the truth or falsehood of the facts related. In its way it can also be called propaganda—in the same sense as a religious tract is propaganda; it seeks to inculcate the religious virtues of penitence and piety. For this very reason, perhaps, there has not as yet been any systematic attempt to estimate the degree of falsification, intentional or unintentional, in what Walton tells us about Donne.

At the outset it should be stressed that Walton's ideals were not those of present-day historical scholarship. We may say, if we like, that he was a Renaissance heir to a greater tradition than ours, that of Thucydides and Plutarch and Livy; if it was needful for his heroes to speak he did not hesitate to put into their mouths what he thought they ought to have said, whether or not there was any evidence that they ever said it, and if a colourful detail would enhance the picture it went in regardless of its authenticity. The classical principle of decorum, of what was, and was not, fitting still dominated historical and biographical writing.

It has to be confessed that Walton commits sins heinous enough to make the hair of a modern scholar bristle with horror. He had no respect for the sanctity of a quotation. Not only would he change it to make it fit better into its new context; he would alter it for the sake of euphony, or to enhance the impression he wanted to convey. In the end the so-called quotation may be saying something quite different from what its author originally meant. To come to specific instances. When Walton wanted to show the "Condition of [Donne's] mind and fortune" when he was living at Mitcham, he quoted two letters.[1] The first was so altered as to be in parts a mere paraphrase; the second is a pastiche of eight extracts from five different letters. Even though it was not actually written until more than two years after Donne had left Mitcham, the first has a date "Aug. 10" and an address "From my hospital at Mitcham" which were added from another letter altogether; the second has a date "Sept. 7" added for the sake of verisimilitude and to suggest, no doubt, that it followed the other letter by less than a month. Yet, in spite of the fact that the two pieces are presented as two entities, it is improbable that there was any deliberate intent to deceive; the letters are introduced by the words "I shall present you with an extract collected out of some few of his many Letters," and the two are linked with the sentence, "Thus he did bemoan himself: And thus in other letters." Walton has, in effect, told the reader what he is doing; yet when the modern reader is given a succinct statement in terms of present-day practice of what Walton has done, the result is a feeling at least of uneasiness and perhaps of downright suspicion.

Another source of uneasiness is to be found in our frequent ignorance of the exact nature of Walton's sources. It is not enough to say that he had the benefit of Wotton's notes in addition to what he himself had collected. We know, indeed, that he consulted some documents (not very many in comparison with the number used for the later *Life of Sanderson*) and that he turned for help to some of Donne's former clerical friends, notably Bishops Morton and King. But there must have been many scraps of information and pseudo-

1. See R. E. Bennett, "Walton's Use of Donne's Letters," *PQ*, XVI (1937), 30–34.

information, picked up from a variety of unidentifiable sources and woven into the fabric of the *Life*, in which fact and falsehood are inextricably mixed. Perhaps the most serious charge that can be fairly brought against him is that he did not check his facts even when they were easily checked, and thus allowed a considerable measure of identifiable error to disfigure his pages. The truth is that Walton only gradually learnt the value of records, and it must not be forgotten that the *Life of Donne* was the first-written of the *Lives*. The original version was, we know, hastily composed, but in spite of the opportunities for subsequent revision Walton made no attempt to retrace his steps; he merely added fresh materials. There is no evidence to suggest that he changed an opinion or altered facts. He was wholly negligent—a modern student might say culpably negligent—of material he might have used.

A single example will suffice:

> Immediately after his return from Cambridge [writes Walton, after telling how the University, at the King's command, made Donne a Doctor of Divinity] his wife died. . . . In this time of sadness he was importuned by the grave Benchers of *Lincolns Inne*, who were once the Companions and Friends of his youth, to accept of their Lecture, which by reason of Dr. *Gatakers* removal from thence was then void: of which he accepted.

Donne received his honorary doctorate in March or April 1615, he was appointed Reader in Divinity at Lincoln's Inn on October 24, 1616, and Mrs. Donne died on August 15, 1617, so that the order of events is wrong. Thomas Gataker resigned the readership in 1611 and was succeeded by Thomas Holloway, whose death created the vacancy that Donne was appointed to fill. And incidentally, Gataker was never Doctor; according to the *DNB* he "refused to proceed D.D.," giving as one of his reasons that "like Cato the censor, he would rather have people ask why he had no statue than why he had one." In 1640, when Walton first drafted this passage, he was living at the corner of Fleet Street and Chancery Lane; a few hundred yards to the west stood the Church of St. Clement Danes, where Donne's wife lay buried and where a mural tablet recorded the date of her death; a few hundred yards to the north was Lincoln's Inn with its archives, where there must also have been among the senior members some who still remembered Donne and the days of his ministration there. Gataker, too, was still alive. One would have thought it impossible for Walton to make so many mistakes within so short a compass, but make them he did.

Three episodes in Walton's account of Donne have already been subjected to rigorous scrutiny.[2] Mr. John Sparrow, writing on the date of Donne's early travels, not only made a careful survey of all the surviving records of Donne's university years and student days at Lincoln's Inn, but carefully compared the successive versions (in the different editions of the *Life*) of Walton's account of the travels. It is quoted below as it originally appeared in 1640:

> About the twentieth yeare of his age, he resolved to travell; And the Earle of Essex going to Cales, and after the Iland voyages, he took the advantage of those opportunities, waited upon his Lordship, and saw the expeditions of those happy and unhappy imployments.
>
> But he returned not into England, till he had staid a convenient time, first in *Italy*, and then in *Spaine*, where he made many usefull Observations of those Countries, their Lawes, and Government, and returned into England perfect in their Languages.

What Walton actually says here is that Donne parted company with a naval expedition in order to continue his travels by passing into Italy and Spain, which is, on the face of it, so absurd that Mr. Sparrow refused to accept it as Walton's meaning. The sentence about Donne's accompanying Essex is, he argues, a kind of parenthesis, and refers to a time after Donne's return to England from Italy and Spain. Yet, even if this is so, it still leaves unanswered a question that seems never to have occurred to Walton. If Donne, about 1593 or 1594, was in Spain for a visit of some length, how did he manage to do so at a time when England and Spain were at war? Did Donne assume the role of a Catholic renegade? Or is Walton merely mistaken in sending him to Spain at this period? It is easier to assume that Donne did not visit Spain until 1605 or 1606 after peace had been made. He was abroad in those years, and English travellers were flocking to Spain now that it was once more open to them.

In examining Walton's account of Donne's journey to the Continent with Sir Robert and Lady Drury in 1611–12, R. E. Bennett found it easy to point out historical inaccuracies. To begin with,

2. John Sparrow, "The Date of Donne's Travels," in *A Garland for John Donne*, ed. Theodore Spencer (Cambridge, Mass., 1932), 131–51; R. E. Bennett, "Donne's Letters from the Continent in 1611–12," *PQ*, XIX (1940), 66–78; I. A. Shapiro, "Walton and the Occasion of Donne's *Devotions*," *RES*, n.s., IX (1958), 18–22.

Walton should have referred to some account of the events of James I's reign (of which there were a number available) to get some of his facts straight; secondly, if he had studied the letters written during Donne's absence on the Continent (they were published in 1651) he would have discovered a number of other errors in his account. But he did neither. Bennett went on to question the story "told me (*now long since*) by a Person of Honour, and of such intimacy with [Donne], that he knew more of the secrets of his soul then any person then living," which was first published in the 1675 edition of the *Life*, about Donne's vision in Paris of his wife with a dead child in her arms. "We may be pardoned," Bennett concludes, "if we give the credit for a good story to a man who not only talked but also wrote about the fish he caught." This is hardly fair; hallucinations do occur, and volumes have been filled with the narratives of such apparently authentic phenomena. The vision may well have occurred, in spite of the inaccuracies among which it is embedded.

Mr. Shapiro, writing of the illness during which Donne wrote the *Devotions*, emphasizes the fact that Walton places it in 1625, whereas it really took place two years earlier. Walton has apparently confused the two illnesses, for Donne was also ill for a time in 1625, though less seriously than in 1623. The significance of Mr. Shapiro's essay lies in the doubts it raises, for, he concludes, "if Walton's personal knowledge of Donne until after 1625 was as slight as this investigation seems to indicate, his account of Donne's life up to that date must be much less authoritative, and may be much less accurate, than is currently supposed."

The thread of inaccuracy, documented in these three studies, runs through the whole of the *Life of Donne*. All the anecdotes related by Walton are specially open to suspicion. David Novarr believes that the story of the origin of *Pseudo-Martyr*, to the effect that it grew out of a command of King James to Donne when the latter was attending him one day at dinner, is based on a deliberate misunderstanding of a sentence in the dedication of that work:

> having observed, how much your Majestie had vouchsafed to descend to a conversation with your Subjects, by way of your Bookes, I also conceiv'd an ambition, of ascending to your presence, by the same way.

"By turning a figure of speech into a personal interview," comments

Novarr, "Walton did not bind himself superstitiously to Donne's words, but even made Donne's words speak not Donne's sense but his own."[3] Novarr may or may not be right (and I am inclined to think that there is probably more behind Walton's story than he concedes), but he expresses an attitude of scepticism that is fully justified by the facts.

The other anecdotes about Donne and James I are even more vulnerable. There is, for instance, the story that the Earl of Somerset sent for Donne to come to Theobalds, where the King was, and bade Donne wait in the garden while he secured for him the gift of an office that had just fallen vacant through the death of the holder, and of the King's obstinate refusal to promote Donne except in the Church. The vacant office was a clerkship of the Privy Council, and it was exactly the sort of office to which Donne's ambitions would have led him. But the date of Donne's introduction to the Earl of Somerset is fairly precisely known (spring 1613), and it can be stated categorically that from then until Donne's ordination less than two years afterwards in January 1615 no Clerk of the Council died. Something is clearly wrong with the tale, though it is difficult to say how much.

Of Donne's appointment to the deanery of St. Paul's Walton tells a pleasant story. Valentine Cary, the previous dean, was appointed to the bishopric of Exeter, whereupon the "King sent to Dr. *Donne*, and appointed him to attend him at Dinner the next day."

When his Majesty was sate down, before he had eat any meat, he said after his pleasant manner, Dr. *Donne, I have invited you to Dinner, and though you sit not down with me, yet I will carve to you of a dish that I know you love well; for knowing you love London, I do therefore make you Dean of Pauls; and when I have dined, then do you take your beloved dish home to your study; say grace there to your self, and much good may it do you.*

Another such story was told of Lancelot Andrewes; it is narrated, with far less skill, by Aubrey, in speaking of his administration of the diocese of Winchester:

. . . which Bishopric he ordered with great Prudence as to government of the Parsons, preferring of ingeniose persons that were staked to poore

3. David Novarr, *The Making of Walton's Lives* (Cornell University Press, 1958), 57–8.

livings and did *delitescere*. He made it his Enquiry to find out such men. Amongst severall others (whose names have escaped me) Nicholas Fuller (he wrote *Critica Sacra*) Minister of Allington, neer Amesbury in Wilts, was one. The Bishop sent for him, and the poor man was afrayd and knew not what hurt he had donne. Makes him sitt downe to Dinner and, after the Desert, was brought in, in a dish, his Institution and Induction, or the donation of a Prebend, which was his way.[4]

It looks as if these are two versions of the same tale, only, as often happens, the names of the participants have been changed.

The final anecdote involving King James refers to Donne's falling temporarily out of favour, for "he was once, and but once, clouded with the Kings displeasure." This happened, Walton makes clear, at the time when the King issued his *Directions to Preachers*. These regulations caused considerable murmuring throughout the country and raised fears that the King was inclining far too much towards popery. Donne, Walton alleges, was accused to the King of spreading such rumours. (Actually, Donne defended the *Directions* from the pulpit at Paul's Cross; James read the manuscript of his sermon, approved it, and commanded that it be immediately put into print.) The King sent for Donne, who successfully cleared himself from all suspicion of disloyalty, and when he had left the King declared to the Council, "My Doctor is an honest man: and my Lords, I was never better satisfied with an answer then he hath now made me: and I always rejoice when I think that by my means he became a Divine." But if Walton is right in saying that Donne was "once, and but once, clouded with the Kings displeasure" he has mistaken the King, for there is a well-documented incident early in the reign of Charles I when Donne was alarmed to find himself in trouble at court over some sentences in a sermon which had been misinterpreted. On April 2, 1627, he received through Laud a command to bring the King a copy of the sermon he had preached the previous day; two agitated letters from Donne to his friend Sir Robert Ker show how concerned he was at the thought that he had given offence where none was intended; and he instantly appealed to the all-powerful Duke of Buckingham, to be assured "by my Lord Carlisle . . . of a gracious acceptation of my putting myself in his protection." Donne, only too aware of the changeable winds of court favour, took imme-

4. Aubrey, *Brief Lives*, ed. Oliver Lawson Dick (London, 1949), 7.

diate pains to defend himself against the worst that might happen. Two days later he had an interview with the King, the outcome of which was recorded by Laud in his diary:

> April 4. *Wednesday*. When his Majesty King *Charles* forgave to Doctor *Donne* certain slips in a Sermon Preached on *Sunday Apr.* 1. what he then most graciously said unto me, I have wrote in my Heart with indelible Characters, and great thankfulness to God and the King.[5]

This surely is the reality behind Walton's anecdote, and the speech of James, reported with such an air of authenticity, is no more than the biographer's embroidery.

It is possible, I think, to trace the various stages in the evolution of one story, and that perhaps the most widely known of those that Walton tells about Donne. The first form of it appeared soon after the event that gave rise to it. In December 1602 (the previous entry is dated December 7) John Manningham wrote in his diary:

> Dunne is undonne; he was lately secretary to the Lord Keeper, and cast of because he would match him selfe to a gentlewoman against his Lords pleasure.[6]

It evidently took some time for the witticism to go the rounds, for it was now December, and Donne had lost his post the previous February, but Manningham's note shows that the witticism was a current one, and there is no evidence to suggest that Donne himself was the source. The next phase is found as long afterwards as 1660, in William Winstanley's *England's Worthies*. Winstanley's life of Donne is a condensation and paraphrase (these are polite terms; today it would be called a plagiarism) of the 1640 version of Walton's *Life*. Modern readers are not likely to notice Winstanley's single addition to Walton's account, but it should be remembered that there was as yet nothing in Walton corresponding to the following sentence:

> In the time of Master *Donnes* melancholy Imprisonment, how true I know not, onely I have heard it often discoursed, that he writ on the window with the point of his Diamond, reflecting on the then present affliction of his Marriage these words, *John Donne*, done and undone.[7]

Two years earlier a fuller (and more picturesque) version of the story

5. William Laud, *Works* (London, 1853), III, 204.

6. *Manningham's Diary*, ed. R. J. Bruce (London: Camden Society, 1868), 99. See also R. E. Bennett, "John Manningham and Donne's Paradoxes," *MLN*, XLVI (1931), 309–13.

7. Winstanley, *England's Worthies*, 301.

had appeared in print, all the more interesting because the teller was no less person than King Charles I. After the battle of Naseby in 1646 the King was for some time the guest at Raglan Castle of the Marquess of Worcester. During this period he was assiduously attended by the Marquess's chaplain, Dr. Thomas Bayly (son of Lewis Bayly, author of the once vastly popular *Practice of Piety*), who took voluminous notes of the table talk of the King and the Marquess. After Charles I's execution and the subsequent death of the Marquess, Bayly published two books based on his notes: *Certamen religiosum, or a Conference between his late Majestie and Henry, Marquess of Worcester, concerning religion* (1649) and *Apophthegme, or witty sayings of the right honorable Henry (late) Marquess of Worcester* (1650). After Bayly's death there also appeared *Witty Apophthegms delivered at severall times by King James, King Charles, the Marquess of Worcester, Francis Lord Bacon, and Sir Thomas More* (1658); though parts of the sections on King Charles and the Marquess of Worcester were reprinted from *Apophthegme*, some additional material was incorporated, including the following anecdote on page 26:

> Upon a Discourse of the singular parts which Doctor *John Donne* Dean of *Pauls*, was indowed withall, he [the King] took occasion to speak of his marriage, who marrying into a rich and honourable Family, being much above his Degree, and against his wives fathers consent, insomuch that the father would give her no Portion, which the Doctor then perceiving, took his pen and writ (and sent it to the old man) in this manner, *John Donne, Anne Donne*, undone, which wrought good effects on the old man.[8]

This is told with much more coherence and point than Winstanley's version. Of course Donne never addressed his father-in-law in these terms; Sir George More carefully preserved the letters he received from Donne after the rash marriage; they are now in the Folger Shakespeare Library, and if such a letter had existed it would be there too. Walton, I think, had read the story in *Witty Apophthegms* and in Winstanley's *Worthies*, and he may have heard oral versions as well that made him prefer the one in which Donne's letter was addressed to his wife. But the fact that the King had related the anecdote (and of course Charles had known both Donne and Sir George More) must have given it an authenticity for Walton that he could not have

8. My attention was first drawn to this passage by Professor F. C. Baxter.

resisted even if he had wanted to. Nevertheless, in view of the history of the tale and its mutations it is very difficult to believe that it had any original basis in fact.

Yet, amid all this uncritical acceptance of doubtful material, Walton embeds facts which have scarcely been recognized as such even where there exists documentary evidence to prove them. There is the remark about Donne's mother, that she "spent her Estate in forraign Countreys"; it can be shown from documents in the Public Record Office just when she and her third husband, Richard Rainsford, left England for Antwerp and when they returned. Again, Walton says that old Mrs. Donne "died in [her son's] house but three Moneths before him." It has been stated more than once by modern writers that Donne's mother survived him, but Walton is nearly right as to the date of her death (it was actually two months before her son's) and she seems to have died not in her son's house but in her granddaughter's, for she was buried at Barking (as the parish register there affirms) from Aldborough Hatch, the home of Constance Donne's second husband, on January 28, 1630/31. In another instance the absence of documentary evidence is significant. Walton distinctly says that Sir Thomas Egerton employed Donne as his chief secretary. Egerton as the head of Chancery, as presiding judge in the Star Chamber as well, and as one of the leading Privy Councillors, must have had a secretarial staff of some size. It is significant, I think, that a search of his papers in the Huntington Library for the years during which Donne was with him revealed neither memoranda nor endorsements in Donne's handwriting. Evidently the routine tasks of preparing documents for submission to his master or of arranging and filing papers were not a part of his duties.

In describing Donne's last illness Walton tells how Donne tried to discharge all the outstanding obligations of his life:

The *Sunday* following he appointed his servants, that if there were any business yet undone that concerned him or themselves, it should be prepared against *Saturday* next; for after that day he would not mix his thoughts with any thing that concerned this world; nor ever did: But as *Job*, so he *waited for the appointed day of his dissolution.*

One would expect Walton to be substantially correct here, for he was in touch with Donne and his household during the last illness, so it is not altogether surprising to find from the register of dealings in cathedral properties and offices that on March 21, 1630/31 (ten days before his death) Donne signed his last documents as dean: a lease of some cathedral property, a grant of the office of Auditor of Paul's to James Singleton and another of the office of Collector of the New Works to Thomas Roper, whom he described in his will as his "faithful servant." Nevertheless it is significant of Walton's constant habit of inaccuracy that March 21, 1631, was a Monday, not a Saturday.

Another statement of Walton's is interesting for what it implies as well as what it states. He describes Donne's grief at the death of his wife, and continues:

> His first motion from his house was to preach, where his beloved wife lay buried (in St. *Clements* Church, near Temple-Bar *London*) and his Text was a part of the Prophet *Jeremy's* Lamentation: *Lo, I am the man that have seen affliction.*

Novarr seems to doubt this statement, on the ground that the surviving sermon on this text clearly belongs to another occasion, but there is no reason why a preacher should not preach more than one sermon from the same text. It is more pertinent to inquire how Donne, the Reader in Divinity at Lincoln's Inn, should have been preaching in the church of St. Clement Danes. Donne was, of course, still living by Drury House, just off Drury Lane, within the parish of St. Clements, and Mrs. Donne died in August at the height of the summer, at a time when he would not have been bound by his obligation to preach twice every Sunday at Loncoln's Inn during term. Furthermore, the rector of St. Clements, John Layfield, a well-known Hebraist who had been one of the translators of the Pentateuch, had died in May; his successor was not appointed until November.[9] It looks very much as if Donne had been filling the vacant pulpit in his parish church as often as he was able during the summer in which his wife died.

In a number of instances where Walton is wrong it is not difficult to see how he made the mistake. After describing Sir George More's anger at his daughter's marriage, he continued:

> he presently engaged his Sister the Lady *Elsemere*, to join with him to procure her Lord [Sir Thomas Egerton, the Lord Keeper, made Baron Ellesmere in 1603] to discharge Mr. *Donne* of the place he held under his Lordship.

9. Parish Register of St. Clement's; G. Hennessy, *Novum repertorium londinense.*

Walton did not know, of course, that Sir George More's sister was dead and that Egerton had remarried. Donne's father, we also learn, "died before his admission into this Society" (Lincoln's Inn); indeed he did—a full sixteen years before—but Dr. John Syminges, his stepfather, died not long before he entered Lincoln's Inn.[10] His father, Walton continues, "being a Merchant, left him his portion in money (it was 3000 l.)." Actually, it has been shown that Donne's inheritance was only about a quarter of this sum;[11] Donne's father left about £3000, but half of it went to his widow and the other half was divided between the two surviving children who reached the age of twenty-one. Walton, an Ironmonger like Donne's father, probably heard the figure from some elderly member of the Company and, not realizing that it was the whole of the estate, mistook it for Donne's share.

Much more serious for their effects on literary criticism in subsequent ages are the statements Walton makes about the dates of Donne's poems:

> The Recreations of his youth were *Poetry* . . . and in those pieces which were facetiously composed and carelessly scattered (most of them being written before the twentieth year of his age) it may appear by his choice Metaphors, that both *Nature* and all the *Arts* joyned to assist him with their utmost skill.
>
> It is a truth, that in his penitential years, viewing some of those pieces that had been loosely (God knows too loosely) scattered in his youth, he wish't they had been abortive. . . . But though he was no friend to them, he was not so fallen out with heavenly Poetry as to forsake that: no not in his declining age; witnessed then by many Divine Sonnets, and other high, holy, and harmonious Composures.

These remarks seemed to be confirmed by Ben Jonson when he asserted to Drummond of Hawthornden that Donne had "written all his best pieces ere he was 25 years old" and declared that "since he was made Doctor" he "repenteth highlie, and seeketh to destroy all his poems." It takes courage to flout such authorities, and for a long time no one thought of questioning them, but it is now fairly well estab-

10. B. W. Whitlock, "John Syminges, a Poet's Stepfather," *NQ*, n.s., C (1954), 465–7.

11. F. P. Wilson, "Notes on the Early Life of John Donne," *RES*, n.s., III (1927), 272–9.

lished that Donne's poetical activities were fairly evenly distributed through his secular years, but that after entering holy orders he composed not more than a handful of poems.[12] Walton has been credited by some modern writers with having had a share in the publication and editing of the 1633 edition of Donne's *Poems*, but even if he only possessed a copy of the volume (in which his commendatory verses were included) he must have been able to see that many of the poems, especially among the verse letters, the epithalamia, and the obsequies, were written between Donne's youth and his ordination. He does, indeed, go so far as to admit that the "Valediction forbidding mourning" was addressed by Donne to his wife before leaving for the Continent with Sir Robert Drury in 1611, but this is his sole concession. He must have known about the *Anniversaries*, but there is no reference to them in connection with Drury. And, incidentally, why is there no reference in the *Life* to Lady Bedford, addressed in so many of the poems? Walton's attitude is far from clear. Nevertheless it is not difficult to see why he made the sharp distinction between early and late poems, between sacred and profane. It was part of his purpose to stress the break in the continuity of Donne's life and to elevate the conversion which brought it about. The contrast between the secular and the holy Donne, the youthful and the mature Donne, was essential to the pattern he was constructing, and literal, stubborn facts were adjusted to fit it.

Two problems remain. The second is probably insoluble, but this discussion can throw some light on, and suggest a solution to, the first. It concerns the date of Donne's "Hymne to God, my God, in my sicknesse." In the 1658 and later editions of the *Life* Walton quotes some lines from this poem, which he says was written on Donne's deathbed, and appends to the title the date "March 23. 1630" (i.e., 1630/31), eight days before Donne died. On the other hand, there is a copy of the poem among Sir Julius Caesar's papers in the British Museum endorsed "D. Dun Dene of Pauls / his verses in his greate / sicknes. / in Deceb. 1623." Mr. John Sparrow has argued for Sir Julius Caesar's date; Mrs. Simpson in rebuttal has defended Walton's;

12. See the dates affixed to the titles in the table of contents of the Nonesuch Donne, and an article by Robert Ellrodt, "La chronologie des poèmes de Donne," *Etudes Anglaises*, XII (1960), 452–63.

and Miss Helen Gardner has surveyed the arguments on both sides in an appendix to her edition of the *Divine Poems*.[13] The problem, Miss Gardner states, is "to decide which of two good witnesses we are to accept." It should be clear to the reader of this paper that Walton is not a reliable witness. In the original edition of the *Life* he said no more than that Donne wrote this poem on his deathbed; this was his impression, but it is more than possible that neither then nor later did he have a definite date for the poem. The man who added dates to the two mosaics that were put forward as letters to illustrate Donne's state of mind during his Mitcham days was quite capable of inserting an appropriate date to add verisimilitude to his assertion that the poem was composed during Donne's last illness. On the other hand, Sir Julius Caesar has given correctly the month of Donne's "greate sicknes"—the sickness during which Donne wrote the *Devotions*; his illness would, no doubt, have been common knowledge at the time (and contemporary newsletters show that it was) but it is not so likely to have been remembered so precisely in later years. Sir Julius Caesar's notation, in other words, seems to have been made at a time quite close to the alleged time of the composition of the poem.

There is further evidence that Caesar must have known a good deal about Donne and indeed knew him personally. In November 1627 Donne and Caesar were both named members of a panel to try a case in the Court of Delegates. Sir Julius Caesar had been Master of the Rolls since 1614, and consequently he lived at the Office of the Rolls. The Rolls Chapel had its preacher, who preached every Sunday during term time, and no doubt the Master attended. But his wife did not; she attended her parish church, and that church was St. Dunstan's-in-the-West. An entry in the Churchwardens' Accounts for 1628–9 for repairs to "the Lady Cesars pew doore" first drew my attention to these facts. In other words, the Caesars certainly knew who Donne was after April 1624, when he became vicar of St. Dunstan's, and it takes no stretch of the imagination to fancy Sir Julius accompanying his wife (out of term time, probably) to hear Donne preach there. But there are several other, and earlier, links. Lady Caesar was a cousin of Donne's former patroness Lady Drury, and

13. John Sparrow, "On the Date of Donne's 'Hymne to God, my God, in my sickness,'" *MLR*, XIX (1924), 462–6; E. M. Simpson, "The Date of Donne's 'Hymne to God, my God, in my sicknesse,'" *MLR*, XLI (1946), 9–15; John Donne, *The Divine Poems*, ed. Helen Gardner (Oxford, 1952), Appendix E, 132–5.

when Lady Drury visited London in the spring of 1622 she stayed with the Caesars, as is testified by a letter addressed to her "at the Roulles." It would have been odd if Donne did not call on her there. Earlier, on August 30, 1621, he speaks of visiting the Caesars.[14] Further, he wrote that as dean he was "under a necessity of preaching twelve or fourteen sermons every year to great auditories at Paul's, to the judges, and at Court," and, though none of the sermons to the judges has survived, it is almost certain that Caesar would have heard one or more of them before Donne's illness of December 1623. All these facts make it clear that Sir Julius Caesar was in a position to know a good deal about Donne, and that he should accordingly be regarded as a reliable witness where Walton cannot be.

The last problem arises out of a contradiction that Walton does not seem even to have perceived, much less tried to solve. Donne states repeatedly that it was James I who first persuaded him to enter the Church. The most emphatic statement comes in the *Devotions*; not only did Walton know the book well, but he even quotes in the *Life* part of the passage that follows:

> Thou [God] through him [the King] hast spoke to me before, then, when he first of any man, conceived a hope that I might be of some use in thy church and descended to an intimation, to a persuasion, almost to a solicitation, that I would embrace that calling; . . . when I asked a temporal office, he denied not, refused not that; but let me see that he had rather I took this.[15]

(If Walton had remembered the last sentence he might have told the story of Somerset's appeal to James rather differently.) Donne's statement is emphatic and precise, but at some time after the appearance of the first edition of the *Life* Walton made the acquaintance of Donne's old friend Thomas Morton, Bishop of Durham, from whom he learnt of Morton's attempt to persuade Donne to enter the ministry in 1607. This event can be dated, because it occurred at the time of Morton's appointment to the deanery of Gloucester. Walton's account is corroborated in the *Life of Morton* by his former secretary Richard

14. See letter to Sir Henry Goodyere: "That place, and Bedington, and Chelsea, and Highgate, where that very good man my Lord Hobard is, and Hackney, with the Master of the Rolls, and my familiar Peckham, are my circumference." Edmund Gosse, *Life and Letters of John Donne* (London, 1899), II, 143.

15. Expostulation viii, in *Devotions*, ed J. Sparrow (London, 1923), 46.

Baddeley, who adds one or two additional details. James's first suggestion that Donne should enter the Church did not come, according to Walton, until after he had read *Pseudo-Martyr* three years later.

Here, rather than in the testimony about the date of the "Hymne to God, my God, in my sicknesse" is a conflict of witnesses not easily reconciled. Donne may simply have forgotten Morton's offer when he was writing the *Devotions*, though that seems hardly likely, or James may have suggested to Donne that he should become a clergyman on some early occasion of which no specific record has survived. It is even possible that Donne meant that James was the first to turn his thoughts seriously in that direction (so that Morton's offer did not count), for in a letter to Sir Robert Ker he wrote: ". . . when I sit still and reckon all my old master's royal favours to me, I return evermore to that, that he *first inclined* me to be a minister [italics mine],"[16] and in his epitaph he spoke of himself as "impulso Spiritu Sancto et hortatu regis Jacobi ordines sacros amplexus anno sui Jesu MDCXIV. et aetatis suae XLII"—as if the impulse and the persuasion were followed after only a short interval by the act. But the puzzle remains; any suggested explanation is at best a guess.

It is probable that we have been measuring the *Life of Donne* by standards which Walton never for a moment dreamt he was expected to maintain. Doubtless he went for information to those he considered the best authorities, but it never occurred to him that their information needed checking. Much of that information must have been oral, and it had all the defects of oral transmission. The charm and sincerity of Walton's portrait of Donne remain, but it is only fair that the seeker after exact information should know precisely what Walton has to offer him.

16. Gosse, *Life and Letters of John Donne*, II, 190.

Some Aspects of Self-Revelation and Self-Portraiture in Religio Medici

N. J. ENDICOTT

THERE ARE STILL ECHOES of Dr. Johnson's scepticism about Browne's sincerity in disclaiming any intention to publish *Religio Medici*, but for various reasons we need not hesitate to accept the statement that it was written "at leisurable hours" for his own "private exercise and satisfaction," "a memorial unto mee." Any peruser of the "depraved" texts of 1642, Browne claimed, would "easily discerne" from "sundry particularities and personall expressions" that the intention was not public, and in his letter to Kenelm Digby he was even more emphatic in insisting that it "could not" have escaped Digby's apprehension that it had been written with no intention for the press. Professor Denonain's text, with it full collations,[1] gives us an idea of how Browne tried to reduce, soften, or disguise some of the more intimate statements of opinion for the authorized text, and also sometimes suggests that the process of making the text less personal may have begun shortly after first composition, a view that is supported by the evidence of a similar process of alteration in much later notebooks. No doubt one or two close friends were thought of as privileged and friendly readers. Publication and fame (to Browne also notoriety) presumably led him to destroy the other pieces "of affinitie," to which he refers as having also been written about 1635, and since we may imagine that the other pieces might have had some of the quality of the *Religio*, it was unfortunate that the latter had so sudden an English and European success.

1. *Religio Medici*, ed. J.-J. Denonain (Cambridge, 1953). All quotations are from this text.

It must have been in its whole character, rather than merely in unguarded details, that the *Religio* seemed to its author too private for general perusal, and while Browne was not in an officially vulnerable position for the expression of heterodox views—as was Donne, for instance, when he consigned *Biathanatos* to a limbo between the press and the fire—he was not as bold a spirit as Donne. In the 1660's or 1670's he described his book (significantly, I think, in a comment on Keck's parallels with Montaigne) as "a peece of myne published long agoe." Amusingly, even here the marginal reference on the opposite verso, "Rel.Med." suggests that though the comment is private, and though Browne by this time presumably preferred to regard himself as the learned author of the *Pseudodoxia Epidemica*, anything written down implies a possible reader. He must have known that the *Religio* had "opened the mind" of a good many tougher minds than that of John Aubrey, who thus acknowledged its part in his own education, and he certainly knew that it was being reprinted and read. In 1669 Edward Browne wrote to his father from Vienna to say that the imperial librarian, Lambeccius, had introduced the book to the Emperor, who had read it with great pleasure and would like to see the English original. Since the edition of 1669 is in the National Library in Vienna it would seem that Sir Thomas sent it over, without inscription, and without corrections, though it calls for some.

By and large, *Religio Medici* is a moderately orderly exploration of Browne's own religious experience and his tentative views on certain aspects of religion and thought. The author is not a theologian, but has read a decent amount of theology and "calls himself a Scholar." He tries to see himself in his time in England and Europe. He tries to assess the relation between reason and faith, especially in resolving problems of biblical interpretation. He meditates on the great "staire or manifest scale of creatures" and the duty of a devout and learned admiration of nature as the art of God. He contemplates the nothingness of the world when seen in the perspective of eternity. If we think of Europe, as well as England, the very great emphasis on tolerance and charity might rather be expected than surprising—there are obvious parallels among thoughtful men of his day—and familiarity with early seventeenth-century literature (not necessarily religious literature) will tell us that many of the minor questions, even some of those regarded as Brownean esoterica, are alive and contemporary. The cessation of oracles; the nature of angels; the *anima mundi*; witches; Fortune and Providence; mortalism; the age of the world: all were subjects of common inquiry. He read the hexameral literature; so did many others. He dispraises Lucian and Machiavelli, and rehabilitates Epicurus; only his phrasing is not commonplace. The famous Hermetic description of God as a circle is referred to and favourably quoted not only by medievals and numerous Renaissance neo-Platonists, but by Rabelais, Montaigne, Pascal, Gassendi.[2] A revealing fondness for little things has been posited from his remark about finding "more curious Mathematicks" (and hence more of the art of God) in "narrow engines" than in prodigious pieces of nature like whales and elephants. But the question was a commonplace. It was debated, for instance, as one of the questions for the M.A. in natural philosophy at Oxford in 1597: *majus est naturae artificium in rebus parvis quam in magis.*[3] Browne himself leads us a little astray by speaking of himself in one context as an "extravagant and irregular head" prone to "old and obsolete errors." The third of the two or three presumably major "Heresies, Schismes, or Errors" by which he had been tempted and "wished it were consonant to Truth and not offensive to my Religion" to maintain, prayers for the dead, was, of course, very contemporary. It was approved by Andrewes; in 1626 Browne could have heard Donne preach on the subject; yet he says he has never positively maintained or practised the belief himself.

Nor was he in any way ignorant of or indifferent to the political events of his time. Our knowledge that the Civil War was about to break out, the violence of the pamplets, as well as the actions, of the next twenty years, the remoteness to us of some of Browne's questions, still lead some critics to imagine that his cast of mind was very rare in his age, while at the same time they rather drastically modify appreciation by adopting the view that, as even Professor Bush implies about later years, Browne went his way without paying too much attention to the struggle going on around him, "living in a timeless world of his own."[4] Professor Huntley extends the second phrase to

2. D. Mahnke, *Unendliche Sphäre und Allmittelpunkt* (Halle/Saale, 1937), *passim.*
3. *Register of the University of Oxford*, ed. A. Clark (Oxford, 1887), II, Pt. 1, 173.
4. Douglas Bush, *English Literature in the Earlier Seventeenth Century* (Oxford, 1945), 336–7.

Browne's tutor, Thomas Lushington, "mathematician and Neoplatonic divine who lived in the unchanging world of form."[5] Except, one might say, remembering a fine anecdote in Aubrey, when he was in the cellar with Richard Corbet, his bishop.[6] Browne's own surviving letters are filled with references to events; one of his "Tracts" is shrewd prophecy of future history; he sends his fourteen-year-old son news of elections in which he gives the number of votes for each candidate. His oldest friend, Whitefoot, underlined what he called Browne's "stochastick" gifts, and said that under given circumstances he might have been another Father Paolo [Sarpi], the "oracle of Venice."

But while Browne was not altogether a remote and meditative eccentric turning over scholastic metaphysics learned at the university and blending it with more recent hieroglyphic or Paracelsan novelties, or, platonically-medical, turning Plato's cave into the womb and jotting down the notion of a dialogue between two unborn twins concerning the world they were to come to, no one would want to dispute the feeling that we enjoy the *Religio* most of all for its extraordinary flavour, and for the feeling it gives us that we are near to a man of a most unusual and enigmatic personality. Yet when we pause to collate and consider more precisely what is meant by Professor Denonain's statement that we have a "detailed portrait" of Browne, Gosse's claim that in the second part we have "pure autobiography" where Browne "gossips as no man except Montaigne had ever gossiped before,"[7] or Coleridge's "fine portrait of a handsome man in his best clothes,"[8] we may find that it is not only a series of impressions of a temperament that we are left with (rather than anything more tangible), but that even these impressions must be interpreted with some caution. It is to be too trusting to suppose that our knowledge that Browne was not intending to publish "nous assure de l'entière

5. F. L. Huntley, *Sir Thomas Browne* (Ann Arbor, 1962), 38.

6. "His [Bishop Corbet's] chaplain, Dr. Lushington, was a very learned and ingeniose man, and they loved one another. The bishop would sometimes take the key of the wine-cellar, and he and his chaplaine would goe and lock themselves in and be merry. Then first he layes down his episcopall hat,—*'There lyes the Dr.'* Then he putts of his gowne,— *'There lyes the Bishop.'* Then 'twas,— *'Here's to thee, Corbet,'* and *'Here's to thee, Lushington.'*—From Josias Howe, B.D. Trin. Coll. Oxon." *Aubrey's Brief Lives*, ed A. Clark (Oxford, 1898), 186. Lushington was one of those who persuaded Browne to go to Norwich; Corbet became Bishop of Norwich in 1632, but died in 1635.

7. Edmund Gosse, *Sir Thomas Browne* (London, 1924), 47.

8. *Coleridge's Miscellaneous Criticism*, ed. T. M. Raysor (London, 1936), 253.

franchise des confidences de Browne, et écarte tout soupçon d'une complaisance envers soi bien fréquente chez les auteurs de *'Confessions'*."[9] The word "I" is used hundreds of times, but this "I" is to some extent a creation, not a person who wants to tell all or introduce himself in his slippers, to say nothing of the further undress proposed by Montaigne.

The notebook comment on the *Religio* as a "peece of myne published long agoe" is in reference and objection to Keck's parallels to Montaigne in the edition of 1656. Browne's desire to be truthful and still express, it would seem, his distaste, not only for plagiarism, but for Montaigne, comes out absurdly in the way in which (for his own satisfaction only, it must be remembered) he considered and corrected his comment on these parallels. "To deale clearly, when I penned that peece [the *Religio*] I had neuer read tw 3 leaues of that Author & scarce any more euer since" reads MS. Sloane 1869 (f.20^r). When copied into MS. Sloane 1879 (f.28^r) it is "To deale cleenely when I penned that peece I had neuer scarce read three six leaues in that Author and scarce any more so much euer since." MS. Sloane 1885 (f.23^r) has an intermediate version sticking to "neuer" and "three." In the famous introductory sentences to the *Essaies* Montaigne tells us (in Florio's words) that it is himself he portrays and that if it had been his fortune to have lived among those nations which are said to live under the sweet liberty of Nature's first and uncorrupted laws he would most willingly have portrayed himself fully and naked. Possibly with Montaigne in mind, though also from a more general aesthetic point of view, Bacon disassociates himself from this view of both life and the essay with, "Besides (to say truth) this same nakedness is uncomely, as well in mind as body; and it addeth no small reverence to men's manners and actions, if they be not altogether open. As for talkers and futile persons, they be commonly vain and credulous withall. . . ." Browne differs emphatically from both: without Bacon's politic and self-advantageous caution; even further from Montaigne's basic naturalism, self-acceptance, and open-eyed unillusioned frankness.

Frankness involves both heterodoxy and public dignity. If, as Coleridge said, Browne is a "fine mixture of humanist, genius, and

9. J.-J. Denonain, *La Personnalité de Sir Thomas Browne*, Publications de la Faculté des Lettres et Sciences humaines d'Alger, XXXIII (Paris, 1959), 10.

pedant,"[10] it is possibly as much the pedant as the man of reserve (and at times propriety) which made him change some of the original "I"s into "we"s, or try to dull some of the personal colour of the original reflections when publication had surprised him or, as later in his life, was being contemplated. When he says in the *Religio* that he could "never divide himself from any man upon the difference of an opinion or be angry with him for not agreeing with me on that from which perhaps within a few days I should dissent myself," it is as natural for us as for Keck to think of Montaigne, though Montaigne goes so much further (*Essays*, II, 12). We do not find this flexibility in the long-posthumously published *Christian Morals*—the only later work which it is relevant to compare with the *Religio*. But the note-books show that while the paradoxical element in his temperament thinned, his sense of the tentative nature of many opinions, and what he described as the Pythagorical metempsychoses in each human life, did not disappear, though it did not get published. A good example of what seems to be the influence of decorum can be seen when we look at the original form of some glowing and well-known reflections on imagination, sense, experiment, reason, and speculation which form part of *Christian Morals*, 11.5:

> There is nothing more acceptable unto the ingenious World, than this noble Eluctation of Truth; wherein, against the tenacity of Prejudice and Prescription, this Century now prevaileth. What Libraries of new Volumes aftertimes will behold, and in what a new World of Knowledge the eyes of our Posterity may be happy, a few Ages may joyfully declare. . . . And therefore, rather than to swell the Leaves of Learning by fruitless Repetitions, to sing the same Song in all Ages . . . many would be content that some would write like Helmont or Paracelsus; and be willing to endure the monstrosity of some opinions, for divers singular notions requiting such aberrations.

In MSS. Sloane 1862, 1885, and 1879 we find successive drafts of this passage as a separate "essay" or reflection, with a personal addition which certainly overgoes the "within a few days" of the *Religio*. "Sing the same song" was at first more contemptuously "cuckoe out the same note," "many would rather" was explicitly "I had rather," and there is a long additional passage in part of which he says:

> . . . to expect constancy of opinions in former and after writings is to forget the difference of men and students allowable for their successive

10. *Miscellaneous Criticism*, 253.

enquiries. . . . A constant tenour of discourse or strict uniformitie of sense & notions from the same elder & junior penns is only expectable from improficient heads . . . time brings not only frequent repentancie in actions butt iterated resipiscency in opinions thoughts and notions. Euen of what I now apprehend I haue no settled assurance. These are my present thoughts this night in England; what they will proue to-morrow when I arise toward China, I may bee yet to determine.[11]

We cannot be too positive in our speculations as to what parts of the *Religio* Browne would rather have kept to himself and his friend, but some comments, illustrative rather than comprehensive, may be hazarded. The generally "Platonic" and Hermetic cast of his thought (preferring an adumbration to a definition which, he thought, did not define) Browne would surely not have felt any need to disguise or apologize for, though the text tells us that he was aware of the disapproval of "the severe Schooles." For such statements as that about his imagined Stoical fortitude, on the other hand, he must have blushed (physically he blushed easily, Whitefoot tells us!) and his "charitable" effusions seem occasionally to betray blemishes of moral complacency so obvious that they ought to have caused uneasiness when seen in print. We certainly see through the modesty of describing himself as having an extravagant and irregular head, and smile (as he may have intended an intimate friend to smile) at the phrase omitted in 1643 about being averse from nothing, neither plant, animal, nor spirit, to say nothing of Italians or Frenchmen. Fortunately we can place beside the easy statement of general tolerance the thoroughly un-English intelligence with which, later, writing to his sons Tom and Edward, he describes France as a place where you not only cast off *pudor rusticus*, but where the people are "sober, diligent, and active," and where the women are "good company." Perhaps to

11. B. M., Sloane MS. 1879, ff. 46–7. There is a marginal gloss on "arise toward China" which reads "Which may bee sayde in some latitude upon the diurnall motion of the earth from west to east." This seems to show that, despite the usual statement to the contrary, Browne was, at least in middle life, a Copernican. In my opinion even when in the early 1640's he wrote, "And therefore if any affirm, the earth doth move, and will not believe with us, it standeth still; *because he hath probable reasons for it, and I no infallible sense, nor reason against it* [italics mine] I will not quarrel with his assertion" (*Pseud. Epid.*, II. 5), he was more than half persuaded. He owned and greatly admired Gilbert's *De Magnete* (1600) in which Gilbert had said "from these arguments therefore we infer, not with mere probability, but with certainty, the diurnal rotations of the earth." *De Magnete*, tr. P. Fleury Mottelay (New York, 1958), 327.

counter statements about the "dullness" of his disposition, and the way this has at least saved him from the wickedly inventive vices of a Nero, he emphasizes his moral struggles and the recurrent battles of Lepanto within himself. There is no real astrological escape from the implications of such phrases as having "the happiness to be borne and framed unto vertue," or "the privilege of a few to be vertuous," in spite of the frequency with which he uses the supposedly objective phrase "it is my temper," but one might add a close contemporary parallel from Lord Herbert of Cherbury explaining that he could not tell a lie, "my soul naturally having an antipathy to lying and deceit." These self-indulgences are balanced by other obviously sincere passages of humility, to say nothing of the original final sentence: "Thy will be done though in my own damnation." Some vanities of the kind I have instanced come in part, it seems to me, because Browne has formalized himself into a kind of person, but we may safely and unsentimentally conclude that he might have been much more embarrassed at seeing them in print for all to read than in seeing his deprecatory boasts about his knowledge of stars and languages. Vain as these boasts may be, moreover, they should not be taken as rendering absurd the preceding remark about pride, pride meaning to Browne something much more arrogant—the vice of a Faustus or Satan.

If there is one reaction that an appreciative and literary reader of the *Religio* is bound to have, after even a single perusal, it is that the book is a marvel of verbal texture. For early (1644 and 1645) comments on the effect of even the Latin version—about which he said they were making *grand état* in Paris—Gui Patin has often been quoted. The phrase "tout gentil et curieux" in his letter may have slightly disapproving overtones, and there is probably some reserve in "fort délicat et tout mystique," but only appreciation in "l'auteur ne manque pas d'esprit; vous y verrez d'étranges et ravissantes pensées. Il n'y a encore guère de livres de cette sorte . . . la subtilité de l'esprit humain se pourroit découvrir par cette voie."[12] Perhaps the most precise, compact, and sensitive comment on the over-all effect is still that of Johnson when in his life of Browne he remarks on "the novelty of paradoxes, the dignity of sentiment, the quick succession of images, the multitude of abstruse allusions, the subtlety of dis-

12. *Lettres de Gui Patin,* ed. J.-H. Reveille-Parise (Paris, 1846), I, 340 and 354.

quisition, the strength of language." Johnson is often praised for hitting the nail on the head; he was usually capable of much more delicate operations—and how right here to end with "the *strength* of language."

This complexity of overtones, and the correspondences between passages in different parts of the book, are time and again such that though Browne is memorable in phrases and sentences, it is very difficult, as well as very mistaken, to isolate some point of thought, or paraphrase in the interest of expository clarity. It is only from the whole effect of the circling movement of his mind, as we follow and participate in the exact phrasing, that we find (or think we find) the author. In addition, the *Religio* is not only a private exercise, but is often "delivered rhetorically, many expressions therein meerely tropical," and it is of course in these mere tropes that we find suggestions of Browne's personality, along with the impersonal enlightenment of metaphor itself. Even when the metaphor is least "far-fetched" we have it: "There must therefore be more than one Saint Peter; particular churches and sects usurpe the gates of Heaven and turne the key against each other *and thus we go to heaven against each other's wills*" (italics mine). Again and again the personal element lies in that turn of ironic humour which is so essential an element of Browne's temperament—ironic humour directed at man and all his prejudices and vanities; directed also at himself more often than is realized, although by some he is thought to be merely naive, as in his remark about bringing up the rear in heaven, or that natural amorousness of all that is beautiful which leads him from the "sweet sexe" to the handsome picture of a horse.[13]

The flourishes of rhetorical bravado, particularly, need to be read in the context of Browne's work and temper as a whole. "It is the microcosm of mine owne frame that I cast my eye on," he says, "as for the other, I use it but like my Globe." "As for the other": what a fine *temporary* waving off of the whole universe in a gesture of compact humour. But one hardly need emphasize Browne's lifelong attention (only this side devotion) to that "other." Even though we may have "all Africa and her prodigies" within us, his appetite for macrocosm-history, archaeology, geography (or herbals), from the

13. Browne owned Carlo Ruini's *Anatomia del Cavallo* . . . (1618), a folio "adornata di bellisime Figure."

ancients to the moderns was prodigious. Time may be but "a parenthesis in Eternity," but "it's good to know as much of it as we can."

There are also many passages hardly, if at all, figurative, which are by their verbal texture as revealing of temperament as some of the direct autobiographal statements of Part Two. One of the most Brownean occurs in the first sentence of the book when he writes of the "indifferency" of his behaviour and discourse and concludes "yet in despight hereof I dare without usurpation assume the honorable stile of a Christian." Almost every word has its weight and colour to express a complex social and personal awareness of his own position in a period of religious controversy which is becoming more acute, but which (at least in certain atmospheres) has still the possibilities of courtesy. The devotional "civility" of his knee, his hat, and hand, later spoken of, is of course complementary, and I hope I am not being too subjective if I suggest that the phrases form an idiosyncratic embodiment of the curious (perhaps rather unreal) before-the-storm civility of Aubrey's remark (in his life of Lucius Cary, Lord Falkland) that poetry and controversy with the Church of Rome were the "studies in fashion in those dayes." Accompanying such personally coloured indirections we have, of course, many straightforward statements; the next paragraph here is a neat if simple formulation of the general Anglican position as a reformed Catholic church.

Browne's partiality to dreams, and mysterious and providential intuitions, his consciousness of the great chain of being in both Christian and Hermetic terms are apparent to any reader. But it is often not altogether easy to say what he literally believes, though, again, he is usually credited with simple credulity. Like most of his contemporaries, learned or unlearned, he had no doubt about witches, the Bible being the corner-stone of his belief. But what is the literal certainty of passages like "I do think that many mysteries ascribed to our inventions have been the courteous revelation of spirits; for those noble essences in heaven bear a friendly regard unto their fellow natures on earth," or "Therefore for Spirits, I am so farre from denying their existence, that I could easily believe, that not only whole Countries, but particular persons, have their Tutelary, and Guardian Angels . . . there is no heresie in it, and . . . it is an opinion of a good and wholesome use in the course and actions of a man's life . . . ," when one puts beside them, from the essay "On Dreams" the doubts of

"*If* there bee Guardian spirits they *may* not bee unactiuely about us in sleepe, but *may* sometimes order our dreams, and many strange hints, instigations or discoueries which are so amazing *may* arise from such foundations" (my italics). Gosse remarks that "Browne declares his confident belief in the Neo-Platonic theory of an undivided and common spirit animating the whole world."[14] The relevant passage (I.32) runs (again with my italics) "Now there *may* be (for aught I know) an universal and common spirit to the whole world. It was the opinion of Plato and is yet of the hermetical philosophers: *if* there be a common nature that ties the scattered and divided individuals into one species, *why may there not be* one that unites them all?" Again one might add a lively sentence from the essay "On Dreams" in which Browne is referring to Plutarch's story of the famous courtesan Lamia, who, with a modern sense of publicity, sued a young man "who had confessed that pleasure from her in a dreame, which shee had denyed his waking senses, conceaving that shee had merited something from his phantasticall fruition and shadow of herself." *If* there be such debts, Browne comments, "Wee owe deeply unto sympathies, butt the common spirit of the world must bee judge in such arrearages." He is not very far from a contemporary passage of ironic humour in which Walter Charlton (repudiating his earlier attitude toward the powder of sympathy) describes the world soul as a kind of universal baggage agent.[15] In contrast to the Cambridge Platonists, all such speculations are play, rather than belief, although they rest on the ethical justification that they are opinions of "good and wholesome use." It is certainly better, for instance, as Browne says, to believe in guardian angels than that there are no angels at all.

I have made the sufficiently obvious comment that a reader of the *Religio* must hold in mind recurrent passages, being at the same time aware of the total character or persona of himself Browne is creating, if only half consciously. This is especially true of the primary temperament he gives himself as one "born under Saturn." Early in the book in a paragraph about religious observance and ritual, he "acknowledges" his "common conversation austere," his "behaviour full of rigour, sometimes not without morosity." A little later he calls him-

14. *Browne,* 40.
15. W. Charlton, *Physiologia Epicuro-Gassendo Charltoniana* . . . (1654), Bk. IV, ch. 15.

self "a melancholy and contemplative nature." On two occasions he speaks of his "solitary and retired imagination." In a paragraph on this world and the next, he says "in expectation of a better, I can with patience embrace this life, yet in my best meditations doe often desire death," to which is added, in the pirated editions and the MSS. only, "It is a symptom of melancholy to be afraid of death, yet sometimes to desire it; this latter I have often discovered in my self, and thinke no man ever desired life, as I have sometimes death." Twice he speaks of the dullness of his reason and the dullness of his spirit. Almost at the end of the book (with a very characteristic blend of urbanity and humour) he says, "At my nativity my ascendant was the watery signe of Scorpius; I was borne in the planetary hour of Saturn, and I thinke I have a piece of that leaden Planet in mee . . . yet in one dreame I can compose a whole comedy, behold the action, apprehend the jests, and laugh my self awake at the conceits thereof."

With some of these phrases too far in the back of his mind, Professor Denonain drives a broad fast modern highway through the curves and contours of Browne's solitary path to say Browne was "avowedly sullen, morose, and melancholy, yet might have fits of cheerfulness. He seems to have been from an early age disillusioned —both sentimentally and intellectually—dissatisfied with his own self, torn by inner conflicts with human nature and human kind . . . all this brought him to the verge of suicide."[16] A case for a psychiatrist, one might say, not much like the "mélancolique agréable" of Gui Patin, or the sensible doctor who described Mr. Alderman Wisse of Norwich as "a meticulous doubting man of a good nature, unwilling to offend God or man and seldome without thoughts to perplex himself and make his life the more unconfortable."

"Best meditations," in its context, gives us the clue to the proper understanding of some of these sentiments, but it is also illuminating to realize that "dullness," "melancholy," "dream," "leaden," (if not "morosity") are in the *Religio* all satellites of Saturn as the influence of that planet was often interpreted in Platonic Renaissance thought. Professor Huntley explains even Browne's remark about his life having been a miracle of thirty years in relation to Saturn and Scorpio: "Born under so unlucky a horoscope Browne looked upon each day

16. *Religio Medici,* ed. J.-J. Denonain (Cambridge, 1955), xiii. This preface is not in the critical edition of 1953.

of his life as a special act of Providence that stayed his natural destiny." This is not far from Gosse's quite undocumentable statement that Browne was an "infatuated astrologer" and hence ineligible for the Royal Society.[17] Instead one may emphasize the fact that not only was "melancholy" generally accepted as a sign of thoughtfulness and imagination, but that in some quarters Saturn was not regarded as primarily malignant. Professor Panofsky, in his study of Dürer,[18] speaks of the Florentine Neo-Platonists (especially Ficino and Pico) as having discovered how highly Plotinus and his followers had thought of Saturn. They even called themselves Saturnians, and showed "immense satisfaction," Panofsky remarks, in the belief that Plato had been born under Saturn.[19] Ficino had not only been born under Saturn in the ascendancy of Aquarius (even more watery than Scorpius) but wrote that "to the spirits that dwell in the spheres of the sublime, who wholeheartedly and sincerely concentrate on divine contemplation, Saturn himself is a benevolent father." Pico, speaking of the way the ancients "cast poetical veils over the face of their mysteries," calls Saturn "the Soul of the World," signifying "intellectual nature, wholly employ'd in contemplations. . . . Saturn makes men contemplative, Jupiter Imperious."[20] Leone Ebreo, in his *Dialoghi d'Amore*, similarly gives various attributes of Saturn, the earthy, the cold and dry, and so on, but says "Besides this, he bestows great intelligence, deep meditation, true science . . . in virtue of the blend of the nature of his heavenly father with that of his earthly mother . . . ."[21]

By comparison with many others of his time Browne shows little or no leaning to judicial astrology; his later connection with Dee was personal, not that of a believer; in *Christian Morals* he is emphatic about not making Saturn, Mars, or Venus guilty of our follies. But

17. Huntley, *Browne*, 3; Gosse, *Browne*, 134.

18. E. Panofsky, *Albrecht Dürer* (Princeton, 1943), I, 165 ff.

19. Plato was also apparently thought to have achieved what in *A Letter to a Friend* Browne called the remarkable coincidence of winding up on the day of his nativity, "the tail of the snake returning into its mouth" on November 9. On the basis of his own astronomical references it is usually said that Browne managed the same feat on October 19, 1682, but he told Aubrey that he was born on November 19.

20. *A Platonick Discourse upon Love by Pico della Mirandola*, ed. E. G. Gardner (London, 1914), 9. The translation is that of Thomas Stanley, published in 1651.

21. *The Philosophy of Love (Dialoghi d'Amore)* by Leone Ebreo, tr. F. Friedeberg and Jean H. Barnes (London, 1937), 134.

for the purposes of a partly "tropical" portrait he may have developed ideas appropriate to a Platonic (rather than astrological) conception of his nativity. He was born under Saturn. When he began to write the *Religio* he had not yet "seen one revolution of Saturn" (that is, thirty years). It was an appropriate time to take a full view and circle of himself, to make a memorial, his education and travels over, and a new circle beginning. One further point. If Saturn and being a piece of that leaden planet suggested "melancholy" musing, lead suggested something more. It inevitably suggested alchemy—lead turned into gold—and then the divine alchemy, an analogy never far below the surface of Browne's mind, and of which the other was often only a symbol. In the Pembroke College MS. of the *Religio*, which, Professor Denonain plausibly argues, seems to represent the earliest extant version, Browne says he has forsaken the ordinary medical and "school" definitions of death as "privation of life, extinction of natural heate, separation etc of soule and body, and have fram'd one in an hermetical way unto mine owne fancie: *est mutatio ultima, qua perficitur nobile extractum Microcosmi,*" "for to mee, that consider things in a natural and experimental way, man seems to be but a digestion, or preparative way unto that last and glorious elixar which lies imprison'd in the chains of flesh etc." It is hard to say why this sentence was omitted, since Browne defies "the severe schools" to laugh him out of other ideas he calls hermetic; but this alchemical metaphor accompanied him, literally to the grave. When his skull was "gnaw'd out" of it, the inscription on the coffin plate was brought to light. It seems very Brownean when it speaks of ". . . *hoc loculo indormiens, corporis spagyrici pulvere plumbum in aurum convertit.*" "Spagyric" is defined in a seventeenth-century alchemical glossary as "that which separates the false from the true, the impure from the pure"; divine alchemy is to change lead into gold, and Browne's lifelong psychological interest in sleep and dreams was part of his sense of life itself as a dream. He was capable of enjoying an ironic smile at his moods of being "weary of the Sunne": "mee thinkes I have outlived my selfe . . . I perceive I doe anticipate the vices of age, the world to me is but a dreame or mockshow, and wee all therein but Pantalones and Anticks to my severer contemplations." But he had as strongly as others of his time the Christian sentiment of waking into life.

One subject especially most congenial to Renaissance Platonism was of course friendship. An orthodox cult for any man of refinement (as Browne puts it, it "fals not on vulgar and common constitutions, but on such as are mark'd for vertue"), to the author of the *Religio* it seems to have been both that and something more passionate, something more than Donne's "second religion, friendship." Even in this relationship is to be seen Browne's intense sense of the individual microcosm with all its mysteries: "so intrinsical is every man unto himself," he writes, "that some doubt may be made, whether any would exchange his Being or substantially become another man." This being so, whatever the friendship, "I am in the dark to all the world, and my nearest friends behold mee but in a cloud." But friendship is one of the "three most mystical unions":

> two natures in one person; three persons in one nature; one soule in two bodies . . . there are wonders in true affection, it is a body of *Aenigmas*, mysteries and riddles wherein two become one, as they both become two. I love my friend before my selfe, and yet methinkes I do not love him enough . . . when I am from him, I am dead till I bee with him; when I am with him, I am not satisfied, would be still nearer him: united soules are not satisfied with embraces but desire each truely to be the other.

Another passage, the first part of which was dropped from the authorized text of 1643, reads:

> There is surely a neerer apprehension of anything that delights us in our dreams than in our wakened senses; with this I can be a king without a Crown, rich without royalty, in heaven though on earth, enjoy my friend and embrace him at a distance; without which I cannot behold him. Without this I were unhappy; for my awakened judgement discontents me, ever whispering unto me, that I am from my friend; but my friendly dreams in the night requite me, and make me thinke I am in his armes. I thanke God for my happy dreames as I doe for my good rest. . . .

The use of the singular in "friend" is perhaps ambiguous, but it is worth noting that in the concluding sentences of the book Browne first wrote "Blesse mee in this life with the peace of conscience, command of my affections, the love of my dearest friend, and I shall be happie enough to pittie Caesar." At a later stage "friend" became "friends," and not until 1643 is the phrase about God added to make the text read "love of thy selfe and my dearest friends." We are almost bound to think of a friendship begun at Winchester or Oxford, rather than later, even though there is any amount of evidence (from dedications and letters) to indicate both Browne's later capacity for friendship, and the fact that it did not depend on similarity of age.

It is probably when he contrasts friendship with filial feelings or ordinary sexual love that we are most aware of the contemplative character of his mind, the reality of his feeling for friendship, and some at least probable features of his family experience. The two most relevant passages are well known:

> I confesse [he observes in one of them] I doe not observe that order that the Schooles ordaine our affections, to love our Parents, Wives, Children, and then our friends; for excepting the injunctions of Religion, I doe not find in my selfe such a necessary and indissoluble Sympathy to those of my bloud. I hope I do not break the fifth Commandment if I conceive I may love my friend before the nearest of my bloud, even those to whom I owe the principles of life. I never yet cast a true affection on a Woman, but I have loved my Friend as I do vertue, my Soule, my God.

The other runs:

> I was never yet once, and commend their resolutions who never marry twice [all MSS. and the pirated editions: "am resolved never to be married twice"]; not that I disallow of second marriages; as neither in all cases of Polygamy . . . I could be content [MSS. and pirated editions: "I wish"] that we might procreate like trees, without conjunction, or that there were any way to perpetuate the world without this triviall and vulgar way of coition; It is the foolishest act a wise man commits in all his life. . . .

Both comments certainly reveal character, and the formal sobriety of the second might make any reader agree with a common modern feeling that no one would guess that the author of the *Religio* was young. Moreover it was inevitably picked up by "journalists" of the day (without doubt to Browne's annoyance), and has ever since had amused annotation. It is a little remote in sentiment; to get a really strong impression of doctors with an intellectual distaste for sex we might look at some of the remarks in early anatomies, for example those of Paré.[22] But first of all, as Professor Leroy says, sensibly and learnedly: "Au surplus le [Browne] railler c'est lui donner le mérite d'une originalité douteuse. Le thème était connu, presque classique.

22. For example, on p. 535 of the English edition of Paré's *Works*, 1691, Bk. 24, "Of the Generation of Man."

Un moraliste, un sage, se devait de l'attaquer, et dans le bon sens: blâmant comme il convient cette ardeur amoureuse, laquelle ne 'laisse à l'homme aucune liberté de raisonner.'"[23] Professor Leroy gives literary parallels from Montaigne and Bayle to Hippocrates (of whom Browne certainly knew every word) whose phrase is "une courte epilepsie." The relation between Browne's original comments on filial obligation and second marriages and his mother's second marriage with a rather typical "low-countries" captain and courtier I have discussed briefly elsewhere.[24]

Although I believe that some notion of Browne's somewhat histrionic approach to himself is central to a proper understanding of the *Religio*, it would be a foolish affectation to imply that one can always only approach his revelation of himself obliquely. There are, of course, a great many revealing and quite straightforward statements about himself in both parts of the book, not merely in the more gossipy second part. If Whitefoot had written his intended memoir rather than notes for it, even though this would have been a memoir about an older man who had entered another metempsychosis, we would have more possibilities of verification. As it is, we have, from Whitefoot and later writing by Browne himself, some confirmations and some questions. Thus (for example, merely) Browne emphasizes his shyness in controversy; Whitefoot tells us how easily he blushed, and Browne is excessively urgent in advising his fourteen-year-old son to learn social ease in France. Browne tells us that he used himself to all diets, humours, climates, "when I am cold I cure not myself by heate"; Whitefoot tells us he always dressed very warmly. Browne speaks of his "untamed affections and confirmed vitiosity," his frame "raised upon a masse of antipathies," the constant "battel of Lepanto" going on within him, and we suspect a dramatic hypostasizing of the human condition; Whitefoot tells us he had no despotic control over his passions. Browne tells us he can weep at a play and gives us a picture of himself weeping at a solemn procession; one of his "Tracts" tells us that he was "often delighted" with the "songs and poems" of southern France when he lived there. He read medicine at Montpellier; he also read Rabelais and other facetious not to say libertine authors.

23. Olivier Leroy, *Le Chevalier Thomas Browne* (Paris, 1931), 157.
24. *UTQ*, XXX (1961), 201–3.

"I have never read a book in which I felt a greater similarity to my own make of mind . . . an affectionate visionary. . . . But then I should tell a different tale of my own heart; for I would not only endeavour to tell the truth (which I doubt not Sir T.B. has done) but likewise to tell the whole truth, which most assuredly he has not done. However, it is a most delicious book . . . ."[25] So Coleridge, and we ask how much truth there is in the first sentence, as well as in Coleridge's assertion of what he would have done. *Religio Medici* is a self-portrait which hides as well as reveals. It presents its author in a way which allows for direct expression of temperament and opinions and also the stylization of seventeenth-century virtuosity. Browne was not too "sincere" to enhance the flavour of his life and role with some rhetorical bravado, and like other characteristic writers of his day he had at times a certain fondness for misinterpretable if not hieroglyphic phrases, giving us an expressive exploration rather than what is innocently called the plain truth. As we have seen, he was not averse to the idea that even his nearest friends (or friend) beheld him but in a cloud.

25. *Miscellaneous Criticism*, 253.

Milton and Cats

GEOFFREY BULLOUGH

THIS ESSAY IS NOT WRITTEN in emulation of the image-worshippers who have discovered that Shakespeare disliked dogs. It is an examination of the relationship between the treatment of Adam and Eve in Milton's *Paradise Lost*, Books IV and VIII, and that in a poem by the Dutch poet-statesman Jacob Cats.

Milton must have known something of Jacob Cats as a statesman, and they may well have met when Cats came over in 1651 on an embassy in hope of settling differences between the Netherlands and England after the passing of the Navigation Act. Fearing the loss of their carrying-trade, the Dutch sent three envoys, with Cats as leader, to negotiate a treaty. The Ambassadors were graciously received in December 1651, and "entertained at dinner again and again" (Masson, *Life*, IV, 371), but close consideration of their proposals was put off for months; meanwhile the sailors of the two countries insulted or fought each other whenever they met, and after Admiral Blake had a brush with Van Tromp in May 1652 the English attitude became bellicose. Negotiations were broken off at the end of June and war was declared in July. Milton's sonnet to Henry Vane the Younger was written at this time, for Vane, as leader of the committee on foreign affairs, had first striven for peace and then brought the negotiations to an end.

As Secretary for Foreign Tongues to the Council of State Milton played some part in these events, since he translated the papers exchanged between the parties. Thus on January 23, 1652, he was instructed to translate from Latin into English a paper of proposals from the Dutchmen, and three days later he was asked to put into

Latin the Council's answer to a previous paper. On March 8 he was bidden to translate articles countering thirty-eight articles submitted by the Dutch, and next day was told to do it within two days. At this time Milton was busy with other work, his eyesight was rapidly failing, and he had been given an assistant, but when negotiations broke down in July he superintended the Latin translation of the Declaration of the Causes of the War against the Dutch.

Milton already had many Dutch acquaintances. He had met Hugo Grotius in Paris in 1638 when on his Continental travels, and Grotius, then Swedish Ambassador to France, had received him kindly. He knew Franciscus Junius who had lived long in England and was there in 1651, returning to Holland in the autumn. At that time intense curiosity about Milton was excited in Holland by his controversy with Salmasius, and Junius was able to give his nephew Isaac Vossius (who sent it on to Nicholas Heinsius) "information about Milton from my uncle Junius, who is on familiar terms with him."[1] According to this, Milton was "a disciple of Patricius Junius," who had been keeper of the King's Library, and still retained his post.

Another Dutch scholar probably known to Milton was Junius Vitius, then a lawyer at The Hague and a writer of Dutch and Latin verse. He was a nephew of Cats and in 1643 had spent some time in England at Hatfield Chase, Cats's country house there. He was Secretary to the Embassy of 1652. Before leaving home he wrote to Heinsius (Jan. 12, 1652) that he looked forward to getting to know Milton, and again after reaching London, "I am resolved to go and see Milton." Also during the negotiations Liewe van Aitzema visited Milton more than once, and nearly two years later corresponded with the poet about getting one of his Divorce pamphlets translated into Dutch.

Masson refers to a tradition that as Secretary for Foreign Tongues Milton was allowed "a weekly table" to entertain important foreigners in London on diplomatic or other business (Masson, IV, 353). So in the first months of 1652 he may have entertained Jacob Cats and discussed poetry as well as politics with him. Later, as public relations became more strained, their contacts are likely to have been official only; and Cats was not a member of the embassy which went to England in 1653 on an unsuccessful peace mission. But Milton retained his interest in things Dutch, and Roger Williams, over from

1. Cf. H. Scherpbier, *Milton in Holland* (Amsterdam, 1933), ch. I.

America in that year on behalf of the Rhode Island settlers, later wrote: "The Secretary of the Council, for my Dutch I read him, read me many more languages" (Masson, IV, 531). So Milton could still read quite well in 1653.

What works in Dutch Williams read we cannot know, or how good Milton's knowledge of the language was previously; but if, as has been argued, Milton afterwards knew Vondel's play *Lucifer* (published 1654) he may also have known some of the poems of Cats, then widely regarded as a better poet than his rival. ("Well, Mr Vondel," said the Bishop of Mechelen, "you are very clever, but still you are no Cats.")

Jacob Cats (1577–1660) belonged to the Zealand school of poets. After studying law at Leyden and in France he became an advocate at The Hague where he first came into notice by defending an alleged witch. He first visited England in a vain search of a cure for a tertian fever which endangered his life. In 1605 he married and went to live at Grypskerke where he farmed and wrote verse. When the dykes were broken at the end of the twelve-year truce with Spain he was obliged to leave his farm and became a stipendiary magistrate, first at Middleburg and then at Dort. His second visit to England was in 1627 on a diplomatic mission, when he was knighted by Charles I. In 1636 he was made Grand Pensionary of Holland and West Friesland, and in 1645 Keeper of the Great Seal. He resigned this post in 1651 but was then sent on his mission to Cromwell. After his return he retired from public work and lived at his villa where he wrote an autobiography, *Eighty Two Years of my Life*.

In politics Cats was a supporter of the House of Orange; in religion a Calvinist. His poetry made him famous for generations, for it was homely, simple, and full of the domestic virtues. His *Emblems* (1618) were often reprinted, and known in England. "An Emblematical Dialogue" (Anna and Phillis) was translated by Thomas Heywood in *Pleasant Dialogues and Dramas* (1637). His *Houwelijck* (1625)—"Marriage"—announces his favourite theme, which he developed in his series of fourteen narrative poems (with prose commentaries) *Trou-Ringh* (1637)[2] ("The Marriage-Ring") in which Cats portrayed

2. *'s Werelts Begin, Midden, Eynde, Besloten in den Trou-Ringh, met den Proef-Steen van den Selven. Door I. Cats* (Dordrecht, 1637). Another edition in 1638 has different engravings and lacks the prose commentaries. Cited and briefly described in W. Kirkconnell, *The Celestial Cycle* (University of Toronto Press, 1952), 608.

the diversity of the marriage state. The work has four parts: Part I contains five stories from Holy Scripture—Adam and Eve, Jacob, Leah and Rachel, Athniel and Ascha, the rape of the daughters of the Benjaminites, David and Abigail; Part II contains classical tales, including Crates and Hipparchia, and Cyrus and Aspasia; Part III includes more modern stories—Princess Emma and Eginart, Ulderick of Bohemia and Phryne—with older tales, Antony and Cleopatra, and Rhodope; Part IV treats of Heavenly Marriage as illustrated in the Song of Solomon, the story of the Virgin and the life of Christ.

Each story is the occasion of discussions about matrimonial problems, set out in dialogue form. Thus the story of Jacob raises questions of polygamy and whether marriage should be based on beauty alone; in that of Athniel and Ascha state-marriages are involved and the power of parents over children; the rape of the Benjaminite women brings consideration of the powers of authority in cases of kidnapping and violence, whether a woman should marry her ravisher, and whether she can possibly feel love for him. David and Abigail raises questions about second marriages, the use of go-betweens, the making of separate wills, etc. The interlocutors are Philogamus, a young bachelor, naïve, impulsive, well-intentioned, and Sophroniscus, an elderly widower, well versed in theology and moral literature. Their discussions should interest students of Milton, since they touch agreeably on problems much deliberated at the time and implied or directly considered in his work.

Thus the first story, *Grondt-Houwelijck* ("The Original Marriage, a Description of the first Wedding held in Paradise between Adam and Eve, the first Parents of all Mankind") is preceded by a short dialogue and followed by a longer one. In the first dialogue Sophroniscus advises Philogamus to marry, in terms which Milton could approve. Philogamus does not want to enter matrimony as the ignorant beasts went into the Ark, without knowing why. Sophroniscus agrees that too many people go into marriage unprepared. Men should not accept hospitality merely in order to eat or for love of novelty. Right-thinking people dine out to be sociable and to enjoy each other's company. Marriage exists not just to satisfy a man's sensual desire for a woman but to provide a sweet and comfortable life in the service of God's Church and of one's country. Cats approves of the broad definition of marriage as "a lawful and indissoluble union instituted by

God so that we may know him as a pure spirit, and serve him in purity, and in order that human beings may be multiplied and God's Church may be gathered from them."

In the following account of "The Original Marriage" I have translated typical passages into blank verse, trying to keep the tone of the Dutch as far as possible.[3] The poem begins (ll. 1–12) with a description of the Creation:

By his eternal Word, out of his lofty power
God cast clear radiance on this marvellous All,
And the dark Night divided from the Day,
That by the light his wonders might be seen.
The earth established stood and separate,
With depths o'erhung and towering heights between.
The Heavens outspread like a fine tapestry,
Bore in their lofty arch the gauge of Time.
For ornament the sky had lucent rays
That stay in Heaven and wander round the world:
The white moon now was seen, the golden sun,
And how these rose and on their course began.

The beauty of the universe and the fitting disposition of the elements and other creatures are shown. Then the Garden of Eden is described (33–61):

A breeze of sweetest kind, blown from the south,
Came wafting on the plain, played in the herbs,
Came sighing in the leaves and other growth.
But never blew a storm out of the north,
For there no tender bloom by winds is blasted,
And no foul mist is found within that arbour,
No harsh frost enters there which bites the cheeks,
No bitter cold that gnaws into the limbs,
There is no dirty fog, no dashing rain,
No lightning-flash, no baleful thunderbolt . . .
Only a pure air fitly temperèd
Draws flowers from foliage, out of flowers the seed.
No harmful weed, no nettles in the fields,
No thistle in the wood to harm the folk,
No aconite or other poisonous herb,
So one could eat all fruits with never a fear.

3. I am grateful to Miss Lucy de Bruyn for assistance in the translation. Without her help I could not have done this work.

No dirty spider spun white webs on the trees . . .
No lazy snail came crawling on the grass;
No toad fat-bellied spat its poison-foam;
No dun-grey mole uprooting round the flowers;
No evil rats with myriad sly feet, . . .
All things that lived came to give joy to men.

The birds praised their Creator, and it is no exaggeration to say that the raven sang like a nightingale. Cats does his best to describe the indescribable, and discusses the Tree of Life and the Tree of Knowledge of Good and Evil which grew in a lovely grove (99–120):

All other growth was planted for the flesh,
But these were for the soul, a holy pledge.
Amid the bed rose up one lovely tree,
Green, sappy, wondrous sound and vigorous.
Upon its boughs no blighted leaf was seen.
It seemed that the world's youth lived in its branches.
A ray from God's high throne with radiant beams
Came from that noble wood continually.
So golden are its leaves and passing fair,
Its foliage hangs like a perpetual crown.
That was a healthful tree; its perfect fruit
All pains, unrest, and sickness could dispel.
With verdure fine it smiled on its great Planter,
And all that's baleful's banished by its scent.
The second tree there (of unusual power)
Is for deep understanding, past our thought;
Its fruit of fairer hue than eye e'er saw,
But yet not made to serve the fleshly taste.
The grounds of knowledge of both good and evil
Repose in the deep mystery of this tree;
But many still believe it came to pass
That a bad spirit oft could there be found.[4]

The universe was good, but (125–42) God was not satisfied until he had made a creature

Of highest skill, endowed with wise discourse,
That looks up Heavenward, with upright limbs.
The Maker went to work, and now He shaped
A morsel of red clay ta'en from the earth,
Whence he brought forth a man, a noble image,
In whom anew he fashioned a small world.

4. Contrast Milton, who makes Satan sit on the Tree of Life, *PL*, IV, 194–6.

The body first was made, that could not move
But rested in the place where it was laid.
It was of pleasant hue and countenance
But yet no life was there suffused throughout.
God breathed, and Adam lived. See now the creature
Whereby this wondrous All's together bound.[5]

So God, like a good host who prepares the tables before his guests arrive, made the world before he created man. "Still this is not enough";

God watches man, sees all that Adam does,
And finds he must not leave him solitary.

So God made Eve (161–84):

He made a slumber deep fall on his limbs
And gently took a rib out of his body
And out of that same bone God wrought it so
That Adam, ere he knew, was given a wife.
The man lay in the arbour in shade of trees,
O'ercome by sleep and so bedazed with dreams
That his dim eye was not awaked until
The gracious work was fully at an end.
Then dawned within his limbs a new sensation;
He glimpsed a something dimly, came more near,
And saw the rarest thing, a fair sweet form,
That straight played through his eye into his heart.
He felt new youth, he felt a different being.
He felt a sweet stir, rising up within him;
Suffuse his blood. He was another man;
He had a new awareness none can tell;
Conscious he was now of the source of life . . .
A fever without pain, heat without burning.[6]

Adam approaches Eve and welcomes her, calling her "My soul, my other self!" The poet describes Eve's reaction rather well (196–216):

How strangely Eve regarded these new things!
She knew not what she saw, but saw with pleasure.
She knew not what a man, or wooer is;
Nor was she drawn towards action by her nature.
She feels her tender mind moved to its depths,
And she is drawn to what she does not know.
She knows not what she feels; her youthful blood
It is that in her stirs and blithely leaps.

5. Cf. *PL*, VII, 505–16, 524–34.

6. Contrast *PL*, VIII, 452–89.

She feels her soul most powerfully moved
Although she cannot give that stir a name.
She stands as though bemused in her amazement,
Uncertain what to do or not to do.
She sees the young man and his handsome limbs,
His breast, his ready frame, his gifts of reason.
She hears a sweet voice speak, in which she joys,
And gives him back the pleasure by her speech.
"What is your name, who come to meet me here?
How must I call you, greet you properly?
I do not know. But what is there I know,
Since but a moment have I been on earth?"

She says that she might call him Brother, or Father, or Keeper, Helpmate, Friend, her true Man, and asks him which style he prefers. He asks her to call him "dear Man" and to take him into her arms. Eve at once begins to temporize. She wishes first to know more about the world around them:

You have informed me how you should be named;
Let us observe what's fitting for us both,
For all things (as I note) have proper bounds.
Naught should be done out of the erring senses,
But through reflection ripe. There's a true measure
On which stands the fair work of Earth and Heaven.

Adam tells Eve how he first beheld Creation (288–300):

I wandered on the plain and in the woods,
Climbed round a hill and went down through the dale.
I walked upon the sand and the rich grass,
Let my eyes stray wherever beauty was.
I saw the fruitful wood, the wild trees,
The beasts within the field, the fish in streams.
The sticky clay I saw, the white seashore,
The royal gold commingled with the sand.
Nearing a rivulet where one might drink
I saw an Onyx gleam within its bed.
I grasped it from the middle of the brook
And stood and gazed a long time at its brightness. . . .[7]

He wondered at the beauty of God's handiwork (309–24), at the

thousand things
Created lovely, all for me alone;

7. Cf. *PL*, VIII, 253–82.

But yet in all the things my eyes surveyed
I found my heart sustained no true delight.
What signifies a tree borne down with fruit,
What is a shining rill wherein to bathe,
What is the richest gem I know on earth,
While I must be alone in these delights?
Moreover how may I the Maker sing
And recognise the source of all this wealth,
The Soul of all the work before my eyes,
While in my curious heart deep sorrow grows?
Whom shall I show the power of God's finger,
And who will prize with me his gracious acts?
Let men say what they will, that life is death
In which they do not find a loving bedmate.[8]

He appreciated God's kindness in making the lower creatures; yet (335–76):

Although their nature I could fully grasp
For none of them I felt complete desire;
They were of stuff too coarse; their flesh was dull;
No help to me; in them no reason dwells.
The form, the noble image of God's mind
Dwells not in lions or in other beasts;
That special grace is given to man alone,
So that he (as he should) for God may live,
And constantly in all things see the Lord,
And homage offer him in every way.
Yet nonetheless I saw the brutish kind
Knew sweet companionship among themselves.
I saw that not a beast so violent was
As not to seek his counterpart, his pair. . . .
I saw the gallant steeds play with their foals.
I saw the mountain goats sport on the rocks. . . .
And why needs more be said? Birds in the trees,
The wild things in the wood, the fish in streams,
Are properly paired and every animal
Feels the sweet warmth of love's interior fire. . . .
Shall the wild herd with their companions play
And shall I be obliged to pine alone,
To be unfruitful in this fertile wood,
Where even the smallest beast finds wonted love?
Shall I ne'er joy in the sweet name of Father,
And never have a fair Maid sleeping by me

8. Cf. *PL*, VIII, 361–7.

Or lead our childish offspring by the hand,
The while my youthful heart burns with new love?
Therefore I feel I need another life.
I need a helpmeet for my comfort given.
I need a bedmate, need a youthful wife,
If my fair bower I am to enjoy to the full.[9]

Adam tells Eve that God heard his appeal and (380–412) understood

That which all flesh and every creature needs.
Then you, sweet flower, were moulded for my joy,
Peaceful to sleep within my loving arms.
The Giver of all good has granted me
The whiteness of your breast, red of your mouth,
Bloom of your youth, and all those pleasant things
Which I in you have marked, that draw me to you.
Let us enact what touches all the world.
For this, dear gift, for this you were created.
  Adam stepped to her then, and with desire
He put his arms about her tender neck.
She looked upon him favourably, but yet
She raised against him her objections.
So quickly thus to do, with little thought
Is in my view too hasty a behaviour. . . .
I am a new growth in this early vale
A tender bloom, a dove without a gall.
Who will untimely pluck fruit from the trees
And not restrain desire till better hour? . . .
Who will a tender rose press with harsh fingers,
Her closed-up bud to pluck in savage haste? . . .
If it may please you, grant me a few days
That I may offer God my tender youth,
And pay him honour as is only right,
And he will smile upon our wedding day.

Adam admires Eve's untutored wisdom and discretion, and agrees that God must be prized above all else (421), but he is insistent (429–40):

But you who God's Will bear inscribed within you,
Know also what a wife should give her man.
Know that her entire will is subject to him
And that his word serves her as a sweet law.
This precept you should aye let guide your acts
That fruitfully you must increase on earth.
That is God's ordinance to you and me,

9. Cf. *PL*, VIII, 381–97.

And so 'tis needful to perform this work.
Beloved, wherefore not? Eternal God
Who strength and life breathed through these faultless limbs
Has fully from the first allowed us two
All things whatever that the moon shines on.

He catalogues God's gifts to him and continues (465–72):

You see indeed the blessings marvellous
Which the Creator has prepared for me.
Come give me then the use of your sweet love,
And you henceforth shall be the Queen of the world.
The whole round earth is not bestowed on us
For us to live here lone and solitary,
No, no, within this garden's earthly vale
Belongs a lusty folk in numbers great.

The fruits of the earth, the animals, are there for man's service (485–92):

For the wise God who wills that his great gift
The world should useful be for human wants,
Wills not that anything by him e'er made
Should useless be and rest unprofitable.
Above all else it is quite out of reason
That you should miserly be of your young limbs,
That you be niggardly of your sweet youth.
My love, give me what you should not withhold.

Eve still demurs, showing an untimely interest in nature and astronomy (501–24):

First let us go and carefully observe
The orderly disposal of God's works,
Of the great sphere which the Creator gave us,
Of all that in the air or earth-bound lives,
Of all the springing wood, of the green trees,
Of all the tribes that rise out of the streams,
Of all the verdure springing from the earth,
Of the flower-harvest blooming everywhere.
For all this let our souls to Heaven rise
And praise with thankful heart the great Creator.
'Tis right that men should pay God reverence
Before they turn their hearts to earthly things.
Let us go gaze upon the beauteous lights
That round the sky take their appointed courses,

Clear, spotless, pure, in numbers wondrous great,
Ornaments of the air and of earth's vale.
Let us the moon behold, her dizzy steeds,
And how her coach rides high above the earth,
And how her pow'r stretches through all the world
And with her swift career great waters pulls.
Let us go find our pleasure in the sun
As he rides by us with his golden car
As he with radiance clear outrides the dawn
Like to a Bridegroom coming from his chamber.

She lengthily likens them to a man given a priceless gift. Should he not admire it, inspect it, and praise the giver? Otherwise the latter will rightly think him ungrateful. So they should spend some time in observation and praise. Once more Adam agrees with all she says (551–2),

Since in whatever favour Heaven sends down
Each part bears imprint of a miracle.

But he turns Eve's analogy against her, saying that the recipient of a priceless treasure will naturally pick out the choicest gem ("Some piece high valued by the giver's self"), and make the most of its blessing, taking the fullest possession of what he is given. The making of man was the crown of God's work, man being a little world in himself, and (579–88), impatiently:

Of all created by the spirit of God
You are most pleasing to my youthful mind . . .
Enough, my friend; resistance serves not here;
To me you're given as my help and joy;
You are my consort and my other self.
Let us together be, as right and proper.[10]

The nuptial bower is now described (589–616):

There was a gladsome dale ringed with fair walks,
Suited to give the eye its fullest wish,
Luxuriant blossoms full of scent and glow
Made it appear a lasting wreath of roses.
In middle of the glade a hillock rose,
Beneath whose mound a noble fountain flowed,
A water without taint, as crystal clear,

10. Contrast Milton's rapid dismissal of Adam's "pleaded reason," *PL*, VIII, 509–10.

That with clear flow wound through the vale entire;
Its bed adorned with various shells, so fair,
No skill could ever make them brighter shine . . .
No slimy moss upon the margins pure,
But only branch of coral, diamonds rich.
The plant that from the strand or water shoots
No clammy thing but only sugar-cane.
The fishes too that in the water float,
Bright as if only gold were their adornment. . . .[11]
In middle of the plain a tree rose up
That seemed created but to please the eye,
So finely bloomed the boughs. Its genial trunk
It bowed when the young bride came walking by.

Thus Paradise took on something of the air of Cockaigne or "Luilekkerland" (617–34):

And if there was a flower which had not bloomed,
It hastily burst out with sweetest scent;
And all the air seems gay with blossom fresh,
Like a young bride only today bestrewed.
Roses themselves sprang blithely from their stalks
To make a garland for her playfully,
So that her living hair that wanton strays
Is finely bound without a maiden's help.
The sweet and handsome pair, involved in talk,
With gradual approach came to this place.
And when the young man saw the lovely glade
(Than which the garden could no finer show),
He stayed there and sat down. Sweet names he used
That issued from the marrow of his being.
He took her in his arms; he sat her there;
He pressed upon her mouth with man's first kiss.
And there began their wedding. The young couple
Again became one who were one before.

The poet tells (654–76) how just as when a king marries his people all make festival,

So goes the matter here. For all creation
Paid Adam homage when Eve was deflow'red.
The earth a nosegay makes of various herbs
And stays in constant bloom the bride to honour.
The water leaps and sings in joyous wise
And rises on all sides in fountain-spray.

11. Contrast *PL*, IV, 689–719.

Filled with sweet scents the air plays round the pair
While strewing over them a shower of roses. . . .[12]
  Besides these come the animals in joy
To view the noble love-match of their King;
And every creature soft or strong in limb
Makes it his task to do them loving honour.
The nightingale and other little songsters
Come with their songs in tribute to the bridal.
The owl that can endure no gleam of sunshine
Comes into light to greet the joyful day.
The bird believed by men to come from Eden
Flies high above as if in happiness,
And lights not there on any tree or bush,
But hovers constant over the young Bride.
The crane comes with her kind all well prepared,
And he, as with a pen, has traced a letter;
Himself his ink, his hand his rapid flight;
The book on which he writes is the blue air.
Highest the Phoenix flies with gilded plumes
And though he never seeks a jolly life,
Comes to the bridal-feast; he wants no bedmate,
But if he breeds must wed himself with death
That makes him new again to fly the higher,
And in his stead another bird does live;
So that he never pairs, or sows his seed,
But dies then in the fire of fragrant herbs.

The insects and the fishes come, the narwhals, the dolphins, which turn somersaults in joy.

But above all the host that in the vales
Or on the mountains high are used to dwell
Or lurk in the woods and feed on herbs alone
Comes too in haste to celebrate the Bride.

A debate soon ensues over the honour of bearing the bride (701–54):

The horse, sagacious beast with noble limbs,
The camel famed for its impetuous tread,
The elephant huge, a very artful beast,
Likewise arrive to enter in the feast.
But this most powerful group began to strive
On which rough back Milady ought to ride;
And each one of the three put forth his claim . . .
And while 'twas sought their dispute to prevent

12. Cf. *PL*, IV, 772–3.

The crocodile before the judgement seat
Advanced and with his full mouth earnestly
Said that this fine chance should be given to him,

for he could bear the Queen of the animals through water as well as over dry ground.

Now while these four together argued thus
Out from the wood a tortoise lumbering came
And halted with the beasts before the Bride.
Then this load-bearer oped his toothless mouth:
"Since a young spouse should never risk her life,
'Tis I should bear our Bride upon my shell.
What here appears is only a raw crew
Inclined to riot and a wild career.
Who does not realize, who knows my shape,
That I am sober, not disposed to run,
And my strong shell a level seat provides
Well suited to a bride or tender maid?" . . .
Then sudden comes a hedgehog from the plain,
A hedgehog with his spines stuck full of fruits,
Till with his load the spiked-one seemed to groan.
It seemed the creature in the grass had rolled
In places where he saw the fairest fruits.
On every spike appeared a pear or apple,
And cherries in between, all neatly set.

The hedgehog too offered Eve its services, for its fruits would be pleasant when she was out with the animal-host. Adam was tactful in praising the diligence and fealty of them all. He told them not to contend, since each should have its turn to serve Eve (777–85):

A camel's fitting on a long, dry journey,
A massive elephant for dignity,
A horse for travel swift, a crocodile
To sport with a young woman in the Nile.
A heavy tortoise' tread shall Eve delight
When she a tender fruit shall bear within her.
The peaceful hedgehog serves with fruit whene'er
A pregnant wife would secret dainties eat.
I shall arrange your various tasks aright.

So reconciled the animals gave themselves up to pleasure (793–820):

That was a golden age; what joyous life
Was granted to mankind and to their herds!
Sinless is man; the beasts are without strife,

> And over all are friendship, peace, and calm. . . .
> Nothing there was on earth or in the sea
> That was not bound together in sweet love,
> Made one in peace. When God is with mankind
> Then men find everywhere their heart's desire,
> And here especially the Three-in-One
> Shows greatest favour to the human-folk.
> Mysterious light ringed round the noble pair
> And all in blessing hovered over them.
> The Spirits of God's host, to whom is given
> Eternally by the Throne of God to move,
> Sing loudly now a happy bridal song
> Wherein a sinless heart may take delight.

The bridal-song follows, with the refrain "Love ye the highest God," a Te Deum of the creatures.

> And lo! the blissful song glads the whole vale,
> Makes glad the noble pair to their souls' depths.
> God's grace they find in them and all their acts.
> See what a joyous feast in Eden's vale
> Before them's set, and shall be so for ever.

The poem ends with a general hymn (841–84):

> O God! O highest Good! Father of all!
> How mighty is your name! Above all clouds!
> How strange your plan! How wondrous your dispose!
> Your praise renowned to all eternity!

The concluding dialogue between Philogamus and Sophroniscus is mainly irrelevant to our purpose, and the triteness of its teaching strikes modern readers as somewhat absurd. But one or two topics discussed are of considerable interest. Philogamus says: "I note that Adam and Eve had fleshly intercourse while in Paradise, which seems to me slightly questionable." Sophroniscus thereupon expounds varying views on the matter: "Certain learned people have written that if our first parents had not sinned there would have been no child-bearing. So, among others, says St. Augustine. Almost all the Greek Fathers agree that in this case there would have been procreation, but not by fleshly union." The example of the Angels is mentioned, who do not practice marital union.

Sophroniscus admits that "it cannot be held as certain that Adam and Eve slept together in Paradise before the Fall." Moses (Gen. iv) mentions it as occurring after the Fall. On the other hand St. Augustine seems to have changed his mind, and "the Scholastic writers concluded that in the primal state fleshly union took place." Cats agrees with them.

Compare with this Milton's several references to physical caresses and the act of love before the Fall (*P.L.*, IV, VIII) and his defence (IV, 750 ff.) of "wedded love," "sole proprietie / In Paradise, of all things common else." His Adam asks about the loves of the Angels, and these are described (VIII, 618–30) as involving a total "Union of Pure with Pure." Obviously the same problems faced writers everywhere who wished to describe the paradisal state. There was a large measure of agreement between Cats and Milton about the nature of marriage.

Another topic arises when Philogamus has "let his thoughts stray upon Eve's clever excuses . . . when Adam wished to approach her as a man. What do you think? [he asks] Has our Writer done well to depict in Paradise a contrary Eve?" Sophroniscus replies that "a courteous refusal on these occasions is not disagreeable." It is certainly better than the direct invitation to sensuality offered to Joseph by Potiphar's wife.

> Wives and spinsters should resemble Parthian horsemen, and shoot while fleeing, that is, surrender while refusing and refuse while surrendering. . . . Honey should be touched only with the tip of the finger and brought thus into the mouth. To use the palm of the hand for such a thing would show little sense. . . . The most skittish of this world's children would not want the way to be too open.

So much for the "sweet reluctant amorous delay" which Milton's Eve shows by running away and coyly shrinking. On their way to the nuptial bower Milton's Eve, like Cats's, expresses delight in natural phenomena and asks Adam why the stars shine at night. Later, when Adam discusses astronomy with the Angel (VIII, 13 ff.) she wanders off, not because she is uninterested, but so that she may hear about it from Adam, who will mingle "conjugal caresses" with scientific discourse. Cats's Eve is rather more independent in mind, although she obeys her husband.

To sum up: Inevitably the two poems have much in common as they expand the material of Genesis in terms drawn from a common Protestant tradition. (Though Cats was a Calvinist his poem is not greatly coloured by Calvin's special doctrines.) It is unlikely that Milton owed much to Cats for his picture of Paradise as on a hill, set in the East, or for anything in his account of the world's creation, the insistence on man's upright posture, the human couple's first impressions of the world, Adam's loneliness, his union with Eve and the rejoicings of nature in it, and the hymns of praise in heaven and on earth. The parallels cited above give no conclusive proof that Milton knew Cats's poem. The differences are more striking than the resemblances. But comparison between the poems illustrates the two poets' participation in the Protestant culture of their century and their individual approaches to theological and moral topics of importance at the time.

Cats's poetic reputation declined as Vondel's increased, and modern criticism has treated him as a bad influence. We must agree with the modern scholar who calls him a "moralizing story-teller in pleasurably garrulous, pedestrian verse which hardly ever departs from the wearisome sing-song of the end-stopped alexandrine with fixed caesura."[13] He resembles Wither more than Milton, and comparison with Milton brings out his limitations; nevertheless his Adam and Eve story *is* pleasurable, with its childlike simplicity and a touch of fantasy best shown in the revels of nature and the contention of the animals.

If Milton did not read the Dutch poem he may well have read a version of it in Latin. Wishing to give his work a wider audience, Cats in November 1633 asked Caspar van Baerle (1584–1648), a well-known scholar and Latin poet, to translate his *Trou-Ringh*, offering him a fee and divers presents. Van Baerle began the task in 1634 and Cats sent his wife some silver and promised his daughter a clavecin. After van Baerle abandoned the work it was completed by Cornelius Boys, and published at Dordrecht in 1643 as *Faces Augustae, sive Poematia, Quibus Illustriores Nuptiae, à Nobili & Illustri Viro, D. Jacobo Catsio . . . conscriptae, Jam à Caspare Barlaeo & Cornelio Boyo Latino Carmine celebrantur*.

The work proved popular and was reprinted in 1653. Dedicated to Princess Elizabeth, the eldest daughter of Elizabeth, Queen of Bohemia, the book has an introductory poem to her in which the "precepts of grave Cats" are praised. A Preface to the Reader

13. T. Weevers, *Poetry of the Netherlands in its European Context, 1170–1930* (1960), 100.

rhetorically sets forth the variety and necessity of love, and the value of marriage, which gives "mutual help and comfort," and unites bodies and minds in companionship. The Preface also points out that the translators have used some freedom and invention in their Latin versions.

This is certainly true of van Baerle's *Paradisus*, which, although about the same length as the original (884 lines), departs considerably from it. Whereas Cats scarcely ever makes an allusion to classical mythology or history, the Latin poem classicizes everywhere. The first few lines contain references to Venus, Cnidus, Cyprus, Ida, Cytherea, Samos, Diones, Hymen, and Juno. When the stars are created, Lucifer, Pleiades, Arctophylax, Hyades, and Leo are named. Whole sections are rewritten. The geographical situation of Paradise is given: "Quosque colit nunc Assur agros" (cf. Milton's "*Assyrian* garden," *P.L.*, IV, 285), and its superiority to beautiful places known later on earth is described in a manner which anticipates Milton's "Not that faire field / Of *Enna* . . ." though the classical allusions are different. The account of the Tree of Life and the Paradise–Golden Age equation are expanded. God himself speaks of Adam's need of a mate, lengthily catalogues the creatures who pair and procreate, says that he will provide a wife for man, and prophesies the spread of their progeny over the continents. None of this is in Cats.

God also tells the pair the meaning of marriage:

> Sors geminis communis erit, quin corpore in uno
> Concordes vivent animae, nec foedera quisquam
> Rumpet & aeterni dissolvet vincula lecti.

The conversation between Adam and Eve is changed. Adam asks her whether she wishes to be called Spouse, Virgin, or Sister, tells her that she is part sister and part daughter to him; and woos her, offering all that he has: "Non est mihi vilis origo," he says, "Ipse Deus pater est." In reply Eve shows greater submission than in Cats:

> Adde quod & dominum Te fas sit dicere, cuius
> Arbitrio submissa regar: quo vindice surget
> Femineae virtutis honos, & tuta manebit
> Fama pudicitiae & socialis gloria lecti.
> Expetimur petimusque duo. quam tu petis, illam
> Jure tuo repetis. . . .

She wishes to mingle with him and to become a wife:

> sed legibus uxor
> Esse velim rectumque sequi. parere marito,
> Non servire, meum est. mandata capessere, quae non
> Fastidit pietas. pariter regnamus, at impar
> Maiestas mea sorte tua est. nihil arrogat ultra,
> Quam minor esse viro mulier.

So Milton insists on their partnership, "though both / Not equal, as their sex not equal seemd" (*P.L.*, IV, 295–6), and makes Eve declare (IV, 634–8):

> My Author and Disposer, what thou bidst
> Unargu'd I obey: so God ordains.
> God is thy Law, thou mine: to know no more
> Is woman's happiest knowledge and her praise.

Van Baerle's Eve goes on to expound the whole duty of a wife, incidentally disapproving strongly of divorce ("divortia censet / Improba, nec volet illa pati"). After the bower has been described,

> hic postquam prisci latuêre parentes,
> Coniugii didicêre modum, plenusque furoris
> Foecundum primus pater exantlavit amorem.

The strong word "furor" would not please Milton, who makes the Angel say to Adam, "In loving thou dost well, in passion not" (VIII, 588). Into the paradisal rejoicings van Baerle inserts a list of the virtues fostered by innocent love (cf. IV, 753–7), and mingles the gaiety of the creatures with classical references. The fable of the contending beasts is reduced to the merest hints, for example,

> Et sola poterat teneram proboscide nuptam
> Tollere subsidens elephas.

An engraving made for the Dutch poem (1638 edition) and copied in the 1643 volume shows the elephant wreathing "his Lithe Proboscis" (cf. *P.L.*, IV, 345–6) among the animals round the rustic throne of Adam and Eve. The poem ends with a hymn: "Disce tuum, veneràre tuum, Natura, parentem," sung, like Milton's at IV, 711, by "heav'nly Quires."

In his use of classical learning, his greater dignity and his succinct and epigrammatic style, van Baerle comes closer than Cats to Milton.

That Milton owed something to the Latin *Paradisus* was suggested long ago, but by a man whose every utterance was made suspect by his confessed dishonesty. This was William Lauder, the Scottish schoolmaster who in *An Essay on Milton's Use and Imitation of the Moderns in his Paradise Lost* (1750) attacked Milton as "the great Plagiary" and a secret pillager of other poets, and supported his contention with citations from modern Latin religious poems such as T. Beza's *Abrahamus Sacrificans* (1599), H. Grotius's *Adamus Exsul* (1601), F. Taubmann's *De Bello Angelico* (1604), C. Barlaeus's *Poemata* (1643), and J. Masenius's *Sarcotis* (1654). Lauder had already written a series of papers for the *Gentleman's Magazine* on the subject and these had attracted the attention of Samuel Johnson, who, moved by Lauder's obvious learning and his pecuniary need, wrote a Preface and Postscript for his volume. Though not signed by Johnson, these were widely recognized as his. Milton enthusiasts, shocked by Lauder's aspersions, hurried to defend their idol, and in 1751 a pamphlet by the Rev. John Douglas (later Bishop of Salisbury), *Milton Vindicated from the Charge of Plagiarism*, convicted Lauder "of several Forgeries and gross Impositions on the Public." Douglas showed that Lauder, relying on the general ignorance about the poets in question, and to enforce the parallels he drew between them and Milton, had interpolated into his quotations from them passages from George Hog's Latin version of *Paradise Lost* (1690).

When Johnson realized the imposture he was furious, and dictated a confession which Lauder signed and published. The discredited man published in 1753 correct texts of several of these authors, including van Baerle's *Paradisus*, but he sank back into obscurity and finally died in poverty in Barbados.

In his original *Essay* Lauder praised the elegance of van Baerle's translation of Cats, "a performance truly sublime," and declared that Milton had "inserted in many places of his *Paradise Lost*" the substance of the *Paradisus*. He cited only one passage, however (and that correctly except for one misprint). This was from God's prophecy to Adam and Eve that their progeny would inherit the earth. It is too long to quote here, but it anticipates some of Milton's references in Books XI and XII to spiritually gifted Old Testament heroes. "In these lines [wrote Lauder] we see the *prima stamina* of the best part of the two last books of *Paradise Lost*, which Milton has enlarged from *Dubartas* and Ross's *Virgilius Evangelizans*. Barlaeus makes mention of *Enoch*, *Melchizedek*, *Noah*, *Abraham*, *Moses*, *David* and *Solomon*, and particularly the last, on account of his wisdom, riches, and building the temple; the three circumstances taken notice of by Milton."

As Douglas pointed out, Lauder often obtained his parallels by omitting long passages of Milton and picking out only those which suited his argument. Milton certainly refers to these biblical characters, but they were traditional ones to choose, and we have only to read Books XI and XII to appreciate the folly of Lauder's main argument. His pamphlet was actuated by vanity, sensation-seeking, and an almost insane animus against Milton. Apart from this it serves as a warning to all source-hunters against the blinkered narrowness of vision which leads to excessive claims. For students interested in the history of ideas and in comparative literature, analogues may be as interesting as sources. Milton may have read Cats and van Baerle or he may not. But the three poems provide instances of resemblance and difference within the tradition of Renaissance religious poetry which illuminate two literatures and deserve further study.

Satan and the "Myth" of the Tyrant

MERRITT Y. HUGHES

IN THIS ESSAY the word *myth* is not used in Jung's sense, or in the sense in which it is used by Mrs. MacCaffrey in *Paradise Lost as "Myth,"* or in R. J. Zwi Werblowsky's *Lucifer and Prometheus*, or in Wayne Shumaker's "*Paradise Lost*: The Mythological Dimension." Nor is the word used as it is by Northrop Frye in his discussions of tragic and comic myth in *Anatomy of Criticism*.[1] Without, it is hoped, undue emphasis upon the Platonism in Milton's political thought, the word *myth* is here applied to the Miltonic conception of the political process as it is stated to Adam by Michael in the last book of *Paradise Lost* when Adam is overwhelmed by the vision of the harm to be done to his descendants by Nimrod and the builders of the tower of Babel:

> To whom thus *Michael*. Justly thou abhorr'st
> That Son, who on the quiet state of men
> Such trouble brought, affecting to subdue
> Rational Liberty; yet know withal,
> Since thy original lapse, true Liberty
> Is lost, which always with right Reason dwells
> Twinn'd, and from her hath no dividual being:
> Reason in man obscur'd, or not obey'd,
> Immediately inordinate desires
> And upstart Passions catch the Government
> From Reason, and to servitude reduce
> Man till then free. Therefore since hee permits

1. Isabel Gamble MacCaffrey, "*Paradise Lost*" *as Myth* (Harvard University Press, 1959); R. J. Zwi Werblowsky, *Lucifer and Prometheus* (London, 1952); Wayne Shumaker, "*Paradise Lost*: The Mythological Dimension," *Bucknell Review*, X (1961), 75–86; Northrop Frye, *Anatomy of Criticism* (Princeton University Press, 1957).

Within himself unworthy Powers to reign
Over free Reason, God in Judgment just
Subjects him from without to violent Lords;
Who oft as undeservedly enthral
His outward freedom: Tyranny must be,
Though to the Tyrant thereby no excuse. (XII, 79–96)*

In the world of the poem the archetypal tyrant is Satan. For the present purpose it is not necessary to consider him as hero or fool, or to meditate on the mystery of evil of which he has been a traditional solution. It is enough to accept him simply as the spirit which Gilbert Murray has called "Satanism, the spirit which hates the World Order wherever it exists." Though our thinking about the problem of evil may be more or less theological, and more or less hopeful than Murray's, we may accept his definition of Satanism as a mysteriously wanton adversary of man in "the great pilgrimage of the spirit [which] from the beginnings of history onward has been on the whole not only a movement from ignorance to knowledge, from collective impotence to collective power, from poverty of life to richness of life, but also in some profound sense a pilgrimage from lower to higher."[2]

If this definition in terms of Satanism seems too abstract to represent Milton's thought about the prince of the devils in the ninth chapter of the first book of his *Christian Doctrine*, it should not be forgotten that in closing that chapter Milton remembered the great tempter's many names: Beelzebub (as Christ called "the prince of the devils," Matthew xii.24), "Satan," or the enemy or adversary of Job i.6; and several more, one of which is "Abaddon, Apollyon," or the "destroyer" of Revelation ix.11. Though the names suggest an identity as elusive as the multiple forms of evil itself, they cannot make the prince of the devils less of a personal evil spirit than his followers, the fallen angels whom Milton describes as reserved for final punishment in hell and yet sometimes permitted to wander throughout the whole earth, the air, and heaven itself. All definitions of Satan concur in making him the destroyer. Rajan, though he observes that Milton's contemporaries held Calvin's view of Satan as a personal "enemie that is in courage most hardie, in strength most mightie, in policies most

*Citations in the text from Milton's poetry are from *John Milton: Complete Poems and Major Prose*, ed. Merritt Y. Hughes (New York, 1957).

2. *Satanism and the World Order* (London, 1920).

subtle," yet thinks that for Milton he was most characteristically "the creature who finds ease 'onely in destroying.'"[3] For the historian, Denis de Rougemont says candidly that the Devil can hardly be more than the "phantom" of human invention which has tormented mankind through "centuries of ignorance." But for de Rougemont Satan is one of "the figures of myth [which] guide us more surely than modern experiment and the analysis of reason." Yet in the end he can define Satan only by opposing him to "the inner order of saintliness, the cosmic order and its immense discourse, the order of the laws sworn to in the commonwealth, the order of language and the order of virtues."[4] De Rougemont's authentication of Satan as a fundamental "myth" of human experience comes close to Mrs. MacCaffrey's recognition that the "aptest epithet" for Milton's Satan "is the Destroyer" (p. 147). But in the destroyer opposed to the cosmic order and the laws sworn in the commonwealth we recognize the "Satanism" which Gilbert Murray opposed to the principles of order and human law which were enunciated by Plato and Cicero. And so in a modest way the ancient myth of man's rational cosmos and its enemies may stand beside the modern myth of the primordial destroyer in de Rougemont's "anthromorphic" world where "reason finds itself disarmed before the brutal eruptions of an evil organized by obscure forces, according to the mysterious logic and the irresistible efficacy of the unconscious."

No demonstration of the Platonic character of Michael's words is needed for readers who are familiar with Plato's theory of the correspondence between the forms of the state and the variety of characters among men, between the tyrannous character of the spirit of entire communities and the vulnerability of their governments to usurpation by tyrants, as this doctrine is laid down in the eighth book of the *Republic*, as it is analysed in the *Gorgias* (468B ff.), and in the *Laws* (272E–273B) is crystallized in the myth of the retreat of the gods of order from the world with the ensuing great earthquake and the destruction of all living beings.

The link with the passage in the *Gorgias* (483D–E) is not the most important, but it is obvious and interesting. In a shrewd exposure of

3. B. Rajan, *"Paradise Lost" and the Seventeenth Century Reader* (London, 1947), 94, 104.

4. Denis de Rougemont, *The Devil's Share* (New York, 1944), 26–8, 220.

the violence of absolute monarchs for whom right is simply their own might, Socrates traps Callicles into approving Darius' conquest of Scythia and Xerxes' invasion of Greece as supreme examples of might making right. Socrates, of course, was taking advantage of an established feeling among his countrymen that—as Aristotle explained in the *Politics* (III.ix.3)—the barbarians were naturally more servile than the Greeks, and the Asiatics than the Europeans, and so they submitted easily to despotism. In the ideal, universal form which Plato gave to his theory of the moral foundation of the State in the *Republic* and in its typically Greek use to explain the prevalence of tyranny in Asia, the theory came to Milton directly; indirectly it came also through many literary channels. In the form of prejudice against the Asiatic tyrants it lay ready to his hand for associative effect in one of the most strikingly placed of his portraits of Satan in the opening lines of the second book of *Paradise Lost*, where the curtain rises on Satan sitting

> High on a Throne of Royal State, which far
> Outshone the wealth of *Ormus* and of *Ind*,
> Or where the gorgeous East with richest hand
> Show'rs on her Kings *barbaric* Pearl and Gold. . . .

Editorial comment on these lines has not stressed their ultimate origin in the *Gorgias* and the *Politics*. Editors have rightly focused attention on Ormus and India as symbols of the contemporary drive of the trading companies, English and Dutch particularly, for control of the trade in jewels and spices which was funnelled through the fabulous port of Ormus on the Persian gulf. So Milton wished his readers to feel about the passage, and that obvious fact is worth consideration by the German critics who have condemned him as a moral accomplice of British imperialism in its early phase. Actually, as B. A. Wright has just observed,[5] the effect of the passage is to throw light both upon Milton's attitude toward Satan as a claimant for heroic honours in the poem and upon the rapacity of the merchant adventurers in the East. Their motives in sending their armed ships to the Spice Islands are like his on his perilous voyage from Hell to Eden. "And so," says Wright, "as Satan starts on his flight towards the gates of Hell and his hazardous quest for the new world of

5. Bernard A. Wright, *Milton's 'Paradise Lost'* (London, 1962), 109.

man, Milton calls up this vision of a voyage from India to the Cape" (II, 636–42):

As when far off at Sea a Fleet descri'd
Hangs in the Clouds, by *Equinoctial* Winds
Close sailing from *Bengala*, or the Isles
Of *Ternate* and *Tidore*, whence Merchants bring
Thir spicy Drugs: they on the Trading Flood
Through the wide Ethiopian to the Cape
Ply stemming nightly toward the Pole.

Wright's interest is mainly in the hazards, not in the prizes, of the eastern voyages which he compared with Satan's; but he is aware that in the tableau in I, 347–9, where the devils rally to "th'uplifted Spear/ Of thir great Sultan waving to direct / Thir course," the moral association of Satan with the traditional tyrants of the East is anticipated. In a note in 1958 Manfred Weidhorn made an elaborate comparison of Milton's Satan with the Xerxes of Herodotus,[6] but did not bring out the full political potential of the implicit image in Milton's text. A year later Jacques Blondel pointed to the comparison in *Paradise Lost*, X, 306–11 of Satan's involvement in the bridge-building of Sin and Death as the final mark of Milton's conception of him as a kind of archetypal tyrant trampling everything sacred under his feet. His act, said the ancients, was a "sacrilège, nefas; de même, les puissances infernales profanent elles aussi la matière, en la pliant a leur volonté perverse pour enchaîner l'homme, comme le roi antique voulut asservir la Grèce."[7]

By making the modern Turkish sultans illustrations or symbols of the tyranny of the arch-tyrant Satan, Milton encouraged his identification with figures on his immediate political scene, and E. M. W. Tillyard was undoubtedly right in saying that his Satan "is partly a Renaissance tyrant."[8] The two concepts were closely linked in the minds of his contemporaries and in *Eikonoklastes* Milton himself made Turkish tyranny the thrice-applied measuring rod for England under the unchallenged unconstitutional rule of King Charles.[9] In

6. In *NQ*, n.s., IX (1958), 389–392.

7. J. Blondel, "Milton: Poète de la Bible dans le *Paradis Perdu*," *Archives des Lettres Modernes*, III (1959), 33.

8. E. M. W. Tillyard, *The English Epic and its Background* (New York, 1954), 433.

9. In chapters x and xxvii (Columbia Edition, V, 170, 282, 283; *Complete Prose Works of John Milton* [New Haven, 1953–], III, 453).

his *Observations on the Articles of the Peace* he repeated a familiar story of an attempt to set up "the Turkish Tyranny" "with best expedition, and least noyse in France."[10] In these references to recent events there is, of course, no exposition of the Platonic political moral implicit in them; but in the entries under "Tyrannus" in the Commonplace Book, where Milton was writing with no controversial motive, he recalls the incident in France and many instances of tyrannous usurpation and abuse of authority in Anglo-Saxon England. In the cool atmosphere of his study at Horton the relation between the evils of tyranny and the vices of society seemed perfectly clear.

It would, of course, be inaccurate to treat Milton's attitude in the entries in the Commonplace Book as simply and consciously Platonic —as it may seem to be in Michael's advice to Adam in the twelfth book of *Paradise Lost.* In the passages which have been quoted from the prose works the pattern of thought is clearly as much religious as it is philosophical; nor would Milton have admitted the distinction. His thinking is always Christian, with all that the Christian world-view implies about the role of human character and divine providence in the affairs of nations. Milton would never have disagreed with the opinion of St. Thomas Aquinas in the *De Regimine Principum* (I.vi.52) that

> . . . it is by divine permission that wicked men receive power to rule as punishment for sin, as the Lord says by the prophet Osee: "I will give thee a king in wrath," and it is said in Job that he "maketh a man that is an hypocrite to reign for the sins of the people." Sin therefore must be done away with in order that the scourge of tyrants may cease.

II

Since in *Eikonoklastes* Charles I was so definitely compared with the proverbial Turkish tyrant, and since in *Paradise Lost* that comparison is implicit in several of the descriptions of Satan, it is easy to conclude that Charles and the sultans were alike ectypes of the Satanic archetype in Milton's mythology. And from such loose application of the principle that things equal to the same thing are equal or identical with each other, it is easy to follow G. Wilson Knight in equating Hitler and Charles as ectypes in the series which

10. Columbia Edition, VI, 253; *Complete Prose,* III, 313.

Milton began with Nimrod—easy, that is, if we agree with Knight that, "as for Charles, he was to Milton precisely what Hitler seems to us."[11] In support of the statement Knight quotes from the first *Defence of the English People*[12] a rhetorical question where Milton asks whether, when the king raves (*quoties delirare libet regi*), the best citizens should not open their mouths in protest.

Chronology prevents Knight from finding Miltonic authority for his inclusion of Hitler among the Satanic ectypes, but his thinking is as sound as was Coleridge's when he wrote in the lecture on *Paradise Lost*:

> The character of Satan is pride and sensual indulgence, finding in self the sole motive of action. It is the character so often seen *in little* on the political stage. It exhibits all the restlessness, temerity, and cunning which have marked the mighty hunters of mankind from Nimrod to Napoleon.[13]

Discussion of Hitler as a Satanic ectype must wait while the one-to-one topical identification of Charles with Milton's Satan is examined. An objection to it is unconsciously indicated by Knight when he generalizes about "the Satanic party" as representing "mankind in its fruitless struggles; in them," he adds, "Puritan revolution and Episcopal idolatry, Cromwellian force and Stuart finery (clearly suggested at I.497–502) are all contained."[14] Topical historical allegory gives way altogether when Charles and the Cromwellian force which destroyed him are both seen as ectypes of Milton's Satan. Nor is the situation helped when Knight declares "the equivalence of Satan to the Puritan party extremely close."

The fact is that attribution of any topical political intention to Milton's epic plan involves irreconcilable hypotheses. The first would entangle the royalism in his aristocratic nature so definitely with the Stuart crown that Charles and his partisans could not possibly be identified with Satan and his followers. But Ross, the analyst of Milton's "royalism," avoids suggesting anything of that kind when

11. G. Wilson Knight, *Chariot of Wrath* (London, n.d.), 170.
12. Columbia Edition, VII, 82.
13. Quoted from *Coleridge on the Seventeenth Century*, ed. Roberta Florence Brinkley (Duke University Press, 1955), 578. In *PQ*, XLI (1962), 307–8, Benjamin T. Sankey, Jr., quotes the longer passage in *The Statesman's Manual*, App. B, where Coleridge gave his reasons for regarding the character of Napoleon as essentially that which "Milton has so philosophically as well as sublimely embodied in the Satan of *Paradise Lost*."
14. *Chariot of Wrath*, 137.

he says that, though traces of "the kingly ideal, the royal 'type,'" are found in Milton's epic plans "well after the last moment in which he might possibly have had respect for the Stuarts," his "epic royalism" was derived "from a sense of the past, from Plato, from Spenser, from Christian tradition—never from Charles."[15]

The second hypothesis, Knight's surmised close equivalence of Satan to the Puritan party, necessarily involves the assumption that one of the leaders of the Long Parliament or of the New Model Army, or of both, should be recognizable in some of the features of Milton's Satan. And in the "mighty chief" whose "Heart / Distends with pride" as he "Darts his experienced eye" through "the armed files" of the devils rallying around him in hell (*P.L.*, I, 566–71), Knight recognizes "indeed, a Cromwell casting an experienced eye over his ironside warriors." But the essence of the scenes in Hell is Satan's enjoyment of a control of his "Synod of Gods" such as Cromwell never enjoyed over his parliaments. And the eulogy of Cromwell in the *Second Defence* leaves no doubt that at least for a very long time he represented the anti-tyrant which George Williamson demonstrates that he always remained for Milton.[16] Ross also recognizes Cromwell as having long been the embodiment of the Platonic ideal of philosopher king, though in the end his image may have been supplanted for Milton by that of John Sobiesky, the saviour of Vienna from the Turks, who was elected king of Poland in the year of Milton's death.

If Milton had intended to make Cromwell and his supporters in the Long Parliament and in the Army recognizable in the persons of Satan and the devils in Books I, II, V, and VI of *Paradise Lost*, he would have had to revise the entire plan of the poem on the general lines of Joost van den Vondel's *Lucifer*. In that play, written in 1654, the action begins with and until the end of the third act consists in manoeuvring among the archfiends Apollyon, Beelzebub, and Belial, to whip up a revolt against God and persuade Lucifer to accept the command of the rebel angels. Lucifer's seeming reluctance even to countenance the revolt is perfectly carried through. Vondel has been understood to have Cromwell's rise to power in England as a kind of objective correlative for the action of those first three acts. The once serious suspicion that *Paradise Lost* was influenced by *Lucifer* cannot be con-

15. M. M. Ross, *Milton's Royalism* (Cornell University Press, 1943), 72.
16. George Williamson, "Milton the Anti-Romantic," *MP*, LX (1962), 151.

firmed. If Milton read the play, as he probably did, he learned from it not to make the conspiratorial scene between Satan and Beelzebub in his fifth book the opening scene in his epic, and not to present Satan first as a politician calculatingly and somewhat hesitantly accepting command in a crisis. If he had followed Vondel's pattern, he would have had to make Satan abject in defeat and might have omitted all infernal scenes, as Vondel did. In Vondel's pattern, if Milton had used it, Satan might seem to be identifiable with Cromwell, but he would have been even more readily identifiable with the far less heroic figure of Shaftesbury, Dryden's Achitophel. In actual life as he participated in the machinations of Cromwell's parliaments, Shaftesbury seems to Morris Freedman to have created an image that would have served Milton as an ideal "'answer' to Vondel's depiction of Cromwell."[17] Indeed, as "an arch opponent of Cromwell," Shaftesbury is skilfully presented in Freedman's study as a figure from which Milton may have drawn his Satan.

It is, of course, possible that the debate in Pandaemonium would not be quite what it is if Milton had not felt as bitterly about the venal factionalism in Cromwell's parliaments as he did when he indicted them openly in his digression in the *History of Britain*. But the dangers of such an assumption are shown by its history in the criticism of *Paradise Lost*. George Whiting has traced a debate on the subject which began in the *London Chronicle* on November 15, 1763, with a bold assertion that in the second book of the poem Milton repudiated his old sympathies by representing the Whigs as the devils. In the series of replies to the suggestion the poem was reduced to a *roman à clef*, and its diabolic figures were consciously or unconsciously turned into actors on the contemporary political scene.[18]

In Walter Bagehot's very different view of *Paradise Lost* we have an example of the dangers of naïve identification of Milton with his rebellious angels. Only by radical misreading of the poem could Bagehot have supposed that Milton's "real sympathy—the impetus and energy of his nature— . . . [slipped] back to the Puritan rebels whom he loved"[19] presumably more heartily when he wrote his epic than

17. Morris Freedman, "Satan and Shaftesbury," *PMLA*, LXXIV (1959), 545.
18. George Whiting, "The Politics of Milton's Apostate Angels," *NQ*, CLXIII (1932), 384–6.
19. Walter Bagehot, "Wordsworth, Tennyson, and Browning," *Literary Studies*, II (London, 1910), 345–6.

he did when he had shared in their counsels under the Commonwealth. By identifying Milton with his rebel angels Bagehot was drifting with the still strong Romantic tendency to identify him with their prince. That way lies the aesthetic, if not the moral, idolatry of Satan which was at its height in 1850 when George Gilfillan proclaimed Satan to be "the most *tremendous conception* in the compass of poetry—the *sublimest* creation of the mind of man."[20] Today we are not sure that we are all of the Devil's party without knowing it, even though Miss Bodkin, speaking in *Archetypal Patterns in Poetry* of Blake's dictum and of the modern feeling of hopelessness against the odds of destiny, does tell us that when a reader is "caught into the theme of *Paradise Lost*, he—like the poet himself—becomes—knowing it or not—'of the Devil's party.'"[21] We hear Northrop Frye saying that "Blake's point is not that Satan is the hero of *Paradise Lost*, but that there is no hero to *Paradise Lost*."[22] We feel A. J. A. Waldock and John Peter plucking at our sleeves to denigrate the mind and the whole artistic integrity of Milton's Satan. On the other hand, anything like romantic admiration of Milton's Satan has now been rendered impossible by the criticism which admires the virtuosity which adumbrates his decay in the early similes describing him and consummates it in the false rhetoric of his temptation of Eve.

Though we may not accept the belittling of Satan for artistic reasons by Waldock's followers or quite like his belittling for moral reasons by the followers of C. S. Lewis, we know that interpretation of Milton's treatment of his myth in *Paradise Lost* must now be cleared of all romantic sentimentality and of the modern psychologism which makes him a reflection of the irrational elements in Milton's own nature. Milton created him as an example of the self-deception and the deception of others which are incident to the surrender of reason to passion. His creation was a deliberate attempt to represent the demon who fell through pride and became the father of lies in the prosecution of his war against God at the expense of mankind. Traditional theology and traditional mythology, the deepest

20. George Gilfillan, *A Second Gallery of Literary Portraits* (Edinburgh, 1850), 20.

21. Maud Bodkin, *Archetypal Patterns in Poetry: Psychological Studies of Imagination* (London, 1938), 234.

22. Northrop Frye, *Fearful Symmetry* (Princeton University Press, 1947), 219.

involvement of Renaissance thought in the problems of the contemplative versus the active life, all are mingled in the myth of Satan in Milton's poem. But the thinking is contemporary as well as traditional. The ceaseless activity of the devils in Hell and Satan's unresting drive through Chaos and the spheres of the newly created universe to the regions of earth and back again to Pandaemonium are examples of the evils of what Bacon had called the "Active Good" in a passage of the *De Augmentis*.[23] Without any thought of direct influence upon Milton in the following passage it is possible to find some light in it upon Milton's feeling that a battle in Heaven with echoes of Hesiod's war of the Titans against the Olympian gods should figure largely in *Paradise Lost*. But the passage also illuminates more fundamental things in Milton's myth of Satan:

> But here it must be more carefully observed, that this active individual good has no identity with the good of society, though in some case it has an incidence into it: for although it many times produces and brings forth acts of beneficence (which is a virtue of communion), yet there is this difference, that these acts are mostly done not with a view to the benefit and happiness of others, but to a man's own power and greatness; as plainly appears when this kind of active good strikes on a subject contrary to the good of society. For that gigantean state of mind, which possesses the troublers of the world (such as was Lucius Sylla, and infinite others in smaller model, who are bent on having all men happy or unhappy as they are their friends or enemies, and would shape the world according to their own humours, which is the true Theomachy), this I say aspires to the active good of the individual (apparent good at least), though it recedes farthest of all from the good of society.

In this passage Bacon wrote for the behoof of men who were intelligent enough to think in terms of the illusions of the active life and the "Active Good." He was extending his favourite doctrine of the idols—especially those of the Market Place and of the Theatre—which are the enemies of the advancement of science. Here they reach to the illusions which darken men's discernment of spirits, their own and those of other men. The essentially Platonic thought is like that of an aspect of Milton's myth of Satan which J. M. Steadman discusses in "Image and Idol: Satan and the Element of Illusion in

23. *De Augmentis Scientiarum*, VII.ii. The translation is from *The Works of Francis Bacon*, ed. James Spedding, Robert Leslie Ellis, and Douglas Denon Heath (New York, 1869), IX, 203–4.

Paradise Lost."[24] Steadman sees Satan the aspirant to divine honours as "Th'Apostate" whom Milton calls an "Idol of Majesty Divine" as he sits in his "sun-bright Chariot . . . enclos'd / With Flaming Cherubim, and golden Shields" (*P.L.*, VI, 100–2). The word *Idol*, Steadman observes, is technical: "In affecting divine honors Satan represented the sort of heroic *eidolon* which Favorinus and Suidas had defined as a fictitious likeness, which Bacon described as a false appearance, and which Plato had classified as a *phantasma* distinguished from a true *eikon* or likeness." Steadman traces the term and the distinction which it represents to several Italian critics—especially to Mazzoni in his *Difesa della Commedia di Dante*—and to a passage in Bacon's *Advancement* which distinguishes fallacious *idola* from true images of virtue of all kinds. The source of the distinction is Plato's *Sophist* and its warning to those who would not give up truth to beware of the *phantasmata* which usurp the recognition due only to true *eikones*. As the admired leader of the fallen angels Satan is an idol in both the Platonic and the Baconian senses. And Steadman aptly adds that "Hell was thronged with such *phantasmata* or *eidola*. The fallen angels, subsequently known by 'various Names, / And various Idols through the Heathen World,' would seduce the greater part of mankind."

III

It is characteristic of Steadman that, instead of following Coleridge's impulse to recognize a contemporary ectype of Milton's Satan, he should look for literary prototypes. Three types of such prototypes occur to him: the "Achilles type," to which Ajax, Turnus, and Rinaldo belong; the shrewdly diplomatic type, of which his only example is Odysseus; and the type of the leader who must have the mixed virtues necessary to preserve order among his followers. His examples are Agamemnon, Aeneas, and Godfredo in the *Jerusalem Delivered*. Other examples of the three prototypes might easily be found in Italian and French epic and romance. Tasso's Saracen challenger of Godfrey's crusaders, the frenetic warrior Argantes, has been suggested[25] as a better example of the first of the three proto-

24. *JEGP*, LIX (1960), 648.
25. By Lawrence Sasek in his unpublished Harvard dissertation, "Satan and the Epic Hero: Classical and Christian Tradition" (1953), 352.

types than the rebellious and proud Achilles himself. In contrast with all his warrior prototypes, says Lawrence Sasek, Satan's absolute fearlessness magnifies him into a superhuman incarnation of human violence and passion. But violence is the least impressive of Satan's characteristics, vital to Milton's conception of him though it may be. It is the tragic element in him which makes him most impressive to us, and of all his literary prototypes the most tragic is undoubtedly Virgil's Turnus, the noble but violent opponent of Aeneas and of his divine destiny in Italy.

In the most recent and most searching of the scholarly comparisons of Milton's Satan with Turnus[26] we are reminded that Turnus was "the specific means Virgil adopts to criticize the standard of Achilles" and that similarly in several situations in *Paradise Lost* Satan is conversely measured against the tragic Turnus of the *Aeneid*. The two are linked by Milton's introduction of Satan towering over his followers "In shape and gesture proudly eminent" (I, 590) as Turnus towers[27] over the forces rallying to his support in troops which are catalogued in Virgil's following lines only less impressively than Satan's legions are catalogued by Milton. Harding is the first commentator to make the link between the two towering figures and the solemn rosters of their followers. But the resemblances between Satan and Turnus continue also in the famous simile (I, 591–9) describing the scene where Satan

> Stood like a Towr; his form had not yet lost
> All her Original brightness, nor appear'd
> Less then Arch Angel ruin'd, and th'excess
> Of Glory obscur'd; As when the Sun new ris'n
> Looks through the Horizontal misty Air
> Shorn of his Beams, or from behind the Moon
> In dim Eclipse disastrous twilight sheds
> On half the Nations, and with fear of change
> Perplexes Monarchs.

Much though the commentators have praised this passage, to which a censor is traditionally supposed to have objected on the ground that it might encourage the superstitious hopes of Charles II's enemies, it

26. Davis P. Harding in *The Club of Hercules* (University of Illinois Press, 1962), 45–52.

27. . . . inter primos praestanti corpore Turnus / Vertitur arma tenens et toto vertice supra est (*Aeneid*, VII, 783–4).

was left for Harding to develop its importance as "part of Milton's grand strategy for the covert discrediting of Satan." Through the first four books of *Paradise Lost* he points out a number of embedded, implied comparisons of Satan with various Homeric heroes—all of them to his discredit. At the end of Book IV they come thickest where (985–9), confronted by Gabriel,

> *Satan* alarm'd
> Collecting all his might dilated stood,
> Like *Teneriff*, or *Atlas* unremov'd:
> His stature reacht the Sky, and on his Crest
> Sat horror Plum'd.

The sky-scraping figure of Satan gigantizes Virgil's comparison of Aeneas to an Appennine peak as he confronts Turnus for their decisive struggle. But Harding notes that the final detail of Milton's description of Satan—". . . and on his Crest / Sat horror Plum'd"—is not drawn from the description of Aeneas, but "distils the essence of Virgil's striking image of the horrible snake-like Chimaera, 'breathing from her throat Aetnean flames,' which adorned the crest of Turnus' helmet." The implied association of Satan and the serpent here and elsewhere has also its latent threat of the doom of the serpent to be bruised by the "seed of the woman" as the serpents Tityos and Typhon were slain by the arrows of Apollo or the thunderbolts of Zeus. But in the scene between Satan and Gabriel the former's fate is openly declared at the climax of Book IV, when it is weighed in God's "golden Scales yet seen / Betwixt *Astraea* and the *Scorpion* sign" in the zodiac. The image of God's scales weighing an individual's fate carried no moral overtone when Hector's death at Achilles' hands or even the defeat of Troy by the Greeks was foretold by it in the *Iliad*, but for Milton's readers it had that quality as definitely as the same figure has it when in Daniel 5.xxvii Belshazzar is warned, "Thou art weighed in the balance and found wanting." It was no accident, says Harding, that Milton "saw fit to end the Fourth Book with a final allusion to Turnus. For the last verse of the book is a skilful reworking of the last line of the *Aeneid* which, briefly, poignantly, and unforgettably, records the death of Turnus and the passage of his soul to the eternal shades: "vitaque cum gemitu fugit indignata sub umbras."

Virgilian criticism has never made the mistake of regarding Turnus as the hero of the *Aeneid*, but it has more and more come to regard him as a tragic figure which its creator fully intended should command pity. In his struggle to hold Lavinia and the Latin kingdom against Aeneas he is magnificent. His disappointments are almost great enough to win the reader's sympathy in spite of his violence. But when all is told, sympathy for him does not extend to approval of his relentless feud with Aeneas and with the destiny of which Aeneas is the symbol. The "rage / Of *Turnus* for *Lavinia* disespous'd" (*P.L.*, IX, 16–17) might make him a tragic hero in Milton's eyes, but his passion is expressly listed with the traditional epic themes which are described in the prologue to Book IX as less heroic than that of *Paradise Lost.* In the end Turnus' rage cuts him off from all possibility of reconciliation with the Trojans and from all hope of being more than an object of pity and terror to the readers of his story.

In the prologue to Book IX Milton says that he must now change the "Notes" or theme of his story to "tragic." The tragedy to be narrated is the sin in Eden, not the sin of Satan or the sins of any of his ectypes in history. It is not necessary to inquire in just what sense Milton used the word *tragedy* here, but it may be extensible from the sin of Adam to the greater sin of Satan, the self-tempted, for which God declared that grace could not be found (*P.L.*, III, 131–2). It is obvious that, as B. A. Wright has most recently reminded us, the fact of Satan's wickedness and impenitence to the end "makes him a great tragic figure"; but he adds the immediate warning that, "although Milton first planned *Paradise Lost* as a tragedy, it is not, as we have it, a tragedy but an epic. The neo-classical theory of the 'forms' is not just pedantry; a writer ignores it at his peril. To regard Satan as the hero of Milton's epic is to stultify the poet's whole intention."[28]

The question may, however, arise as to whether a tragic figure may not play a great and essential though subordinate role in an epic. Victory of some kind–hard-won, perhaps hardly worth winning, but indefeasible–is the proper theme of epic. A defeated epic hero is a contradiction, but defeated opponents or anti-types of the hero are indispensable in an epic where cosmic and absolute actors are the principals. Of such opponents or anti-types of the truly heroic or good, Satan must be the supreme example. In an essay to which Wright refers on the page which is in part quoted above, Miss Helen Gardner traces the emergence of the Satanic tragic hero from Marlowe's

28. *Milton's "Paradise Lost,"* 54.

Faustus and Middleton's Beatrice-Joanna and Shakespeare's Macbeth to Milton's Satan.[29] All the four tragedies involve the progressive isolation of the hero by his own deeds and resolutions. The most striking parallel with Satan is Macbeth, with his self-revealing soliloquies and his painfully conscious approach to the point of no return. To some extent he is also like Satan because he is a public figure, a usurper as well as an abuser of power and therefore by classical definition doubly a tyrant. Pride or ambition is the passion which motivates the first crime of both figures, but their accumulating wickedness with progressive hardening of the heart is due to the almost inevitable consequence of their public stations.

IV

As the romantic myth of Satan has yielded to the criticism of historical scholarship and to modern psychological approaches to *Paradise Lost*, a new myth of a peculiarly political, tragic Satan is emerging. The basic conception may be less Miltonic than we suppose, but it is certainly to be found in Vondel's *Lucifer*, which was deliberately planned to expose the interplay of snowballing popular resentment of an act of authority as it is exploited by astute leaders to accumulate the mass support and passion necessary for open revolt. But it is essentially the same kind of process of conspiracy interworking with mob psychology that Raphael reports Satan as sparking first in the mind of Beelzebub on the night following the presentation of the Son as God's vice-gerent in Heaven. "New Laws," says Satan (V, 679–91),

> thou see'st impos'd;
> New Laws from him who reigns, new minds may raise
> In us who serve, new Counsels, to debate
> What doubtful may ensue; more in this place
> To utter is not safe. Assemble thou
> Of all those Myriads which we lead the chief;
> Tell them that by command, ere yet dim Night
> Her shadowy Cloud withdraws, I am to haste,
> And all who under me thir Banners wave,
> Homeward with flying march where we possess

29. "Milton's 'Satan' and the Theme of Damnation in Elizabethan Tragedy," *Essays and Studies by Members of the English Association*, I (1948), 46–66.

The Quarters of the North, there to prepare
Fit entertainment to receive our King
The great *Messiah*, and his new commands. . . .

Moving swiftly among Satan's myriad hierarchies, Beelzebub scatters "Ambiguous words and jealousies" (V, 699–701). Loyalties are confused by his intimation everywhere

That the most High commanding, now ere Night,
Now ere dim Night had disencumber'd Heav'n,
The great Hierarchal Standard was to move.

When the signal is given the habit of unquestioning obedience to "thir great Potentate" blinds the mass of his hierarchies to his "lies," and instantly they become a revolting army on the march. By a trick of semantics their leader has been transformed into their idol, their divinely commissioned potentate has become "the most High." When we meet them again later in their experience though earlier in Milton's narrative, more powerful semantic drugs prove capable of blinding them to the meaning of their defeat. While still in Heaven on the eve of battle they have heard Satan declare that their being was not owing to God, that they were "self-begot, self-rais'd" by a "quick'ning power" of their own "when fatal course / Had circl'd his full Orb" (V, 860–2). Defeat in Heaven has not purged their minds of the illusion that they are the spontaneously generated "Ethereal sons" of the celestial soil, and in Hell they are ready to listen with Beelzebub to Satan's doctrine that "by Fate the strength of Gods / And this Empyreal substance cannot fail" (I, 116–17). Since God solemnly addresses the loyal angels in Heaven as "all ye Gods" (III, 341), Beelzebub may well feel secure against any suspicion of flattery when he addresses the council of devils in Pandaemonium as "Synod of Gods" (II, 391). In the *Christian Doctrine* I.v, Milton observed that "the name of God is not infrequently ascribed, by the will and concession of God the Father, even unto angels and to men."[30] But, as J. C. Maxwell observes, an ambiguous play with the title *gods* is central in Satan's temptations of his followers and later of Eve, for they are both structured around the central text of the story of the temptation in Eden, "Ye shall be as gods."[31] In the abuse of that one word is all the lure and logic of Satan's flattery of his legions.

30. Columbia Edition, XIV, 245. 31. NQ, CXCIII (1948), 242.

Before his hosts in Pandaemonium Satan is the archetypal demagogue. Comparison with "Hitler addressing one of his monster rallies, with all the trappings of banners, uniforms, and insignia," seems to justify Daiches' assertion that "The whole debate as it develops in Book II is a classic presentation of the abuses of democratic assembly."[32] The archetype includes both demagogue and audience. "Hell's totalitarianism," Broadbent rightly says, "is most obvious in the devils; Satan, though in the created world he occasionally turns humane, in Hell is predominantly a *führer*."[33] But it is a question whether Milton was as much concerned as we are today about mob-psychology and its part in the evolution of dictatorships. Yet that view of the debate in Hell is clearly much closer to Milton's thought than is Chateaubriand's notion that "Cromwell and his associates served as Milton's models for his portraits of the infernal crew"—a notion which Kenneth Muir calls "absurd."[34] Milton, of course, had no more respect for the univocal horde of devils than he had for the members who might be elected to a popular assembly which a member of the revived Rump Parliament proposed in the political crisis in September 1659: such an unwieldy body, said Milton, could convene "only now and then to hold up a forrest of fingers, or to convey each man his bean or ballot into the box."[35] The mere numbers of Satan's inner council of a "thousand Demi-Gods on golden seats" (I, 796) would have seemed to Milton to be a travesty of a responsible governing body.

If to the end of his life Milton continued to regard Cromwell as an anti-tyrant (as he certainly did in the *Second Defence of the English People*), then certainly it was not to represent Cromwell that he conceived his figure of Satan. Nor do the four main participants in the infernal debate, Moloch, Belial, Mammon, and Beelzebub, readily match any of Milton's contemporaries. Their function is to provide a foil and a setting for Satan's original proposal of an assault by a single champion, himself, upon the world which rumour said was to be created, and upon its inhabitants. His strategy and his courage are to stand out against the evasive policy of essential surrender to defeat of Belial and Mammon, and Moloch's rash demand for a direct assault upon Heaven. Their speeches and Beelzebub's following preparation

32. David Daiches, *Milton* (London, 1957), 166.
33. J. B. Broadbent, *Some Graver Subject* (London, 1960), 78.
34. Kenneth Muir, *John Milton* (London, 1955), 129.
35. *A Readie and Easie Way*; Columbia Edition, VI, 131.

for the gesture which is to make Satan forever Hell's unchallengeable ruler are magnificent in themselves—so magnificent that Gilbert has said that Milton developed the situation "for its own sake with great pleasure and with little thought of its connection with other parts of the poem, except in the character of Satan."[36] But the value of the debate in Hell is more than vindicated if it adds anything of value to his characterization.

As characterization it is indispensable, for it dramatizes Satan as an idol set in contrast not only with God but with Milton's life-long ideal of the true orator of the breed that was once

> renown'd
> In *Athens* or free *Rome*, where Eloquence
> Flourish'd, since mute.... (IX, 670–2)

When Satan approaches Eve in the garden his assumed stance is the false image of such an orator, but the comparison fits him equally well as he stands "with Monarchal pride / Conscious of highest worth" (II, 428–9), ready to make his final pitch for power in Pandaemonium. When he returns from earth triumphant in Book X it is to receive the absolute homage of the "consulting Peers / Rais'd from thir dark *Divan*" (X, 456–7). Again there is the implied comparison with a Turkish sultan as a type of absolute ruler. And, as Zera Fink has observed, the authority which Satan has gained in *Paradise Lost* is reaffirmed by acclamation of the devils in council in *Paradise Regained* (I, 111–13) when

> Unanimous they all commit the care
> And management of this main enterprize
> To him their great Dictator.

Indeed, Fink regards the entire poem as "an expression of Milton's lack of faith in dictatorship as it was conceived in seventeenth century political thought."[37]

To shift the suggestion to *Paradise Lost* and regard Satan there as in any sense the archetype of ectypes like Napoleon, Hitler, or Lenin, clearly involves the risk of overweighting the political potential of the poem and also of thinking uncritically in terms of Paris, Nuremberg,

36. Allan H. Gilbert, *On the Composition of Paradise Lost* (University of North Carolina Press, 1947), 104.
37. Zera S. Fink, *The Classical Republicans* (Northwestern University Press, 1943), 195–6.

or Moscow. The ectypes are sure to be chosen on grounds personal to the reader even though he may think that Milton, if he could be with us at this hour, would surely concur in the identification. In the poem Milton names only one ectype, Nimrod. But in the way he refers to some of the passionate heroes of the classical epics he implies that others are to be found in history as well as literature. Links with actual life are to be inferred from Satan's distinct though fleeting resemblances to Achilles, Turnus, and others. But besides Nimrod another historical ectype of Milton's dictator-Satan has been confidently identified in the pattern of *Paradise Lost*: William Blissett points out that Milton's Satan seems to reflect the "Satanic in Lucan's Caesar" which had left its print upon Ben Jonson's *Catiline* and several other Jacobean plays.[38] Blissett's parallel between the *Pharsalia* and *Paradise Lost* is a rather shadowy one between Satan's voyage through Chaos and Caesar's effort to cross the storm-tossed Adriatic to get reinforcements before the battle of Pharsalia. Both passages, that in Book II of *Paradise Lost* and that in Book V of Lucan's *Civil War*, are very long, and the parallels are acknowledged to be "in general conception rather than in details of execution." The most convincing evidence adduced is a final group of four short passages from *Paradise Lost* which reveal "the Caesarian in Milton's Satan." None of them has a verbal parallel in the *Civil War*, but a definite link of one of them with the Caesar of recorded history is possible through Plutarch's *Life of Caesar* (xi.2). It is the passage (I, 261–3) where Satan declares that in his

> choice
> To reign is worth ambition, though in Hell:
> Better to reign in Hell, than serve in Heav'n.

Milton was certainly aware that to illustrate the point that Caesar's master passion was ambition Plutarch had recalled a story that when passing through a mountain village he had said that he would prefer the first place in such wretched surroundings to the second place in Rome. The transfer of those words from the supreme type of human ambition to Satan seems to have been traditional. In the *Adamo Caduto* of Serafino Salandra, Satan declares that he has deliberately preferred reigning in Hell to remaining in Heaven.[39] The verbal parallel is not exact, but no one familiar with Plutarch's anecdote could fail to make the link with it from Milton's passage or from

38. William Blissett, "Caesar and Satan," *JHT*, XVIII (1957), 222–32.
39. (Cozenzo, 1647), Act II, Scene i.

Salandra's. Probably the link was also intended by Vondel when in the second act of *Lucifer* he made Lucifer exclaim:

> Better it were by far
> To be the first Prince in a lower Court
> Than second, or still less, in heaven's Light.[40]

But it is one thing to recognize ectypes of Milton's Satan in Nimrod and Julius Caesar, and perhaps another to link him with the political dictators who have involved their countries in wars against humanity in the twentieth century. The distinction is a fine one and it involves a difference between Milton's first readers and ourselves. Rajan indicates what it is when he warns against modern sympathy for Satan's "Promethean qualities" which to many of us cover the flaws in his moral and intellectual arguments, his appeal to "just right and the fixt laws of Heav'n" and his outcries against God's "tyranny." "Other politicians," Rajan concludes, "have made claims somewhat similar, and Satan's assertions as the champion of Liberty would amuse, rather than perplex, those who were brought up to think of him as the first Liar."[41]

For modern readers who approach *Paradise Lost* with Milton's basically Platonic conception of the government of the state and of the soul as matters of what Milton called "right reason," there is no mystery in the successful rebellion of the Father of Lies against the divine "tyranny" in the name of liberty. But for a reader who comes to the poem with Broadbent's ambivalent psychological view of its author, the repudiation of the traditional conception of epic heroism in the prologue to Book IX itself shares "a flickering remote beauty with Pandemonium, the *ignis fatuus* in which Satan glides to tempt Eve, the glister of the forbidden fruit itself."[42] At the climax of Satan's review of his troops (I, 571–3), when

> his heart
> Distends with pride, and hardning in his strength
> Glories;

at this "moment of deepest involvement in the grandeur of the devils," Broadbent thinks that "the reader finds himself thrown by the enormous weight of that 'Glories' into identity with a fascist Satan." This

40. See the translation in Watson Kirkconnell, *The Celestial Cycle* (University of Toronto Press, 1952), 374.

41. *"Paradise Lost" and the Seventeenth Century Reader*, 95–6.

42. *Some Graver Subject*, 97.

is all the likelier to happen if the reader is imbued with Sir Herbert Grierson's dissatisfaction with Milton's God as an absolute ruler and with his concern lest Milton's confidence in the justice that he preached in his regicide tracts should end in a dangerous doctrine, "one that might be used to justify Lenin or Mussolini or Hitler alike."[43] If Milton's political tracts are brought into the interpretation of his poem, anything is possible unless the longest view is taken. That view, as Barker so deliberately takes it, must recognize constant conviction of "the harsh Puritan belief in the duty and privilege of the righteous to impose the divine will on the unregenerate mass," but it must also remember that the "very centre of Milton's thought on liberty" was always faith in "the Creator of natural freedom" and in "the Redeemer of both spiritual and natural freedom" to whom he appealed in the added final paragraph of the second edition of *The Readie and Easie Way to Establish a Free Commonwealth.*[44]

The Milton who wrote the closing sentence of the *Way* and had Michael teach Adam the lesson of the government of reason in the souls of citizens as the key to political freedom was not speaking with irony. In *Paradise Lost* as a whole he was a deliberate ironist in structure, characterization, and style. In his treatment of the devils of Books I and II as what Broadbent calls a basis "for satire of the underside of tyranny"[45] he seems to the present writer to be more of a satirist than an ironist, though the line may be hard to draw. To Mrs. MacCaffrey, they seem, as they do to G. Wilson Knight, to "represent mankind in its fruitless struggles," and to be involved with Satan in an irony, which like all irony, "is fundamentally tragic: it calls out simultaneously our sympathetic emotions and our critical intellects. Hence," she says, "all arguments as to where our sympathies lie in the early books of Milton's epic are vain; they lie *both* with the follies of the fallen, and with the rigor and discipline that are necessary to our salvation as reasonable beings."[46] In view of God's condemnation of all the rebel angels as "self-tempted" (*P.L.*, III, 130) and therefore beyond grace, Mrs. MacCaffrey seems to strain the *conscious* ambivalence of Milton's irony in drawing the "underside of tyranny." He would be less gracious to the horde of devils and, *a fortiori*, to

43. H. J. C. Grierson, *Milton and Wordsworth: Poets and Prophets* (New York, 1937), 63.

44. Arthur Barker, *Milton and the Puritan Dilemma* (University of Toronto Press, 1955), 273, 289.

45. *Some Graver Subject*, 87.

46. *"Paradise Lost" as Myth*, 182–3; cf. Knight, *Chariot of Wrath*, 137.

Satan, although it seems from his soliloquies that Milton would approve all that Arnold Stein says in his brilliant study of the "trap of leadership" in which Satan finds himself caught. The private Satan who himself is Hell is the obverse of the public Satan who is admired in Pandaemonium.

But *Paradise Lost* cannot be read as a justification of Satan and his ways either to man or God. That conclusion unexpectedly emerges from Miss Ann Lodge's rigorously objective study of him as a classic case of paranoia in "Satan's Symbolic Syndrome."[47] Her procedure is simply to observe the resemblances of Satan's self-portrayals in his soliloquies and in his speeches in Pandaemonium to Brickner's list of the "major symptoms of paranoid behaviour: megalomania, the need to dominate, persecution complex utilizing projection and exaggerated self-reference, retrospective falsification, and an absolutely logical, though delusional, character of thought." She ends with a prognosis which rests upon the basic assumption in *Paradise Lost* that angels and men enjoy an inviolable original freedom unless they "enthrall themselves" (III, 125). The enthralment of the rebellious angels is paranoid because, rather than being a revolt against an arbitrary divine decree, it "is analogous to disobeying a law of gravity," and amounts simply to "defiance of their environment." "It is with this outlook," she says, "that Milton so stresses obedience. It represents not so much a becoming humility as the only deeply realistic approach to action."

Miss Lodge is impartial between the psychiatric theories of therapy for paranoids which oppose the doctrine that "the physician's love heals the patient" to faith in a "realistic and merciless environment as sometimes the best treatment and the best physician." When a paranoid achieves power, however, and when he is institutionalized by society, she regards his case as all but hopeless. The records of her great historic paranoids—Ivan the Terrible, Napoleon, Marx, Stalin, and Captain Nemo[48]—offer no hope for the cases of men caught in the trap of leadership. There is nothing in *Paradise Lost* to encourage Origen's view that Satan will ultimately be saved. In its modern form, as proposed by Giovanni Papini, that view attracts Miss Lodge because

47. In the *Psychoanalytic Review*, XLIII (1956), 411–22.

48. The inclusion of Nemo seems as odd as the omission of Balzac's Vautrin, that embodiment of "l'archange déchu qui veut toujours la guerre" and possesses "tous les sentiments humains, moins un seul, celui de repentir." *Le Père Goriot* (Paris, La Renaissance du Livre, n.d.), 182.

it asserts the freedom of even the perverse will and implies the inexhaustible love of God. Milton, of course, would have included it among the heresies with which he said that Origen's works were "thick sown."[49] In *Of Christian Doctrine* he expressly denied it.[50] The more symbolically the myth of Satan is understood in *Paradise Lost*, the more unequivocally final his ultimate exclusion from all society except his own must be, unless the poem is to end in pessimism. On Miss Lodge's showing, the paranoid character of Milton's Satan is not such as to encourage modern critics who fail to recognize in that "megalomaniac and destructive spirit" anything less than "a superlative prophetic picture of the world of conquerors of our time."[51]

In substance, if not in style, Miss Lodge's prognosis in the case of the archetypal paranoid is as prophetic as Michael's apocalyptic metaphor describing Satan as doomed to be finally dragged "in Chains / Through all his Realm: and there confounded" left (XII, 454–5). And in substance the psychiatrical prognosis comes close to Satan's own analysis in his most revealing soliloquy when he confesses that "Where wounds of deadly hate have pierc'd so deep," only a "worse relapse" could follow any attempt at reconcilement (IV, 98–100). That soliloquy reviewing his private experience on the way to the tyrant's fall into the trap of leadership is simply the obverse of the public experience of the society which Michael describes to Adam as doomed to servitude "When upstart Passions catch the Government / From Reason."[52] Though Michael's style in prophesying the end of the archetypal paranoid may be apocalyptic, his metaphor is no more lurid than the facts of Waterloo and of Hitler's death in Berlin: it is from the historical record of the careers of Satan's ectypes that Miss Lodge draws her unfavourable prognosis in his case. And actually in her psychiatric prognosis of the probable end of the myth of Satan her thinking is as Platonic as Michael's, for her fear that Satan is incurable corresponds with Plato's mathematically established demonstration of the supreme misery of the man of tyrannical nature who is so unfortunate as to become an actual tyrant.[53]

49. In *Of Reformation*; Columbia Edition, III, 21.
50. Columbia Edition, XVI, 363.
51. The words are from Douglas Bush's *"Paradise Lost" in Our Time* (Cornell University Press, 1945), 55.
52. *Paradise Lost*, XII, 88–89. For the context see p. 130 above.
53. *Republic*, IX, 578C ff., and 587D–E.

Milton and Sacred History: *Books XI and XII of* Paradise Lost

H. R. MACCALLUM

MICHAEL DRAYTON, well embarked on the second book of *Moses his Birth and Miracles*, startles his reader by interrupting an account of the Egyptian plagues in order to reflect on the perils of writing poetry about sacred history. If he is to escape the critic's poisoned breath, he protests to his Muse, he must have guidance,

> Lest too concise injuriously we wrong
> Things that such state and fearfulnesse import,
> Or led by zeale irregularly long,
> Infringe the curious liberties of Art. (161–4)

The reader, aware that only two of the ten plagues have so far been accounted for, might be forgiven for feeling that zeal is already in danger of overwhelming art completely. The question of reconciling the authority of sacred truth with that of art, however, was a very real and pressing issue for seventeenth-century religious poets.

It has frequently been contended that Milton fails to resolve this conflict in the history of the world with which he closes *Paradise Lost*. Addison, who found much to admire in the last books, nevertheless felt that there are passages in Book XII where "the Author has been so attentive to his Divinity, that he has neglected his Poetry."[1] Among modern critics, C. S. Lewis has shown the strongest antagonism to the history, which he repudiates as an "untransmuted lump."[2] While few critics have followed Lewis to this extreme of condemnation, many have felt that the last books should have less matter and more art.

1. *The Spectator*, no. 369.
2. *A Preface to Paradise Lost* (Oxford, 1942), 125.

Recently this traditional view received a sharp check with the appearance of an imaginative and very persuasive essay on Milton's history by F. T. Prince.[3] Prince maintains that the history reveals Milton's intuitive grasp of the ebb and flow of the reader's attention. In the last movement of a long work, he argues, the reader inevitably feels that the imagination is satisfied and the curiosity appeased. Milton deftly utilizes this shift in attitude by supplying a subject-matter which suits the new mood. The vision of the future is peculiarly appropriate to the autumnal atmosphere, the sense of chastened interest and sober concentration, which develops toward the close of Book X.

Prince's defence has found support in a fine analysis of the last books by J. H. Summers in *The Muse's Method*.[4] This study examines the dramatic manner in which the history of the future completes the education of Adam. The present essay explores further the parts of Milton's history in the hope of contributing to an understanding of the unified structure and dramatic form of the last books. It should be remembered, however, that the art of these books cannot be considered in abstraction from the context of Christian belief about history within which the poet is operating. Only by seeking a full awareness of this context can we appreciate how Milton, by acts of selection and arrangement, has made doctrine coalesce with aesthetic pattern. Such an appreciation should in turn enable us to see more clearly the dramatic logic which controls the stages and the form of the history.

One of the most significant patterns in the account lies in the divisions of history. These conform, not to the classical ages of man, but to the traditional Christian chronology of the world in which history is envisaged in terms of six ages, corresponding to the six days of creation. This traditional scheme was given authority by St. Augustine, and a clear statement of the view is to be found in his *Contra Faustinum*:

In the creation God finished His works in six days, and rested on the seventh. The history of the world contains six periods marked by the dealings of God with men. The first period is from Adam to Noah; the second, from Noah to Abraham; the third, from Abraham to David; the fourth from David to the captivity in Babylon; the fifth, from the captivity to the

3. "On the Last Two Books of *Paradise Lost*," E&S, n.s., XI (1958), 38–52.
4. *The Muse's Method* (London, 1962), ch. 8.

advent in lowliness of our Lord Jesus Christ; the sixth is now in progress, and will end in the coming of the exalted Saviour to judgement. What answers to the seventh day is the rest of the saints,—not in this life, but in another, where the rich man saw Lazarus at rest while he was tormented in hell; where there is no evening, because there is no decay. On the sixth day, in Genesis, man is formed after the image of God; in the sixth period of the world there is the clear discovery of our transformation in the renewing of our mind, according to the image of Him who created us, as the apostle says. As a wife was made for Adam from his side while he slept, the Church becomes the property of her dying Saviour, by the sacrament of the blood which flowed from His side after His death.[5]

Subsequent theologians and biblical exegetes often wrote with such a scheme in mind, although they did not always agree as to the extent and boundaries of each phase. G. W. Whiting, who has drawn attention to the presence of the traditional scheme in Milton's history,[6] shows its popularity by citing an impressive list of historians who employ it. His illustrations stretch from Isidore of Seville to *Du Bartas His Devine Weekes and Workes*, and the chronological table published in the Geneva Bible.

Seventeenth-century examples are frequent, and the view is particularly popular with theologians who are exploring the typology of the Bible. Thus it is invoked by Thomas Taylor in *Christ Revealed: or the Old Testament explained* (1635), and it is central to *The Figures or Types of the Old Testament* by Samuel Mather (published posthumously in 1683). Mather's treatment of the subject is worth summarizing.[7] Having divided history into the old dispensation and the new, he finds in the former two chief periods: the first extends from Adam to the reception of the law by Moses; the second, in which religious tradition achieved written expression, extends from Moses to John the Baptist. The period before the law, when the Church was in its infancy, is then further articulated into three dispensations, from Adam to Noah, from Noah to Abraham, and from Abraham to Moses. In the second "grand period" four dispensations are discovered, from Moses to the temple, from the temple to the captivity in Babylon, from the captivity to the construction of the second temple, and from the second temple to the coming of the Messiah. Each of these phases

5. *The Works of . . . Augustine*, ed. M. Dods (Edinburgh, 1892), V, 208–9.
6. "The Pattern of Time and Eternity," in *Milton and This Pendant World* (University of Texas Press, 1958), 169–200.
7. *The Figures or Types of the Old Testament* (London, 1705), 22 ff.

is marked by covenants between God and his chosen people, and each contains types of Christ. Mather thus finds two periods more than Augustine, one arising out of his desire to make Moses central, the other emphasizing the Babylonian captivity. Both additions suggest his Puritan viewpoint.

The history of the world revealed to Adam by the angel Michael conforms to the traditional scheme.[8] Sometimes the divisions are clearly marked, sometimes they are only implied, but the presence of the pattern is undeniable. After the visions which culminate in the history of the flood, Michael formally marks the transition from the first age to the second (XII, 6–7):

> Thus thou hast seen one World begin and end;
> And Man as from a second stock proceed.

This new world rapidly loses its pastoral simplicity, and Michael, having described the tyranny of Nimrod and the construction of the tower of Babel, draws the conclusion (XII, 105–6):

> Thus will this latter, as the former World
> Still tend from bad to worse. . . .

God now withdraws his presence from the nations and selects a particular race which is to spring from the faithful Abraham. This step introduces the third age, which includes the captivity of the chosen people in Egypt, their wanderings in the desert, and their triumphant entry into Canaan. The outlines of the fourth and fifth periods are blurred. The fourth begins when David receives the promise that his throne shall endure forever, and ends in the Babylonian captivity. The fifth age, ushered in by a reaffirmation of the covenant made with David, receives only thirteen lines in which Michael describes the return to Jerusalem and the struggle between Onias and Joshua for the high priesthood. The Incarnation opens the sixth age, which contains the life of Christ and his Church, and ends with the dissolution of Satan's "perverted world" and the inauguration of an endless Sabbath of joy and bliss. We have come to the "world's great period." Milton has followed the sixfold pattern defined by Augustine; he does not, like Mather, make the period from Moses

8. Milton normally thought of biblical history in terms of phases which reveal a rhythm of fall and reformation, as can be seen in his polemical use of examples and types in the anti-episcopal tracts.

to David a distinct age. Yet there is a significant disturbance in the development of the narrative just after the description of the entry into Canaan. In response to a question from Adam, Michael turns back in his account to provide a fuller description of the purpose of the Mosaic law. He then returns without pause to the history of Canaan. Thus one is left with the impression of an extra age which is not acknowledged by the structural divisions of the history. In this way Milton provides the characteristic Puritan stress on the Mosaic law as a watershed in history, enabling us to see the threefold design which Mather mentions—an age of patriarchs, an age of law, and an age of gospel.

In *Contra Faustinum* Augustine was attempting to refute the Manichaean view that the God of the Old Testament is not that of the New. The two testaments, he argues, present a continuous revelation: "In every page of these Scriptures, while I pursue my search as a son of Adam in the sweat of my brow, Christ either openly or covertly meets and refreshes me."[9] This traditional view was stressed with great energy by the Puritans. Richard Sibbes, whose writing contains much that is characteristic of the central stream of English Puritanism, puts the matter clearly in *The Excellency of the Gospel Above the Law*:

> What is the scope of the whole Scriptures but Christ? from the first promise of the blessed seed, The seed of the woman shall break the Serpent's head, Gen.iii.15, to the end of the book. . . . He is that Spirit which gives life unto all the Scriptures. Moses without Christ is but a shadow without a body, or a body without a soul. Take away Christ, what was the brazen serpent? What was the ark? What were the sacrifices? . . . The kings, and priests, and prophets, they were types of Christ. . . . Christ is the spirit of all. And the Scripture without Christ it is but a mere dead thing; it is but a shell without a kernel. . . .[10]

This comes very close to the heart of Michael's treatment of history.

When this theory of Christ's typological presence in the Old Testament is brought into conjunction with a stylized theory of historical periods, a fairly complex situation emerges. Since the Old Testament periods (whether or not exactly five in number) are typologically related to the New Testament, they will also be related to each other

9. *Works*, V, 224.

10. *The Excellency of the Gospel above the Law*, in *Complete Works*, ed. A. B. Grosart (Edinburgh, 1862–4), IV, 207.

by various correspondences of design. The basic pattern of fall, judgment, regeneration, and renewal is repeated cyclically from age to age, each new world being born out of the ruins of the old through the man of faith. Yet there is progress, too, a movement from implicit to explicit, "from shadowy Types to Truth, from Flesh to Spirit" (*PL*, XII, 303).

There was general agreement among Protestant commentators that, as Mather put it, the first gospel light was preached to Adam in "that great and blessed Promise, that *the seed of the Woman should break the Serpent's head*."[11] Michael has been instructed to "intermix" this covenant in his history of the future (XI, 115–16), and he makes it a dominant motif. The seed of the woman is made relevant to Abraham (XI, 148–50), to the ceremonial law (XII, 232–4), to Joshua (XII, 310–12), and to David (XII, 327). Finally, the fulfilment of the prophecy is shown in the account of Christ's birth and redemptive act, an account which makes repeated use of the terms of the prophecy. As Adam's eyes are gradually opened, a series of subsidiary promises mark the stages of the process and point in an increasingly specific manner to the nature of the promised seed. Christ fulfils all the prophecies, offering the promise of life to "all who shall believe in his redemption" (XII, 406–7) and the final hope of a world purged and refined by fire. Milton's dexterity in handling this material shows how thoroughly he had mastered the Protestant approach to the Bible. "Seek therefore in the Scripture," as Tyndale remarked, "chiefly and above all, the covenants made between God and us; that is to say, the law and commandments which God commandeth us to do; and then the mercy promised unto all them that submit themselves unto the law."[12]

As the history develops, events and figures gain in significance by their typological suggestiveness. The opening tableau of Cain and Abel is itself a kind of dumb show which reveals through mime, and in cryptic fashion, the essentials of the drama to come. The reference to the "cleft Wood" on which Abel's sacrifice is placed has obvious overtones. A clearer prefiguration of Christ is found in Enoch, "the

11. *Figures or Types*, 7.
12. "Prologue to the Book of Genesis," in *Doctrinal Treatises and Introductions*, ed. Henry Walter, Parker Society (Cambridge, 1848), 403.

only righteous in a world perverse." He has another function, however. Beset by foes, Enoch is saved by divine intervention:

> Him the most High
> Rapt in a balmy Cloud with winged Steeds
> Did, as thou saw'st, receive, to walk with God
> High in Salvation and the Climes of bliss,
> Exempt from Death; to show thee what reward
> Awaits the good. . . . (XI, 705–10)

In *De Doctrina Christiana* Milton invokes the popular theory that Enoch and Elijah typified perfect glorification, the former before law, the latter under it.[13] In the poetic account of Enoch's translation Milton has remembered Elijah, for the picture of Enoch "Rapt in a balmy cloud with winged steeds" draws upon the biblical passage describing Elijah's translation.[14]

The story of the flood is resonant with typological implications, and only the more important ones can be mentioned here. Crucial is the typology by which Noah prefigures Christ. Michael hints at this theme by calling Noah "the one just man alive," but it is Adam who establishes it clearly when, at the triumphant conclusion of Noah's voyage (XI, 876–78), he rejoices

> For one Man found so perfect and so just,
> That God vouchsafes to raise another World
> From him, and all his anger to forget.

In traditional typology the ark itself is a prefiguration both of Christ and of his church, and these identifications can be felt in Michael's description (XI, 819–21) of how Noah built

> a wondrous Ark as thou beheld'st
> To save himself and household from amidst
> A world devote to universal rack.

The same associations are present when Adam sees that during the

13. *De Doctrina Christiana*, XVI, 337. (All citations from Milton's prose are to *The Works of John Milton*, ed. Frank Allen Patterson [New York, 1931–8], 18 vols.; citations from Milton's poetry are from *John Milton: Complete Poems and Major Prose*, ed. Merritt Y. Hughes [New York, 1957]). Thus Mather writes of Enoch that he was "a most illustrious Type of Christ's Ascension into Heaven" before the Law, adding that the Jews "had but two in all, Elijah under the Law, and Enoch before the Law" (*Figures or Types*, 67).

14. See II Kings 2.xi.

flood all mankind "in one small bottom swum embarked" (XI, 753). Here we might remember Milton's endorsement of the tradition, sanctioned by I Peter (3.xx–xxi), in which the flood is taken as a type of baptism, and his view that baptism is a figurative representation of our death, burial, and resurrection with Christ.[15] Noah in the flood suggests both Christ's act of atonement and the baptismal rite whereby the Christian commemorates that act in "the profluent stream" (XII, 442). But Noah's trials should remind us of other phases of history. Adam, before he realizes that Noah will be saved, laments (XI, 777–9) that

> those few escap't
> Famine and anguish will at last consume
> Wand'ring that wat'ry Desert. . . .

The language used here invites us to think of the chosen people in search of Canaan. We are also expected to connect these words with Adam's later expression of concern over the Church after the death of Christ (XII, 480–3):

> what will betide the few
> His faithful, left among th'unfaithful herd,
> The enemies of truth; who then shall guide
> His people, who defend?

Finally, the account leads the reader to remember the beginning and the end of time. The description of the flood subsiding echoes the account of the creation of the world out of chaos by the Son (VII, 205 ff.); the ark grounded "on the top of some high mountain" (XI, 851), together with the imagery of nature's rebirth, suggests the garden of Eden; the emphasis on a "world restor'd" (XII, 4) points forward to the time when all things will be made new. Through typological implication the history of the flood has become a microcosm of human history.

The account of the ten plagues with which Moses subdues the Egyptians contains a number of images which recall the description of Hell in Book I. The passage also suggests the signs and judgments of the Book of Revelation. This prefiguration is clearly implied when Milton, picking up a phrase from Ezekiel 29.iii, refers to Egypt as "the

15. *De Doctrina Christiana*, XVI, 191. In *Tetrachordon* (IV, 136) Milton approvingly notes that "Eusebius . . . compares the state of the Christians to that of Noah and the Patriarchs before the Law."

River-dragon" (XII, 191). (In the *Reason of Church Government* he connects "that huge dragon of Egypt" with the dragon of Revelation.[16]) It is possible, too, that his picture of Moses passing between "crystal walls" of water should awaken memories of the "sea of glass" and the river "clear as crystal" in Revelation.[17] The subsequent description of the Ark of the Tabernacle in which the "holy One" dwelt with "mortal Men" (XII, 248) points forward to the temple at Jerusalem, to the Incarnation, and to the living temple of the heart.

With the story of the quest for the promised land Milton's typological intention becomes more explicit. Moses is described as bearing "in figure" the office of mediator. His ceremonial laws are "types and shadows." Joshua, leading the chosen people into Canaan, typifies Jesus, leading the blessed into Heaven. This typology is, of course, completely traditional and sanctioned by the New Testament. The same types are considered by Milton in *De Doctrina Christiana*.[18]

As well as treating some of the major episodes in such a way as to bring out their figurative implications, Milton weaves into the narrative certain motifs which reinforce his typology. One of the most persistent of these is cloud imagery. At the beginning of the history is the cloud of steam which rises when the fire from heaven consumes Abel's sacrifice; at the end, the cloud of glory in which Christ descends to purge the world by fire. We also hear of the "balmy cloud" which carries away Enoch, the cloud and rainbow by which God signifies that he will not destroy the earth by water, the cloud and pillar of fire which guide the Israelites through the wilderness, the cloud over Sinai, and the clouded Ark. In *De Doctrina Christiana* Milton notes that Christ's final advent is "uniformly described" as a time when he comes with the clouds of heaven.[19] Thomas Taylor is more expansive on the subject. God, he observes, was often pleased to manifest his presence by clouds: "As when he sets his bowe in the cloud as signe of his favour: God in a cloud appeared to Moses, God appeared in the cloud upon the Oracle, Christ in the Mount was transfigured in a bright cloud; in his ascending he was taken out of their sight in a

16. *The Reason of Church Government*, III, i, 275.

17. The image, which comes from Sylvester's *Bartas His Devine Weekes and Works*, appears to have impressed Milton for it is found in his early translation of Psalm 136.

18. *De Doctrina Christiana*, XVI, 111.

19. *Ibid.*, XVI, 359.

cloud: And in his coming againe to judgement, he shall appear in the clouds."[20]

Despite motifs of this kind, Milton does not give prominence to the typology of objects. The dominant feature of his typology is the Pauline and Augustinian emphasis on the men of faith as prefigurations of Christ. Abel, his faith approved, shall lose no reward, "though here thou see him die / Rolling in dust and gore"; Enoch, whose translation has already been mentioned, is "the only righteous in a World perverse"; Noah is "the only son of light / In a dark Age"; Abraham is the "one faithful man" through whom all nations will be blessed; Moses, as we have seen, is a figure of the Mediator. The model for such typology is to be found in the histories of the saints in the Epistle to the Hebrews (11–13), and Stephen's speech before the Sanhedrin in Acts (7.i–liii). The author of the Epistle to the Hebrews sets out to illustrate the doctrine that faith is "the substance of things hoped for, the evidence of things not seen." His examples comprise a short history of the world. Beginning with Abel, Enoch, Noah, and Abraham, he sweeps down history through a cloud of witnesses to Christ, the "author and finisher of our faith," and concludes by hinting at the second coming. It is in terms of the lonely men of faith who realize that in this world God has no continuing city, that Milton, like the writer of the Epistle to the Hebrews, records the history of the world.

Milton's use of biblical typology directs attention to his rationalism and his Puritanism. This can be seen very clearly if we contrast his practice with that of George Herbert. The Anglican poet is also concerned to turn the outward or the institutional into a figure of the inward and private; he does not insist on this transformation in the same manner, however, for he lacks the Puritan sense of urgency and he sympathizes with the medieval schematic method of reading the Bible. Thus he is interested in the prefigurative function of objects, examining the symbolic nature of Aaron's vestments ("Aaron"), seeing manna as a type of the Scripture ("The Bunch of Grapes"), and stressing the typical significance of rocks, grapes, and seas. He is not averse to the kind of type which depends on external or allegorical resemblances, as when he compares Samson bearing the doors away to Christ on the cross ("Sunday"), and he likes to make typical relations

20. *Christ Revealed, or the Old Testament Explained* (London, 1635), 222.

explicit, as in "The Bunch of Grapes." Milton, on the other hand, seldom emphasizes the prefigurative function of objects, avoids external or allegorical analogies, and evokes typical relations by indirect means, by the allusive use of imagery, or by nuances of language. A similar restraint is to be found in Marvell's use of types. His "Bermudas" is ostensibly a fanciful picture of religious exiles in the New World, but language and image contrive to evoke a whole series of biblical analogues, so that the island becomes associated with the garden of Eden, the promised land, and the Temple. Marvell, Miss Wallerstein has suggested, is "a rationalist, if we use rationalism in the sense of objectively oriented and critical, not readily surrendering the imagination to a great chain of symbol or extended myth."[21] Much the same observation could be made about Milton.[22]

Milton, of course, is not writing an abstract discourse on sacred history, but the last movement of an unusually dramatic epic. The organization created by historical periods, types, and promises is only the foundation for the unity which he achieves by making the whole history serve the education of Adam. As J. H. Summers has observed, the learning of what is to happen simply provides the occasion and the raw materials of Adam's enlightenment.[23] It should be added, however, that the very arrangement of these materials creates a dialectical pattern of ascent which leads Adam from type to truth, from flesh to spirit.

Dialectical argument is of course basic to Milton's major poems, but its most interesting theoretical account is to be found in the divorce tracts. There, in an attempt to circumvent the most obvious interpretation of Christ's injunction against divorce (Matthew 19.vi), Milton evolves a significant theory of Christ's method of teaching. It is a theory which has far-reaching implications, and which provides the answer to problems that had haunted Milton through the tracts of the early forties. Christ, he argues, employed in his teaching a strategy of indirection. He did not teach all things at all times, and

21. *Studies in Seventeenth-Century Poetic* (University of Wisconsin Press, 1961), 340.

22. As I have attempted to show elsewhere, Milton believed that schematic symbolism is dangerous and liable to enslave the imagination and force the spirit ("Milton and Figurative Interpretation of the Bible," *UTQ*, XXXI [1962], 397–415).

23. *The Muse's Method*, 190.

on occasion he even allowed his audience to mistake his meaning; yet he did not "omit to sow within them the seeds of a sufficient determining against the time that his promised spirit should bring all things to their memory."[24] He spoke often in monosyllables, rather than in continued discourses, leaving the work of drawing together his remarks to "the skilful and laborious gatherer."[25] He was oracular, speaking in parables and gnomic utterances, employing condensation, exaggeration, ambiguity, and paradox.[26] These devices are used to drive his followers from the letter to a spiritual apprehension of truth. Thus Christian liberty is not simply a precept of the New Testament; it is expressed in the very texture of the Gospel, in its "drift and scope."[27]

A similar strategy is found in Michael's education of Adam, and an awareness of its operation increases one's sense of dramatic conflict and psychological complexity in the last two books. Michael's aim is to bring Adam to a full and spiritual understanding of the Son's prophecy concerning the war between the seed of the woman and the serpent. He leads Adam toward this goal by a series of graded steps, each one but the last inconclusive, and each consequently capable of misinterpretation. Yet as he proceeds he does sow within Adam "the seeds of a sufficient determining," so that by the close of the story every part takes its place in a total design. He does not teach oracularly, of course (one might feel that his pleasure in lecturing is a little too obvious), but the events themselves, whether presented in vision or simply recounted, provide the material on which he and Adam must practise the art of gatherers. He employs ambiguity, sometimes appearing to mislead Adam deliberately in order to crystallize the false interpretations which must be rejected, and he uses the "powerful art of reclaiming" employed by Christ in which excess is administered against excess, bending the crooked wand the contrary way, "not that it should stand so bent, but that the overbending might reduce it to a straightness by its own reluctance."[28]

24. *Tetrachordon*, IV, 188.

25. *The Doctrine and Discipline of Divorce*, III, ii, 491.

26. See, for example, Milton's discussion in *Tetrachordon* of the "trope of indignation" (IV, 169), of proverbs (IV, 136), of contradiction (IV, 136 ff.), and in *Divorce* his comments on brevity (III, ii, 449 ff.).

27. *The Reason of Church Government*, III, i, 184. The attempt to formulate the roles of letter, reason, and spirit in the anti-episcopal tracts led Milton into severe difficulties. The passage here cited anticipates his later solution.

28. *Tetrachordon*, IV, 174.

A full exploration of this dialectic is beyond my present scope,[29] but a few examples may prove useful. The process, it should be noted, has two main movements. The initial movement is designed primarily to expose the spiritual bankruptcy of natural man, and its religious teaching seldom goes beyond that natural theology which, in a liberal view, is available to all men through the light of nature. The closing movement, which entails a change of method, is concerned with spiritual regeneration through grace, and its emphasis falls on the revealed truths of Christianity. Together the two movements form the main thesis and antithesis of the dialectic.

Michael's aim in the first movement can only be understood if we bear in mind Adam's spiritual state at the moment when he receives the angelic visitor. The clue lies in a speech in which the Father (with a rather too explicit account of the mechanics of grace) comments on the signs of repentance now visible in the human pair; Adam, says the Father (XI, 90–9),

> . . . sorrows now, repents, and prays contrite,
> My motions in him; longer than they move,
> His heart I know, how variable and vain
> Self-left. Lest therefore his now bolder hand
> Reach also of the Tree of Life, and eat,
> And live for ever, dream at least to live
> For ever, to remove him I decree,
> And send him from the Garden forth to Till
> The Ground whence he was taken, fitter soil.

In *De Doctrina Christiana* Milton distinguishes between natural and supernatural renovation, and defines the former as a state in which repentance and faith, present only in a natural mode, are "accompanied by a trust which is in like manner natural, and often vain."[30] Just such an unstable state has now been achieved by Adam and Eve, although the dry theological category is brought to life in the poem. Having forgiven each other and acknowledged their guilt, they reveal their change of heart in prayer. Yet the inconclusiveness of the change is apparent in the way that the new hope carries them to a wishful, partially vain, optimism. Adam, remembering the Son's

29. Milton's lasting interest in the subject is proved by *Paradise Regained*, where Christ, "the living oracle" (I, 460) employs the "trope of indignation" and most of the other devices described by Milton in the divorce tracts. Christ's attitude is of course more radical than Michael's, and he takes for his starting point those principles which Adam grasps only at the end of his education.

30. *De Doctrina Christiana*, XVI, 361.

promise, is now convinced that the offended Deity has become "placable and mild / Bending his ear" (XI, 151–2), and asserts that "the bitterness of death / Is past" (X, 158–9). He anticipates that God will now teach them to "pass commodiously this life, sustain'd / By him with many comforts" (X, 1083–4). Eve, too, assumes that the worst is over. "Here let us live though in fall'n state, content" (XI, 180). Although their determination arouses pity and even respect, their trust is clearly in vain because they have not confronted the way in which their act has changed reality. Moreover their attitude is terribly insecure, and, as so often in Milton's late poems, the impulse to presumption is closely related to the tendency to despair. Michael, when he first appears, prefaces his bad news with words of comfort in which he points to the hope of redemption. Adam and Eve are so shocked by the news of their forthcoming exile, however, that they momentarily abandon hope, ignoring the great theme which Michael has introduced (XI, 251 ff.).

Michael's first task, then, is to help Adam to achieve patience. With this end in view, he dwells on the loss of those "two fair gifts" with which Adam was endowed, Happiness and Immortality (XI, 58–60). Death is the chief theme of the vision of Abel, the subsequent allegorical vision of the Lazar House, and the picture of war in the heroic age. The treatment of the sons of Lamech and Seth centres on the theme of pleasure, and pleasure is again considered in the picture of the "luxury and riot" of the heroic age. Through these scenes, Michael manipulates Adam's mood in such a way that he fluctuates between extremes of emotion. Adam, for example, has shown a tendency to slight death and to assume too easily that its bitterness is past. In order to understand the spiritual sense in which this is true, he must first realize the fleshly sense in which it is false. His chief reaction to the story of Abel is one of sheer horror at the fact of death, and this horror is increased by the subsequent vision to the point where he trembles on the verge of rebellion or despair. Having led Adam to this brink, Michael now, in a series of steps, persuades him to adopt an attitude of stoic disdain toward death (XI, 553–4):

> Nor love thy Life, nor hate; but what thou liv'st
> Live well, how long or short permit to Heav'n.

Michael also wishes to correct Adam's tendency toward hedonism. Again he leads him to an extreme, this time an extreme of false joy.

First Adam is shown two examples of the "arts that polish life," music and metal work, and then a scene which combines revelry, music, and ceremony to form an image of sensual and civilized delight. "True opener of mine eyes, prime Angel blest," exclaims Adam, unaware of the ironic overtones of his remark, "Here Nature seems fulfilled in all her ends." Having elicited this crystallization of error, Michael delivers a swift and crushing condemnation of Epicureanism. Adam's earlier Robinson Crusoe-like hope that God would provide shelter and fire did not extend to such refinements as metal work, but the "arts that polish life" emerge very naturally out of the attempt "to pass commodiously this life," and Michael has now checked the tendency to see the significance of history in terms of the mastery of environment.

The next scenes are drawn from a later and more decadent historical epoch. The nomadic period gives way to a civilization of villages and walled cities. Adam, who can be deceived by pastoral delights, lacks the corruptions of sophistication, and he sees at once the falsity of martial heroism and the true courage of Enoch. Being less concerned with immediate problems, he has more thought for the future, and his reactions are now primarily those of a father for his children. As the history of the flood continues, the alternation of joy and despair brings home to Adam not only the ramifications of his own sin, but the surprising and bewildering ways in which Providence brings good out of evil.

After he has finished the story of the flood, Michael pauses to see if his pupil has any comments. Adam remains silent. The brief event (it was added only in 1674) mirrors perfectly both Adam's bafflement (the complexity of the problem is beyond any solution he can suggest), and his expectant sense that some further revelation is to be made. This sets the stage for the countermovement, in which Michael will reveal the matters of faith which make supernatural renovation possible. As he resumes the story, however, one has at first a strong sense of continuity. Once again we are shown a fairly blameless pastoral world, living according to the law of nature, but sacrificing cattle and crops to God, which is corrupted and destroyed by city dwellers. This new era, however, is not a new heroic age, but the age of empire, and Nimrod and his crew represent a form of evil far worse than anything encountered earlier. Everything about the building of the tower of Babel, from the bitumen of hell used as mortar to the punishment visited upon the builders, reminds one of Hell. The episode shows mankind becoming satanic, turning earth into both an empire and a bridgehead for the invasion of heaven. The chaos and violence of the heroic age could be met by a flood which, appropriately, suggests the "dark Illimitable Ocean" (II, 891–2) of Chaos; the perverted order of Babel—to be reasserted again and again in history—requires a different kind of answer.

It is to this answer that Michael now proceeds. As he describes the election of Abraham a new sense of direction and urgency enters the narrative. Adam, listening to the "gracious things" (XII, 271) that follow, quite understandably has little comment to offer. But his brief remarks serve to reveal the angel's strategy in leading him from flesh to spirit. His exclamations of joy indicate the growth of awareness; his questions, and his tendency to overleap the mark, suggest the difficulties of spiritual vision. "Now first I find / Mine eyes true op'ning" (XII, 274), he exclaims on hearing of the entry into Canaan. This time the words convey no irony, for he is right. Yet his conception of the blessing which Abraham will bring to all nations is clearly too literal, as he will find much later (XII, 447 f.), and like the younger Milton he obviously believes that the end of history is imminent. These misconceptions give piquancy to the question in which he asks why the Israelites, with whom God now dwells, have need of so many laws, for these argue "so many sins" (XII, 283).

The next resting point in the narrative follows the account of the Incarnation. Here (XII, 368–71) the angel seems to mislead Adam deliberately:

> A virgin is his Mother, but his Sire
> The Power of the most High; he shall ascend
> The Throne hereditary, and bound his Reign,
> With earth's wide bounds, his glory with the Heav'ns.

Adam has just been told that the Messiah was born "Barr'd of his right," and if he remembers the earlier lessons concerning ceremonies and types, he might be suspicious of taking Michael's words literally. But he has yet to grasp that the power and the kingdom are not of this world (XII, 383–5):

> Needs must the Serpent now his capital bruise
> Expect with mortal pain: say where and when
> Thir fight, what stroke shall bruise the Victor's heel.

Michael now has the perfect opportunity to emphasize the spiritual nature of the conflict (XII, 386–9):

> Dream not of thir fight,
> As of a Duel, or the local wounds
> Of head or heel: not therefore joins the Son
> Manhood to Godhead.

The next logical step is from the powers of Christ to the powers of the Christian, and Adam takes it when he asks how the followers of Christ will fare after the resurrection (XII, 482–4):

> who then shall guide
> His people, who defend? Will they not deal
> Worse with his followers than with him they dealt?

He is, of course, remembering the supernatural aid which was given to the Israelites by angelic powers and by the pillar of fire and the cloud. The penultimate truth of the dialectic is established when he learns that the Christian's armour is spiritual, his consolations inward, and that he worships at living temples (XII, 485 ff.). At the close, man and angel summarize, in antiphonal chorus, the lessons of history. Adam's view now touches and becomes the true vision of life. The last step in Michael's argument is that in which he urges Adam to transform knowledge into deeds and active virtues. The final realization of the spirit lies in the ideal of the "paradise within thee, happier far."

Two further observations on the form of Milton's history can now be made. The first concerns the shift from vision to narration which occurs at the opening of Book XII. Critical opinion has inclined to the view that the visions succeed as poetry because of their vein of realism, but that the narration fails because it relies too much on abstractions. Yet the technique in each of the last two books is remarkably appropriate to its subject. Book XI, which centres on the spiritual bankruptcy of natural man, presents an episodic story. Events are relatively self-contained, and continuity is achieved simply by the fact that each new phase of history is worse than the last. The method of presentation is visual, emblematic, and rather static: Abel and Cain provide an introductory dumb show; the heroic age is presented in a series of pictures which have been likened by A. S. P. Woodhouse to the panels of Achilles' shield;[31] the story of Noah, while a more sustained drama, is told in straightforward chronological order and tends to resolve itself into a sequence of pictures. Michael's relation of events in Book XII appears at first to continue in the spirit of the visions. The story of the tower of Babel is told in a way which preserves the chief features of the earlier mode of presentation. But this initial continuity only emphasizes the deliberateness with which Michael changes his narrative method as he turns in the next episode from nature to grace, from man's inability to save himself to God's plan for man's redemption. A new sense of urgency is felt at once. This story, we realize, has continuity and form: a beginning, middle, and end. Although the characters change, they are all subordinate to an emergent design and linked by typology to the real hero of the story. In the background, of course, the endless ramifications of the fall continue. The cycle leading from pastoral simplicity to sophisticated decadence repeats itself again and again. But this panorama of futility serves only to throw into sharper relief the process which gradually brings about the accomplishment of God's will.

Michael's manipulation of time in this second half of the history is partly responsible for the new and dynamic sense of direction. The basic pattern is one in which we are first shown a moment of triumph, and then led back in time to a survey of the trials which preceded it. Thus, for example, the story of the Jews' escape through the Red Sea begins with a summary of the destruction of Pharoah and his army:

> the Sea
> Swallows him with his Host, but them lets pass
> As on dry land between two crystal walls
> Aw'd by the rod of Moses so to stand
> Divided. . . . (XII, 195–9)

Michael lets himself be carried back by this rhetorical switch to an account of the "obdurate" King's pursuit; he then gradually returns to the figure of Moses who

> once more his potent Rod extends
> Over the Sea; the Sea his Rod obeys;
> On thir imbattl'd ranks the Waves return
> And overwhelm thir War. (XII, 211–14)

31. "Pattern in *Paradise Lost*," *UTQ*, XXII (1953), 125–7. Woodhouse draws attention both to the general likeness of the vision to the panels of Achilles' shield, and to the specific parallel between *PL*, XI, 580–673 and *Iliad*, XVIII, 490–535.

We have completed a loop in time. The whole passage, however, is contained within a figure of similar design. This opens when Michael briefly describes how Moses and Aaron will lead the Israelites "With glory and spoil back to thir promis'd land" (XII, 172). Having designated the outcome of the escape from Egypt, he proceeds to recount the event in detail, reaching the actual entry into Canaan close to one hundred lines later.

This device of placing the end before the beginning is employed on a number of occasions, but the most striking examples are those in which Michael leaps to the end of time and describes the purging of all things by fire and the creation of new heaven and earth. The first two anticipations are connected to events which have traditionally been seen as of eschatological import, the flood, and the entry into the promised land; the next two follow the histories of the Incarnation and the Crucifixion; the final account concludes the narrative. The effect of such revolutions in time is to suggest that when history is seen from the viewpoint of eternity, it is no longer linear. The ends to be brought about by Providence exist from the beginning. Thus the second movement of the history has a sense of time quite foreign to the first movement. Addison was off the mark when he suggested that the shift from vision to narration is "as if an History-Painter should put in Colours one Half of his Subject, and write down the remaining part of it."[32] The contrapuntal movement of time in the narration suggests an analogy to music rather than to painting.

What, finally, can be replied to the common criticism that the history of the world is "curiously without proportion"?[33] The first period of the world receives almost as much space as the remaining six. The history of the Jews from the election of Abraham to the entry into Canaan is shorter than the story of the flood, and Christ's life and death makes a still briefer narrative. Is there any significance to this pattern, or is Milton, like an inexperienced student at a history examination, simply running out of time?

The answer is that the proportions of the story reveal Milton's concern with decorum. Events are seen through the eyes of Adam, and this involves a reversal of normal perspective. Events farthest from

32. *The Spectator*, no. 369.

33. D. C. Allen, "The Legend of Noah," in *Illinois Studies in Language and Literature*, XXXIII (1949), 154.

us are those closest to Adam: they stand in the foreground of his vision, and are correspondingly large. Events which come late in time, even though of great magnitude, are foreshortened; the diminished scale in which the life of Christ is presented testifies to the span of time over which it is seen by Adam, a span so great that it is reduced to iconographic simplicity. The whole design might be compared to that of a Baroque staircase in which various illusionistic devices are employed to increase the sense of distance. This effect of perspective contributes subtly to the "autumnal atmosphere" which F. T. Prince sees as a final artistic triumph.

The biblical epics of the seventeenth century cast little light on the sacred history with which Milton closes *Paradise Lost.* He did not, like Drayton, feel torn between art and truth. To find illuminating analogues we must turn to the metaphysical poets. Herbert, despite a different temper of imagination, provides particularly useful parallels. He, too, makes biblical subject-matter serve the principle of progression from flesh to spirit. The very structure of his poetry reveals his interest in that dialectic which leads, by sudden peripeteia, from law to gospel, outward nature to inward grace, fear to love. With Anglican emphasis, and within the scope of short lyrics, he is concerned with the same theme which Milton presents in epic dimensions and from a Puritan point of view.

Structural and Doctrinal Pattern in Milton's Later Poems[1]

ARTHUR E. BARKER

I

THE DOCTRINE OF CHRISTIAN LIBERTY which Professor Woodhouse has shown to be of such crucial significance in Milton's prose, as in radical Puritan revolutionary theory,[2] serves as a focus for Milton's developing preoccupations and might provide interpreters with a further means of clarifying the cruxes of his later poems. Though the

1. This essay forms part of a study, too long to be published in this volume, in which the application of the doctrine of Christian liberty to Milton's later poems is preceded by an extensive interpretation of the public prose and of the implications of the revisions to *De Doctrina Christiana* in their bearing on my central argument, here replaced (as section I) by a short summary.

2. "Puritanism and Liberty," *UTQ*, IV (1934–5), 395–404; "Milton, Puritanism and Liberty, *UTQ*, IV (1934–5), 483–513, especially 487, note 7; "Puritanism and Democracy," *Canadian Journal of Economics and Political Science*, IV (1938), 1–21; *Puritanism and Liberty* (London, 1938); review of Haller, *Rise of Puritanism*, *American Historical Review*, XLV (1945), 123–5; "Background for Milton," *UTQ*, X (1940–1), 499–505; "Seventeenth-Century Radicals," *UTQ*, XV (1945–6), 98–101; "Religion and Some Foundations of English Democracy," *PhR*, LXI (1952), 503–31; *Milton the Poet* (Toronto, 1955), 12.

Subsequent references to these studies are by title and page. Where no author is indicated for other items, the author is Professor Woodhouse, save for bracketed references for Milton in the text, to volume and page of *Works* (Columbia), unless otherwise indicated in notes. The omission of acknowledgments of debts to other authorities (which students will easily recognize as requiring throughout heavy annotation) may be forgiven and postponed to another occasion, in favour of an effort to acknowledge, to such extent as is at least indicatively possible, the debts demanding appropriate recognition on this occasion, among which, as some readers will be aware and others will readily perceive, must be counted the accumulation of unidentifiable debts of many years of close relation—going back indeed to undergraduate inability to attempt an answer to the question, on an examination set by Professor Woodhouse in 1932, as to whether Milton should be thought a Puritan or a Christian rationalist.

phrase does not occur in the poems, and though scholarship rightly associates the doctrine chiefly with the radical Miltonic assertions of "private or domestic liberty" and liberty of conscience, its revolutionary Miltonic development, with its associated complex of doctrines, and the centrality of these for both books of *De Doctrina Christiana*, may suggest the possibility of its having contributed significantly to the structure of the later poems and the terms out of which their representation of experience develops its meaning. The manuscript of *De Doctrina* illustrates Milton's continuing preoccupation with these doctrines and the cruxes presented in their terms by the political and later prose; and his reconsiderations pass directly into the later poems and may be found to have a relation to many of the interpretative cruxes—from "heroism" through irony and the Miltonic association of biblical figurality with neo-classical form—with which criticism is currently much concerned.

The prose experience very nearly induced Milton to believe that human history and experience are merely purgative; but the prose itself makes sufficiently clear the convictions preventing him from resting in this conclusion and from accepting an ultimate principle of segregation.[3] Its preoccupation is much less with liberty than with the responsibility that makes liberty, Christian and natural, possible, and differentiates it from licence.[4] Whereas his revolutionary contemporaries tend to turn to transcendent absolutes, theological or naturalistic, his concern is increasingly with the individual religious experience—on which the revolutionary dynamic originally depended.[5] For him the revolution is a way of keeping open and opening further the possibility of the knowledge of true liberty through a willing response to what he supposed the ways of God, as they operate for men, in time and through nature, to clarify its dependence on constant truths. Such truths depend for him on a divine law, inherent in the nature of things natural and human, however distorted and imperfect; all historical dispensations, even in their failures and perhaps then most, progressively reveal this law. The Gospel's clarification of

3. Cf. "Puritanism and Democracy," 9–10, 12; "Milton, Puritanism and Liberty," 487–94, 511–12; review of Wolfe, *Milton in the Puritan Revolution*, *JEGP*, XLI (1942), 104.

4. "Milton, Puritanism and Liberty," 499–500.

5. Cf. *Puritanism and Liberty*, [56]; "Milton, Puritanism and Liberty," 497–500; review of Haller, *Rise of Puritanism*, 124–5; *Milton the Poet*, 24.

this law and abrogation of its partial and incomplete institutional manifestations is the basis of Christian liberty,[6] which must manifest itself in truly human actions and relations. However parodied in the perverse responses of his opponents, it remains a "law of sociable parts united in one body" implied by Milton's sociable prelapsarian Spirit and the spirit he implies for human relations even in the postlapsarian state. Revolutionary frustration induced Milton to clarify his belief that discriminating human values are matters at once of natural and spiritual relation, since even degenerate history is contained within the order of nature as the order of nature is contained within the order of grace. He may have learned this experiential lesson too late to allow him to readjust his views and to return to some notable degree of participation in the frustrating life of institutions; but this theme is the chief burden of the revised manuscript of *De Doctrina* and of the humane mimesis developed during what was allowed him of retirement during his sixties.

The poetic significance of Milton's developing notions about the process of regeneration on which Christian liberty depends for him is not obscured but underlined by our interest in the historical (or modern) bearing of his revolutionary arguments and our interest in his handling of doctrines of less obviously immediate experiential significance which, however, ultimately serve only as buttresses for orientations of this focal problem. Most of what he wrote, consciously or unconsciously, ironically or naïvely, points to the matter, so that, as Professor Woodhouse has said,[7] he seems always to be making his way, through whatever lapses, deluges, or thickets, towards the later poems. The extant revisions and additions made in the manuscript of *De Doctrina* all focus attention on his preoccupation with redemption and the process of regeneration and the Christian liberty resulting from the process; the most obvious clusters of revisions occur in the chapters on Christ's mediatorial office, on man's "natural renovation" and "calling," on his "supernatural renovation" and "regeneration" and "being planted in Christ," on the Covenant of Grace, including Law and Gospel, on Christian liberty. "Natural" renovation is the process through which God invites all men to a knowledge of true propitiation

6. Cf. "Puritanism and Liberty," 401; "Milton, Puritanism and Liberty," 488.
7. "Milton and his Readers," *UTQ*, XVIII (1948–9), 204; *Milton the Poet*, 13; "The Argument of *Paradise Lost*," *UTQ*, XVI (1946–7), 435.

and worship, a calling which includes such as have never heard of Christ, since they are called through what they can know of God, if they will, simply from his creation, though their responsive faith in God is made possible by the redeeming Christ they know not (XV, 344, 346–8, 403–5). "Regeneration" is the effect of the "supernatural renovation" which follows a willing and believing response to calling with the repentance that this must induce; it extends the process of natural renovation which cannot be extended without it. What supernatural renovation restores, in men who exercise their responsibility, their naturally renovated and their new powers thus to obtain salvation, is the divine image. Milton was never moved to revise his belief that the unwritten Law of God is that "law of nature" given to the first man, of which remnants and a kind of reflection remain in all men's hearts, and which in the regenerate is day by day being renovated in the direction of its primitive (or prelapsarian) perfection. But his continuing concern for the Christian liberty related to it is evidenced by revisions which stress the abrogation of the whole Mosaic Law by the Gospel to emphasize the law in the renovated heart as the basis of true liberty, and this in turn depends upon what Milton thinks the demonstrable continuity of a providence which makes possible similar responsibilities and opportunities under every dispensation, not only under the prelapsarian and Christian but under all dispensations (with their appropriate differences) in between. What God consistently gives his responsive creatures is an opportunity to respond to his providential processes—and to all creatures his own good time. Towards this the most significant revisions of *De Doctrina* are making their way.

II

Milton's later poems elaborate and represent his notions about the process of regeneration by filling in, mimetically, what *De Doctrina* leaves confused, its operation even under pre-Christian dispensations. Whatever the poems may do with the treatise's heresies about the Son, Creation, and so on,[8] the function of these remains—what it was in

8. Nothing in Milton is, in the end, "indifferent" or "peripheral" to his main theme; but there are limits to such percipience and comprehension as ordinary readers can muster in response, and the relations of his "major" heresies to his theme demand special knowledge. See "Notes on Milton's Views on the Creation: The Initial Phase," *PQ*, XXVIII (1949), where what is perhaps of most immediate

the treatise—the buttressing of the conviction that God's accommodating ways to men, as they are illuminated in Scripture and however wrathfully left-handed they may seem to the unresponsive, are manifested in the demanding and sustaining process of responsive individual natural and supernatural experience as it develops in time. The poems use, without any substantial change whatever and indeed in literally prolonging echoes, all the doctrines to which the manuscript revisions call attention. In general they use the doctrines focusing on the incompleteness of earlier dispensations and the consequent appearance of discontinuity between successive dispensations to provide the poems with their structural patterns and circumstantial details; but the development of the mimetic action depends on the implications of the doctrines and revisions concerned with response to the developing continuity of God's ways through all dispensations. "Christian liberty" nowhere appears in the later poems, not simply because the exhaustion of frustrated controversy has wearied Milton with the spectrum of the seventeenth century's confused and futile fragmentation of it, but because decorum and theology alike render it inappropriate in the representation of experience under pre-Christian dispensations. Yet "Christian liberty" is what the poems are about. Their aim indeed is to re-focus the fragmented bands of the spectrum in a unified ray, illuminating any individual's experience, by inducing seventeenth-century Christian readers to realize the point of God's continuous ways by mimetic participation in the responses or failures of response of other men (or indeed of angels, since all creatures are involved) to their process, as it manifested itself in the circumstantially contrasting but essentially and developingly related conditions of other dispensations, and as these point towards the

relevance to the point in hand would seem to be, 227–8, the "neutral" yet "potential" quality of the first, far-from-nought matter (cf. "Pattern in *Paradise Lost*," *UTQ*, XXII [1952–3], 124)—though through the Satanic eye it seems simply disordered rather than "unordered," and especially Milton's insistence on the "voluntary" (if also rational) creative act, 213–14, on the "dregs" to be purged away and the problem of evil, 229–30, and on "potentiality," 223–4, 234. See the recent articles by W. B. Hunter, especially *HTR*, LII (1959), 9–35, on the Son, especially on the theories of "subordinationism" and the Son's participation in the Father's will and of "predominance" and the union of the two wills in Christ (with implications for both the married relation and the church inviting the expectation of significant elaboration). Such discernible revisions in the manuscript as bear on these matters would seem to relate them to the process of renovation. Here I have to record my debt to the work in progress of my research assistants, Mr. Lindsay A. Mann and Miss Mary Elizabeth Merril, of Champaign-Urbana.

clarifications of responsibility available to Christians because they all involve covenants progressively, though adequately enough for what their times demand, implying the New Covenant (as it implies its own ultimate fulfilment).

Since God's ways to men (or angels) are continuously constant but developing, the essentials of the response demanded remain constant but essentially imply their continuous development, from one dispensation to another, from one segment of individual experience to another. On the one hand is the universal process of God's ways; on the other the process of individual experience which fulfils itself in the degree to which it corresponds with God's ways as they manifest themselves in successive dispensations. Hence the terms of the poems are the developing structure of universal history and the individual's response to experience. Though at first sight recent English history seems to be frustratedly excluded, it is of course not so. The licenser was rightly troubled by his perception at least of the tail of the comet that fills kings with fear when they hear the Gospel speaking much of liberty. The echoes of the prose in the diatribes against tyrants, hirelings, women, by Samson's chorus, the young Christ, Michael—who is of course very precisely summarizing for his immediate purposes the conclusions of the frustrated political prose and especially the tracts of 1659 on conscience— established a relation between the prose and the poems and set the pattern of recent irresponsible history very firmly, by something more than implication, in its place in the apparently universal pattern of the degenerate beat of tyrannical and anarchical history. But the rhythm which contains this beat is, for Milton, really universal; and this is chiefly recognizable, in the clear light of the comet's body, through the corresponding rhythm of responsive individual experience, thrown into relief by irresponsible contrast. Hence the focus of the poems is on the individual (though by no means in isolation); and their systematic theology and transcendent vision are used in the representation of the psychology of what Milton thinks true religious experience under any dispensation—a subject experience had evidently taught him, with others in his period, to think Protestantism very much needed to include in its curriculum since its tendency, however initially humble or despairing, to ascribe all responsibility to God's secret will and pleasure had had such confusing consequences. As the Christian dispensation fulfils, though by discontinuous continuity, earlier dispensations, so Christian liberty depends on a response which fulfils, and not simply by contrast, the responses demanded by earlier dispensations. The response the mimesis invites from its seventeenth-century reader is not simply an analogous response. Rightly or wrongly, Milton does not segregate his theory of poetry and its function from his theory of the process of regeneration or his view of religious experience or irreligious experience. As his prose parallels and prefatory comments indicate, Aristotelean Italianate words like "katharsis" or "decorum" always imply for him their meaning in the context of the regenerative process as his northern mind understands it, since poetry is an imitation of this accommodatingly purgative and illuminating art of God. Indeed, the "literal" is opposed to the "literary" and the "poetic" and the recognition of this, or failure to recognize it, is part of the process of experience represented by the mimesis. In the process of the response it invites, image and meaning become inseparable, as do genre and meaning,[9] for he is not using pagan images or classical genre to convey a simply contrasting Christian theme: as he thinks the classical genres, when they were well used, the product of a developing response to the law of nature to which a supernatural dimension is added by the corresponding prophetic and poetical parts of Scripture, so he thinks the Christian theme fulfils what was truly responsive in the classical. Since, as *De Doctrina* says (XV, 199), all acts are good and evil is only obliquity and anomaly in terms of the right direction it thus illuminates, the obliquities and anomalies of actions under other dispensations only serve to illustrate the direction to be more clearly revealed by the Gospel, by which, according to *recta ratio*, Christians are required to bring into action the natural and supernatural gifts of the Spirit, pregnantly working in all dispensations.

Thus Milton's late (and somewhat ambiguously espoused) companion pieces both depend, for their doctrinal significance, their circumstantial decorum, their sustaining structure and development, not simply on the everywhere implied contrast and relation between

9. "Pattern in *Paradise Lost*," *UTQ*, XXII (1952–3), 109, 114; "Tragic Effect in *Samson Agonistes*," *UTQ*, XXVIII (1958–9), 205; "Some Reflections on How to Read Milton," *SCN*, XVI (1958), 8–9.

Christian liberty's Gospel and the Old Dispensation but on the contrast and relation between the Law and the Prophets.[10] Samson's experience is so far from having no middle that it is in effect all middle, as Judges, following after Law, in the Chronicles of time from giants onward, must imply the poetical and prophetic to follow; and the process of his response to experience thus leads him from the childhood of law and its despairing uncertainty, resulting from apparent failure, to a recognition of what the Law underlines through failure: the real significance of the original call to the use of natural powers in merely national and physical heroism. It is not simply Samson's suicidal fulfilment of himself in the end as vista-vision national folk-hero that gives the mimesis its significance but what this doubly retributive fulfilment after failure implies. This implication is underlined by Samson's special Nazarite concern for the requirements of the Law, which itself is underlined by the Old Testament preoccupations and difficulties of the chorus of Ebrewes. The point for everybody is that his failure and despair, as impinged on by the incidents of the poem, lead him to recognize God's constantly renovating calling and to respond in a way which further contradicts and undermines the dictates of the Law yet indicates its fulfilment and the significance of his earlier "national" callings and failures. Whether or not Milton had or had not any higher-critical awareness of the stratifications in the version of the story in Judges, of its naturalistic Paul-Bunyanesque origins, its elaboration in terms of God's Law for and covenant with his chosen people in whatever Dead-Sea scrolls, and its prophetic overtones, he was certainly aware that the aim of conflicting patristic and later commentary was to get out of the story the full implications of what the author of the Epistle to the Hebrews saw in it—and in comparable illegal actions by other Old Testament heroes, such as a

10. The question of the dating of the composition of *Samson* must here be ignored, as chiefly, in the absence of documentation, a question of "internal evidence" and hence "interpretation": Woodhouse, "Historical Criticism," *PMLA*, LXVI (1951), 1063; "Samson Agonistes and Milton's Experience," *Transactions of the Royal Society of Canada*, Series III, vol. XLIII (1949), Sec. 2, 157–60; *Milton the Poet*, 14. It must suffice to express the impression that, whenever the poem was *begun*, it was "finished" (no doubt like the "undergraduate" and "graduate" academic exercises and many other of Milton's writings) just before it was sent (late) to the printer—and indeed perhaps (as in other cases) just before the presses stopped printing. Doctrinal and emotional differences between the companion pieces remain a matter of free opinion; but at least *PR*, 639 and *SA*, 1733 and their contexts are related in the right order.

favourite of the prose, David and the shew-bread. Milton's manipulation of the story in terms of the percipient Greek tragic genre[11] (or more percipient Revelation) organizes it to induce the katharsis and the illumination involved in such actions in an audience which rightly sees Samson as a Hebraic Hercules but whose humanism is inclined to read him back down below the level of insight attained even by Greek tragedy or nationalism. The best gloss we have on this manipulation and on Milton's prefatory expressions of opinion about the use and implication of Greek tragic convention (and its limitations), may be found in *De Doctrina's* chapters on calling and renovation, repentance and faith, and their sustaining extension in supernatural renovation towards Christian liberty. These suggest, especially as to Law and Gospel, that the strictly preserved Greek and, what is more important, Hebraic decorum of the piece—underlined by the chorus which is, if nothing else, in every way decorous—is designed to focus on the progressively realized fact that it is not Samson's resistance to the repetition of temptations alone (triple or otherwise)[12] that is of primary importance but what makes this negative resistance possible, his progressive response to the renewed calling of the renovation of his natural powers and thence his awareness of new faculties that, as Hebraic Hercules, he stupidly never dreamed he potentially had—until he recognizes that his real strength was never in his hair but in the living God and that all his actions have been perverse and inadequate parodies of the significance of his calling, as his sacrifice of his hair and natural power to love of Dalila was a parody of another kind of sacrifice, which he might, even in domestic relations with an unbeliever, have better imitated. Hence his being led to something extraordinary under the Law, like the other figures cited by Hebrews and *De Doctrina*.

Each of Samson's temptations is itself a parody related to the Law and containing distorted elements of the truth of what is really demanded under the Law. They reminiscentially underline, ironically,

11. "Tragic Effect in *Samson Agonistes*," *UTQ*, XXVIII (1958–9), 205.

12. Review of Krouse, *Milton's Samson*, *MLN*, LXVI (1951), 118, for the traditional view that the moral centre of interest, in Samson's sin and repentance, is incompatible with the prophetic emphasis on him as a "type" of Christ; "Samson Agonistes and Milton's Experience," *Transactions of the Royal Society of Canada*, Series III, vol. XLIII (1949), Sec. 2, 162–72, for *Samson* as "a study in regeneration," and "Tragic Effect in *Samson Agonistes*," *UTQ*, XXVIII (1958–9), 206–7, 213, on freedom of will and God's providence.

the increasingly parodic quality of Samson's own earlier acts, chiefly motivated by the impercipient preoccupation with his function as national hero and his own natural strength which made him his own idol. Hence Manoa's well-intentioned but senile offer of juvenile ransom, the braggart parody of Harapha's challenge, and even more centrally Dalila's apologetic parody of deeds answerable to a loyalty higher than the merely patriotic. The process of Samson's fumbling but repentant response to the implications of these parodies—which causes the choral commentators so much uneasiness—marks the stages in the renovating movement out of despair and beyond the Law. The process is marked by, among other things, the changes in Samson's tone of voice which become most complex at the centre, in response to Dalila, blending other notes with indignation in a way perplexing to both severity and sentiment. The double-scened "act" that follows indicates that the righteous indignation that must greet Harapha is not inconsistent with the quite uncharacteristic gentleness—though there was the boy—of the effort to reassure the beaten chorus of the ultimate rightness, despite the apparent repetition of obliquity, of the culminating action to which he is being called.

Such reassurance is not easy to induce or come by, for uneasy poetical messengers and their audiences. It perhaps can only be achieved, each for himself after what support others have intentionally or unintentionally provided, in such moments as that in which, as we hear, Samson stands alone and waiting, with head bowed and arms outstretched between two stony pillars. One of the striking (and evidently self-restrained) effects of the later poems is that they move towards such moments of silence, in which the reader is left to decide, in terms of his response to the controlled mimetic movement, what is happening and is meant. Manoa and the Hebrew chorus do not quite tell us the meaning, but only that the moment is to be remembered and the meaning of its new aquist sought after the event.

If the movement and the moment may be glossed in terms of *De Doctrina*'s renovation towards Christian liberty, this does not mean that Samson possessed "Christian liberty," or that he is, without important distinctions and reservations, a "type" of Christ or even of the Christian. He cannot possess Christian liberty, by definition, because he is acting under the as-yet-unabrogated dispensation of the Law, the demands of whose decorum must be preserved at whatever sacrifice, since they may provide a fulcrum for some though a stumbling stone to others. As a revision in the manuscript of *De Doctrina* observes, under the Law those who trusted in God were justified by faith "but not without the works of the Law" (XVI, 150). So Manoa; if with limited and even neo-classical percipience. But the implication of the spirit in which in his time Samson fulfils himself and the Law requires further comment. A type is significant both for its contrast with and its likeness to what it types, by being itself according to the decorum of the circumstances of its dispensation in time and an indication of what the process of time moves towards. As to human individuals or types, despite frustration, Milton never lost his conviction that the fulfilment of the particular is the end of the experiential process, not its being swallowed up in some vaguely indefinable over-soul of meaning. In his way and time, Samson is the type of what the Christian may be the type of in his way and time, fulfilling the letter of the type by bringing into appropriate action the gifts of the Spirit. Even the typical destruction of temples or rebuilding of them appropriate to one dispensation may prove inappropriate to another; but the spirit of the type continues to fulfil itself, appropriately to God's secular ways, in time. Hence the chorus: with its culminating implications at least of the Prophets, perhaps even of the Epistle to the Hebrews.

Paradise Regained similarly, with differences, rests on the contrast and relation between the Law and the Prophets and the abrogation and fulfilment of the Old Dispensation by the New, its movement depending on the recognition by Milton's young Jew in the temporary isolation of the empty wilderness his people have so often passed through, that history (including the history of his separated people) has reached the time in which the letter of the Law is to be abrogated and the prophetic spirit begins to be clearly fulfilled through his fulfilment now in time of the redemptive act undertaken for all men, even transgressors, by the Son the Christ incarnates. The Satanic temptations, despite their balanced and elaborated drama and splendour, are hardly even of negative significance and are of somewhat less significance, save by their obliquity and anomaly, than those presented to Samson by insufficiently percipient or perverse humans. They are always on the point of futile irrelevance and deserve something less than the detached inattention or glancing attention the young Jew politely but bluntly affords them, to the offence of those who would sentimentalize over and stand upon ceremony with irrecoverable and subhuman evil, determined to frustrate its own possibility of redemption. Satan's increasingly frustrated response to the situation does of course illustrate *De Doctrina*'s comments on the wilfully unregenerate, for he has no sense of present continuity, in history, time, his own experience, and his concern is perhaps less with what the young Jew is and is in process of recognizing[13] than in obscuring the contrast between what he himself was and is, and why. Hence the temptations he offers do not have the significance they might have if they simply reduced the Messianic function to the level of the Apocrypha, or the kind of temporal salvation promised by the Law, or the natural values of the pagans. Satan is more confused than the text of *De Doctrina* or even the angriest prose ever was as to the relations between these. He cannot even understand the letter of the Law; he does not even know with the wisest of the pagans that he knows not; and he is beneath the level of unresponsive perversity under the law of nature, for he is under its self-damned angelic equivalent and repetitiously distorts, in fictitious shows, what he hears in the young Jew's observations. Yet he is the instrument of providence: his anomaly, in its very meaningless tendency to nonentity, indicates in what terms acts are always good. What the young Christ hears, across the Satanic obliquity, is the calling in his waiting heart as it answers the approving voice he attends to. Hence, often with not unamused irony, he literally repudiates and rejects nothing. He accepts the calling to fulfil in himself all that has gone before in time and all of which the Satanic temptations are confusedly parodic. Christ does not much attend to the parody. If other men can learn of good only through parodic evil, he has the unique human power to learn good from good. He attends to what is parodically confused by Satan, the meaning of the historical, legal, and prophetic signs in which he has been educated, though by teachers less able than he to interpret them fully and whom—as is, thanks be, often the case with students—he can teach. If many readers, intent on learning the common human lesson in the common way, think the poem undramatic, involving no crisis or crux for this reason, it may yet be seen as a mimetic process, at least point-

13. *Milton the Poet*, 27; "Theme and Pattern in *Paradise Regained*," *UTQ*, XXV (1955–6), 173–4.

ing to a painful and frustrating crux. The datum the young Jew is responsively in process of clarifying and extending for himself points directly to this crux. He knows it in historical terms through its obscure shadow in the Law and the Prophets; there is never any doubt that he will clarify its meaning, and the poem certainly goes about to induce a false sense of dramatic crisis through the false crises of the temptations. The dramatic crux is not in the poem: it is implied by it, in what is pointed to by the shadow and what will be pointed to by the shadow of the young Jew as he stands on the pinnacle of the old temple. Despite his knowing good by good, his responsive submission of will, and his acceptance of pain, he must know human despair (beyond even Job's[14]) and meet it in himself to offset it, in God's time.

Thus the structure of the poem does not depend on the apparently balanced and centrally elaborated sequence of hierarchical but circularly staggering temptations, though of course their pattern throws its pattern into relief by conflicting with the marking of the divisions of its progressive movement by the four books—if only because the first and the last trials are really the same, waiting obediently on God and true self-dependence having proved to be the same thing. Yet the pattern of the temptations is not significantly oblique and anomalous simply in terms of the past. Even a lost archangel is confusedly concerned about the future. Unconsciously—and hence the order chosen—Satan is acting as the instrument of Christ's calling by the parodic Lenten foreshadowing in his temptations of the events and teachings of ministry to which the young Jew is called through all shadows, by the illumination of signs through word and deed, through the last banquet and the realities of the storm in the heart in the garden. In a sense, indeed, the temptations parody the cycle of experience of the Christian year. Yet the parody is confused, and would remain so without the consistent datum developed by the young Christ's progressive recognitions in the four books. What illuminates the significance of the ministry is his developing response to the call as it comes to him from his meditation on the recorded experience of his own people; and each of the poem's four books will be found to centre on and conclude with some significant aspect of the process of natural and supernatural renovation as *De Doctrina* attempts to define these.

14. "Theme and Pattern in Paradise Regained," *UTQ*, XXV (1955–6), 168.

Mary and the disciples, obscurely faithful and however uncertainly responsive in their degree to experience, are waiting to have the principles of *De Doctrina* illustrated for them in the actions of the ministry. Whatever the later Milton thought of the Christian year, thirty-five of the thirty-nine Articles, or the liturgy of the English prayer-book, his young Christ is in process of becoming, in the terms of the collect for the second Sunday after Easter, both a sacrifice for sin and also an ensample of godly life. The ministry that leads to the sacrifice providing redemption must also provide an existential example, the more dramatic for not being needed by the actor, of the response required for the process of regeneration. Our difficulties with this (despite or because of *De Doctrina*) have perhaps really very little to do with Milton's anti-trinitarianism or his decisive stand on the inseparability of the two natures in Christ and on his being at every point the subject of temptation and sacrifice in both. These massively heretical flying buttresses may certainly be found lending their support (with many orthodox pillars) somewhere below the Gothic temple's spire that, in the poem, is about to be topped off with its living sign. But, despite the revisions, *De Doctrina* will only partially make clear their relevance to the main point. Though it is on its way in that direction, it does not quite make clear that the process of regeneration involves an imitation of the process of redemption that makes it possible. Regeneration does not necessarily follow from redemption; yet they are inseparable. This significance of the inward oracle in deeds answerable depends on such further understanding as the poem represents of the implications of "All our Law and Story, strew'd with Hymns." Christ's reflective observations are in effect exegetical comments on the Scriptures he is meditating on; hence they are always rather more than one jump ahead of the Satanic temptations. But even the final recognition, after the echoing of yet another Old Testament situation and phrase, comes again in a moment of silence, broken by the summary by the angelic chorus of the clarification to come, from the Gospels through to Revelation, which the young Christ confirmingly hears before he returns to his mother's home to fulfil every jot and tittle before returning to his father's.

What is remarkable about the poem is its having with such serene decorum developed its pointed mimetic movement from a situation which might very well seem obviously predetermined, in order to demonstrate that in all human activity in time, even throughout the career of the young Jew who will leave the Spirit in the hearts of his disciples, growth and increase in stature, wisdom, spirit, in the sight of God and men, requires a willing participation based on a sensitive doctrinal understanding of God's ways in the past that will support a confidently prophetic trust in the future.

III

Though the action of *Paradise Lost* has nothing directly to do with Law and Gospel (save in its last book, and then only by prophecy since the dispensation under which Adam lives will end with the many-coloured post-diluvian covenant), the poem reflects their pattern of continuity and discontinuity, elaborating a correspondence suggested but left undeveloped and unclarified in the treatise, in terms of prelapsarian and postlapsarian and the law of nature in its double function. The prelapsarian state is related to the state of Christian liberty to which Christians are called, though now through woe, under the Gospel, and in which the prelapsarian law of nature is day by day being renewed in its primitive brightness. The unresponsive postlapsarian state is that in which the law of nature operates for Adam as for all unregenerate Gentiles, with the same force as the Law has only for Jews. The responsive postlapsarian state under fallen Adam's dispensation is that in which the law of nature also operates renovatingly in a way comparable, however imperfectly, to its original operation but with additions extending its prelapsarian operation. If Michael's summary prophecy of Law and Gospel seems a little thin to us, especially after the rather thin vision of what will characterize Adam's unparadised dispensation, and if the two later poems seem to some efforts to fill the gap more adequately, that is perhaps the consequence not simply of the intractibility of Milton's material, or of a falling off from inspiration, or of the poem's somehow not having quite adequately embodied or extended the developing conclusions of *De Doctrina*, but of our not having recognized that its conclusion is the meaning whence the poem was derived and that this is implied in every incident and passage and in every stage in Adam's continually developing experience. It was no doubt a perilous task to attempt, whether in prose or rhyme, to represent the meaning of the whole of Scripture and human experience (including the unmentioned but oft-implied failure of the English people) by folding it back into the stratified opening chapters of Genesis to demonstrate its continuity; but after all nothing succeeds like failure well met, even *in medias res*.

At least the recognition that Adam's experience is everywhere mimetically illustrating, by parallel, obliquity, or directly, *De Doctrina*'s process of re-novation and re-generation might save one from some pitfalls; and, so saving, might make clearer the light reflected, fierce as a comet, by the brandisht sword. To begin with, it might suggest how the emphatic insistence on the present unavoidableness of all our woe, the fruit of disobedience, prepares for the expanding insistence that our time of woe is also the time of the growth and development of the redeeming seed, by being turned towards the surprising "Sing" through the "till" which has not only the syntactical position but more than the complex of meanings associated with the Virgilian *dum*, including the meaning sometimes implied by Middle English "till" in the seventeenth century—"during the time in which" or "while." To end with, it might disabuse us of some notions about "the fortunate fall" which—however they may be true in fact and so may be employed to save interpreters much critical woe and might have saved Milton much had he read experience so—are inconsistent with the distinction between "redemption" and "regeneration." Michael's way of dealing with Adam's expression of the notion is no doubt best; but, despite him, the notion is cheerfully echoed by many of the best interpreters of our time, with woeful consequences. The "paradox" may well be used, as by many of the intelligent Fathers, to underline the wonder of God's so loving the world. But, for the perceptive, it has only the ironic effect of at once underlining, as it does for Adam, the dreadful fact that the Fall was in no sense fortunate. What was fortunate was God's redemptive love. Michael can ignore Adam's paradoxical expression of wonder because it immediately induces in responsive Adam before the words are out of his mouth the right question: "But say . . . !" What will happen to the faithful left among enemies in a world and time of woe? The answer to this has of course to do with the Spirit and its writing the law in the heart, and with what most concerns Adam and the reader—daily life and the existential situation and getting on with one's wife.

Vision and prophecy may seem to run thin because they are not what is immediately significant for the poem (or *De Doctrina*): it is Adam's response that is significant; and this will be found a not inadequate representation, in terms of his particular situation, of the continuous rhythm of the response to renovation whose stages are systematically defined in *De Doctrina*, and which, in the poem, has hesitatingly begun earlier, with Adam's response to judgment that is also calling, and has been proceeding ever since. But of course (though the treatise's detail will clarify the process of the last three books) the poem does not need *De Doctrina*. It has already, in its own mimetic terms (sometimes with direct and sometimes with ironic support of doctrine) exemplified by repeated parallel and contrast, and in every one of its incidents, the kind of response demanded under these circumstances from Adam. Satan[15] illustrates throughout the wilful refusal to respond to calling, though he is not, properly speaking, renovatingly called till Book IV. His condition in the opening books is analogous to the condition fallen man would have experienced if no fortunate call had resulted from God's love. This results from the Son's response to calling, mimetically set up in terms of Law and Gospel. Milton's God, who is otherwise unknowable save through the accommodating ways described in *De Doctrina* (XIV, 31–9), adopts the *persona* of the wrathful God of the Old Testament—a certainly somewhat risky piece of stage-managing on his part and the poet's at least for such as are unwilling to include considerations of doctrine in their response to mimesis. His exaggerated, egocentric anger is an ironic parody of all that has been obliquely and anomalously said of him by the perverse Satan in the opening books; and it is also in a sense a humbling of himself in taking on the appearance of Satan's God for the purpose in hand. The purpose is to call the Son in a way which invites him to a free act of participation in the Father's will and of confirmed free agency. The Son's (*not* yet the young Jew's) response is instructive: it includes understanding of the theological crux (as to justice and mercy) the Father has formally (though ironically) posed, preconsideration of the woeful state of unredeemed fallen men, foreboding imagination of what his participation will involve for himself (in some of Milton's most moving lines,

15. On Satan's neither comprehending nor desiring "Christian liberty," see *Milton the Poet*, 23. Cf. "Pattern in *Paradise Lost*," *UTQ*, XXII (1952–3), 113–14; and "Theme and Pattern in *Paradise Regained*," *UTQ*, XXV (1955–6), 172.

drawn from the New Testament that, in terms of the poem's time, will be written about the Incarnate Son), the expression of resolute and submissive faith in the Father, and of course an act of will. The process, with the situation and state it puts the Son in, merits the comment of the Father and the angelic chorus. The "high degree of humanization and individuation" in the handling of the devils, Eve, Adam,[16] is thus to be seen also in the representation of the Son (and as making the rest possible). And of course the state is the equivalent for the Son, of Christian liberty, as the process is the equivalent of the renovating process that will follow upon willing response to calling. In the daring mimesis of this scene, "drama" and "doctrine" are so far from being at all in conflict (or any more separable than the two natures in Christ or soul and body in man) that the only problem is to find critical terms—*not* "sugar-coated," "fused," "integrated," or even "embodied" (though the last is perhaps best)—that do not carry suggestions of a separability which is the result of our critical method and nomenclature, not of Milton's poetic practice.[17] This is underlined by the (somewhat heretical and even somewhat self-contradictory) representation of Satan's being "called," as a consequence, immediately thereafter. Like a Gentile angel—who has never heard of "Christ" and is so degenerated from his former powers of perception that he cannot remember in his partial revival in the opening books, what was the occasion of his rebellion and by what person he was expelled from heaven—he learns enough, from Chaos and what Uriel tells him and he himself sees of Creation, to know God sufficiently and to be called under the Law of partially renovated angelic nature. His meditations at the beginning of Book IV sufficiently illustrate the refusal to believe of those who are called without the Law or the Gospel, and who in consequence have no one to blame but themselves. He will of course be called again continually, by signs, but his response is ever the same. So it is, one way or the other, with the experience of every other person in the poem, unfallen or fallen: with the leaders of the fallen angels in the Satanic council; with Abdiel, who responds to the call, though with a degree of self-righteousness

16. "Milton and his Readers," *UTQ*, XVIII (1948–9), 204.

17. "The Historical Criticism of Milton," *PMLA*, LXVI (1951), 1040; cf. "Notes on Milton's Views on the Creation," *PQ*, XXVIII (1949), 231; *Milton the Poet*, 3, 21–2. On the Son, cf. "Milton and his Readers," *UTQ*, XVIII (1949–9), 204; "Pattern in Paradise Lost," *UTQ*, XXII (1952–3), 119–20; *Milton the Poet*, 21–2.

not unadmired by some critics who recognize its relation to the self-righteousness of Milton's reforming prose yet do not develop the implication that the angel's admirable response only sets him in a position to recognize, with the other unfallen angels, the inadequacies of his own notions, the limits of still developing angelic percipience, the ultimate futility against evil even of mere angelic power, and so the necessity of waiting on God and his time and the proper fulfilment of purpose by the appropriate instruments against evil which do not include, even in the angelic sense, the war that but endless war still breeds. Even Raphael learns much in his effort to respond adequately to his call. His effort fails (and before the end of his poetical discourse with Adam he knows vaguely and in sensitive troublement of mind that it has failed), because he does not yet understand the meaning implied by the Son's willing response to the call to sacrifice and so (blushingly) cannot quite explain the implications of angelic and human love. Yet he learns much, both from his own rehearsal of the War and Creation, about justice and mercy and the Son, and from Adam's responsive relations and doubtful or wondering questions and his own answers. He himself is on the point of learning in what sense Earth may perhaps (there are qualifying conditions) be but the shadow of Heaven. He is of course, as many have lately said, the "Orphic" poet of prelapsarian nature; and his two poems represent the prelapsarian naturalistic Orphicism of which remnants and as it were a reflection remain in all pagan Orphic poets (though, to use Sidney's phrase, in a full wrong divinity), and in the pagan myths (as Milton's now pejorative, now sympathetic use of them, throughout makes clear). Yet the inadequacies of Orphicism are illustrated by the inadequacies of even prelapsarian Orphicism. It cannot quite get to the responsive root of the matter, though it can provide and induce in Adam, as an unfallen Gentile under the law of nature, a clearer sense of the conditions of his calling than Satan can get from Uriel. The contrast between Raphael as poet and Michael[18] underlines the limitations of the Orphicism of Milton's own Renaissance contemporaries and the difficulties he is striving to overcome in his own mimetic method—in which the Orphic has the subordinate function of illuminating the preoccupation with response. Orphic poetry is concerned with supranatural transcen-

18. "Pattern in Paradise Lost," *UTQ*, XXII (1952–3), 118.

dentals as they are mythomystically shadowed forth in external nature. It cannot quite, in its terms, induce the response to nature and time and what lies before us in our daily lives which Raphael knows it should be his function to induce in Adam. But Raphael is the poet of the past merely: he operates through Dame Memory and her angelic daughters, and his chief contribution is to induce Adam to rehearse and to try to explain the significance of his memory of finding himself created and of the response that followed. Raphael is left by God to perform his task as best he may with his own developing powers.

Michael is sent to reveal to Adam what shall come in the future, as God enlightens his angelic mind in terms appropriate to Adam's response to expulsion from Paradise and its implications. He is the Miltonic poet accommodating the truths of Christian experience to fallen man. So long as postlapsarian Adam can be sustained in the repentant process of response to renovation by being led to envision what his sin implies for men by the force of Michael's sword and harsh words, he can deduce from experience the first and greatest commandment. But, by a complex derivation, "obey" implies "to hear and willingly respond." The angel adds what follows from prophecy, to send man into a world of purgatively frustrating woe—after a moment of mixed reflective silence—to learn, through continuously repentant and obediently faithful response to calling and the operation on memory of renovated and added powers, how to continue to grow and to increase the sum through the performance of the deeds answerable to the second, whose spirit he likewise broke, under his dispensation, in favour of the letter. Whether he does or does not have "Christian liberty" is again a nice doctrinal point meriting further research in terms of the student's concerns.

Adam's response, not only postlapsarian but prelapsarian, is everywhere the poem's central concern, as this response illustrates, by parallel or contrast, the response demanded by the process of renovation in those under the Gospel. Though Adam's postlapsarian response, towards which the whole poem moves, is of course what is of prime relevance, the gloss on the representation of his prelapsarian state provided by *De Doctrina* might help to illuminate the bearing of the poem's representation of the "paradisal" state on this central concern. The gloss is not so much in the treatise's chapter on unfallen man (with its concern with the divorce some interpreters would appear to think Adam should have demanded as soon as Eve faulted) but in the implications of the chapters on renovation and Christian liberty. What it will offset is the inclination to a slackly nostalgic, if not phantastically mythomystic, misinterpretation of the paradisal conditions in which man is set after his creation in nature, and (what goes along with this) the mistaken reading (of which foreboding vestiges continue to appear even in the most sensitive appraisals of the poem) that every prelapsarian human action involves a foreshadowing of the inevitable lapse and the bitterness of all our woe. Every incident in the poem does of course imply the possibility of Fall, as Milton's God says in his wrathfully theological *persona*. But it does so because the invitation to willing response implies freedom to refuse response; and the Satanic eye cannot perceive that (as this involves all men, even the "good," in frustrating woes after the Fall, though perhaps Christ knew no "fear"), so it involves before the Fall a paradisal (or heavenly) responsibility to be fulfilled with innocent joy but not without responsive effort and some difficulty to be overcome. Every prelapsarian incident in the poem involves for Adam and Eve (as for all its other creatures) a "calling," and every prelapsarian incident illustrates the possibility of refusal. But what is significant about these incidents is not that they forebode the Fall but that they illustrate the kind of active response that is according to the norm of right. Milton's Creator does not punish his creatures for the limitations and even degrees of impercipience he has given them, even *un*fallen, to use instrumentally in the development of the potentialities they have as his image, only for wilfully not so using them. It is purposeful growth towards completing that is implied, not only by the Orphic Raphael, but by every prelapsarian incident; and what this implies is the renovation, despite sin though through woe, of the fallen but responsive and the infusing of new faculties and dimensions of perception. This is true—to follow the chronology of historical time rather than the significant sequence of the mimesis—of Adam's response to the calling of his coming to created consciousness, of his argumentative (and certainly risky) plea to God for an appropriate companion, of his response to Eve's loveliness, of Eve's response to Adam's calling her from contemplation of the reflection of her beauty's reflection of the image of God in the beauty of creation to recognition of his reflection of that in God of which beauty is but a sign, of her response (tutored by Adam) to her phantastic dream, and of Adam's response to Raphael's tutorial warnings, and so forth. What the mimetic sequence of these prelapsarian incidents illustrates is the process of prelapsarian growth, through man's being lifted up out of mere nature to be planted in God's garden, and being given two commands, one negative, one positive, beyond the nature and natural law of his creation, to cultivate himself and it in these double terms. This process illustrates, in prelapsarian terms, developing action in accordance with the law of nature's line of right, with which action fulfilling the gift of the Holy Spirit is continuously analogous (and more than segregatedly analogous) under the Gospel. The Fall is simply an action oblique and anomalous, though all actions in themselves are good. Every prelapsarian human action in *Paradise Lost* is so far from foreboding the Fall that it stands in the sharpest continuous contrast with it, to underline the fact that the Fall is, as to right action, a parodic obliquity and anomaly. The moment at which it occurs is clearly marked, though the perception of what is involved in it depends on recognition of the right line Adam has taken up to that point, not without the difficult and even hazardous necessity of working out his response each time. He is quite right to acquiesce in Eve's insistence on her responsibility as an individual (though female) human being, though here, as often before, he has to work his way through uncertainty, and the possibility of mistake is of course, as ever, already implied by his uneasiness. His response to this challenging call is not quite adequate, yet it is not "fallen." Eve's response to temptation of course illustrates the process of mistaken response, and should be glossed, in the logic of its steps, and as a parody of each preceding prelapsarian response, by *De Doctrina* on this process. But her fall is not *the* Fall. Though the command about the tree applies to her, it was originally given to Adam alone. The Fall occurs (and the sin original is completed) when Adam determines his response to her deceived situation. But the determination occurs in another of the significant Miltonic moments of silence, whose implications we have to work for in terms of the whole poem and its parallelingly contrasted incidents. The moment is that in which Adam, meeting returning and deceived Eve and hearing her tale, stands "amaz'd, / Astonied . . . and Blank, while horror chill / Ran through his veins" and the garland wreath'd for Eve slips from his slack hand, shedding all the thornless and now faded roses. All that follows is apologetic explanation, which does not explain the fondness (or foolishness) that allows him to be overcome by female charm. It is not "uxoriousness," or anything else definable in classical terms, that is the centre of Adam's fall: it is heart-failure or failure of nerve, so to speak. But what the moment of horrified silence marks is chiefly despair, the consequence of a mistaken response to the situation. The response assumes that because his happiness and Eve's lies in their own arbitrament, it depends on themselves. But Eve's happiness depends on him, and his depends on the faith in God that slips, with the roses, from his slack hand, in his failure to believe that Satan can no more win on earth than in heaven, and why he cannot. The explanation of this failure, the origin of evil, remains a problem;[19] but it is the nature of evil in the present existential situation that is the poem's concern, and the likeness of falling Adam's despair to ours. In consequence of it, he cannot tell what faith in God calls on him to do in this situation. What he is called on to do the reader who has the Law and the Prophets and the Gospel can tell better than he, who has never heard of "Christ" (but only of the Son in the chariot of wrath and as the instrument of creation); yet the primitive brightness of the law of nature in his heart, with the command about the tree and the institution of marriage, and Raphael's efforts should have been enough. How? The point of the situation and the question is in the response of the reader who knows more than Adam; but Adam knows enough to make his explanation an obliquely and anomalously romantic parody of the right act. He falls because, in despair and lack of faith in a loving God, he lets deceived Eve and the roses down, through the egocentric character of his imagination in its response to her difficulties. The real defect of *Paradise Lost* is not that it presents any duality, whether in actions or in arguments, but that it depends so much on such ironic parodies making such demands on the response of the reader. But what is being parodied is nevertheless plainly there in the poem, in the character of each prelapsarian response and in the sequence of prelapsarian responses under the law of nature; and it is outlined clearly in the response of Adam (rather than of Eve, who has, as ever, good natural instincts but is apt without tutoring to go off the further line of right) to the

19. Cf. "Notes on Milton's Views on the Creation," *PQ*, XXVIII (1949), 230, note 31.

natural renovation which begins with the clothing judgment and the spiritual renovation which follows, through Michael, in consequence of Adam's painful but willing response to the partial renovation of his natural faculties, as *De Doctrina* has systematically laid these out.

This does not mean that *Paradise Lost* presents no problems: poetic mimesis of the stature of Milton's is not least an imitation of experience in presenting the reader with many thorny problems and with an example of a sound response to experience making good use of its own faults and failures. Many of these, time being what it is, are intensified by the historical necessity of determining what Milton's seventeenth-century terms mean and of translating them, as he tried to do, into terms appropriate to the audience. Many also are presented not only by the inadequacies of our critical terminology and its implications but what these inadequacies often parody—the seventeenth-century problem of representing continuity by the use of dualistic terms (ultimately derived from Plato and the dialectic of transcendentalist and materialist footnotes on him), like *externam et inter[nam]*, *naturali et spirituali,* and so forth. Even the revisions of *De Doctrina,* following on the prose, make no great success of heretically climbing out of this dualistic crux: perhaps separations and divorces, *a mensa et thoro* at least, are still too much in Milton's mind. What helps to save Adam is that at least his parody is in no such terms, but in parodic terms of the indissoluble unity of what God has joined. Sentimentalism is at least preferable to brutality. Thus the mimetic method of *Paradise Lost* can do better than the systematically analytical method of *De Doctrina* in representing the continuity that demands a continuously developing response from men. Yet even here dualistic terminology constantly threatens to let Milton and his critics down, especially when the dualism tends to be resolved by the period in terms of its inferior term.

A prime defect of the terminology both of *De Doctrina* and of *Paradise Lost* is that it does not sufficiently clarify the problem of the response of all the mind's irradiated powers to generation and regeneration. Though the poem's mimesis does better than the treatise's systematic analysis of the developing prelapsarian norm, and though the emphasis of both on the will as well as the discursive intellect is illuminating, one essential operation involved in the response to renovation seems to remain unclear. The "right reason" we sometimes mistakenly identify with right academic intellection involves not only choice, which also is reason, but memory and imagination. This is not inadequately illustrated by the response of the Son, the efforts of Raphael, Adam's response to Michael's vision and prophecy, the poem's invocations, and by contrast with the chimeric phantasies of the Satanic mind and its distortions of memory. Adam can, at an early stage in his prelapsarian development, speak of Fancy and mimic Fancy in terms of willing waking percipience and phantastic dream. But the high-raised phantasy of the early poems finds no place in the later, or in *De Doctrina*, no doubt because the anarchies of the revolution had taught Milton what undifferentiated triumphant high-raised fantasies, on thrones of royal state or among the confused herd, could issue in. Yet Adam and Eve learn in the prelapsarian and post-lapsarian state by God-given dreams and induced visions (and by poetry) in the response to which Fancy must play a right-rational part. The later Milton would seem to have accepted, on the whole, the commonplace sixteenth- and seventeenth-century suspicion of Greek fancy (and its synonymous Latin imagination) as phantastic and vain and the sources of perversity. But clearly the author neither of *Areopagitica* nor of the later poems accepted the tendency to explain this vain phantasy of lunatics, lovers, sectaries, and other irrational persons in terms simply of the close relation between the imagination and the degenerate senses responsible for the Fall. The senses are not responsible for the Miltonic Fall. The Fall is a failure of the whole man and the whole mind. Analytical commentary on the mimesis of the later poems is constantly running into this gap in nomenclature—and as constantly falling into gloomily neo-Stoic or fantastically neo-Platonic misinterpretations as a consequence. Yet if *De Doctrina*, insensitively used, only serves to underline this gap, it also serves, properly used, to illuminate the fact that the mimesis of the later poems is chiefly concerned with the psychological process of response which leads to Christian liberty in charity, or to the state of mind in which Adam, with hand no longer slack, leaves Paradise to go on with the process of response to renovation in the world at large, with Eve who has been dreaming once more. The point is perhaps somewhat illuminated by the observation in *De Doctrina* that, though all believers do not have the gift of prophecy, "the Holy Spirit is to them an equivalent and substitute for prophecy, dreams, and visions," Joel 2:xxviii; 2 Cor.

3:iii, 5:vi; James 1:xxi (XVI, 118). It is at this point that doctrine and mimesis, systematic theology, poetic, and poetic practice come inseparably and determinedly together for Milton. It is happily not necessary to escape from this critical crux by asserting, with many current interpretations, that poetry and dogma must be segregated in Milton because there is an unbridgeable gap between them; nor even to conclude sadly, out of uneasiness over mythomysticated lapses or abstracted hiatuses in the sustained response Milton's poetry demands, that his developing comments on Scripture at best provide only an uncertain guide to his notions about his poetry. His theology can illuminate and sustain his poetry and his poetry illuminatingly applies and extends his theology because his theory of renovation and his theory of poetry are, at the responsive and responsible heart of the matter, quite inseparable. The *ratio . . . charitatis* without which Christian liberty is an absolutely dead thing includes, as expelled Adam, the young Jew, and monumental Samson learned, each in his way and time, the exercise of what commentators on Milton since the eighteenth century have steadily reduced below or exalted above the level of the sympathetic imagination.[20] But Milton believed, in his version of the Augustinian tradition, that Christian liberty involved and indeed depended on the right reading of the significance conveyed by signs and a homiletic effort, however oblique and anomalous, to induce in others a continuously developing right reading of the significance of signs in terms of the soul of all the rest.[21] It is heartening to reflect that one may confidently look to the communications of years of productive release from the demands of participation in institutional administrative responsibilities, merited by more than notable national and humanistic literary activity in and outside the classroom, to develop yet further the bearing of the Woodhousean version of the Pauline principle. *Velut arbor aevo. . . .*

20. *Milton the Poet*, 28; "Collins and the Creative Imagination," *Studies in English by Members of University College, Toronto*, ed. M. W. Wallace (Toronto, 1931), 69–71, 121, 125.

21. H. R. MacCallum, "Milton and the Figurative Interpretation of the Bible," *UTQ*, XXXI (1961–2), 397–8, 410.

The Correspondence of the Augustans

HERBERT DAVIS

IN AN AGE which regarded polite conversation as one of the most important arts of human life it is hardly surprising to find more attention being given to that other form of conversation which may be carried on through correspondence; and that this should come to be recognized as something worth preserving and fit perhaps in due time to be published for the delight and benefit of a larger audience. It had long been customary for letters of public interest on affairs of state and diplomacy and even private letters of famous persons to be preserved and used in memoirs and histories and in religious controversies; and the epistle both in verse and prose was a recognized form, of which there were sufficient admirable examples in Latin and French and English. But it was not I think until towards the end of the seventeenth century in England that collections of letters began to appear, containing the correspondence of contemporaries with such titles as *Miscellaneous Letters of Eminent Men of the Age*, or of literary men, poets and dramatists, as in *Familiar Letters on several Occasions* by Dryden and his friends. And at the same time there began to be provided for a less sophisticated audience numerous letter books which offered instruction and examples of the epistolary art.[1]

1. *Academy of Eloquence with Letters amorous and moral*, 1683; *Wit's Academy: With Letters on all occasions fit for Ladies Gentlemen and others*, 1684; *Letters of Religion and Vertue to several Gentlemen and Ladies to excite Piety and Devotion*, 1695. See *The Complete Letter Writer in English*, by Katherine G. Hornbeak, with an excellent bibliography (Smith College Studies in Modern Languages, Northampton, Mass., 1934); and for Tom Brown's many publications of familiar Letters, original and translated, see *Tom Brown of Facetious Memory*, by Benjamin Boyce (Harvard University Press, 1939). See also "Familiar Letters," in *Literary Bypaths of the Renaissance*, by E. N. S. Thompson (Yale University Press, 1924).

There is still little enough here to indicate what a large and prominent place collections of private letters would occupy not only among the books printed during the eighteenth century, but among the family papers and archives in manuscript that continue to be discovered and made available to enlarge our acquaintance with all those who left any mark on their generations at that time.

It is only as the result of the intensive search for papers and documents which has been going on for the last fifty years that the full extent and variety of the private correspondence of Pope and Swift and their friends has been revealed; and when we look at the most recent editions of their correspondence[2] we find that many of the letters written by them or addressed to them are still missing and have probably been lost. Nevertheless we can now observe the characteristics of this art of letter-writing as practised by the eminent men of the age, poets and wits and churchmen and politicians, and by the varied circle of their friends and patrons and acquaintance—ministers and courtiers, duchesses who could not spell, blue-stockings and learned citizens' wives, country gentlemen and parsons. We can, moreover, read many of these letters, printed from the original autographs, exactly as they came into the hands of their first recipients, unrevised and uncorrected; we can read such replies as are available; we can compare letters sent out to very different sorts of correspondents on the same dates, sometimes with echoes or repetitions, sometimes with modifications or even contradictions. We can obtain from the whole correspondence of a writer's lifetime a many-faceted vision of his personality as its different surfaces are presented to those around him, first to those of an older generation somewhat veiled, then shining more brilliantly in the midst of a larger circle of contemporaries, and later glowing with a softer radiance as these give way to a younger generation offering homage or seeking patronage.

For a biographer there can hardly be any documents more reliable, more valuable and more essential than the whole corpus of a writer's correspondence, once the full texts are available—if it is properly used, not to afford carefully selected illustrations for some preconceived judgment, but to provide in its entirety the detailed evidence of many

2. *The Correspondence of Alexander Pope*, ed. George Sherburn, 5 vols. (Oxford, 1956), cited as P. *The Correspondence of Jonathan Swift*, ed. Harold Williams, vols. I–III (Oxford, 1963), cited as S. I have been given permission to use the page proofs of vols. IV–V, which are now being printed.

different witnesses to check our hasty impressions and to prevent us from misinterpreting things which were said in a certain way for a particular person at a particular moment. It is this particularity which gives its unique character to the personal letter, and distinguishes it from other forms of familiar writing. A letter has an address and a date; it is written for a certain recipient, and may often be concerned with matters of that particular time. Its whole style is conditioned by this. And if it is one of a series of letters to the same correspondent it may also be affected by a sort of momentum which will have been given by their previous interchanges. For instance, Swift rarely forgets in his later letters to Bolingbroke that he is writing to one whom he had called Aristippus, because he had begun as a great minister, was then sent into exile and at last allowed to "retire to the country and be a pattern of hospitality, politeness, wisdom and virtue" (S, II, 332). Naturally this relationship provides the theme for Bolingbroke's reply, where he talks of Aristippus and Seneca and Cato and Lucan and Virgil and Plato. And in the following years he tends to give Swift a picture of his life of study and retirement which he knows will be approved; he continues to echo the theme of Aristippus: "he is still my favourite among the philosophers; and if I find some faults in him, they are few and venial." He is not wholly unaware of the importance of these letters, which will provide posterity with a notion of his character. Therefore he warns Swift not to pay him too many compliments "for fear of passing for partial in y[r] paralells, which has done Plutarch more hurt than it has done good to his grecian Heros" (S, II, 414).

Perhaps it was not to be expected that any of the Augustans could write letters to their more distinguished friends without the consciousness that they would most likely be published in a collected edition of their works. Swift taunts Pope with this in a letter of 26 February, 1729:

> I find you have been a writer of Letters almost from your infancy, and by your own confession had Schemes even then of Epistolary fame. Montaigne says that if he could have excelled in any kind of writing, it would have been in Letters; but I doubt they would not have been natural, for it is plain that all Pliny's Letters were written with a view of publishing, and I accuse Voiture himself of the same crime, although he be an Author I am fond of. They cease to be Letters when they become a jeu d'esprit. (S, III, 373)

Pope protests too much, when over and over again in his early letters to Caryll he repeats that he writes without any conscious art:

> You see my letters are scribbled with all the carelessness and inattention imaginable; my style, like my soul, appears in its natural undress before my friend. 'Tis not here I regard the character of a wit. (*P*, I, 155)

A few weeks later he speaks again of "so many things freely thrown out, such lengths of unreserved friendship, thoughts just warm from the brain without any polishing or dress, the very *déshabille* of the understanding" (*P*, I, 160). But he is really only making comments on the art of letter-writing between friends, which may therefore appear equally well in a letter to Caryll as in a letter to Addison some months later:

> I am conscious I write with more unreservedness than ever man wrote, or perhaps talked to another. I trust your good nature with the whole range of my follies. (*P*, I, 185)

And he can say pretty much the same on another occasion to Congreve:

> Methinks when I write to you, I am making a confession, I have got (I can't tell how) such a custom of throwing my self out upon paper without reserve. (*P*, I, 274)

When protesting most vigorously that he is writing with the utmost carelessness, he is in fact trying to do his best to provide what he thinks is required by the canons of Epistolary Art. And he gives himself away by his revisions and his rearrangements when he comes to publish the letters afterwards. He can transfer parts of one letter or a postscript to take the place of a rather trivial paragraph in a letter to a different person, because he is writing familiar essays to show his wit, which will fit one correspondent just as well as another. This is not true later when he is writing to Swift, and he explains delightfully how this happened in his letter of 29 November, 1729:

> This letter (like all mine) will be a Rhapsody; it is many years ago since I wrote as a Wit. How many occurrences or informations must one omit, if one determin'd to say nothing that one could not say prettily? I lately receiv'd from the widow of one dead correspondent, and the father of another, several of my own letters of about fifteen or twenty years old; and it was not unentertaining to my self to observe, how and by what degrees I ceas'd to be a witty writer; as either my experience grew on the one hand, or my affection to my correspondents on the other. Now as I love you

better than most I have ever met with in the world, and esteem you too the more the longer I have compar'd you with the rest of the world; so inevitably I write to you more negligently, that is more openly, and what all but such as love one another will call writing worse. (S, III, 362)

This is not only a very shrewd comment on his own epistles but it enables him very naturally to offer Swift a pretty compliment in a manner which he would appreciate. The deprecatory judgment "writing worse" suggests the careless unreserve with which it was permissible to allow a sincerity of feeling to be shown. But at once the thought of others reading these letters comes into Pope's mind and prompts him to add: "I smile to think how Curl would be bit, were our Epistles to fall into his hands, and how gloriously they would fall short of every ingenious reader's expectations!" (S, III, 363). Yet he never requests that his letters should be destroyed, which would obviously have been the safest way to keep them out of Curl's hands. In fact, they both knew, as well as their correspondents, that this deprecation was a pretence; and that their Epistles, like Pliny's and Cicero's whom they are constantly quoting, would be preserved and published for the delight of posterity. But this made it all the more necessary to remember that it was the art of the good letter-writer to keep the illusion of spontaneity, of "thinking aloud or talking upon paper."

Finally, in a letter to Swift, dated 9 April, 1730, from Pope and Bolingbroke the idea of publication is frankly brought forward. Pope says he has kept some of Swift's letters and some from other friends, and has thought of putting them together in a volume, just for his own secret satisfaction—"do not therefore say, I aim at Epistolary Fame; I never had any Fame less in my head; but the Fame I most covet indeed, is that which must be deriv'd to me from my Friendships." Then Bolingbroke takes up the theme: "I seek no Epistolary fame, but am a good deal pleased to think that it will be known hereafter that you and I lived in the most friendly intimacy together." In the best Augustan manner we are reminded of the epistolary writers in Roman times and their particular contribution to our knowledge of their great contemporaries:

Pliny writ his letters for the Publick, so did Seneca. . . . Tully did not, and therefore these give us more pleasure than any which have come down to us from Antiquity, when we read them, we pry into a Secret which was intended to be kept from us, that is a pleasure. We see Cato, and Brutus, and Pompey and others, such as they really were, and not such as the gaping Multitude of their own Age took them to be, or as Historians and Poets have represented them to ours, that is another pleasure. (S, III, 387–8)

There can be no doubt of their intentions, and of the dilemma in which they found themselves. There was always the danger, perhaps greater for Pope, of being disturbed by the consciousness that anything that he wrote might be preserved for a witness against him. And this I believe is liable too often to spoil the quality of his letters.

Arbuthnot and Gay are the least affected. They do not write carelessly, but they have regard always to the person they are addressing. It is wise to remember, when we read Arbuthnot's letters to Swift, that they share the same delight in irony. They address one another in a way they know very well each will understand. Apart from this there is an extreme directness and sincerity between them; there can be no doubt of the complete understanding they maintained during their five and twenty years acquaintance. Arbuthnot seems to have been a person valued by his friends without any reservations at all. He was enjoyed as a delightful companion and respected as a man of character and integrity. Perhaps as a mere amateur in letters, with an unchallenged reputation in his own profession, he never aroused any feelings of jealousy. But there were moments when he could write with a rare warmth and depth of affection, as in his reply to Swift's letter of farewell at the time of the death of Queen Anne:

Dear Freind the last sentence of your letter quite kills me: never repeat that melancholy tender word that you will endeavour to forgett me. I am sure I never can forgett yow, till I meett with, (what is impossible) another whose conversation I can so much delight in as Dr Swifts & yet that is the smallest thing I ought to value you for. That hearty sincere freindship That plain and open ingenuity in all your commerce, is what I am sure I can never find in another alas. I shall want often a faithfull monitor one that would vindicate me behind my back and tell me my faults to my face. god knows I write this with tears in my eyes. (S, II, 122)

It is so different from the tone of the letter which Ford took to Swift in Dublin in the summer of 1716 where Pope plays upon the idea that a friend in Ireland is like a friend in another world,

whom (popishly speaking) I believe constantly well-disposed towards me and ready to do me all the good he can. . . . A protestant divine cannot take it amiss that I treat him in the same manner with my patron Saint. (S, II, 211)

Swift of course does not miss the chance to make good use of such an opening:

> You are an ill Catholick, or a worse Geographer, for I can assure you, Ireland is not Paradise, and I appeal even to any Spanish divine, whether addresses were ever made to a friend in Hell, or Purgatory.

He lives in fact in an obscure scene of which Pope would know nothing, and so has nothing to write about—except a Quaker poet in Dublin, and the thought that had come to him that Gay might try a set of Quaker-pastorals. This form of ridicule he feels is not exhausted and he tosses off another suggestion, which may have led to the *Beggars' Opera*: "Or what think you of a Newgate pastoral, among the whores and thieves there?" (S, II, 214–15).

Gay, in his letters to Swift, takes upon him the duty of sending news and gossip about his friends; he says little about himself, except perhaps to promise that he is following Swift's advice to revise his work and finish it as well as he can. He writes always without pretentions and without malice or guile. Only we may feel sometimes when he is writing to Swift that he allows himself little asides which he knows will be rightly understood and relished. Swift is always admonishing him about the care of his money, and hopes he will soon be rich enough to have some little place of his own, either in town or in the country. He replies that he is afraid of getting into debt: "I cannot bear to pawn five pounds worth of my liberty to a Taylor or a Butcher; I grant you this is not having the true spirit of modern Nobility, but tis hard to cure the prejudice of education." As to more writing, he hesitates from fear of incurring the displeasure of his superiors, "for I cannot for my life think so well of them as they themselves think they deserve" (S, III, 384–5).

The best of these letters between Pope and Swift and Arbuthnot and Gay are those which follow Swift's memorable visit to London in 1726, when he left behind the manuscript of *Gulliver's Travels* to be printed. His visit had renewed his ties with his old friends; and the correspondence that followed has inevitably the quality of a conversation that is being continued which had gone on merrily all through the months they had spent together. We even find Swift reminding them that when they were together he could never get in a word, because of the stream of talk from Pope and Gay. This sounds a little unlikely but it gives him an excuse to have his say now that he has a pen in his hand. He had provided them with plenty to talk about, and they are joined by others of his acquaintance, all in their several ways under the spell of the creator of Lemuel Gulliver. He complains that he could not understand their strange talk at all until a bookseller happened to send him a book of Travels, two volumes of 700 pages, which he was forced to read through in order to be able to interpret a few lines in their letters. These letters began to arrive in November 1726 and are soon followed by others from Mrs. Howard, the Earl of Peterborough and Lady Bolingbroke; and there was talk of others, either lost or intercepted. He was delighted to hear from Peterborough who had described "the strange distempers that rage in this nation," said to have been "brought about by the black Art and by the spells of a notorious scribbling Magitianï who had appeared in several shapes—att one time a Drappier, att another a Wapping Surgeon, sometimes a Nardac, sometimes a Reverend Divine" (*S*, III, 191–2). And Mrs. Howard, who had signed herself "Sieve Yahoo" in her letter of November 17, received a suitable reply from the Dean from Dublin dated November 27 and also an acknowledgment from Lemuel Gulliver, written from Newark on the next day, asking her "to reconcile him to the Maids of Honour whom they say I have most grievously offended" and begging leave "to lay the crown of Lilliput at your feet, as a small acknowledgment of your favours to my book and person" (*S*, III, 190). Only Bolingbroke, according to Gay, was inclined to "blame the book as a design of evil consequence to depreciate human nature." But he too wrote to Swift early in 1727, warning him not to break his engagement with them to spend the next summer between Dawley and Twickenham: "what matter if you are deaf, what matter if you cannot hear what we say? you are not dumb, & we shall hear you, and that is enough" (*S*, III, 200).

Shortly after this Pope wrote to report that their joint *Miscellanies* were printed off (though the two volumes did not appear until June) and speaks of them in terms which might well be used to describe their correspondence:

> I am prodigiously pleas'd with this joint-volume, in which methinks we look like friends, side by side, serious and merry by turns, conversing

interchangeably, and walking down hand in hand to posterity; not in the stiff forms of learned Authors, flattering each other, and setting the rest of mankind at nought: but in a free, un-important, natural, easy manner; diverting others just as we diverted our selves. (S, III, 201)

That was certainly the kind of impression he wished to give when he arranged some twelve years later to gather together a selection of letters written by them and their friends, between the years 1714 and 1738. I am not here concerned with the story of how this happened,[3] but wish to draw attention to the very different impression we are now given with the whole range of their correspondence before us. For it has been added to in some rather striking ways, and now provides us with a great variety of splendid examples of the epistolary art of the Augustans.

First, there are the letters from a group of ladies, like Lady Elizabeth Germaine, Lady Carteret and her mother Lady Worsley, Mrs. Howard (later the Countess of Suffolk), the Duchess of Queensberry, Martha Blount and Esther Vanhomrigh, which give us an opportunity of comparing the quality of their writing with that of their correspondents, the poets and men of letters. We may hesitate to treat as a mere compliment Swift's own remark about the excellence of Esther Vanhomrigh's letters, "which I never look into without wondering how a Brat who cannot read, can possibly write so well" (S, II, 335–6). She can put things to him so shrewdly: "tell me did those curcumstances crowd on you or did you recolect them only to make me happy. . . . " She can write in a way that could not but have rent his heart:

with the utmost distress and confusion I behold my self the cause of uneasie reflections to you yet I can not comfort you but here declair that tis not in the power of arte time or accident to lessen the unexpressible passion which I have for — — — don't flatter your self that separation will ever change my sentiments for I find my self unquiet in the midst of silence and my heart is at once pierced with sorrow and love. (S, II, 357, 363)

Even set down awkwardly in print with their curious spellings and entire absence of punctuation her letters fully justify Swift's astonishment and explain the hold this fascinating and passionate creature

3. For an account of the first printing of the letters of Pope and Swift, see Maynard Mack, *The Library*, 4th ser., XIX, 465, and Vinton A. Dearing, *ibid.*, XXIV, 74.

continued through so many years to have upon him. His replies to her are often awkward and sometimes difficult by reason of his restraint and his fear of giving himself away; but when she complains of his puzzling her with difficult writing, he only threatens to give her more of it.

There is no difficult writing in his letters to Lady Elizabeth Germaine or Mrs. Howard, who perhaps more than any even of his closest friends allowed themselves to amuse him in the same terms which he used to them. He begins a letter to Mrs. Howard (14 August 1727):

> I wish I were a young Lord, and you were unmarryed. I should make you the best husband in the world.

She immediately replies:

> I did desire you to write me a love letter but I never did desire you to talk of marrying me.

And she finishes by giving him orders in the very manner in which he always delighted to demand obedience from the ladies. After giving him that advice which was to cause so much trouble between them later on—not to leave England until she had seen him—she insists that he should let her make a courtier of him:

> I have been a Slave twenty years without ever receiving a reason for any one thing I ever was oblig'd to do. and I have now a mind to take the pleasure once in my life of absolute power which I expect you to give me in obeying all my orders without one question why I have given them. (S, III, 230, 231)

There is nothing quite like this short exchange of letters between them in August 1727—the answers returned almost immediately—the same strokes played on both sides until the short game is finished. She claims equality with him since she shares the two misfortunes of a bad head and deafness, which he is always complaining about, but which have never made her peevish.

The easy terms in which this exchange of letters had been carried on must be remembered when the correspondence is resumed three years later. Swift wrote first in November 1730, when it was rumoured that she would be leaving the Court, to congratulate her "for being delivered from the toyl, the slavery, and vexation of a favorite," and to complain of the treatment he had received as well as Gay from the Queen her Mistress. He blames her also for acting towards him "too much like a Courtier," and lets her see plainly that he felt he had been taken in. He allowed her so much virtue as could be expected in a lady, a courtier and a favourite—"as to Freindship, Truth, Sincerity, and other trifles of that kind, I never concerned my self about them, because I knew them to be only the lower morals, which are altogether useless at Courts" (*S*, III, 424–5). She did not reply, but the following summer he wrote again, to congratulate her on her title, and also to mention the three letters "in relation to one Mrs Barber" which had been sent to the Queen over his signature. He has heard that Pope and the Countess herself had maintained that he was entirely innocent, "which indeed was but bare justice in you both, for he is my old friend, and you are in my debt on account of the esteem I had for you." To be suspected of behaving in this ridiculous manner seems to him so severe a censure that he asks that this letter be shown to the Queen, and takes the liberty of stating very plainly what his feelings are towards her Mistress and herself. "One who asks nothing, may talk with freedom; and that is my case. I have not said half that was in my heart; but I will have done" (*S*, III, 483–4).

There was certainly some excuse for her to be angry, and in her reply Swift must have recognized an ability to express her scorn in words as bitter and contemptuous as his own. She stated with the utmost directness her purpose of revenge:

> You seem to think that you have a Natural Right to abuse me because I am a Woman and a Courtier; I have taken it as a Woman and a Courtier ought, with great Resentment.

Then she proceeds to rally him, to make fun of him, to pour scorn on "this Monitor of Princes, this Irish Patriot, this Excelent Man at Speech and Pen"; and after showing that she has enough courage to fight him with some of his own weapons, she offers him honourable articles of peace to sign, but insists first that he should own he had been unjust to her:

> If I cannot justifie the advice I gave you from the success of it; yet you know I gave you my reasons for it . . . if the Principle was false you ought not to have acted upon it; so you have only been the Dupe of your own ill Judgment and not to my falshood. (S III, 498–9)

This letter was endorsed by Swift: "Countess of Suffolk. Sept 25th 1731 Answrd Octbr 20th 1731" but his reply was dated "Octr 26th." These dates certainly suggest that he had been "leaning on his elbow" for several days– "a posture never used except when I was under a necessity of writing to Fools, or Lawyers, or Ministers of State, where I am to consider what is to be said!"—even though he denies it, because he is writing to a person whom he still esteems. At least he wrote with some difficulty, though he repeats a good deal of what he had said before. Again he asks her to put the Queen in mind of what had passed between them in the presence of Dr. Arbuthnot, and to assure her that he will have no hand in any further State-scribbles; "looking upon this Kingdom's condition as absolutely desperate, I would not prescribe a dose to the dead." Even this powerful and memorable phrase had been used before in a conversation with the Lord Lieutenant. He repeats his account also of other things that had taken place when he was last in England, finally taking his leave of both ladies with some formality, not forgetting that he is addressing the "Groom of the Stole to Her Majesty at St. James's," and allowing himself a little very carefully calculated courtier's rhetoric:

> As to the Queen, whom I never offended, since it would be presumption to imagine I ever voluntarily came into her thoughts; so it must be a mortification to think, when I happen to be named in her presence, it is usually to my disadvantage. (S, III, 499–501)

His friends felt that he was being unfair to one who had had only good intentions towards him. None protested more vigorously than Lady Elizabeth Germaine, who writes with no hesitation and no concern at the frowns she might bring to his countenance. Moreover she knows him well and has some shrewd hits:

> Im sorry to find our tastes so different in the same Person, as every body has a Natural Partiality to their own opinion so tis surprising to me to find La: Suffolk dwindle in yours who rises infinitely higher in mine the more and the longer I know her, but you say you will say no more of *Courts for fear of growing angry* and indeed I think you are so already since you level all without knowing them, and seem to think that no one that belongs to a Court can act right. I'm sure this can't be really and truely your sense because it is unjust, and if it is I shall suspect there's something of your old Maxim in it (which I ever admired and found true) that you must have offended them because you dont forgive. . . . (S, IV, 85)

This was written towards the end of 1732, when they had been exchanging letters frequently since her friends the Duke and Duchess of Dorset had arrived at Dublin Castle, whom she had boldly recommended to him, and offered her services as a sort of informal secretary whenever he might have any recommendations for the Lord Lieutenant. She hopes to see him in England and is ready for him in any of his various shapes, but her choice would be "the Parson in Lady Betty's Chamber." This reference to those early verses of his about Mrs. Frances Harris, written to amuse the household of her father the Earl of Berkeley, was clearly intended to remind him of her affection for him when she was only a child, which gives her a right to treat him with some familiarity, or to chide him for his injustice to her friend, and report fresh evidence that she had just had of the kindness of her heart:

> I wish with all my heart as a judgment upon you, that you had but seen her as I did when the News of your Friends Death came, for though you are a proud parson, (yet give you, Devil, your due) your a sincere, goodnatured, honest one. . . . (S, IV, 150)

I do not know whether it was because of the freedom she takes with him, or because Swift had indeed made some use of her as a sort of go-between in some of his dealings with the Lord Lieutenant, that she wrote to him in 1735, urgently requesting him to burn all her letters. Perhaps the publication of his *Works* in Dublin at that time had reminded her that he was famous enough for his correspondence to be in danger of getting printed. At any rate she wrote:

> I must recommend to you an affair which has given me some small palpitations of the heart which is, that you should not wrap up either old shoes or neglected sermons in my Letters but that what of them has been spared from going toward making Gin for the Ladies, may henceforth be committed instantly to the flames, for you being stigmatized with the Name of a Witt, Mr Curl will rake to the Dunghill for your Correspondence. (S, IV, 342)

This gave Swift an opportunity for a delightful compliment which he was not slow to offer her, though it probably did not give her much confidence that her letters were very safe in his hands. They were obviously written very easily in the fashion of the great lady who does not need to worry about her idiosyncracies of spelling, and he complains sometimes that her writing was hard for his eyes; but they were written to chide him when it was necessary, or to express her thanks, or as he felt, to give him pleasure:

> As to the letters I receive from your Ladyship, I neither did or ever will burn any of them, take it as you please: For I never burn a letter that is entertaining, and consequently will give me new pleasure when it is forgotten.

And then he adds another comment, in that annoying and condescending fashion he was very fond of using in his letters to young ladies:

> I confess also that I have read some passages in many of your letters, to a friend, but without naming you, only that the writer was a lady, which had such marks of good sense that often the hearers would not believe me. (*S*, IV, 344)

It is well to remember, when we are considering the epistolary art of the Augustans, that they may not have been unaware that the letter they were writing might sometimes be read aloud by the recipient to a few of his friends, or might be kept to provide fresh entertainment when the first reading of it had been forgotten.

Probably no one even of the greatest ladies of his acquaintence ever wrote to the Dean without some attempt to entertain him and give him pleasure. Even Lady Worsley, the mother of Lady Carteret, who admits that she is a great-grandmother, pays her court by reminding him of the share she had once had in his heart and claims that she deserves to be remembered "better than all those flirting Girls you coquett with." She had been most jealous of one whom she disdainfully refers to as "dirty Patty," whom he had seen so often when he was staying with Pope during his last visit to Twickenham. And to all this Swift answers very meekly:

> She was the onely Girl I coquetted in the whole half year that I lived with Mr. Pope. . . . She was a neighbour's child, a good Catholick, an honest Girl, and a tolerable Courtier at Richmond. I deny she was dirty, but a little careless, and sometimes wore a ragged gown, when she and I took long walks.

Then he turns to thank her for the escritoire she had sent him—the work of her own hands—and indulges in his usual ironies and graceful compliment. He hears on all sides excessive praise of her handiwork, but

> although what they say be perfectly true, or indeed below the truth, yet if they had ever seen or conversed with Your Ladyship, as I have done,

they would have thought this escritoire a very poor performance from such hands, such eyes, and such an imagination. (S, IV, 77)

Even the Duchess of Queensberry, who had never met him, and only began a correspondence with him through their mutual friend Gay, is soon on very familiar terms with him; and after Gay's death they continue to write and tease one another. He admits that in a letter to Pope he had mentioned good qualities which she seemed to have; but after all he had never even had a glimpse of her since she was a girl, and her letters might be "false copies of her mind." She quickly tosses this back to him, as if their letters were a pleasant conversation:

> I deny I am touchy, yet am going to seem so again by assuring you my letters are never false copies of my mind, they are often I believe imperfect ones of an imperfect mind, . . . tho I will not take upon me to declare my way of thinking to be eternally the same Yett whatever I write is at that instant true. (S, IV, 141)

This is another point we should bear in mind, when we are considering the truthfulness of statements that we may find in letters, and the weight of authority that such statements should be given. We must allow for imperfect copies of what is in the mind of the writer, and recognize also that views and opinions however emphatically stated may possibly be only "at that instant true."

It should hardly be necesary to add that in much of this correspondence a very favourite form of wit, to be indulged in and to be improved upon at every opportunity, is that sort of irony which Swift always claimed to have introduced among them. He himself makes use of it almost invariably whenever he is writing a letter of thanks for presents that were made to him. When he receives from the daughter of the Archbishop of Armagh a present of butter and a pig, he threatens that he will let everyone know that the sole daughter and child of his Grace is so mean as to descend to housewifery, and that her writing and spelling are quite ungenteel, more like a parson than a lady. And when another young lady in Ireland makes advances to him and sends a gift of shirts "to the Hercules of the age"—as she calls him—he threatens that he will make a journey into the country the next summer to expostulate with her for all the unprovoked injuries she has done him.

Pope writes in the same manner after the summer they had so

happily spent together in 1726: "I may say that you have used me more cruelly than you have done any other man; you have made it more impossible for me to live at ease without you . . . " (*S*, III, 156). But the most sustained example of it is to be found in a letter from Lord Bathurst, which was calculated to give Swift pleasure by providing a sort of parody of his own manner, done with great gusto. Lord Bathurst says he is determined to plague and pester him in such a way that he will be sure to draw a reply. He then proceeds to show that all Swift's verse is borrowed—the style from Dryden and Waller, the thoughts from Virgil and Horace; and as for his prose writings which they make such a fuss about, they are only slight improvements on Cervantes and Rabelais: "I have twenty other points to maul yu upon if yu provoke me but if you are civil and Good natur'd & will send me a long, a very long letter in answer to this I will let yu alone a good while . . . " (*S*, III, 406). In his reply Swift protests that he has never been attacked "in so tender a point, nor by weapons against which I am so ill able to defend myself." "I pretend to have been an improver of Irony on the subject of Satyr and praise: but I will surrender up my title to your Lordship" (*S*, III, 410).

Such forms of the epistolary art as these are naturally limited for use among a group of friends, who have become familiar enough through conversation with one another's habits of mind and play of humour; they assume a considerable freedom and ease and informality, which shows itself often even in the penmanship of some of these noble lords and ladies who allow themselves every liberty in their spellings, abbreviations and punctuation. But the epistolary art must also provide very different forms from these, such as are required between strangers, or on more formal occasions. One which was much in use at this period was the letter of solicitation, written to a patron for a place on behalf of oneself or of a friend; and equally necessary a form which the patron might use in his reply. In Swift's correspondence there are some excellent examples, from the early letter of Sir William Temple recommending his young secretary Swift to Sir Robert Southwell for a place to the many letters written by the Dean of St. Patrick's on behalf of his friends to various Lord Lieutenants from Carteret to Chesterfield. Hidden beneath the necessary formality are a variety of different tones, nicely calculated to fit the tastes of the recipient. With Carteret he is on such friendly terms, and has such respect for his integrity and his intelligence, that he can risk using all his powers of humour and raillery. With Chesterfield he is more cautious, permitting himself only a slight touch of playfulness, so that his irony is not too obvious; and the interchange of letters between them shows that there is a possibility of an adequate understanding of each other, and a sort of courtier-like elegance is maintained. He adopts a different manner—"a style very different from what I use to my friends with titles"—in asking the Duke of Chandos to present to Ireland the ancient records relating to that Kingdom, which were in his possession; and he is very angry when all his civilities and compliments on the fame of the Duke's generosity meet with no response.

There is one other kind of letter at which we might expect Swift with his powers of satire and invective to excel: the letter in which the intention is to hurt an opponent or to hurl defiance at an enemy. He is likely to be at his best when he is addressing his immediate superiors —the bishops and archbishops—whenever they had been so ill advised as to try and assume an authority over him, which he refused to recognize. For in his letters as in his pamphlets he is stirred to exert his powers most of all perhaps when he is faced by petty tyranny or authority claiming to assert itself against the laws of God and man. On two occasions Bishop Evans at his visitation of St. Patrick's refused to admit the Dean's proxy, and made personal reflections on the Dean for his absence. On the first occasion Swift was content to remind the Bishop that he had not deserved such treatment, since he had been more than ordinarily officious in his respects to him from the time of his first coming over, though he had nothing to hope or fear from his Lordship. But the second time he took full advantage of the opportunity to express his utter and complete defiance, and to let the Bishop know plainly that in any circumstances he would avoid being present at his visitation:

> and by the grace of God, I am still determined to absent myself on the like occasions, as far as I can possibly be dispensed with by any law, while your Lordship is in that diocese and I a member of it. (S. II, 389)

This may seem a very trivial matter, a foolish squabble over ecclesiastical authority; and it was not very different when some years later while Swift was away on his last visit to England the Archbishop of

Dublin adjourned his visitation, until a proxy should be provided for the Dean. But here was a demand for which there was no justification whatever:

> it is a thing wholly new and unheard of, let the consequences be what they will, I shall never comply with it. . . . My proceeding shall be only upon one maxim: Never to yield to an oppression, to justify which no precedent can be produced.

An Archbishop must be taught to know the difference between servitude and proper obedience:

> My Lord, I have lived, and by the grace of God will die, an enemy to servitude and slavery of all kinds: And I believe, at the same time, that persons of such a disposition will be the most ready to pay obedience wherever it is due. (S, III, 210)

This kind of letter is equally conditioned by the character of the person to whom it is addressed. It takes on something of the form of a duel in which the writer is entirely concerned with the necessity of discovering his opponent's weakness, and using this to triumph over him; while at the same time he shows his own perfect mastery and skill.

These letters were first printed by Deane Swift twenty years and more after Swift's death, and the manuscripts have still not been discovered; they were presumably printed from drafts or copies found among Swift's papers. We may be sure that he would have had no objection to appearing before posterity, not merely as Pope would have shown him in the company of a few friends, exchanging pleasantries and compliments, but also as he was in his more formal letters, bargaining with governors and members of the House of Lords on behalf of his friends or in the interests of Ireland, or facing his accusers and defying those who tried to use their authority to break his proud spirit.

Pope and the Great Chain of Being

F. E. L. PRIESTLEY

IT HAS NEVER BEEN VERY FASHIONABLE to treat Pope seriously as a philosopher, and the *Essay on Man* has been a particular target for comments ranging from the patronizingly supercilious to the completely contemptuous. The most common charge is that Pope is writing about things he does not understand. Bolingbroke's assertion that the poet "understood nothing of his own principles nor saw to what they naturally tended" is quoted with acquiescence by Bonamy Dobrée,[1] as it has been by many others. Johnson's verdict, that "never were penury of knowledge and vulgarity of sentiment so happily disguised," has tended to become the general verdict, nowadays with emphasis on the "happily disguised"—that is, on the poetic excellence as distinct from the intellectual. Johnson, it will be remembered, once refuted Berkeley by kicking a stone, a performance which ought to cast grave doubts on his qualifications as a critic of philosophical ideas. It would not perhaps be difficult to question the credentials of many of those who dismiss Pope's philosophical pretensions so lightly—one could, for example, quote Dobrée, "In the main Pope gives a vision of the clockwork universe implied, if not exactly stated, by Locke,"[2] as evidence of a misunderstanding of both authors named, or John Laird's "Locke was very nearly a critical positivist."[3] But even to prove the incompetence of all the critics would not prove Pope's competence —Berkeley could still be a bad philosopher even if Johnson did not know how to refute him.

1. Bonamy Dobrée, *The Early Eighteenth Century* (Oxford History of English Literature, vol. VII; Oxford, 1959), 540–1.
2. *Ibid.*, 541.
3. John Laird, *Philosophical Incursions into English Literature* (Cambridge, 1946), ch. III, 41.

And it is by no means certain that Pope has been damned as a philosopher solely by the incompetent. I think, however, it is fair to say that he has often been damned on misunderstandings and misinterpretations, and it is with some of these that I wish to deal.

Nearly all critics have found difficulty in relating the first epistle of the *Essay on Man* to the other three. They have tried either to impose the pattern of the Great Chain of Being throughout the poem or have given up and decided that Pope oscillates between the Great Chain and a quite different constitutive idea. Now it is quite obvious that Pope uses elements of the doctrine of the Great Chain in the first epistle, and Crousaz was right in seeing a relation between Pope's ideas and Leibniz's,[4] even if he was wrong about how it got there. And Lovejoy was right in seeing that the *Essay on Man* had a place in the history of the Great Chain of Being.[5] But Pope's Epistle I takes on a very modified appearance if one asks another question about it. If one asks, not what there is in common between Pope's doctrine and Leibniz's, or how much of the tradition of the Great Chain he expresses, but how his doctrine differs, or what elements of the tradition he does not express, one gets perhaps a clearer view of what Pope is doing.

As C. A. Moore suggests,[6] followed more recently by Dobrée, it is quite possible that both Pope and Bolingbroke "had recently read King's *De Origine Mali*, to which fresh attention had been drawn by Law's translation." If they indeed did so, they would have read one of the most complete of the many expositions of the doctrine.[7] And the essential point about the complete doctrine is that it is ontological and *a priori*. In the phrase by which the doctrine is known, The Great Chain of Being, the most significant word is the last. For it is not merely a doctrine of a great chain, not merely a *scala naturae* (although it is that also). Nor is it a chain of *beings*, that is, of entities or existences. It is an ontological hierarchy: that is, it explains differences of degree in the *scala naturae* not in physical terms, primarily,

4. J. P. de Crousaz, *Examen de l'Essai de M. Pope sur l'Homme* (Lausanne, 1737).

5. A. O. Lovejoy, *The Great Chain of Being* (Harvard University Press, 1936), chs. VI and VII.

6. C. A. Moore, "Did Leibnitz influence Pope's *Essay*?" *JEGP*, XVI (1917), 84–102.

7. William King, *De Origine Mali* (Dublin, 1702); English translation by Edmund Law (London, 1729).

but in metaphysical, ontological terms. Again, the *scala naturae* can be derived *a posteriori*, from the classification and ordering of observed particular entities. The Great Chain is derived *a priori*, from axioms about the nature of Being. There can be only one perfect, self-sufficient Being, and it must be from this one perfect Being that the necessitating logical ground for all other Being must be derived. Since there can be only the one perfect Being, all created Being must be imperfect in degree of Being. From these first principles it is argued that, since Being in any degree is a good, as opposed to not-Being, the best scheme of created Being would be that which included every possible degree of Being, from that closest to perfection to that closest to not-Being, or nothing.

All this will be very familiar to readers of Lovejoy's *Great Chain of Being*. It is also part of the scheme, again by deduction from the *a priori* axioms, that it should include the two principles of continuity and plenitude: that no possible kind of being should be absent, that there should be no gaps in the chain. "Missing link" here had a somewhat different meaning than it acquired in the next century; in the *a priori* chain a missing link was an impossibility; in the evolutionist's *a posteriori* chain, a great many links were missing.

Another important aspect of the doctrine is indicated by the title of King's work, *De Origine Mali*, and by that of Leibniz's, *Theodicée*. The Great Chain theory starts, not with an attempt to make an orderly arrangement of natural phenomena, not with a *scala naturae* as an exercise in taxonomy, but as an explanation of the origin of evil, a demonstration of divine justice. Milton justified the ways of God to men through the theology of the Fall; Archbishop King did it through the metaphysics of Being. This involves treating evil in negative terms, as imperfect Being, or deprivation of Being. If Milton found difficulties in his theological treatment in the problems of foreknowledge, foreordination, and free will, King and his fellow ontologists, in demonstrating the necessity of imperfection, hardly fare better.

And it is important to remember that this *is* a demonstration, and that the *a priori* argument, proceeding deductively from self-evident truths or axioms, carries with it in the first half of the eighteenth century the prestige of certainty attached to mathematics. King and his fellows are offering a certain explanation, not only of how the created world originated, and the principles upon which it is created, but of how and why God created it, and why he could not have created it otherwise. It is this demonstrative *a priori* ontology which is the essential element of the Great Chain of Being, and which distinguishes it from the mere *scala naturae*. And it is only necessary to outline it in this fashion to recognize at once that this is certainly not the dominant doctrine in Pope's Epistle I.

In the first place, there is no sign in Pope of the doctrine of the nature of Being from which the whole structure is derived—no definition of perfect, self-sufficient Being, whose overflowing goodness imparts all degrees of Being to his creations. There is none of the confident demonstration that God could not have created a different universe:

> He, who through vast immensity can pierce,
> See worlds on worlds compose one universe,
> Observe how system into system runs,
> What other planets circle other suns,
> What varied Being peoples every star,
> May tell why Heaven has made us as we are.

This is surely an explicit repudiation of the Great Chain philosophers, who boldly "tell why Heaven has made us as we are." It is also an implicit repudiation of their method, since the conditions Pope lays down for understanding the cosmos, conditions which he goes on to explain are impossible for man to meet, are those of *a posteriori* proof, not of *a priori*—a proof, that is, from a knowledge of particular phenomena. He has made his rejection of *a priori* reasoning clear at the beginning of the Epistle:

> Say first, of God above, or Man below,
> What can we reason, but from what we know?

And he goes on to define "know" in *a posteriori* rather than *a priori* terms:

> Of Man, what see we but his station here,
> From which to reason, or to which refer?
> Through worlds unnumbered though the God be known,
> 'Tis ours to trace him only in our own.

It is only necessary to recall Samuel Clarke's demonstration of the Being and Attributes of God,[8] the Being *a priori*, the Attributes

8. *A Discourse concerning the Being and Attributes of God . . .*, 1705–6 (Boyle Lectures).

a posteriori, to recognize how sharply Pope is limiting our knowledge to *a posteriori* here.

All the same, he goes on at once to speak of the "great chain":

> Is the great chain, that draws all to agree,
> And drawn supports, upheld by God, or thee?

The crucial question is whether he is using the phrase with its full ontological context. Since he goes on to rebuke "presumptuous Man" and to ask him a question to which the full doctrine of the Great Chain would offer an easy answer, the implication is that the "great chain" as Pope speaks of it is not the Great Chain as King conceives it:

> Presumptuous Man! the reason wouldst thou find,
> Why formed so weak, so little, and so blind?
> First, if thou canst, the harder reason guess,
> Why formed no weaker, blinder, and no less?

In the complete doctrine of the Great Chain, the second question is no harder than the first, the answers to both being in fact identical. Pope is clearly thinking here, not in terms of continuity and plenitude, but of Being as a free gift of God, granted to unworthy man who is ungratefully critical of what he has received.

As I have said, the crucial question is the extent to which the full doctrine of the Great Chain of Being enters into the poem. It could be argued (and has been) that Pope is oscillating from one doctrine to another. I do not think so, and I now come to the passage which will, I hope, clarify my conception of Pope's procedure:

> Of Systems possible, if 'tis confest
> That Wisdom infinite must form the best,
> Where all must full or not coherent be,
> And all that rises, rise in due degree;
> Then, in the scale of reasoning life, 'tis plain,
> There must be, somewhere, such a rank as Man:
> And all the question (wrangle e'er so long)
> Is only this, if God has placed him wrong?

At first glance, this looks like a direct expression of the doctrine of the Great Chain, with its principles of plenitude and gradation. But a closer and more thoughtful reading reveals a significant variation. In this passage, what is logically the conclusion of the *a priori* argument on which the Great Chain of Being is constructed, the conclusion that this is the best of *possible* worlds, becomes instead a premise. Moreover, the premise is given a conditional form: "Of Systems possible, *if* 'tis confest / That Wisdom infinite must form the best. . . ." *If* this is granted, then it must follow that there must be such a rank. Now logically this is a significantly different procedure from that of the Great Chain philosophers. For them, Pope's premise is a logically demonstrated conclusion, derived from *a priori* truths, and a conclusion which rules out Pope's question, or, indeed, is meant to answer it. For Pope, the proposition that infinite Wisdom *must* create the best of possible worlds is not a demonstrated conclusion, but a reasonable premise. What makes it reasonable? Primarily, I think, the unreasonableness of its negative. The world is divinely ordered or it is not divinely ordered; if it is not, then it is incoherent, unintelligible, and human thought about it is irrelevant. The *a posteriori* reasoning whose validity Pope accepts depends itself on an assumption of order in Nature, and for Pope, as for most of the eighteenth-century thinkers, order in Nature is the result of and the evidence of Divine Providence. This order is not completely demonstrable *a posteriori*, since, as Pope constantly reminds us, we cannot know the whole of Nature, or, as a part of it, understand the whole. Ultimately our assumption of order must rest on faith, or, as some in the century would say, on probability. It may be significant that Pope uses the term "confest" here; in the Nicene Creed "confiteor" is used in the sense of "acknowledge and accept the doctrine" (of baptism).

To thinkers of our own day what I have just argued may not seem significant. It is our pragmatic habit to describe those who arrive by very different paths at the same conclusion as being in agreement. In the eighteenth century, to be in agreement meant to have followed the same paths to the same conclusion, and some of the bitterest arguments are between those who would accept each other's conclusions if it were not so necessary to reject the premises from which they had derived them. Alternatively, quarrels were based on the assumption that the expressed conclusion must have entailed a fixed set of premises. This explains why it is so easy to assume, when Pope expresses conclusions belonging to the Great Chain theory, that he has arrived at them by the usual ontological argument. By now it should be clear that this is not so, and that there is a fundamental disagreement between Pope and the ontological philosophers. He is willing to accept and to use many of the concepts belonging to the Great Chain theory, but never willing to accept its system of ontological logic, its certainty of demonstration, its confident elucidation of how the Divine mind and powers operate. In fact, he uses the concept of the necessary limitation of the creature to undermine the *a priorism* from which it is usually derived:

> Know thy own point: This kind, this due degree
> Of blindness, weakness, Heaven bestows on thee.

Given the limitation, the degree of blindness, man can know only partly, must trust and affirm by faith,

> Safe in the hand of one disposing Power,
> Or in the natal, or the mortal hour.
> All Nature is but Art, unknown to thee;
> All Chance, Direction, which thou canst not see;
> All Discord, Harmony not understood;
> All partial Evil, universal Good. . . .

These are affirmations, not demonstrations—the emphasis falls on "unknown," "canst not see," "not understood."

Yet at a number of points in the poem Pope seems to be speaking, with the same sort of confidence as the ontologists, of the cosmic scheme of creation.

> See, through this air, this ocean, and this earth,
> All matter quick, and bursting into birth.
> Above, how high progressive life may go!
> Around, how wide! how deep extend below!
> Vast chain of Being! which from God began,
> Natures ethereal, human, angel, man,
> Beast, bird, fish, insect, what no eye can see,
> No glass can reach; from Infinite to thee,
> From thee to Nothing.—On superior powers
> Were we to press, inferior might on ours:
> Or in the full creation leave a void,
> Where, one step broken, the great scale's destroyed;
> From Nature's chain whatever link you strike,
> Tenth or ten thousandth, breaks the chain alike.

Here is not only the phrase, "Vast chain of Being," but what seems the quite usual elaboration of it. But even here, where the ontological implications seem at their strongest in the Epistle, certain phrases attract our attention. The suggestion that a void *could* be left in the full creation is at variance with the ontological doctrine in much the same way as the question whether God has placed man in the proper rank. In the ontological system, each place is filled by ontological necessity; each creature occupies its particular place by virtue of what it is, not by virtue of what it does, and even less by its willingness to occupy that place rather than another. Pope's suggestion that it is within the realm of possibility for us to "press on superior powers," and his very use of the term "powers" here, are incompatible with the ontological demonstration of the necessity of all degrees of being.

It might be supposed, perhaps, that Pope is here merely being rhetorical, and sacrificing strict philosophy for effect. It is more plausible, I think, that he is again talking in terms other than those of the strict Great Chain doctrine. This is suggested by the line: "Where, one step broken, the great scale's destroyed." The "great scale" is, of course, the *scala naturae*, a ladder with steps. It is easy enough to confuse the great chain and the great ladder, but they are not identical, and the implications of the images are not the same, nor are their histories. (The attachment of the chain metaphor to the Platonic tradition, and the ladder to the Aristotelian, is, I suppose, largely a historical accident; one can see ways in which the ladder fits the Platonic better than the chain. The separateness of the degrees of being, in spite of the principle of continuity, fits the steps of a ladder better than the mutually involved links of a chain; the ladder carries with it firmer implications of a hierarchy than a chain, and so on.) As we have seen, Pope juxtaposes the two images, and again the question arises whether this is a deliberate part of his expression or mere confusion. Let us recall again that the notion that the act of a creature could make a void in the system of creation is incompatible with the Great Chain ontology. Even more so is the notion that it could destroy the whole system. If Pope's mind is working as he writes these lines, it is clearly working in another context. What that context is the following lines suggest:

> And, if each system in gradation roll
> Alike essential to th'amazing Whole,
> The least confusion but in one, not all
> That system only, but the Whole must fall.
> Let Earth unbalanced from her orbit fly,
> Planets and Suns run lawless through the sky;

Let ruling Angels from their spheres be hurled,
Being on Being wrecked, and world on world;
Heaven's whole foundations to their centre nod,
And Nature tremble to the throne of God.

What is at once noticeable about this passage, with its vivid picture of the dissolution of cosmic order into chaos, is that the kind of order it is speaking of is not the kind of order depicted in the Great Chain of Being—it is not an ordered hierarchy of different degrees of Being, an order established by ontological necessity, but the much more familiar kind of order, empirically observed, and established *a posteriori*, of the celestial system. And the context here is primarily that of the astro-theologian. The "amazing Whole" is that of earth, planets, suns, "world on world," held in a system of orderly motion. When Pope describes the way in which, in the "amazing Whole," "each system in gradation" rolls, he is clearly using "gradation" in a quite different sense from that of the Great Chain. The "dread Order" he here pictures as being broken is that observed by the astronomer.

Now there is no ontological, or any other kind, of necessity about this order. Newton, like nearly every other thinker of his time, took the view that the observed order of motion of the celestial bodies was an order imposed by divine fiat; it need not have been imposed at all, and it need not, if imposed, have been the particular order we observe. Another order, with a different mathematical law of gravitation, and correspondingly different kinds of orbits, could have been given to the system. As Newton himself put it: "It may be also allow'd that God is able to create Particles of Matter . . . perhaps of different Densities and Forces, and thereby to vary the Laws of Nature, and make Worlds of several sorts in several Parts of the Universe. At least, I see nothing of Contradiction in all this."[9] Since it is not a necessary, inevitable order, since it is originally dependent on Will, and since it involves a kind of ordering which is not ontological, but physical, it has nothing in common with Great Chain theory as such. The catastrophe Pope describes so vividly is precisely the same as that which Newtonians like Whiston ascribe to the suspension or withdrawal from the Universe of the "continued exercise" of the Divine and Immaterial Power upon which its order depends: "If the Almighty should supersede or suspend this his constant Providential Power for one single Hour, all the

9. *Opticks* (1730 ed.), Bk. III, Qu. 31; first added in 1706.

World would be dissolv'd and dissipated, and all the noble Bodies therein, Suns, Planets, Comets, Vegetables, and Animals would at once be destroyed, and perish at the same time."[10] That the order is conceived of by Pope in Newtonian terms is further suggested by setting a passage from Newton himself against one of Pope's most famous passages, which follows almost directly the one I have just quoted. Here is Newton:

Such a wonderful Uniformity in the Planetary System must be allowed the Effect of choice. And so must the Uniformity in the Bodies of Animals, . . . also the first Contrivance of those very artificial Parts of Animals, the Eyes, Ears, Brain, Muscles, Heart, Lungs, . . . and other Organs of Sense and Motion; and the Instinct of Brutes and Insects, can be the effect of nothing else than the Wisdom and Skill of a powerful ever-living Agent, who being in all Places, is more able by his Will to move the Bodies within his boundless uniform Sensorium, and thereby to form and reform the Parts of the Universe, than we are by our Will to move the Parts of our own Bodies. And yet we are not to consider the World as the Body of God, or the several Parts thereof, as the Parts of God. He is an uniform Being, void of Organs, Members or Parts. . . .[11]

And here is Pope:

All are but parts of one stupendous whole,
Whose body Nature is, and God the soul;
That, changed through all, and yet in all the same;
Great in the earth, as in th'ethereal frame;
Warms in the sun, refreshes in the breeze,
Glows in the stars, and blossoms in the trees,
Lives through all life, extends through all extent,
Spreads undivided, operates unspent;
Breathes in our soul, informs our mortal part,
As full, as perfect, in a hair as heart;
As full, as perfect, in vile Man that mourns,
As the rapt Seraph that adores and burns:
To him no high, no low, no great, no small;
He fills, he bounds, connects and equals all.

The single difference in expression is Newton's "We are not to consider the World as the Body of God," and Pope's "Whose body

10. William Whiston, *Sermons and Essays* (London, 1709), 209.

11. *Opticks* (1730 ed.), Bk. III, Qu. 31. The query was added in the Latin edition of 1706, but the last two sentences of the quotation were not added until the second English edition of 1718.

Nature is, and God the soul." Newton is trying to guard himself against the implications of his use of the term *Sensorium*, and against charges that he has made God merely the *anima mundi*. Pope uses the term "Nature," which is much more comprehensive than "World." But in spite of what seems like a direct contradiction, I think Pope's doctrine and Newton's are essentially the same. Both see Nature as a system of finite matter in infinite space. Throughout the whole of this infinite space is the omnipresent divine Spirit, source of all life, motion, force, and order. Each thinks of the relation of the divine Spirit to the created material world as in some way analogous to the relation of the human soul to the human body. Each tries to guard against implications resulting from carrying the analogy too far, or applying it too literally. Pope's main defence here is in the inclusion of "the rapt Seraph that adores and burns," which reminds the reader that God, although he animates material Nature, transcends it, as Newton also would insist. In fact, of course, neither is putting forward a pantheist doctrine; they both preserve a sharp dualism which distinguishes God from his material creation.

The way in which this passage of the Epistle echoes Newton's passages in the *Optics* and in the General Scholium of the *Principia* has often been noted, but I do not think the significance has been brought out. The significance is, as I have said, that the Newtonian doctrine represents a quite different context of thought from the Great Chain, with a quite different concept of cosmic order, of the origin of cosmic order, and of the principles underlying that order. And also quite different possibilities of interpreting man's attitude to the order. Since the Newtonian order is based upon divine choice, and could have been otherwise, it is possible for man to challenge the divine Will, and, as it were, criticize the divine arrangements, which is hardly the case in the Great Chain theory, where things could not possibly have been otherwise. At least there is a difference between challenging the inevitable and challenging a voluntary act.

It is fitting in this context, then, for Pope to introduce the familiar Christian analogy of the body and its members:

> What if the foot, ordained the dust to tread,
> Or hand, to toil, aspired to be the head?
> What if the head, the eye, or ear repined
> To serve mere engines to the ruling Mind?

Just as absurd for any part to claim
To be another, in this general frame:
Just as absurd, to mourn the tasks or pains,
The great directing Mind of All ordains.

Pope is as aware as we are that this analogy is usually applied to political society, that it usually expresses an organic view of political society. He is deliberately suggesting an extension of the analogy. The function of each part of the "general frame" is ordained by the "great directing Mind of All," somewhat as the foot is "ordained" the dust to tread—the connection established by the repeated word "ordain" emphasizes the fiat of the divine Will. The organic analogy also establishes an order, not of Being, as in the Great Chain, but of function; parts are defined in terms of tasks, not of degree of completeness of being. It is rather doubtful whether the analogy permits a true hierarchy. Foot, hand, eye, ear, head, all serve as "mere engines to the ruling Mind" in the body; by analogy, all the parts of Nature serve as mere engines to the "great directing Mind of All." If there is a limited hierarchy in the suggested superiority of head to foot, this is certainly not the detailed and completely graduated hierarchy of the Great Chain. There is rather the sense of an organic unity[12] to which every part is necessary, and it is in this framework that we can fit the lines:

To him no high, no low, no great, no small;
He fills, he bounds, connects, and equals all,

and match to them the description of God:

Who sees with equal eye, as God of all,
A hero perish, or a sparrow fall,
Atoms or systems into ruin hurled,
And now a bubble burst, and now a world.

12. There are, of course, doctrines of organic unity in Leibniz and in Spinoza, but they seem to have significant differences from Pope's both in origin and in function or implication. Spinoza and Leibniz are primarily concerned with the relation of the One and the Many, and each revives a version of the doctrine of substantial forms. Spinoza wishes to move from *corpora simplicissima* to composite individuals which retain their identity despite change of their component *corpora simplicissima*, and thence to "proceed to infinity," to "all nature" as "one individual whose parts, that is, all bodies, vary in infinite ways without any change of the individual as a whole" (*Ethics*, II, Lemma vii)—that is, to God as *natura naturata*. Leibniz, wishing to avoid a doctrine of God as the substantial form of the world or *anima mundi*, moves as it were from the middle down, from dominant monad to subordinate monad, each subordinate monad a dominant one to the smaller, *in infinitum*. These doctrines have little in common with that expressed by Pope.

The view of the created cosmos Pope presents is closely dependent on this organic analogy, and on the theme of the pervasive power of divine Providence. It is not surprising, then, to find him in the third Epistle substituting for the Great Chain of Being the phrase "a chain of Love":

> Look round our World; behold the chain of Love
> Combining all below and all above,

and introducing the analogy, becoming popular, of the divine Love and the force of gravitational attraction:

> See plastic Nature working to this end,
> The single atoms each to other tend,
> Attract, attracted to, the next in place
> Formed and impelled its neighbour to embrace.
> See Matter next, with various life endued,
> Press to one centre still, the general Good. . . .
> Nothing is foreign: Parts relate to whole;
> One all-extending, all-preserving Soul
> Connects each being, greatest with the least;
> Made Beast in aid of Man, and Man of Beast;
> All served, all serving: nothing stands alone;
> The chain holds on, and where it ends, unknown.

And again in the fourth Epistle, the chain is the chain, not of Being, but of divine Love which leads man to God; the good man, untaught, will find bliss as he

> looks through Nature up to Nature's God;
> Pursues that Chain which links the immense design,
> Joins heaven and earth, and mortal and divine; . . .
> Learns, from this union of the rising Whole,
> The first, last purpose of the human soul;
> And knows, where Faith, Law, Morals all began,
> All end, in Love of God, and Love of Man.

This is again the language of the *a posteriori* philosophers, the astro- and physico-theologians, who see in the particulars of Nature evidence of divine Providence, of divine Love. The passage is echoed later by one in Book IV of the *Dunciad*, and by the note Pope and Warburton attached to it:

> Those who, from the effects in this Visible world, deduce the Eternal Power and Godhead of the First Cause, though they cannot attain to an adequate idea of the Deity, yet discover so much of him as enables them

to see the End of their Creation, and the Means of their Happiness: whereas they who take this high Priori Road . . . for one that goes right, ten lose themselves in Mists, or ramble after Visions. . . .

And the Goddess of Dulness adjures the sons of men to

See Nature in some partial narrow shape,
And let the Author of the Whole escape:
Learn but to trifle; or, who most observe,
To wonder at their Maker, not to serve.

Her follower speaks scornfully of those who reason *a posteriori* from experience:

Let others creep by timid steps, and slow,
On plain Experience lay foundations low,
By common sense to common knowledge bred,
And last, to Nature's Cause through Nature led.
All-seeing in thy [Dulness'] mists, we want no guide,
Mother of arrogance, and Source of Pride!
We nobly take the high Priori Road,
And reason downward, till we doubt of God. . . .

It is in the name of Dulness, Mother of arrogance and Source of Pride, that her follower rejects the *a posteriori* for the high *a priori* road; and it is with the triumph of Dulness that Chaos is restored at the end of the *Dunciad*, "And universal Darkness buries All."

It is small wonder, then, that in the first Epistle of the *Essay on Man* one finds constant attacks on "Man's pride and dulness," his presumption. "Go, wiser thou!" the poet ironically advises,

and in thy scale of sense,
Weigh thy Opinion against Providence;
Call imperfection what thou fanciest such. . . .
Snatch from his hand the balance and the rod,
Re-judge his justice, be the God of God.

It is not for man to write a theodicy, to pass judgment on God. It is not for him to scrutinize God:

Know then thyself, presume not God to scan;
The proper study of Mankind is Man.

That is, of course, precisely why this is an Essay on Man, not an essay (like Clarke's) on the *Being and Attributes of God*, or (like King's) on *The Origin of Evil*. In this first epistle, Pope has set the limits of his subject; he has, as he promised in the opening, explored "the giddy heights . . . / Of all who blindly creep, or sightless soar." He has suggested what conjectures we can make "of the Nature and State of Man with respect to the Universe," but the promise of the title of the epistle is itself ironic, as is most of the opening. The optimistic demonstration of the Great Chain theorists was hardly likely to be any more convincing to Pope, given his experience of life and his satirical temper, than to Swift, Voltaire, or Johnson.

None of the *Essay on Man* is constructed around the Great Chain of Being as a main constitutive idea. Pope's real view of the nature of things and of the nature of man is presented in the line: "But ALL subsists by elemental strife," and in the opening of *Windsor Forest*, where the Windsor countryside becomes a symbol of the universe:

> Here hills and vales, the woodland and the plain,
> Here earth and water seem to strive again;
> Not Chaos-like together crushed and bruised,
> But, as the world, harmoniously confused:
> Where order in variety we see,
> And where, though all things differ, all agree.

It is this dynamic balance of opposites[13] (note that "strife" appears in both passages) into a harmony, and not the static order of the Great Chain that seems to Pope to represent the observed reality. What we immediately observe is of course the strife; evil is not simply negative, the weeds are as real as the flowers. We must affirm a plan in this mighty Maze; and as with the injunction, "Know then thyself," Pope proceeds to his study of Man, to what we can know—the nature and state of man with respect to himself as an individual, with respect to society, and with respect to happiness—he organizes what he sees around this constitutive principle of the "elemental strife." It should by now be evident that the structure of the first epistle is distinct from that of the other three, but is yet not primarily the ontological structure of the Great Chain; it is dealing with the ultimately unknowable, and disposing of those who arrogantly profess to know it. This is why there is somewhat the same note of irony in the opening

13. Again, there are doctrines of strife in Spinoza and Leibniz, but they involve essentially the problem of "compossibles," the survival of the ontologically fittest. The struggle in Pope's "conflict" is not for survival, since the survival of both opposites creates the harmony—harmony is seen itself as a dynamic tension, as in "chiaroscuro."

"Let us . . . vindicate the ways of God to Man" as there is in the later:

> Yes, I am proud; I must be proud to see
> Men not afraid of God, afraid of me. . . .

And yet Pope has, in a sense, vindicated the ways of God to Man, albeit in a sense very different from that usually suggested by the phrase. He has affirmed the divine Order, man's creatureship under the divine Love, and has offered some of the *a posteriori* evidence of divine Providence. There may be significance in his echoing of only half of Milton's phrase: if he has not justified the ways of God to men, he has asserted eternal Providence.

The Three Forms of The Prelude 1798-1805*

J. R. MACGILLIVRAY

THE PRELUDE was first published in 1850, shortly after Wordsworth's death. The composition of the poem, as distinct from its revision, had been completed forty-five years earlier, in 1805. It was revised on three occasions afterwards, the latest in 1839, and many minor changes were made, and a few larger ones. The fair copy of 1839 was the manuscript which was sent to the printer in 1850.

The next important date in the history of the poem was 1926, when Ernest De Selincourt published his edition "from the manuscripts, with introduction, textual and critical notes." The poem as it had been completed in 1805 was printed there for the first time, on verso pages opposite the corresponding lines of the well-known work of 1850. This convenient confrontation and the elaborate textual apparatus made it possible for the student to observe significant changes in thought and expression in Wordsworth's greatest poem over nearly the whole period of his literary life. However, neither De Selincourt's introductory account of the early history of *The Prelude*, nor Helen Darbishire's revision and correction of it in 1959, nor the textual apparatus, useful as it is, makes it clear that the poem of 1805 was not the first version of the autobiography, but rather the third. It had first been composed in 1798–1800 as a poem in two parts, less than one thousand lines in length. By the end of 1801, Wordsworth had decided to enlarge the poem and to give it a different

*In an earlier form, this paper was read at a meeting of Section II of the Royal Society of Canada at McMaster University on June 4, 1962.

emphasis. After working on it only rarely in the next two years and then continuously in February and March, 1804, he had almost finished it, in five books, when he changed his plan once more, and went on to write the much longer poem which he first completed the following year. Each of these three poems had its particular biographical extent and literary organization. The first poem was incorporated somewhat less than perfectly in the second, and the second in the third. In this paper I intend to trace the early history of the autobiographical writing which became *The Prelude,* to distinguish the three forms which it took, and to indicate how some puzzling features of the poem of 1805 and later can be explained as unassimilated survivals from the two earlier poems.

First a difficulty in designation should be mentioned. From the beginning of its composition until shortly before its publication, more than half a century later, the poem in each of its forms remained without a title. It was referred to in such terms as "a Poem . . . on my early life or the growth of my own mind" or "the poem to Coleridge." It was Mrs. Wordsworth, after her husband's death, who gave the work its name: *The Prelude, or Growth of a Poet's Mind; An Autobiographical Poem.*[1]

It was intended both to *relate* and to *be* a prelude. It was to relate the beginning of the poet's imaginative life, eventually down to the year of the publication of *Lyrical Ballads,* when he was twenty-eight years old. It was to be a prelude to a much longer and more ambitious poem which he hoped would be his greatest literary achievement, a work never completed—hence the long delay in publication. We first hear of the plan for the great poem and the beginning of its composition in March 1798. "I have been tolerably industrious within the last few weeks. I have written 1300 lines of a poem which I hope to make of considerable utility. Its title will be *The Recluse; or views of Nature, Man, and Society.*"[2] A few days earlier he had mentioned the poem without indicating the primary title: "My object is to give pictures of Nature, Man, and Society. Indeed I know not any thing which will not come within the scope of my plan."[3]

1. Christopher Wordsworth, *Memoirs of William Wordsworth* (London, 1851), I, 313.
2. *The Early Letters of William and Dorothy Wordsworth,* ed. E. De Selincourt (Oxford, 1935), 190. Hereafter referred to as *Early Letters.*
3. *Ibid.,* 188.

Of the plan of *The Recluse* at this stage we learn no more than that. It was both extensive and vague. It may have originated in the mind of Coleridge, so productive of large schemes. Certainly for many years he was to continue to show an almost proprietary interest in the project. Since the previous summer (1797), the two poets had been living near each other in Somerset. An established friendship had been followed by mutual dependence for intellectual and literary stimulation. They had wandered over the neighbouring Quantock Hills together or down to the shore of the Bristol Channel—where a government spy with a Bardolph nose, sent to find out what those suspected radicals were discussing so frequently, was incensed to learn that they were talking about him. He was sure he heard them, several times, refer to Spy Nozy.[4] In November, accompanied by Dorothy Wordsworth, they had walked as far as Lynmouth, on the

4. *Biographia Literaria*, ed. J. Shawcross (Oxford, 1907), I, 126–7. The government spy was once thought to have been a comic invention by Coleridge, but there actually was such a person. His name was G. Walsh, his instructions and reports are in the Public Record Office (H.O. 42/41), and he was sent to keep under surveillance the Wordsworths who had just settled at Alfoxden.

From the Globe Inn, Stowey, where he had established himself, "Spy Nozy" Walsh wrote on August 15, 1797:

"I had not been many minutes in this house before I had an opportunity of entering upon my Business, By a Mr. Woodhouse asking the Landlord, If he had seen any of those Rascalls from Alfoxton. To which the Land lord reply'd, He had seen Two of them yesterday. . . . I told Woodhouse, that I had heard somebody say at Bridgewater that They were French people at the Manor House. The Land lord & Woodhouse answer'd No. No. They are not French, But They are people that will do as much harm, as All the French can do."

I know nothing further about Woodhouse. Evidently he was no stranger at the village pub (though perhaps not a regular), a man of firm opinion and vigorous expression, and, no doubt, a staunch Tory. Only the temptations of rhetoric and his audience, we may be sure, made him assert that these English fellow-countrymen of his could ever be as rascally and noxious as the French.

Though there is no question about Spy Nozy, there is one about Spinoza. Were Coleridge and Wordsworth actually discussing him frequently in the summer of 1797 when the spy was shadowing them? The earliest mention of Spinoza in Coleridge's letters is to be found two years later, after his return from Germany, when he was happily "sunk in Spinoza" (Sept. 30, 1799) and commented on his own Spinosism "if Spinosism it be and i' faith 'tis very like it" (Dec. 24, 1799). The first reference in the notebooks is even later. At a much earlier date, however, in the winter of 1797–8, a few months after the spy's visit, Wordsworth was revising "The Ruined Cottage," as mentioned below, and expressing there in his additions to the poem his sense in youth of a living world of external nature, when the very rocks seemed to be permeated by the divine mind, when the vitality of both man and nature seemed to be modes by which the unknown God expressed his own being in particular ways. It may be that Wordsworth had discovered Spinoza by this time and recognized some points of similarity with his own thought. However, I cannot recall any mention of Spinoza in Wordsworth's letters and notebooks, early or late.

border of Devon, and during the first evening as they tramped along they had planned and begun to compose as a joint effort *The Ancient Mariner*. Day after day they retraced the well-worn paths between Coleridge's humble cottage on the edge of Nether Stowey and the handsome country mansion of Alfoxden, three miles to the west, where the Wordsworths had obtained a year's tenancy at a nominal rent which even they could afford. And always they discussed poetry and literary plans. In the three weeks that began with the first reference to *The Recluse*, as Dorothy Wordsworth's journal shows, there were not more than three days in all when Wordsworth and Coleridge did not see each other.

At this time, in March 1798, both poets were thinking of publishing, but neither had yet considered the joint volume of poems which was to appear in only a few months, the famous *Lyrical Ballads*. Coleridge was negotiating with Cottle of Bristol for a third and much revised edition of his poems, but he also proposed a volume to be made up of his unpublished tragedy *Osorio* and Wordsworth's *The Borderers*. In addition to his tragedy, Wordsworth's only sizable literary commodities were two fairly long narrative poems of social comment, "Salisbury Plain" and "The Ruined Cottage." The latter poem, recently revised and enlarged, was probably now thought of as eventually to form part of *The Recluse*.

"The Ruined Cottage" had been finished, Wordsworth then believed, in the previous summer. It was the pathetic story, in blank verse, of the misfortunes of one family in a time of unemployment, scarcity, and war. The central character was a woman whose husband was driven in the desperation of penury to take the King's shilling, leaving her and their children in the cottage which, as it gradually falls into ruin, becomes the suggestive counterpart of a ruined family. The sympathetic observer and narrator was a pedlar of philosophic cast of mind, whose occasional returns to the neighbourhood accounted for the observed stages in the decline of Margaret's fortune. The pedlar was little more than a narrative convenience when the poem was first finished, merely the poet's source of information and a quite secondary figure in the story. But by the beginning of 1798 Wordsworth had become dissatisfied with the poem. The pedlar was, in a way, the poet's surrogate, and he probably found it necessary to explain how so unlikely a person had become a sensitive and imaginative observer of life. So he began to enlarge the poem with a history of the boyhood of the pedlar, in Cumberland, the region of the poet's birth, and particularly with a history of the growth of his imagination. The composition went on rapidly, in January and February. The sombre story of Margaret and her ruined cottage was joined to another story, related with subtlety and passion, about a youth's feelings for the world of nature. By March 5, Dorothy Wordsworth reported that the poem had grown to 900 lines and "The Pedlar's character now makes a very, certainly the *most*, considerable part of the Poem."[5] Wordsworth could have had no idea where the new theme would lead him. However, we can recognize in about 250 lines of MS. B of "The Ruined Cottage" the first clear statement of some dominant ideas and the anticipation of some parts and episodes in *The Prelude.*[6]

I shall make only summary reference to a few points of similarity. Here, as in *The Prelude*, Wordsworth distinguishes stages in the development of an imaginative mind, and records a boy's passionate joy in the world of nature and in the very experience of being alive. In all nature the youth came to recognize life and the presence of mind, even in the very rocks:

> Even in their fixed and steady lineaments
> He traced an ebbing and a flowing mind,
> Expression ever varying. (106–8)

At last,

> From Nature and her overflowing soul
> He had received so much, that all his thoughts
> Were steeped in feeling. He was only then
> Contented, when, with bliss ineffable
> He felt the sentiment of being, spread
> O'er all that moves, and all that seemeth still. . . .
> Wonder not
> If such his transports were; for in all things
> He saw one life, and felt that it was joy. (238–52)

This final passage in the story of the pedlar's youth was afterwards transferred to the second book of *The Prelude*. The only change was the substitution of *I* and *my* for *he* and *his*. The youth described in "The Ruined Cottage" was really the poet himself.

The most memorable literary accomplishment of 1798 for both

5. *Early Letters*, 176.

6. MS. B of "The Ruined Cottage" is printed at length among the notes to *The Poetical Works of William Wordsworth* [V]: *The Excursion, The Recluse*, ed. E. De Selincourt and Helen Darbishire (Oxford, 1949), 379–404.

Coleridge and Wordsworth was the publication of *Lyrical Ballads*. Wordsworth's share in the joint project was to demonstrate what could be done to make events from humble and rustic life described in a deliberately, even defiantly, plain language into poetry of permanent interest and appeal. The experiment was hardly a success, and it was tacitly abandoned or the conditions much altered thereafter, though the reasoned and stubborn apologia first published with the second edition in 1800 gave the literary public for a long time, perhaps down to our own day, the ineradicable belief that the most typical poetry of Wordsworth is to be found in *Lyrical Ballads*, 1798, and all his critical ideas in the preface of 1800. Yet the best poem by Wordsworth in the volume was not in the least of the sort in question. The *Lines Composed a few miles above Tintern Abbey* was written when *Lyrical Ballads* was already in the hands of the printer, and it was added as an afterthought. The Wordsworths were in Bristol to see the poems through the press and in mid-July went for a few days up the Wye Valley into South Wales, a region which the poet had visited once before. The literary result was the composition, in one day, of an autobiographical poem of reminiscence and speculation, a poem in which he traces the stages in the development of his mind and feelings, and expresses a sense of a living universe of man and nature pervaded by the power of the unknown Being,

> A motion and a spirit, that impels
> All thinking things, all objects of all thought,
> And rolls through all things—

motion and spirit, the ultimate mysteries of the physical and the biological realms, and beyond them a "something," for the name of God does not occur in the poem.

The themes which Wordsworth had first used in MS. B of "The Ruined Cottage" and to which he had given the first formal poetic expression in *Tintern Abbey* could not be ignored for long. In the autumn, Coleridge, his disciple Chester, and the Wordsworths went to Germany to spend the winter. Financial circumstances and temperamental preferences sent the first pair to the social gaieties of a North German town and the Wordsworths to a thrifty solitude in Goslar, near the Harz Mountains. In a foreign land, shut out from society by poverty and a merely elementary knowledge of German, with few books to read, Wordsworth was compelled to draw on his inner resources of memory and thought. One day, probably late in October, he opened one of the pocket-notebooks he had with him (the one in which he had already written a report of Coleridge's and his interview with Klopstock in Hamburg and in which Dorothy had entered her journal of the trip from Hamburg to Goslar) and on the last recto page of the notebook he began to write:

> Was it for this
> That one, the fairest of all rivers loved
> To blend his murmurs with my nurse's song
> And from his alder shades and rocky falls
> And from his fords and shallows sent a voice
> To intertwine my dreams. . . .

He was writing the beginning of *The Prelude*. The "this" of his question, the end toward which nature and fortunate circumstance had conspired, was that the child whose earliest memories were of the garden-terrace back of the house, washed by the Derwent "fairest of all rivers," should mature in mind and imagination to become the poet Wordsworth hoped to be. He continued composing, using pages and parts of pages in an order often confusing to the student who would follow him, but in general setting down passages of reminiscence alternated with others of interpretation or of generalization about the early development of a poet's imagination. Several of the most memorable passages of the first book of *The Prelude* are there in their earliest form, in the notebook now designated JJ.[7]

7. Miss Darbishire's transcript of the drafts of *The Prelude* in MS. JJ will be found at the end of *The Prelude*, ed. E. De Selincourt, 2nd edition, revised by Helen Darbishire (Oxford, 1959), 633–42. My quotations from the poem are from this edition, and from the text of 1805 unless otherwise indicated.

The passage quoted above from MS. JJ, the passage which I have referred to as the beginning of *The Prelude*, corresponds to I, 271–6 of the 1805 text and I, 269–74 of 1850. The question of when, and under what circumstances, lines 1–270 were composed is an old and famous problem for Wordsworthians. I do not know that anyone has yet found a satisfactory solution. Merely to present the problem in all its aspects would require another paper as long as this. The earliest manuscript in which the introductory passage appears is MS. M, a fair copy made in the spring of 1804. In all the previous ones–JJ, the *Christabel* Notebook, U and V (1798–1800?) –the poem begins in the same way, with the half-line "Was it for this."

Though *The Prelude* may be said to have had its real beginning in Goslar in the autumn of 1798, with the first draft of these lines in MS. JJ, a few passages now in the poem had certainly been written earlier, notably the lines on the youth of the Pedlar first composed for "The Ruined Cottage" and the episode of the meeting with the discharged soldier on the road at night, now at the end of Book IV of the poem.

When the travellers returned to England the next summer (1799), Wordsworth should have gone on with *The Recluse*, the poem which he and Coleridge had decided was to be his most ambitious work. But he felt unprepared, perhaps inadequate for the task. The quite indefinite extent and unpredictable content of a work called "Views of Nature, Man, and Society" might well have given him pause. In a lost letter to Coleridge, to which we have part of the reply, he must have announced that he was first going to expand and complete the poem begun in Germany about the growth of his imagination, that it was to be a poem addressed to Coleridge as a personal record between friends and fellow poets, and that although it would be a composition complete in itself and could be so published, he expected to publish it only when *The Recluse* was finished and as an appendix to that poem. Coleridge was less than enthusiastic, though he did not directly oppose the scheme: "O let it be the tail-piece of 'The Recluse'! for of nothing but 'The Recluse' can I hear patiently."[8] So in the autumn and winter of 1799–1800, the first winter at Grasmere, Wordsworth added greatly to the work begun in Germany, completing a poem in two parts, of about 960 lines, addressed to Coleridge, and describing the early development of a poet's mind. This poem survives in two manuscripts, one complete (MS. U), the other lacking only the first 54 lines of the second part (MS. V). It has never been published, though many of its readings are given in the De Selincourt–Darbishire variorum edition, and most of the poem, revised, rearranged, and in some parts broken up, appears somewhere in *The Prelude* as published, mostly in Books I and II, but also in Books V, VIII, and XI.

In this proto-*Prelude* of 1798–1800 one observes a much more unified theme and a much stronger sense of formal structure than in the poem completed first in 1805 and published in 1850. The time covered is restricted to childhood and school days only. The single theme is the awakening of the imagination. Each of the two parts has its own limit in time: the first being of childhood and to the age of about ten, the second until the end of school days when the narrator was seventeen. The whole poem, and each separate part, shows an unusual number, for Wordsworth at least, of devices of formal

8. *Collected Letters of Samuel Taylor Coleridge*, ed. E. L. Griggs (Oxford, 1956), I, 538.

structure, used, I think, with considerable success. In the First Part, for example, of which the first two hundred lines had been largely written, or at least drafted, in Germany, we find, as I have mentioned earlier, alternating passages of reminiscence and of comment, or reflection, or psychological generalization. The reminiscences are varied to represent, not only the particular activities of the child, usually at play, but activities of each of the four seasons, of day and night, morning and evening, within doors and without, in society and in solitude. We begin with "the five year's Child" who "made one long bathing of a summer's day" and go on next to the boy who aspired to be "a fell destroyer," snaring woodcocks in the moonlight when

> The frost and breath of frosty wind had snapp'd
> The last autumnal crocus . . . (I, 312–13)

or later to the same boy, with his friends or alone, skating on a winter evening:

> while the stars,
> Eastward, were sparkling clear, and in the west
> The orange sky of evening died away. (I, 471–3)

Always, in every remembered episode there is the primary matter-of-fact event usually described vividly and with a sense of joy, but there is also the secondary event that really mattered, in the boy's mind and imagination, the awareness of beauty or mystery or of purposeful power and life in all the world of nature about him. These moments of imaginative intensity, Wordsworth would say, of insight, come rarely, and sometimes on unlikely occasions. Here, for example (I, 339–50), the poet remembers the boy-mountaineer risking his life on a rock-face for no better purpose than to rob a raven's nest:

> Though mean
> My object, and inglorious, yet the end
> Was not ignoble. Oh! when I have hung
> Above the raven's nest, by knots of grass
> And half-inch fissures in the slippery rock
> But ill sustain'd, and almost, as it seem'd,
> Suspended by the blast which blew amain,
> Shouldering the naked crag; Oh! at that time,
> While on the perilous ridge I hung alone,
> With what strange utterance did the loud dry wind
> Blow through my ears! the sky seem'd not a sky
> Of earth, and with what motion mov'd the clouds!

Toward the end of this First Part of the poem of 1798–1800, three memories are recorded of a quite different character, of the boy's first glimpses of the dark side of life, his first awareness of death. These are the memories of watching the recovery of the body of a drowned man (an episode now in Book V of *The Prelude*) and the two illustrative "spots of time" (later transferred to Book XI of the poem), of the child's fears when left alone, near the Border Beacon of Penrith, at the place where a murderer had been hanged at the scene of his crime, and the particularly poignant memory for Wordsworth from his school days of his impatient wait in the wind and the rain near Hawkshead, at the beginning of the Christmas holidays, for the horses which his father was to send to carry him and his brothers home to the anticipated gaieties of the season, unaware that before the holidays would be over his father would be taken ill suddenly and die.

The Second Part of the poem of 1798–1800 generally corresponds to the second book of *The Prelude*. Here too we observe the use of contrast as a formal feature. In four episodes the noisy athletic activities of the "boisterous race" of schoolboys at play are associated and contrasted with the occasional experience of "calmer pleasures" by at least one of their number. To mention only the last of these four—after a noisy afternoon of bowling on the green at the fashionable "White Lion" at Bowness, by Windermere, with indecorous juvenile shouts that "Made all the mountains ring," darkness fell on the lake and stillness broken only by the music of a flute played from across the water by one of their number:

> Oh! then the calm
> And dead still water lay upon my mind
> Even with a weight of pleasure, and the sky
> Never before so beautiful, sank down
> Into my heart, and held me like a dream. (II, 176–80)

Wordsworth tries also in this part to trace systematically the stages in the development of his mind, more fully than he had attempted for the Pedlar in "The Ruined Cottage" and for himself in *Tintern Abbey*, and to distinguish between the contributions of reason and imagination. But he soon gave up the attempt, remembering that he was writing for Coleridge who was far more practised than he was in these speculations:

> Thou, my Friend! art one
> More deeply read in thy own thoughts. . . . (II, 215–16)

A good many things are included in *The Prelude*, and others omitted for the same reason, that the poem was addressed to Coleridge. This early version reaches its climax when the youth of seventeen can be described in words originally written of the Pedlar, and quoted above, that "all his thoughts were steeped in feeling." He was ready in mind to try to learn the art of poetry.

This poem was finished and put aside. It was complete in itself, but it was not to be published except with *The Recluse*. We hear no more of it for two years, until in December 1801 Dorothy Wordsworth made a brief reference in her diary to the composition "of the third part" of the poem to Coleridge. Evidently the two-part poem of 1798–1800 was to be enlarged. Over a year later, in January 1803, there is another even slighter reference. Then another year passes. In mid-January 1804, after a visit of several weeks with the Wordsworths, Coleridge set out for London and eventually to the Mediterranean region where he was to spend more than two years, mostly at Malta, for the recovery of his health. About two weeks after Coleridge left Grasmere, Wordsworth wrote to Francis Wrangham: "At present I am engaged in a Poem on my own earlier life, which will take five parts or books to complete, three of which are nearly finished."[9] On March 6, in a letter to De Quincey, he reported: "I am now writing a poem on my own earlier life; and have just finished that part in which I speak of my residence at the University. . . ."[10] Writing to Coleridge the same day to report progress he said: "When this next book is done, which I shall begin in two or three days' time, I shall consider the work as finished."[11]

This second poem which had evidently been planned as to length and form, and to a large extent composed, was never finished—or rather before it could be finished Wordsworth changed and enlarged the scheme once more and went on to write the much longer work in thirteen books completed in 1805. We have no manuscript of the second poem to correspond to U and V, the fair copies of the first. We

9. *Early Letters*, 355. 10. *Ibid.*, 370. 11. *Ibid.*, 368.

have a few references in letters, the most helpful of which I have quoted in part. We have also one notebook, W, containing perhaps 700 lines of autobiographic verse in about a dozen discontinuous passages plus minor drafts and jottings written over a period of two years and a half; but in what order the passages were composed is not always discernible, and only a few of them can be dated with moderate certainty.

Several points, however, about the second form of the poem seem quite clear. Wordsworth became dissatisfied with the original two-part poem because it related nothing about the influence of books and formal education upon his imagination in childhood and youth. In notebook W he composed a considerable amount on this subject, much of it now in Book V of *The Prelude*. He wrote in ridicule of the educational theorists who would give the child only factual and improving books. He was ponderously ironic about the model child in moral and didactic tales (like Thomas Day's famous *Sandford and Merton*)—a diminutive man, obedient, unselfish, industrious, and prodigiously learned.

> Briefly, the moral part
> Is perfect, and in learning and in books
> He is a prodigy. . . .
> With propositions are the younker's brains
> Filled to the brim, the path in which he treads
> Is chok'd with grammars. . . . (V, 318–20, 323–5, W).

His master, the educational theorist, is ever on the watch to restrain him within limits as if he were a stray domestic animal in the village pound:

> Some busy helper still as on the watch
> To drive him back and pound him like a Stray
> Within the pinfold of his own conceit. . . . (V, 360–2)

A few years ago, David Erdman discovered and published a letter, written in 1797 to William Godwin by Thomas Wedgwood, afterwards the friend and patron of Coleridge, suggesting the establishment with Wedgwood money of a sort of Centre for Child Study and Controlled Education where a truly efficient formal education could be given by shutting the child away entirely from the confusing complexities of nature ("the child must never go out of doors or leave his own apartment"), where he could learn only what the educational theorists in charge chose to teach him, when they thought he was properly conditioned to learn.[12] The most incredible feature of this remarkable letter was that Wedgwood confided to Godwin that he was thinking of offering the wardenship of his projected institution to a bright young man whom he had not actually met—his name William Wordsworth! All this, of course, came to nothing, except perhaps Book V of *The Prelude*. It may be significant that in January 1803 when we know that Wordsworth was engaged, briefly, on the second form of the poem, Thomas Wedgwood had come north with Coleridge to spend a month in the Lake District. He could be a reminder of the preposterous among theories of education.

The original two-part poem to Coleridge, then, was enlarged to be about the development of the imagination under the dual influence of nature and books. There are at least two passages in notebook W (passages now in the fifth book of *The Prelude*) where the key words appear linked together and capitalized, Nature and Books. Wordsworth's remarks afterwards about his first year at Cambridge (now Book III) were to carry his formal education far enough to allow for all he had to say on that subject, and the poem was to be completed in one book more which was to include two striking passages, one now in the fourth book, the other at the beginning of the final one. They both appear in an early stage in notebook W. The first passage is the description of scene and feeling as he crossed Hawkshead Moor returning home from a party in a glorious summer dawn during his first Long Vacation from Cambridge and recognized that he was called and dedicated to poetry.

> Ah! need I say, dear Friend, that to the brim
> My heart was full; I made no vows, but vows
> Were then made for me; bond unknown to me
> Was given, that I should be, else sinning greatly,
> A dedicated Spirit. On I walk'd
> In blessedness, which even yet remains. (IV, 340–5)

The other memory first recorded in notebook W is of climbing Snowdon in the darkness until he found himself suddenly in the

12. David V. Erdman, "Coleridge, Wordsworth, and the Wedgwood Fund," *Bulletin of the New York Public Library*, LX (Sept. and Oct. 1956), 425–43, 487–507.

light above the clouds, which the poet interpreted as an allegory of the imagination. As this passage is preceded by the heading "5th Book," it seems clear that even at this time Wordsworth had decided that this episode should introduce the conclusion of his poem. So we may surmise that the second poem to Coleridge was to be about a poet's education, by nature and by books, down to the end of his formal education when he was twenty. It was to reach its climax and conclusion in the allegorical experience by night on Snowdon and the recognition of a poet's dedication in the splendour of dawn and sunrise. Again, the poem was to be of comparatively limited extent and of a clearly discernible formal structure.

Only a few days after March 6, 1804, when Wordsworth told both Coleridge and De Quincey that his poem was almost finished, he must have decided to enlarge it further. Some weeks earlier, Coleridge had asked the women of the Grasmere household to make him a fair copy of all Wordsworth's unpublished poetry to take with him to the Mediterranean. In February and March they were engaged on this very demanding task. The packets of manuscript which they prepared survive, MS. M. The last section transcribed is of Books I-V of *The Prelude*, and *they are in the order and otherwise substantially the same as in the 1805 text*. This fair copy of five books on the new and final plan must have been completed by about March 20. Incidentally, this is the first manuscript in which one finds the first 270 lines of Book I of the poem.

By the time Coleridge had received the fair copy of five books, Wordsworth was well on with the sixth. After a long rest in the summer he took up the task again and finished it the following May.

Of the theme and structure of the published poem, much has been written, and I would only make a few comparative generalizations. Although no one could question Wordsworth's assertion in the last book that the theme of the imagination "hath been the moving soul of our long labour," this central interest in *The Prelude* is often obscured by somewhat peripheral matters of political, social, and intellectual history. There is a good deal of external autobiography, of particular places, people, and public events. It may be that the particularities in the first of the books about life at Cambridge (March 1804) indicated the new direction. More than once the poet showed that he was aware of writing a chronology of external events when he should have tried to concentrate on the inner events which had been of the greatest importance in the first two plans of the poem.

Several features of the published poem, including oddities and anomalies, can be understood better when we are aware of the history of the writing. From Book I, 270 to the end of Book II still makes a poetic unity which the general reader may recognize without knowing that here we have still a large proportion of the earliest poem. It is odd, however, that the farewell to Coleridge which was its formal conclusion still remains at the end of Book II. Many readers have wondered why the poet after writing of his life at Cambridge should in Book V, on "Books," say so much about tales for children and nothing about books read at the university and after. The inadequate explanation, of course, is that this section was written to pair with the education of the child by nature, in the second plan of the poem, and was, incidentally, composed before he wrote anything about Cambridge. Also, anyone reading Books IV, V, and VI can see that VI appears to follow right after IV and that V is an interruption in every way. Again, the explanation is that the scheme of the second poem has not been sufficiently suppressed in the third. Books IV and VI were written in that order, and most of V had been composed earlier than either for another poem. Some readers may also have observed that Book III, about the poet's first year at Cambridge, includes a great variety of description and comment, but Book VI, entitled "Cambridge and the Alps," tells hardly anything about the last two-and-a-half years of his academic career. The explanation is that Book III was written for the second plan of the poem and was intended to be complete in itself. It left little to be related afterwards when the poet found it necessary to provide more chronological autobiography.

In the Preface to *The Excursion* (1814), Wordsworth wrote of *The Prelude*, then still unnamed and unpublished, and of *The Recluse* that "the two Works have the same relation to each other, if I may so express myself, as the ante-chapel has to the body of a gothic church." An architectural comparison is appropriate, but *The Prelude* seems to me to be rather more like a work of domestic than of ecclesiastical architecture. The first building was a well-proportioned structure of moderate size, varied yet congruous in its parts. But the owner, as often happens, came to think that it lacked some essential features for his satisfaction and decided to extend the edifice, changing its design and more than doubling its size. However, before this had been completed, no doubt encouraged in his extravagance by his wife and by his sister who had a great interest in these matters, he changed the plan again and, extending the building in several directions, he finally made it very much larger than he had ever envisaged. Visitors nowadays to this massive and complex structure may sometimes lose their way in its connecting passages or stumble at some abrupt change of level in different parts, but the amateur student of this kind of architecture can enjoy a harmless pleasure in discovering how the whole edifice was put together. As often happens in old-world building, some of the material used quite evidently antedates the earliest part of the triple structure. Some of it derived from a ruined cottage; some may be traced back to Tintern Abbey.

John Stuart Mill and Jeremy Bentham, with some Observations on James Mill

J. M. ROBSON

GEORGE GROTE MILL, irritated by his brother John's coolness, accused him, in their father's words, of being "mysterious"; John was stung to retort that James Mill had said far worse things about other members of the family, and that he himself had nothing to be mysterious about.[1] Here, as in most of John Mill's quarrels with his family, one cannot but be on the family's side; at least one can understand why James Mill, puzzled by so few things, must have pondered over the result of his educational experiment. His intention, and Jeremy Bentham's, was to make the "poor boy . . . a successor worthy of both of us,"[2] and he spared no pains and gave few pleasures to ensure the result. The gloom of the Mill home has undoubtedly been over-estimated, but for the eldest children at least cakes and ale came far behind Q.E.D.'s.[3] In the company of adult males, of course, James Mill was accepted as

1. British Library of Political and Economic Science (London School of Economics), Mill-Taylor Collection, XLVII, f.47r&v. Cf. Mill's admission to a "close & reserved" character in a rejected passage from the early draft of his *Autobiography*, in Jack Stillinger, ed., *The Early Draft of John Stuart Mill's Autobiography* (University of Illinois Press, 1961), 184.

2. James Mill to Bentham, 28/7/12, in Bentham's *Works*, ed. Bowring (Edinburgh, 1843), X, 473.

3. While John Mill's account of his father and of family life is not to be accepted without reservation, the passages in the *Early Draft* cited by Professor Stillinger in his "Introduction" (13) cannot but chill one's sympathy for the father of a not-ungrateful son.

witty, incisive, and companionable,[4] and it might be argued that his limitation of the franchise (in his *Essay on Government*) to males over forty years of age really defines the limits of his friendship. He was anxious that John should jump the gap in years and join the favoured company, and the boy's first appearances in contemporary records indicate that he was thrust forward socially as well as intellectually, as became a future ally.

Jeremy Bentham was more kindly towards John, though little more complimentary except in so far as the boy fulfilled his elders' expectations. His attitude is fairly revealed, allowance being made for his habitually light tone, when he writes to his brother Samuel to say that when John visits France, Samuel "may shew [him] for 6d a piece and get rich."[5] The expectations were fulfilled for many years, as precocity succeeded precocity, but finally the apostle looked more and more like an apostate, criticizing when he should have copied, straying when he should have led.

Mill's contemporaries were aware of the hopes built into his education, and were quick to deprecate or praise his seeming desertion of the Benthamite ship in the 1830's. Both opinions may be seen in Caroline Fox's reference to Bowring's speaking of John Mill "with evident contempt as a renegade from philosophy," and her comment, "Anglicè—a renouncer of Bentham's creed and an expounder of Coleridge's."[6] Mill was sensitive about his ambiguous position, and all his comments on Bentham should be read with this sensitivity in mind.

Sensitive or not, however, he had no doubt that he was uniquely qualified to assess Bentham. His right to judge is implicit in his major article in the *London and Westminster Review*; his claim had been established by his being asked to write Bentham's obituary notice in

4. See, for example, the remark by John Mill: "It was a fine thing for me to hear him [Conversation Sharp] and my father converse; some of these confabs are published in Sharp's 'Essays and Conversations'—a favourite good thing would often make its appearance." Caroline Fox, *Memories of Old Friends* (2nd ed.; London, 1882), I, 146–7.

5. British Museum Add. MS. 33,545, f.381r. Quoted by Anna J. Mill, *John Mill's Boyhood Visit to France* (University of Toronto Press, 1960), xiii.

6. Caroline Fox, *Memories*, I, 216. See also Place's remark: "I think John Mill has made great progress in becoming a German metaphysical mystic," and Harriet Grote's description of him as "that wayward intellectual deity" (both quoted in Graham Wallas, *Life of Francis Place* [London, 1918], 91, 91n). On the other side, see William Empson's review of Bentham's *Works* (*Edinburgh Review*, LXXVIII [Oct., 1843], 516), where Mill is praised for having "broken away" from his narrow training, and "asserted his philosophical independence."

the *Examiner*, as well as a critique of Bentham for Bulwer's *England and the English*, and a memoir or brief life for Bowring's edition of Bentham's *Works* (an honour which he refused).[7] Others accepted this claim: Alexander Bain, for example, says, "No one possessed the qualification of Mill for setting forth Bentham's merits and defects. . . ."[8] Recently, attempts have been made to undermine Mill's assessment, mainly on the grounds that he does almost as little justice to the range of Bentham's thought in his review article as he does to the subtlety of Coleridge's in the companion article.[9] But these attempts, while useful in directing attention to Bentham, are queerly mistaken in their attitudes towards nineteenth-century review articles, which seldom even pretended to be balanced or analytic accounts of the works supposedly under consideration. Nonetheless, one may legitimately wonder whether John Mill, for all his obvious qualifications, was really a fair judge of Bentham. Certainly to understand his judgment, one must look at the history of their relations, a history in which at first James Mill is much more important than his son.

James Mill seems to have met Bentham in 1808, when the former was thirty-five years old, the latter sixty, and John Stuart two. At the period of their first meeting, James Mill had been driving his pen furiously in London for six years; soon thereafter, with a view to improvement in all ways, he was walking furious miles through London to dine with Bentham. Then in 1810 Bentham offered the Mills a refuge in the house in his garden.[10] This proved unsatisfactory,

7. In November 1837, John Mill was asked by Tait, the publisher of Bowring's edition of Bentham's *Works*, to write a memoir for the edition. He refused, mainly on two grounds; he wanted to discuss Bentham on his own terms in his own *London and Westminster Review*, and he wished "to avoid getting into a hornet's nest." (Francis E. Mineka, ed., *The Earlier Letters of John Stuart Mill*, in *Collected Works*, XII [University of Toronto Press, 1963], 357–8.) He also tried unsuccessfully to exclude the *Introductory View of the Rationale of Evidence* (ed. James Mill) from the edition, or to relegate it to a subsidiary position, perhaps in an attempt to protect his father's reputation, even though the editor remained anonymous. (*Ibid.*, XIII, 368.)

8. *John Stuart Mill* (London, 1882), 55. Cf. Leslie Stephen, *The English Utilitarians* (London, 1900), III, 3.

9. See, for example, the ill-judged remarks by Mary P. Mack in *Jeremy Bentham* (London, 1962), and compare the more considered judgment of Alan J. Milne in his University of London thesis (1952), "Coleridge and Bentham as Political Thinkers."

10. In a volume presented to Professor Woodhouse, a piece of Miltoniana cannot be misplaced. This house, occupied by Milton when he was Cromwell's secretary, was frequently pointed out by Bentham to those who visited his garden, as the home of "the prince of poets." One interested visitor was the American minister in London,

and after only six weeks,[11] the Mills moved to Newington Green, whence Mill continued to march during the winter and spring months to the Hermit's retreat in Queen Square Place, Westminster. Also from Newington Green to Bentham, appropriately enough, came the earliest extant letter from John Mill, aged six, asking to borrow Hooke's *Roman History*[12]—and even more appropriately, the letter seems to have been enclosed in the one from James Mill to Bentham accepting the latter's offer to look after John should James die. The intimacy had ripened from the time in 1809 when Bentham took Mill and his growing family to Barrow Green for the summer months. This practice continued until 1814, when Bentham rented Ford Abbey in Devon, where he, with the Mills, spent the months from July well into January, until the opening months of 1818.

These workdays, for holidays they were not, provide most of the extant biographical information about the Mills, and fairly early John appears in the account, usually not lumped with "Mrs. Mill and the brats," but as "my poor boy," and then "John." The regular routine and the supply of library and domestic help made the great educational experiment possible, but while the experiment went on in Bentham's house, little of it went on under his eye. The precocious, proud, awkward boy, his conscience always speaking in his father's voice, might occasionally play chess, or even battledore and shuttlecock, with

Richard Rush, whose interest was rewarded: in Bentham's Account Book his amanuensis records, under date 17 August, 1821: "R[ichard] D[oane] sent to Mr. Rush, 51 Baker Street at his desire with a piece of wood, wh. constituted the prime support of the ballustrade of the staircase of No. 11 York Street, now held by J. B. under the Dean & Chapter of Westminster. To be presented by Mr Rush to the Philadelphian Museum—No. 11, as above, being the House recorded as having had *Milton* for its inhabitant, and the piece of wood, (as there is every reason to believe), having been habitually pressed by Milton's hand in the course of his travels, in his state of blindness up and down the staircase of the ballustrade, of which it constituted the prime support." For the next day, there is this entry: "Came a letter of thanks from Mr. Rush 51 Baker St. for the Ballustrade of Milton's—can't give it to the Philadelphian Museum—must reserve it for his own House in Philadelphia." (British Museum Add. MS. 33,563, ff.85v–86r.) Rush recalls the episode and describes the "relic" in his *Residence at the Court of London* (3rd ed.; London, 1872), 288n: "It was composed of four twisted columns. Many years afterwards the author had it worked into his own staircase at Sydenham, at the foot of the stairs, topped with a silver plate indicating its history, as 'The Milton Balustrade.' It is still preserved in the possession of the writer." Is there any present record of this piece of the true balustrade?

11. John Plummer, "Remarkable Men: John Stuart Mill," *Cassell's Illustrated Family Paper*, n.s. 2 (16/9/65), 87. Mill probably gave Plummer the facts for this short biography.

12. Mineka, *Earlier Letters*, XII, 3.

the eccentric old man who himself had been a precocious, proud, awkward boy with a domineering father, but neither can have had at the time (up to John's twelfth year) much understanding of the other.[13] Although the children were heard as well as seen, the household, in sensible nineteenth-century style, was dominated by adult needs. Of his family, James Mill writes to Ricardo in 1815, "the history is two words—*semper idem*. We study, walk, eat, drink and sleep, and that is all."[14]

Actually, that was not quite all, unless Bentham is included in the family. From the beginning, James Mill and Bentham were close collaborators, though they were master and disciple rather than friend and friend. Mill fitted into a pattern—or perhaps more accurately, established one—for Bentham, comically vain always, tried to create pseudo-parental relations with almost all his younger allies. Soon after meeting Bowring, he writes: "he and I are son and father."[15] Of course he never dared offer to Mill (or Ricardo) such addresses as those to Brougham—"TO MASTER HENRY BROUGHAM!—NAUGHTY, NAUGHTY BOY!—Pap for you? Oh no! no more of that—you would only puke it up again"—but he was able to say: "I was the spiritual father of Mill, and Mill was the spiritual father of Ricardo: so that Ricardo was my spiritual grandson."[16] (It is worth remembering, when considering the relation between John Mill and Bentham, that while John addressed Sarah Austin as "Mütterlein," signing himself "Ihre Söhnchen," she addressed Bentham as "Dearest Grandpa," and even "Dearest Greatgrandpa."[17]) Although James Mill did not rise to this

13. Almost the only trait of Bentham's that the Mill children seem to have remembered was his kindness; see Caroline Fox, *Memories*, I, 162, citing conversation of 9/4/40.

14. Dated 10/10/15, in David Ricardo, *Works*, VI (Cambridge, 1952), 309.

15. Bentham to Blaquiere, 11/12/20, University College, London, Bentham MSS., x.60; quoted in G. F. Bartle, "Jeremy Bentham and John Bowring," *Bulletin of the Institute of Historical Research* (University of London), XXXVI (May 1963), 28. Cf. *ibid.*, 30.

16. Bentham, *Works*, XI, 36–7, and X, 498. James Mill, in his turn, tried to educate Ricardo as he educated John, insisting that he keep a journal when travelling, write practice speeches before entering the House of Commons, and work and work again at his economic writings.

17. British Museum Add. MS. 33,546, ff.15r, 17r (2/7/24 and 19/7/24). Harriet Grote, another of John Mill's substitute mothers, addressed Bentham as "My dear Father Hermit" (*ibid.*, f.55r [18/12/25]). It should also be remembered that Mill's judgments of his father were based on a very unequal relation, and were not candidly expressed. See Stillinger, *Early Draft*, 13, and the passages there cited. The judgments were also inadequately based; he knew very little about his father's early

sort of badinage, he certainly was treated as a favourite son for more than a decade.

Bentham was characteristically only too willing to define the relation; in 1828, for example, he writes to Rammohun Roy that James Mill has "numbered himself among my disciples" for twenty-three or twenty-four years, and has been "receiving my instructions" for more than twenty.[18] This is much too strong, especially with reference to the previous ten years, but James' and John Stuart's later attempts to deny this relation are pointless in view of the evidence, which is conclusive—or establishes James Mill's duplicity. In his *Fragment on Mackintosh*, published three years after Bentham's death, James Mill (anonymously and in the third person) says of himself in relation to Bentham, that he was not a man "who took any body for a master," though he was attracted to Bentham "by the sympathy of common opinions, and by the respect due to a man who had done more than any body else to illustrate and recommend doctrines . . . of first-rate importance to the happiness of mankind."[19] But twenty-six years earlier, in 1809, he signed letters to Bentham, "Your zealous pupil," and "Your affectionate pupil."[20] In 1814, when Bentham "extracted umbrage" from Mill's spending time with his old school-friend, Joseph Hume, instead of with the Master, Mill's reply (an attempt to right the matter) refers to "that system of important truths of which you have the immortal honour to be the author, but of which I am a most faithful and fervent disciple—and hitherto, I have fancied, my master's favourite disciple," and continues, "nobody at all [is] so likely to be your real successor as myself. . . ."[21] Later in the same year

---

career, as is seen in the remarkable letter written to David Barclay asking for information about James Mill for Andrew Bisset's biography of him in the *Encyclopaedia Britannica*. (Mineka, *Earlier Letters*, XII, 315.) When Barclay visited James Mill in London in 1810, not a word was said about Scotland when Mrs. Mill and John were present, "but, the moment they left the room, Mill burst out in eager enquiry after everybody in Logie Pert," his birthplace. (Alexander Bain, *James Mill* [London, 1882], 110.)

18. Bentham, *Works*, X, 590.

19. *Fragment on Mackintosh* (London, 1835), 124. John Mill's denial is in his *Autobiography* (Columbia University Press, 1924), 71; see also Stillinger, *Early Draft*, 68n.

20. British Museum Add. MS. 33,544, 433r, 451v.

21. 19/9/14, quoted in Bain, *James Mill*, 137, and in less full form in Bentham, *Works*, X, 481–2. Cf. *ibid.*, 603 and 606, where Bentham describes James Mill as "one of the earliest and most influential of my disciples." Perhaps they were looking for a triple security in the succession when James Mill named his second son (born 1814) James Bentham Mill.

he describes Bentham to Francis Place as "by far undoubtedly the first philosopher in existence."[22]

Early in the Ford Abbey period, the intimacy between Bentham and the Mill family became year-round, when Bentham obtained for them 1 Queen Square, which adjoined his own property. This move also made Mill more dependent on him, and the financial arrangements between the two caused Mill's friends some anxiety.[23] John Mill later righteously repudiated the suggestion that his father was Bentham's dependent, but of course James Mill did owe in money terms a good deal to Bentham for both country and town residences (though for about two years one-half of the rent of 1 Queen Square seems to have been paid by Mill's friend Thomas Thomson, the chemist, who lived in the Mills' house from about 1815 to 1817).[24] At all events, a letter from James Mill to Place in 1818 indicates Mill's view of the relation not long before he achieved financial independence through his *History of India* and subsequent appointment to the East India Company. Some repairs being made to the property, under Place's supervision, Mill writes:

Ought I to permit so much expence to be incurred on my account when it may not be in my power to fulfil the expectations grounded upon it—this I do indeed feel to be a weighty consideration, but on the other hand there are considerations too—If this proposal has a reference to my abode it shews he thinks my being near him a thing of no small importance to his happiness and though I have no doubt he would soon learn to do without me, yet I could not forgive myself if I did anything to impair his happiness for any considerable part of his now contracted time—Another thing is, it is really a source of happiness to myself to be near him, & though there are no small incapabilities [*sic*] between us I could not part from him without a good deal of emotion. The union in intellectuals, which is perfect, with the first man for intellectuals in his age, cannot fail to be a source of pleasure, and in the morals and sympathies with a good many clashings between him and me, there is also much in his character to love, his sincerity and simplicity of character it would not be easy to match and there is nothing which goes so far as these two qualities in laying the foundation of attachment.[25]

22. British Museum Add. MS. 35,152, f.110v; copy in the hand of Francis Place, Jr.

23. See Wakefield to Place, 17/8/14, quoted in Wallas, *Place*, 68.

24. Bain, *James Mill*, 156–7, 162.

25. British Museum Add. MS. 35,153, f.50r; copy in the hand of Francis Place, Jr.

Here one can sense Mill's gradual movement away from Bentham, but they remained useful to one another for another ten years. The frequency of their intercourse can be judged by references in Bentham's letters and Account Books to Mill's dining at Queen Square Place, borrowing books, and running small errands. The books passed between the houses in large batches for years, until Bentham, whose Account Books in the 1820's are increasingly lists of lent, given, and purchased books, evidently came to believe that the traffic was one-way. The result was another serious quarrel between them, in 1827, when Bentham sent his nephew George to collect books from Mill's shelves when he was out of the house. Mill's resentment was expressed in a letter concluding in his highest manner: "Among the virtues which Mr. B. has discovered in his nephew, Mr. M. cannot forbear adding his testimony to the handsome manner he has of doing things." (It is worth noting that a "List of J.B.'s books at Mr. Mill's," dated four months before this quarrel and containing some six hundred titles, ends with a group in John Mill's hand.[26])

By this time their relations had definitely cooled, partly because after Bowring's meeting with Bentham in 1820 there was little room in Bentham's affection for anyone else. One of Bentham's disaffected "reprobates" (amanuenses),[27] John Flowerdew Colls, remarks that no one, among Bentham's "*once*-numerous friends and associates . . . ever offered a thousandth part of the incense of this nature [flattery] at the shrine of his vanity than this gentleman [Bowring] was in the constant habit of intoxicating him with, either by his pen or with his tongue."[28] Angered by Bowring's machinations concerning the *Westminster Review*, and conscious of his own increased importance through personal influence and the India House, James Mill finally resigned his part (and John resigned his) in the *Westminster* (which was founded and maintained by Bentham's money). For the last few years

26. University College, London, Bentham Papers, x.186 (22/2/27), and *ibid.*, x.187–8 (16/10/26).

27. Had James Mill died earlier, John might well have joined this numerous band, which included Colls, Walter Coulson, Herbert Koe, Edwin Chadwick, William Stockwell (who, at age 12, was Bentham's barber), Arthur Moore (who swore to Bentham's will), and more, six of whom are listed but not named, or identified only by initials, in Bentham's *Works*, X, 572–3.

28. *Utilitarianism Unmasked* (London, 1844), 9. In a lugubrious aside referring to himself and Bentham, Colls, who had become a clergyman, says that he has "put off the old man" (5).

of Bentham's life there is no record of reconciliation, though the Mill family continued to live in 1 Queen Square for about two years before moving to Kensington.

The apparent breaking-off of relations between James Mill and Bentham has been generally accepted as entailing a similar break between John Mill and Bentham. But there is some evidence to suggest, if not to establish, that John Mill was not a party to the estrangement. For example, he was very friendly with Edwin Chadwick, one of Bentham's amanuenses. The draft of Bentham's will is corrected in a hand that at least strongly resembles John Mill's; the corrections in this hand (there are others) indicate not only a knowledge of Bentham's cramped and erratic scrawl, but also of names of servants and works which would be within John's knowledge. Also in the will there is a bequest of "a ring with my effigie—and some of my hair" to "John Steward Mill" and twenty-five others—not including James Mill.[29] And the placing of the obituary in John Mill's hands, when there were many others capable of writing it (Chadwick was sub-editor of the *Examiner* at the time), as well as its highly eulogistic tone, indicate a continued fond relation between them.[30]

It cannot be maintained that Bentham came between father and son, but it is possible to argue that there was a special feeling between the spiritual god-father and the messiah, dating back to the summer tour of 1813 which John Mill recalls warmly in his *Autobiography*, and certainly strengthened by Bentham's arranging the boy's year in France (1820–1) with Sir Samuel Bentham and his family.[31] After his return from France, John Mill began a course of reading under John Austin, Bentham's best legal disciple, and soon began his serious writing career in the *Westminster*, contributing articles made from

29. University College, London, Bentham Papers, clv.30. In his letter offering to look after John Mill, Bentham spells his middle name "Stewart," thus possibly showing an ignorance of James Mill's early connection with Sir John Stuart. If the corrections in the will are by John Mill, it is odd that he did not alter the spelling; it is not odd that it was misspelt by the amanuensis (as distinct from Bentham) as John Mill and his friends did not commonly use the name until much later.

30. A very tenuous bit of evidence linking them is perhaps found in a letter to Bentham from W. B. Adams ("Junius Redivivus"), who became friendly with John Mill in the early 1830's, giving Bentham "the credit of having first taught that author [Adams] 'to think and look beneath the surface of human transactions'. . . ." Bentham, *Works*, XI, 75.

31. See the fine introduction by Anna J. Mill to *John Mill's Boyhood Visit to France*.

Bentham's opinions in James Mill's tones. Living across a wall from Bentham, his other activities had an obvious reference: he spoke at the Mutual Improvement Society, of which Bentham was Honorary President,[32] founded the Utilitarian Society, of which Bentham was patron and secular diety, and defended the true faith in debates at the Co-operative Society and in the London Debating Society. And one cannot forget that Bentham shared John Mill's views about female franchise, as opposed to those of James Mill in the *Essay on Government*, and undoubtedly looked with favour on the activities of the younger group of Radicals forming around John. A rare expression of Bentham's opinion of John Mill is found in an unpublished criticism of the *Essay on Government*, commenting on the exclusion of males under forty years of age from the electoral franchise. Bentham writes:

> Continually under his eye while penning this paper our exclusionist had before him a youth who at the age of 18 was beyond all doubt by appropriate aptitude in every shape fitter for a situation of the sort in question in the legislative Assembly of his country than a vast majority of those by whom it is filled: a son to whom by the instruction given him by his father, without any [*undeciphered word*] whatsoever this extraordinary aptitude had been given: and by whom at that same age, no inconsiderable part was acted in the disposal of the lot of a hundred million of human beings.[33]

32. For references to this rather elusive Society, see Bentham, *Works*, X, 488–9, 505–6; a letter of James Mill's, referring to the correspondence found in the former of these, indicates his interest in the Society (British Museum Add. MS. 35,153, f.13r). The sad story of Colls' interrupted participation in the Society's activities can be found in University College, London, Bentham Papers, clxiii.48.

33. University College, London, Bentham Papers, xxxiv.303. Bentham also says that the *Essay on Government* will give a "selfish and tyrannical husband" an excuse "for aggravating the already universally existing tyranny of the male sex over the female," and a selfish father an excuse "for converting into puppets . . . the minds as well as bodies of his children of both sexes." I am indebted for the reference and for help with the deciphering to Dr. J. H. Burns. (About Bentham's hand I can only agree with Hazlitt: "He is a kind of Manuscript author—he writes a cipher-hand, which the vulgar have no key to." *Spirit of the Age* [3rd ed.; London, 1858], 43.) The reference to John Mill's part in the government of India is typical of Bentham's interest in the Hindus. While writing his *History of India*, James Mill drew heavily on Bentham's library, and Bentham saw himself, through the Mills' application of his tenets, as a vicarious and posthumous ruler of the sub-continent. India often appears in his correspondence, and he nearly joined the East India Company in some capacity early in his career. Bentham's father Jeremiah for some years rented property in Leadenhall Street to the Company (British Museum Add. MS. 33,563, ff.235ff.).

Clearly, of all these connections, the legal one was most immediately important, especially if one understands law to bear the intimate relation to morals indicated in the title and text of Bentham's *Introduction to the Principles of Morals and Legislation*. As John Mill says in his *Autobiography*, his education up to 1821 "had been, in a certain sense, already a course of Benthamism," and he had studied Bentham's Chrestomathic Tables while in France,[34] as well as his father's Benthamite account of jurisprudence in the *Supplement to the Encyclopaedia Britannica*. But not until he read Dumont's French redaction of Bentham—and, although he does not make the point clearly, until he saw the details and applicability of the utilitarian doctrine through Austin's tutoring—did he reach a "turning point" in his mental history. Bentham's work "gave unity to my conceptions of things," he says in a well-known passage. "I now had opinions; a creed, a doctrine, a philosophy; in one among the best senses of the word, a religion; the inculcation and diffusion of which could be made the principal outward purpose of a life."[35]

Read in the context of Mill's later life, this passage seems a legitimate comment on the direction of his thought as a moralist, but those who gave him the heady draught were at the time thinking of a career in law. As Mill says, just before the passage above quoted: "My father, notwithstanding his abhorrence of the chaos of barbarism called English Law, had turned his thoughts towards the bar as on the whole less ineligible for me than any other profession. . . ."[36] It is indeed surprising that he did not become a lawyer; there was the strong influence of Bentham and Austin, and James Mill himself, in spite of his "abhorrence," had felt a yearning for the law. When just beginning his London career, he wrote to Thomas Thomson to say that he

34. *Autobiography*, 45. In the *Early Draft* (74), "in a certain sense" reads "in a great measure". (In all quotations from the *Autobiography*, unless otherwise indicated, the reading of the *Early Draft* is not for present purposes significantly different from that of the Columbia edition.) The reference to the Chrestomathic Tables is in Anna J. Mill, *John Mill's Boyhood Visit to France*, 29.

35. *Autobiography*, 47. In the *Early Draft* (75–6), "one among the best senses" reads "one (& the best) sense". It is interesting to compare this passage with Bentham's account of the effect on him of reading Book III of Hume's *Treatise*: "I well remember, no sooner had I read that part of the work which touches on . . . [the foundation of virtue in utility] than I felt as if scales had fallen from my eyes." *Fragment on Government* (London, 1776), 46n.

36. *Autobiography*, 45.

might offer a course of lectures in jurisprudence, as preparation for which he should enter the Inns of Court.[37] This plan bore fruit only in his editing of Bentham's *Introductory View of the Rationale of Evidence* in 1809, and in the article on jurisprudence mentioned above, but as late as 1818 he was still thinking of writing on law:

> You do not know, perhaps, what is my presumption on the subject of law. The next work (after the History [of India]) which I meditate, is a History of English Law, in which I propose to trace, as far as possible, the expedients of the several ages to the state of the human mind, and the circumstances of society in those ages, and to show their concord or discord with the standard of perfection; and I am not without hopes of producing a book readable by all, and if so, a book capable of teaching law to all.[38]

James Mill had not entirely dismissed the possibility of a legal career for John even after the latter's appointment in the India House in 1823. In a further letter to Thomson, he says that the hours in the India House would permit John still to "keep his hours as a student of law. . . ."[39] But John seems not to have entered at the Inns, although he attended Austin's lectures at University College some seven years later. Many of his associates in this period had legal training, of course, including George Bentham, who entered Gray's Inn in 1826, though his distinguished later career was as a botanist.[40] Others of the young men connected with both Mill and Bentham who had legal training, such as Chadwick, Richard Doane, and David Ricardo, Jr., must also have inclined John in this direction. And, most important of all, again following in his father's path, he spent at least a year in editing Bentham's *Rationale of Judicial Evidence* between 1825 and its publication in 1827.

It perhaps had long been in Bentham's mind that John should join the chosen many who were privileged to edit his manuscripts, but it was almost a signal honour—and I think evidence of a special relation —that he should insist that the editor's name appear on the title-page.[41]

37. Dated 13/3/02, in Bain, *James Mill*, 37–8.

38. Quoted in Andrew Bisset, "James Mill," *Encyclopaedia Britannica*, 7th ed., XV, 79.

39. Dated 22/5/23, in Bain, *James Mill*, 207.

40. Here is another link between the Benthams and John Mill, who continued his early interest in amateur botany until his death. George Bentham cultivated Mill's enthusiasm in France in 1820–1, and Jeremy himself, though not a field botanist by any means, was an assiduous sender of the seeds of useful and ornamental plants to many parts of the world.

41. See Mineka, *Earlier Letters*, XII, 18–19.

The list of those who prepared Bentham's manuscripts for publication is almost as impressive as their willingness to remain anonymous: apart from Dumont, Bowring, and James Mill, the company includes Richard Smith (15 titles), Place, Grote, Bingham, Doane, Chadwick, George Bentham, Wooler, and Hobhouse. As Graham Wallas remarks: "One service which all Bentham's disciples were allowed to perform was the writing of Bentham's later books."[42] John Mill shared the usual attitude of these editors: he was grateful for the opportunity, and comments almost exclusively on the virtues of the work and the benefits he obtained from it.[43] He strongly objected to Bentham's insistence that his name appear on the title-page,[44] and managed to suppress it when the work was reprinted in Bentham's *Works*, adding at that time to the "Preface" an apology for "the air of confident dogmatism" in some of the notes and additions, excusable only by "their having been written in very early youth," and by his belief that that tone was "accordant with the spirit of the work itself, and in Mr. Bentham admissible. . . ."[45] So much did he worry about this matter that he wrote to J. H. Burton asking that the words "and, in Mr. Bentham, admissible" be added to the draft of the paragraph, to avoid "the appearance of censuring the tone of the work, which I am very far indeed from intending."[46] And in the *Autobiography* he is still apologizing: "The controversial part of these editorial additions

42. Wallas, *Place*, 83. J. H. Burton, another lawyer with extensive experience of Bentham's papers, says that he left the task of preparing his later works for the press "to others, in the belief that the produce of his labours had intrinsic value, and would, through the assistance of editors, be adapted to the uses of society. Actuated by this feeling, when he had laid out his subject for the day, he laboured continuously on, filling page after page of MS. To the sheets thus filled he gave titles, marginal rubrics, and other facilities for reference: and then he set them aside in his repositories, never touching or seeing them again." ("Introductory Notice," *Benthamiana* [Edinburgh, 1843], x.) Cf. the slightly less complimentary account by Coleman Phillipson, in *Three Criminal Law Reformers* (London, 1923), 148, which includes the remark: "his literary vanity—in marked contrast to his philosophical vanity—was so small, that he freely allowed his friends and disciples to put them into systematic form."

43. *Autobiography*, 80–2. One might make the small point that in revising the text, where he had written simply, "I undertook this task" Mill adds—his memory perhaps failing—"gladly" before "undertook" (*Early Draft*, 105). His contemporary account of his editing work ("Preface" to the *Rationale of Judicial Evidence* [London, 1827], I [v]–xvi) may be compared with Richard Doane's similar description in his "Note by the Editor" to Bentham's *Principles of Judicial Procedure*, *Works*, II, [2].

44. Mineka, *Earlier Letters*, XII, 18–19, and *Autobiography*, 81.

45. "Preface" to *Rationale*, in Bentham's *Works*, VI (Part XI, 1839), 203.

46. Mineka, *Earlier Letters*, XIII, 368 (23/1/38).

was written in a more assuming tone than became one so young and inexperienced as I was: but indeed I had never contemplated coming forward in my own person; and as an anonymous editor of Bentham, I fell into the tone of my author, not thinking it unsuitable to him or to the subject, however it might be so to me."[47]

The editing, Mill says, improved both his knowledge and his style, and he must be right. It seems also to have marked the end of his serious devotion to law. That he remembered the work is seen in a letter to Cliff Leslie in 1869, where he says he agrees with Leslie "in going the complete length with Bentham as to the admissibility of evidence," adding, "The one point on which alone B seems to me to be wrong is in allowing the judge to interrogate."[48] But he could hardly have forgotten Bentham's opinions on these points, which are the rationale of the *Rationale*. More significant are letters to Burton in 1838 and Cole in 1854, in the former of which he says he is not "acquainted with many law books," and in the latter, "I am very little acquainted with recent writings on Jurisprudence."[49] But the most abiding effect of the editing (apart from its furthering Bentham's reputation, as the editing is very good), curiously was to make him less a Benthamite, for if, as seems indubitable, the extreme labour contributed largely to his mental crisis in 1826–7, it drove him to poetry and "German metaphysics."

From this time until Bentham's death in 1832, though it may be assumed that John Mill was not estranged from him, there certainly was a lessening of devotion. After his mental crisis Mill turned to new friends and new books, most of which represented a revolt more against the privileges of the older generation than against the privileges of the aristocrats, and which encouraged personal development rather than the destruction of systems. It is more than a pun to say that Positivism appealed to Mill because it was not negative. He soon began to associate his intellectual heritage with the eighteenth century, and for many years "Benthamism" and "the philosophy of the eighteenth century" were synonymous for him. And Macaulay's attack on James Mill led John about 1830 to rethink his position concerning

47. *Autobiography*, 81.
48. Draft letter, Johns Hopkins; printed in H. S. R. Elliot, ed., *Letters of John Stuart Mill* (London, 1910), II, 186.
49. Mineka, *Earlier Letters*, XIII, 368; and from a transcript kindly supplied by Professor Mineka.

method, logic, and proof, and to develop ideas about them which were certainly an advance over those of his elders, ideas which find a firm place in nineteenth-century thought while remaining—and this is finally important—in the centre of the empirical tradition.

Three days after Bentham's death on 6 June, 1832, Dr. Southwood Smith delivered his celebrated dissectorial oration, its rhetoric gratuitously punctuated by thunder and lightning. In the audience was James Mill, and—almost certainly—John Mill, either fresh from writing, or about to rush off to write, Bentham's obituary notice for the *Examiner* of the next day.[50] With this obituary, Mill began his long attempt to put the "Auto-Icon" in its proper niche.[51]

The year after the eulogistic obituary, his unsympathetic "Remarks on Bentham's Philosophy" were published as an anonymous appendix to Bulwer's *England and the English*; two years later he wrote his review of Sedgwick, a defence of utilitarianism which does not deal with Bentham (his father forced him "to omit two or three pages of comment" on utilitarianism which James Mill "considered as an attack on Bentham & on him").[52] Three years later again, in 1838, his review article on Bentham's *Works*, while it gave offence to more rigid

50. There are close parallels between the printed version of Smith's oration (*A Lecture Delivered over the Remains of Jeremy Bentham, Esq., in the Webb-Street School of Anatomy & Medicine, on the 9th of June, 1832* [London, 1832]) and John Mill's obituary of Bentham. The opening biographical accounts are in places word for word (though Smith's is fuller), and some images and passages are parallel. For example, Smith writes (21): "The general admission is, that the law of England, as it is, cannot stand; that it must be taken down, and re-constructed. Glory to the hand that has destroyed it! Glory to the hand that has built up the beautiful structure reared in its place!" Mill says that the task of "utterly eradicating" the English law, "and sweeping it away" became "the task of his own [*sic*] existence: glory to him! for he has successfully accomplished it." (There are obvious parallels here also with the article on Bentham in 1838.) But the most striking resemblances are seen in the quoting of the same two anecdotes about Bentham in both accounts in identical language, and—as I shall show later—the important coincidence that Smith quotes (26n–28n) a passage from Bentham's *Introduction to the Principles of Morals and Legislation* which became Mill's favourite quotation. Unhappily, I cannot show the exact relation between these two documents; it is clear that one or the other author at least knew the other's opinion.

51. For an account of Bentham's curious physical remains, see C. F. A. Marmoy, "The 'Auto-Icon' of Jeremy Bentham at University College, London," *Medical History*, II (April 1958), 77–86. Bentham's blend of whimsy and dedication, which must have puzzled both Mills, is nowhere better seen than in his printed but unpublished *Auto-Icon; or, Farther Uses of the Dead to the Living* (London, [1842?]). The "Uses of the Dead to the Living" were devised by Southwood Smith (see *Westminster Review*, II [July 1824], 59–97).

52. Stillinger, *Early Draft*, 158n.

Benthamites, is much less critical than the Bulwer Appendix; in "Coleridge," in 1840, he attempted to redress the balance without jumping on the Benthamite scale; in Book VI of his *Logic* (1843) he delivers his verdict on the shortcomings of the school's method; he makes incidental remarks in his letter to the Editor of the *Edinburgh Review* (1844) objecting to Bentham's ill-considered judgments of James Mill. Eight years later, reviewing Whewell, he is much more firmly committed to Benthamism; finally in 1854, working on both the *Autobiography* and the essay later published as *Utilitarianism*, he gives his favourable mature judgment. There are of course many references to Bentham in Mill's other works and in his letters, and a few illustrative biographical anecdotes,[53] but these are the principal documents.

Mill himself recognized his seesaw, saying in his Preface (1859) to *Dissertations and Discussions*:

> the review of Mr. Sedgwick's Discourse, taken by itself, might give an impression of more complete adhesion to the philosophy of Locke, Bentham, and the eighteenth century, than is really the case, and of an inadequate sense of its deficiencies; but that notion will be rectified by the subsequent essays on Bentham and on Coleridge. These, again, if they stood alone, would give just as much too strong an impression of the writer's sympathy with the reaction of the nineteenth century against the eighteenth: but this exaggeration will be corrected by the more recent defence of the 'greatest happiness' ethics against Dr. Whewell.[54]

Opinions about this qualification and requalification will vary, but

53. Probably the most important is his reported objection to Carlyle's denunciation of Benthamism in his lecture on the Hero as Prophet (Richard Garnett, *Life of Carlyle* [London, 1887], 171). If one accepts this story, it certainly illustrates Mill's ambivalent feelings, for eleven days later Caroline Fox, after hearing Carlyle's lecture on the Hero as Man of Letters (which contains a second attack on Benthamism) with Mill's sister Harriet, went back to the Mills' house, where "Several busts of Bentham were shown, and some remark being made about him, John Mill said, 'No one need feel any delicacy in canvassing his opinions in my presence'; this indeed his review [of Bentham in 1838] sufficiently proves. Mrs. Mill gave us Bentham's favourite pudding at dinner!" And two weeks later, on 3 June, 1840, she found the Carlyles chatting happily at the Mills' (*Memories*, I, 188–9, 203). See also David Masson's account of Mill's saying with a smile, in a conversation about Bentham in 1843, "And I am Peter, who denied his Master." Masson, *Memories of London in the 'Forties* (Edinburgh, 1908), 35.

54. *Dissertations and Discussions* (London, 1859), I, iv-v. Cf. *Autobiography*, 153, where the sentence beginning "Now, however, when a counter-reaction appears to be setting in towards what is good in Benthamism," is not in the *Early Draft* (166). In the Columbia MS., "appears to be setting in" is interlined for the cancelled "has begun to set in".

certainly none of the judgments of Bentham up to the 1850's is alone entitled to acceptance. The complicated reasons for the apparent changes of opinion can here only be suggested, not investigated. The changes, I would argue, are the combined result of polemical considerations and personal history. Much of the strength of Mill's early criticism of Bentham derives from his fear of what he might have become, had his path remained as strait as that of Bowring and his Westminster Reviewers. (Often this projected picture of himself is Mill's real target, not Bentham or the actual Benthamites.) Having rejected the narrowness, but not the aim, he tried to create a new Radicalism, in Parliament and through the *London Review*, and in so trying, he had to attract new adherents without repelling the old. Two personal events, his love for Harriet Taylor and the death of his father, influenced his judgment in subtle as well as obvious ways, bringing him ultimately closer to his intellectual origins while immediately distancing him from them.

At the beginning of the 1840's, the decade that established his independent fame, his steadier position is indicated in his acceptance of what is finally of value for him in "nineteenth-century" schools of thought ("Coleridge," 1840), his incisive comments on sociological, political, and ethical method (*Logic*, Book VI, 1843), and his indignant letter to the Editor of the *Edinburgh* (vol. 79 [Jan., 1844], 267–71). It may seem curious to cite such divergent pieces as evidence of steadiness, but here the differences are in approach and are not contradictory, for Mill had learned to separate judgment of personal worth and intellectual stature from judgment of the value of parts of systems—had learned, as he and others have said in other circumstances, to abhor the sin but not the sinner.

In the 1850's his steadiness is even more apparent in his comments on Bentham and utilitarianism: the assessment in "Whewell" is of a piece with those in the *Autobiography* and *Utilitarianism*. Bentham and James Mill are accepted as having an important place in public philosophy, the former having special eminence in legal reform, the latter significant because of his personal influence. The last tributes are warm both in the final version of the *Autobiography* and, for James Mill, in the Introduction and notes to the second edition of the *Analysis of the Phenomena of the Human Mind* (1869), which was published as an act of filial piety as well as of public utility. In the case of both Bentham and James Mill, John Stuart Mill felt that his earlier criticism had been too soon and too strong, and he did his best to amend the damage he thought he had done.

I have up to now intentionally ignored one important consideration. Bentham had his greatest impact through his writings, on John Mill as well as on others. So, in spite of their long acquaintance and intimacy, it should be asked: which of Bentham's works had John Mill read, and which had he read with care and excitement? The frequency of allusion to Bentham's writings in Mill's works suggests a confident awareness of all aspects of his thought, and Mill's library (now in Somerville College, Oxford), which must have contained more of Bentham's writings when James Mill was alive, still has a complete set of Bowring's edition, the five volumes of the *Rationale of Judicial Evidence*, and separate copies of the *Fragment on Government*, the *Introduction to the Principles of Morals and Legislation*, and *A Protest against Law Taxes*. A comparison of Mill's major writings on Bentham to see which works are cited and quoted in them, while tiresome, is also instructive.[55]

1. *Morals and Legislation* (a, b, c, d)
2. *Book of Fallacies* (a, b, c, e)
3. Dumont's redactions (a, b, e)
4. *Fragment* (a, c, e)
5. *Rationale of Evidence* (a, c, e)
6. *Civil Code* (c, d)
7. *Defence of Usury* (a, c)
8. *Deontology* (c, d)
9. *Influence of Time and Place* (c, d)
10. *Judicial Establishment* (a, e)
11. *Constitutional Code* (c, d)
12. *Influence of Natural Religion* (e)
13. *Panopticon* (a)
14. *Promulgation of Laws* (c)
15. *Springs of Action* (c)

It should be noted that the obituary notice (written, like the "Remarks," before the publication of Bentham's *Works*) follows a conventional pattern in listing the "principal works." In "Bentham,"

55. In the following list of Bentham's works I use short titles; the letters in parenthesis following each title indicate the document by Mill in which it is mentioned, as follows: a=obituary notice, b="Remarks on Bentham's Philosophy," c="Bentham," d="Whewell," e=*Autobiography*.

which is a review of the first four Parts of Bentham's *Works* (volumes I and IV, not I and II), Mill mentions only six of the seventeen works contained in these Parts (he ignores Parts III and IV), but includes five not therein contained.[56] Whenever he cites the *Deontology* it is only to deny that it gives a true record of Bentham's ethical opinions.[57] While his treatment of the *Defence of Usury*, the *Influence of Time and Place*, and the *Table of the Springs of Action* (which was edited by James Mill) indicates a careful reading of them, they are not used by him except in limited contexts or for illustration. His account of the *Analysis of the Influence of Natural Religion* in his *Autobiography* leaves no question about its importance to him (and work needs to be done on the influence of Bentham's religious views on the two Mills), but his reticence about religious matters limits his reference to it. Dumont's redactions are mentioned only in passing,[58] except in the *Autobiography*, where the passage treated comes from the *Introduction to the Principles of Morals and Legislation*. Of the other works by Bentham, none is treated in any sort of detail except—and this is the crucial point—the *Introduction to the Principles of Morals and Legislation*. Moreover, almost all his references are to one chapter, in fact one *passage*, in that work. In his *Autobiography* he says, commenting on his first appreciation of Bentham's thought:

What thus impressed me was the chapter in which Bentham passed judgment on the common modes of reasoning in morals and legislation, deduced from phrases like 'law of nature,' 'right reason,' 'the moral sense,' 'natural rectitude,' and the like, and characterized them as dogmatism in

56. Items 2, 5, 7, 8, 11 in my list. Bentham's *Works* were issued in Parts from 1838 to 1843 and published together, in eleven volumes, in 1843.

57. See, for example, Mineka, *Earlier Letters*, XII, 236 (14/10/34); "Bentham," *Dissertations and Discussions*, I, 364–5; and "Whewell," *ibid.*, II, 463. Cf. Stephen, I, 325, and Thomas Whittaker, *Report on the Bentham MSS. at University College, London, with Catalogue* (London, 1892), 4, who support John Mill's contention, as do the present editors of Bentham's manuscripts. The best comment is in a letter from Place to Wheatley: "It is no work of my very dear and good old master, but of that wild poetical surface man Bowring." (Wallas, *Place*, 84n.)

58. The most important of these redactions is the three-volume *Traités de législation civile et pénale* (Paris, 1802), which contains, Vol. I: *Principes généraux de législation, Vue générale d'un corps complet de lois*; Vol. II: *Principes du code civil, Principes du code pénal*; Vol. III: *Suite des principes du code pénal, Mémoirs sur le Panoptique, De la promulgation des lois, De la promulgation des raisons des lois, De l'influence des tems et des lieux en matière de législation*. It is interesting that as editor of the *London Review* Mill defended Dumont against a slighting attack by Carlyle in his "Mirabeau"; see *London and Westminster Review*, 4 & 26 (Jan., 1837), 390n–391n.

disguise, imposing its sentiments upon others under cover of sounding expressions which convey no reason for the sentiment, but set up the sentiment as its own reason. It had not struck me before, that Bentham's principle put an end to all this. The feeling rushed upon me, that all previous moralists were superseded, and that here indeed was the commencement of a new era in thought.[59]

The passage in Bentham is too long for complete quotation here, but a shortened version will indicate its mode of attack:

1. One man says, he has a thing made on purpose to tell him what is right and what is wrong; and that it is called a *moral sense*: and then he goes to work at his ease, and says, such a thing is right, and such a thing is wrong—why? 'because my moral sense tells me it is.'
2. Another man comes and alters the phrase: leaving out *moral*, and putting in *common*, in the room of it. . . .
3. Another man comes, and says, that as to a moral sense indeed, he cannot find that he has any such thing: that however he has an *understanding*, which will do quite as well. . . .
4. Another man says, that there is an eternal and immutable Rule of Right. . . .
5. Another man, or perhaps the same man . . . says, that there are certain practices conformable, and others repugnant, to the Fitness of Things. . . .
6. A great multitude of people are continually talking of the Law of Nature. . . .
7. Instead of the phrase, Law of Nature, you have sometimes, Law of Reason, Right Reason, Natural Justice, Natural Equity, Good Order. Any of them will do equally well. . . .
8. We have one philosopher, who says, there is no harm in any thing in the world but in telling a lie: and that if, for example, you were to murder your own father, this would only be a particular way of saying, he was not your father. . . .
9. The fairest and openest of them all is that sort of man who speaks out, and says, I am of the number of the Elect. . . .[60]

This is undoubtedly the "portion of Bentham's 'Introduction'" which John Mill was reading when studying under Austin;[61] its effect

59. *Autobiography*, 45–6. In the *Early Draft* (74) "passed judgment on the common modes" reads "examined the common modes"; "others under cover of sounding expressions" reads "other people by the aid of sounding phrases" ("others under cover of" is a late alteration in the definitive Columbia MS.); and "It had not struck me . . . all this" reads "This struck me at once as true".

60. Bentham, *Introduction to the Principles of Morals and Legislation* (London, 1823), I, 29n–31n. Mill appears to have used this edition (the one now in his library) rather than that in Bentham's *Works*, I, 8n–9n, into which Bowring has inserted the names of the various moralists attacked.

61. Mineka, *Earlier Letters*, XII, 13.

appears first in his own work in 1827 in a note to the *Rationale* (I, 126n–127n), where he says that such phrases as those attacked by Bentham are "*covers for dogmatism*" and "cloaks for ipse-dixitism" (Bentham's own terms); assigning those who employ them to the "*dogmatical school* of ethics," he distinguishes them from "those who think that morality is not the province of dogmatism, but of reason, and that propositions in ethics need proof, as much as propositions in mathematics." In his obituary of Bentham, Mill writes: "Mr. Bentham's real merit, in respect to the foundation of morals, consists in his having cleared it more thoroughly than any of his predecessors, from the rubbish of pretended natural law, natural justice, and the like, by which men were wont to consecrate as a rule of morality, whatever they felt inclined to approve of without knowing why." And, although I have not been able to show that Mill had any part in the composition, it is at least striking that it is this very passage which Southwood Smith prints as a footnote to his *Lecture Delivered over the Remains of Jeremy Bentham*.[62]

The extent of John Mill's apostacy in the next year is nowhere better demonstrated than in his criticism of this crucial passage in his "Remarks on Bentham's Philosophy":

> The principle of utility . . . stands no otherwise demonstrated in his writings, than by an enumeration of the phrases of a different description which have been commonly employed to denote the rule of life, and the rejection of them all, as having no intelligible meaning, further than as they may involve a tacit reference to considerations of utility. Such are the phrases 'law of nature,' 'right reason,' 'natural rights,' 'moral sense.' All these Mr. Bentham regarded as mere covers for dogmatism; excuses for setting up one's own *ipse dixit* as a rule to bind other people. 'They consist, all of them,' says he, 'in so many contrivances for avoiding the obligation of appealing to any external standard, and for prevailing upon the reader to accept the author's sentiment or opinion as a reason for itself.'
>
> This, however, is not fair treatment of the believers in other moral principles than that of utility.[63]

In "Bentham" he is less sure; quoting part of the same sentence about "avoiding the obligation of appealing to any external standard," he says "we could scarcely quote anything more strongly exemplifying both the strength and weakness of his system of philosophy" than

62. See note 50 above.
63. Edward Lytton Bulwer, *England and the English* (London, 1833), II, 322.

the passage as a whole, which he reproduces at length. He then comments:

> Few, we believe, are now of opinion that these phrases and similar ones have nothing more in them than Bentham saw. But it will be as little pretended, now-a-days, by any person of authority as a thinker, that the phrases can pass as reasons, till after their meaning has been completely analysed, and translated into more precise language: until the standard they appeal to is ascertained, and the *sense* in which, and the *limits* within which, they are admissible as arguments, accurately marked out.[64]

In "Whewell" he again quotes the passage, this time at even greater length,[65] without any introductory qualification, and follows it with three pages of argument against Whewell and in strong defence of Bentham. And seven years later, in his reprint of "Bentham," he alters the comment of 1838 quoted above, retaining only the first and last words:

> Few will contend that this is a perfectly fair representation of the *animus* of those who employ the various phrases so amusingly animadverted on; but that the phrases contain no argument, save what is grounded on the very feelings they are adduced to justify, is a truth which Bentham had the eminent merit of first pointing out.[66]

Mill's treatment of this passage obviously bears out my earlier contention that in his middle age, his personal doubts over, he returned again to his early enthusiasm for Bentham. He saw himself—and here the passage from the *Introduction* is most important—as Bentham's ally in a continued battle against just the kind of variable and unverifiable moral judgments attacked by Bentham. Once he had decided that Bentham's ethics needed correction by the addition of a private morality founded on personal development, he was able fully to appreciate the virtue of Benthamite thought in the public area where mischief was still caused by fools and knaves who hid their sinister interests under loosely formulated moral appeals, or mistook words for facts.

The differences between his political philosophy and that of the

64. *London and Westminster Review*, 7 & 29 (August 1838), 477.

65. *Dissertations and Discussions*, II, 467–70; Mill quotes three additional paragraphs at the beginning, and drops one at the end. There is no difference in his comment between the versions of 1859 (*Dissertations and Discussions*) and 1852 (*Westminster Review*, n.s. II [Oct., 1852], 349–85).

66. *Dissertations and Discussions*, I, 344–5.

Philosophical Radicals of pre–Reform Bill times, while considerable, are more circumstantial than essential. His aims were the same, although the practical situation was seen by him in such altered light that he may be viewed as repudiating all their direct proposals. He certainly no longer saw the main political problem as the dethroning of aristocratic power, and his conception of "securities" (his elders' key term) is similarly modified by his belief that the problems of the future were those of maintaining freedom within a social democracy and intelligence on top of it. But these new dangers were entailed by the beneficial changes which his elders wrought; they could not have countered dangers which did not exist for them.

About most other areas little need be said. He continued to be his father's disciple in associationism. The contributions of Bentham and James Mill to political economy were recognized by him, but recognized as outranked in importance by those of Ricardo, McCulloch, Senior, Adam Smith, and Malthus. Throughout his life he praised Bentham for inspiring legal reform and for his practical and theoretical grasp of the law, and he correctly saw that Bentham's main contribution as well as his main interest was in law.[67] But while he devoted a good deal of his criticism of Bentham to eulogy of these reforms, the activity held only an abstract charm for him.

More important to him was the question of method. He never praised his father's method, being too aware of its limitations, as pointed out by Macaulay and others, including himself. But for Bentham's "method of detail," which is almost as seriously inadequate when compared with John Mill's own more sophisticated and complete approach, he has high praise. He connects it with the dialectic of Plato, the questioning of nature by Aristotle and Bacon, the "negative" philosophy of the eighteenth-century sceptics and empiricists, and with the normal activity of those periods in history which, following the St. Simonians, Comte, and Coleridge, he called "critical," "transitional," and "progressive." What he was praising was not the detail of Bentham's method, or its universal applicability, but the very

67. Roughly one-half of Bentham's manuscripts are on legal matters; of the other half, a large batch is concerned with the Panopticon struggle, much with abstract speculation on logic and language, and only a small proportion with ethical questions as distinct from legal ones. Cf. A. Taylor Milne, *Catalogue of the Manuscripts of Jeremy Bentham in the Library of University College, London* (2nd ed.; London, 1962), *passim*; and Whittaker, 1.

use of method by Bentham in ethics, politics, and sociology. Here again the relevance of the passage from the *Introduction* which Mill quotes so often is apparent. The intuitionists' lack of method rules out progress in ethics and sociology, and without progress there can be no utility. As Mill grew older, he saw more clearly that the work of negative philosophers was far from done; earlier he had expected an "organic state," in St. Simonian terms, to be soon instituted, making the work of destruction and protection unnecessary. While he never lost faith in the institution of a better order, he became less confident of its imminence (especially after Harriet's death in 1858).

And finally, of course, as he grew older and more famous he had less fear of being dismissed simply as "one of the Benthamites"; more and more often James Mill was referred to as the "father of Mr. Mill" than John was referred to as the "son of Mr. Mill." So John could acknowledge his debt without being ruined by the acknowledgment. Never having been a child himself, he could not attain the childlikeness (or childishness) of Bentham, but he finally did not object to the idea that the child had been father to the man.

The Idea of Reform in Newman's Early Reviews

LAURENCE K. SHOOK

INTEREST IN THE PURELY SCHOLARLY WORK on John Henry Newman can only be stimulated by the recent releases in Fredson Bowers' *Studies in Bibliography* of the identification of so many anonymous contributors to the *British Critic*. The first inkling of what the Wellesley College researchers were doing for those interested in Newman came in Walter E. Houghton's letter in the *Times Literary Supplement*, April 15, 1960, p. 241, when seven book reviews or "critics" written by Newman for the *British Critic* were announced. Now Esther Rhoads Houghton, in a most useful general catalogue of identification of *British Critic* articles, presents these seven articles again, along with seventeen others known for some time to be by Newman. Mrs. Houghton explains how Newman and his friends bargained with editor James Shergold Boone for approximately sixty-four pages an issue where members of the Movement could express their views "exempt from the Editor's censorship." She also points out how important for the recent identifications is the Pusey House list of the *British Critic*'s contents and contributors which supports and supplements the two partial lists drawn up by Newman and others and preserved at the Oratory.

It will be some time before these reviews are adequately assessed in their full context. Not all of them will prove to be significant. Indeed, one or two, the review of Elliott's *Travels* for example, would appear to be quite worthless, possibly done in haste to meet deadlines. A few, however, and notably the reviews of Le Bas's *Life of Archbishop Laud*, Burton's *The History of the Christian Church*, and

Jackson's English translation of Guerike's *Life of Francke*, are not only precious items in themselves but seem to have value for the study of Newman's opinions and attitudes during the critical years between 1836 and 1841 when the *Tracts for the Times* and the *Library of the Fathers* were still appearing and when Newman was going through the agony which took him to Littlemore and ultimately to Rome. The first part of this article indicates in merest outline the schema employed by Newman in the seven newly identified reviews. The second part brings forward some considerations which they occasion.[1]

I

1. *British Critic*, XIX (April, 1836), 354–380: Art. VI, The Theological Library, Vol. XIII, *The Life of Archbishop Laud*, by Charles Webb Le Bas. This would appear to be Newman's first contribution after contracting for space. It lends itself to a threefold division as follows: (i) pp. 354–357 ("In this volume . . . distinct from one another."), reflections on the "pseudo-Protestant" rejection of ecclesiastical history; (ii) pp. 357–373 ("But it is time to turn . . . in him who endured it."), assessment of Laud as Reformer; (iii) pp. 373–380 ("The imperfections . . . during evil times."), excerpts dealing with Laud's trial and execution.

2. *British Critic*, XX (July, 1836), 209–231: Art. X, *The History of the Christian Church from the Ascension of Jesus Christ to the Conversion of Constantine*, by the Rev. Edward Burton. (i) pp. 209–213 ("The unexpected and immature death . . . form a judgment of it."), general comment on the decline of the influence of the High Church and Low Church parties both among Oxford Divines and the Episcopal Bench and on the rise of Latitudinarian secularism; (ii) pp. 213–214 ("The work before us . . . moralist or divine."), a succinct and almost tabulated statement of the virtues of Burton's book, for example, its efficient scholarship and synoptic approach, and, more emphatically, of its limitations, especially its lack of unity as a book, its want of plan or scope, its failure to interpret events and facts; (iii) pp. 214–231 ("Dr. Burton commences . . . edification of their own."), a list of topics treated in the volume, followed by

1. Esther Rhoads Houghton, "*The British Critic* and the Oxford Movement," *Studies in Bibliography*, XVI (1963), 119–137. For the phrase quoted see 119, n.2.

generous excerpts without commentary, as "the most respectful course to our author."

3. *British Critic*, XXII (July, 1837), 94–116: Art. V, *The Life of Augustus Herman Francke* etc. from the German of H. E. F. Guerike, by Samuel Jackson; with an introductory Preface by the Rev. E. Bickersteth. Largely an analysis of religious movements of the seventeenth and eighteenth centuries, in the form of a long refutation of Bickersteth's Preface; it is best taken as falling into only two divisions. The review gives few excerpts. (i) pp. 94–114 ("The Pietists of Germany . . . or the visible Church.") rejects the view that there is a close parallel between German and English religious movements since the Reformation; (ii) pp. 114–116 ("One word . . . translated very carelessly.") points out omissions and mistranslations which reduce the value of the English version. The first part can be subdivided as follows: (*a*) pp. 94–99, an outline of the course of German Protestantism regarded as the appearance of two pietistic movements, the first Luther's which levelled off into the dogmatic formalism of the seventeenth century, the second the Pietism of Spener and Francke at the end of the seventeenth century which heralded the era of rationalism; (*b*) pp. 99–108, the assertion, based on Dr. Pusey's "Essay on German Rationalism," that the English High Church was never very much like the pre-Francke Lutheran Church and that evangelical religion is itself susceptible to formalism; (*c*) pp. 108–113, claims that Francke's at times admirable spirituality is often expressed in "rich and glowing Catholic language" quite as open to the charge of latent popery as anything uttered by English churchmen of whatever caste; (*d*) pp. 113–114, statement that neither dogma in the sense of "*human* doctrine *enforced*" nor ordinances which are "not from Christ" are characteristic of the English Church.

4. *British Critic*, XXV (April, 1839), 305–320: Art. II, *Travels in the three Great Empires of Austria, Russia and Turkey*, by C. B. Elliott. A straightforward indivisible review, consisting of excerpts and ironical commentary, of a travel book by a "comfortable" Englishman of "ultra-Protestant" views.

5. *British Critic*, XXVI (October, 1839), 440–453: (1) *Ancient Christianity, and the Doctrines of the Oxford Tracts*, by the author of "Spiritual Despotism," Part I; (2) *Brief Memoirs of Nicolas Ferrar*, collected from a narrative by Rt. Rev. Dr. Turner and edited by T. A.

Macdonogh. (Two books reflecting contrary opinions on the practice of celibacy are here reviewed. In a letter to Anne Mozley, Newman assigns to this review the short title "Taylor versus Ferrar."[2] One part of the review seems to have been written by R. F. Wilson, the other by Newman. Mrs. Houghton's suggestion that Taylor first reviewed the Ferrar book and that Newman then added the review of Taylor's, including the section defending celibacy, is convincing. Newman's sympathetic attitude towards celibacy is well known; but that he could write with the engaging humour displayed here in his treatment of Taylor is not nearly so well known. Indeed, if the authorship of the first part of "Taylor versus Ferrar" can be irrefutably established, the piece must assume genuine importance in any general assessment of Newman's literary achievement.) 1. (i) pp. 440–444 ("We do not intend . . . repent his temerity.") is a *tour de force* dealing seriously yet amusingly with an incompetent writer whose unfinished work associates the Tractarians with the late Fathers of the Church—Cyprian, Tertullian, Chrysostom, Ambrose, Augustine—who, it is maintained, have departed from the Christianity of the pristine Church at Carthage, Alexandria, Rome, Athens, and even fall far short of the medieval Church of Rome, and *a fortiori* of that "of our own Protestant worthies"; the reviewer regards Taylor's position as inconsistent and tells him he is involved in a ridiculous sort of self-refutation by which he must, like the circus entertainer, "finish his exhibition by eating himself up." (ii) pp. 444–448 ("We will notice in passing . . . so odious a controversy.") deals in detail with Taylor's contention that the notion, held Taylor asserts from Apostolic times, that celibacy is a higher state than matrimony has plunged the Church into theological error, moral perversion, superstitious usage and hierarchical usurpation. 2. The second part of "Taylor versus Ferrar," which seems to be Wilson's, proceeds as follows: (i) summary of Ferrar's career up to his going to Little Gidding, (ii) statement of Ferrar's views on celibacy, (iii) the naming of some contemporary Churchmen approving or disapproving of Ferrar's experiment, (iv) regret that opposition to celibacy is so strong in the Church of England.

6. *British Critic*, XXVII (January, 1840), 24–39: *The Court of King James the First*, by Dr. Godfrey Goodman, to which are added

2. See E. R. Houghton, *ibid.*, 131 n.

Letters illustrative, and now first published from the original MSS by John S. Brewer. This review of Brewer's edition of the hitherto unpublished memoirs of Bishop Goodman, who had achieved a certain notoriety when imprisoned by Parliament in 1640 under suspicion of Romanism, and who was among the twelve bishops imprisoned by the Puritans during the forties, consists of a series of excerpts each preceded by a brief appropriate reviewer's comment. The items dealt with are as follows: Queen Elizabeth's sense of personal security and her freedom of movement among her subjects in her declining years; Raleigh's "last" letter to his wife; the Gunpowder Plot and the despair of papists generally; neglect and exploitation of Church properties by administrators; preferment hunting and the love of lucre; the career of Antonio de Dominis, Italian archbishop of Spalato who became an Anglican, recanted, and died suspect back in Italy. The first of these items has special interest in that it elicits from Newman a strong refutation of the notion that Elizabeth regarded herself as Head of the Church.[3]

7. *British Critic*, XXVIII (July, 1840), 160–176: (1) *The Pro testant Exiles of Zillerthal*, translated from the German of Dr. Rheinwald by J. B. Saunders; (2) *Persecution of the Lutheran Church in Prussia from 1831 to the Present Time*, chiefly translated by J. D. Löwenberg. This review is only interesting for the technique employed: the juxtaposing of two accounts of the persecution of Protes-

3. Goodman reports an Italian visitor's remarking "that it was a wonder to see an old woman, the head of the Church, being seventy years of age, to dance in that manner. . . . " Newman retorts (p. 27): "We are sorry to spoil the mirth, or diminish the wonderment, of the Italians, but we beg leave to state that the queen had no such dignity to support during her galliard as the headship of the Church; nay, that she herself had a great dislike of this title, as being an unwarrantable interference with religion: Henry the Eighth, indeed, among his other excesses, had been bold enough to assume it; but Mary had repealed Henry's statute; and though Elizabeth seems to have repealed Mary's with many others of her sister's statutes, and thus accidentally revived the title; yet that this was an accident, and that the title, if formally legal, does not constitutionally belong to the crown of England, is proved by a number of incontrovertible facts, and acknowledged by the most unbiassed authorities. Instead of 'Head of the Church,' Elizabeth took the title of 'Supreme Governor,' and that expressly as having, as Burnet informs us, 'a scruple about it.' Jewel says the same, writing at the time of Elizabeth's accession, and adds, *suo periculo*, that 'that title could not be justly given to any mortal.' This implies, of course, that the Zurich and Geneva people disliked it, as indeed might have been conjectured; and it is as certain that the title was offensive to Roman Catholics; indeed Burnet informs us, that Elizabeth declined it 'to mitigate their opposition.' No pretensions then could have met with a more rough protest, on all hands than did those of the English Crown to be Head of the Church on the accession of Elizabeth."

tants in such a way as to show how unsatisfactory and contradictory are the apologetics provided by books of this kind. 1. Pp. 160–162 ("The former of these . . . Exiles of Zillerthal.") deals with Reinwald's account of the group of families of Zillerthal which sought to be formally registered as Protestants and had ultimately to move elsewhere in order to be so registered. Newman does not find the action of either Catholic Church or government authorities particularly harsh and feels that Saunders' interest in the affair is less one of sympathy for the Zillerthalers than eagerness to point out a demonstration of the "dominancy of the priesthood" of the intolerant Romish Church. 2. Pp. 162–176 ("The proof of this surmise . . . anti-Catholic government of Prussia.") deals with Löwenberg's account of the persecution carried on by the Lutheran Church and the Prussian government against Lutherans who rejected the new union of Reformed and Lutheran Churches and adhered simply to the Confession of Augsburg. The juxtaposition is so made as to present Catholic persecutors as less objectionable than Protestant.

I find in the preceding reviews evidence of a preoccupation on Newman's part with various aspects of the idea of reform in relation to the historical Reformation: the books selected for review lend themselves to a discussion either of reform itself or of the Reformation; Reformation (i.e. ultra-Protestant) churches are constantly being shown to be neither analogously situated nor identical with the English Church; the Church of England, like that of the Fathers, is not confined by the limitations of any given reforming founder but can embrace a Reformer like Laud, a Romanizer like Goodman, an ambivalent floater like Antonio de Dominis; Reformation attitudes towards celibacy, community life, dogma can sometimes be humanly inadequate; spirituality, whether reform or Reformation, can employ a language open to the charge of popery. The following section presumes the reality of such a preoccupation and uses it for further analysis of the mind of Newman.

II

The preceding examination of these reviews, illogical no doubt in that there is no very strong reason for isolating them from other reviews known to have been done by Newman during these same years, reveals nevertheless what seems to be a contribution to the very old problem of the origin of Newman's theory of doctrinal development. How did Newman who had once put such store by the notion of the antiquity of the Church of England come to alter his interpretation of the Vincentian Canon and admit the element of change or, as he qualified it, "Development" into his doctrinal analysis of Christianity? For Newman's friend James Mozley the answer was simple: Newman had compromised with the Latitudinarians and had become, in this regard at least, a liberal Christian. There is something of Mozley's judgment in any explanation of Newman's action which emphasizes his adopting the pattern of contemporary evolutionary thinking.

Modern scholars tend to find Newman's action much more complex. F. L. Cross has provided what has become the classic explanation. In 1933 he proposed the thesis that "it was merely a personal quandary which forced the idea of development upon Newman, and that it was from a seventeenth century source—the Bull-Petavius controversy—that Newman derived the idea."[4] In other words Newman experienced within himself pretty much the same conflict as had gone on between the two noted controversialists, the Jesuit Dionysius Petavius (Petau) for whom historical statements of doctrine were subject to change, and the Anglican theologian, later Bishop of St. David's, George Bull, who joined forces with Bossuet in defence of the splendid consistency claimed for the doctrinal positions of pre-Nicene, Nicene, and post-Nicene Fathers. "The issue which divided Bull and Petavius," writes Cross, "was the very issue which divided the pre-1841 and the post-1841 Newman."[5] The validity of the parallel, however, does not force the conclusion, and Newman seems to have been blown by other winds.

Owen Chadwick has recently made the plausible suggestion that Newman's theory of Development derives from the conjunction of several forces and notably three: (1) the methods and insights (though not the principles) of the German historians as met in Guizot, Thirlwall, and Milman, and as stated later in the *Edinburgh Review* by John Stuart Mill; (2) the quasi-evolutionary philosophy

4. F. L. Cross, "Newman and the Doctrine of Development," *Church Quarterly Review*, CXV (Jan., 1933), 245.
5. *Ibid.*, 255.

of Drey and Möhler (Catholic theologians of a somewhat liberal temper at the University of Tübingen) which inclined him to an essentially critical rather than apologetic approach to theology, an approach to Church doctrine in its totality as an historical unfolding of divine revelation; (3) a mode of argument learned from Bishop Butler which, however, emphasized an "antecedent probability" and was less disposed to draw on analogies with natural religion or scientific observation.[6]

It is important in approaching this question to keep in mind that Newman was not especially aware of any violent change in his own theological outlook during the years 1835–1845. As Chadwick puts it, his "sense of continuity remains."[7] He felt, however, that others were changing: "A new school of thought . . . was sweeping the original party of the Movement aside," and again, "these men cut into the original Movement at an angle, fell across its line of thought"; but when it came to himself, he said: "The whole man moves"; and of himself in relation to others: "A sort of defence which they might call a revolution, while I thought it a restoration."[8] What could have caused Newman to think that his theory of Development (which seems to be the issue in the preceding statements from the *Apologia*) was really not a change but the restoration of a position perhaps long familiar and in some way constantly held?

A contribution towards the answer to this question, and in part to the larger and more complex one of the origin of "Development," can be formulated from Newman's writings prior to 1841, including in a special way the seven reviews listed above. It will come, not from positive statements about Development itself, but from that preoccupation with reform referred to above. It consists in a notion of reformation, perhaps uniquely his among members of the Movement, derived not so much from the Reformers but rather more directly from the Fathers, a notion of reformation in which the pattern of Development can be said in some way to inhere. The reviews deal constantly with two notions, first, that there is incompatibility between traditional Christianity and the spirituality of the Reformation, that is, that both Luther's and Calvin's concepts of salvation through Christ call for a

6. Owen Chadwick, *From Bossuet to Newman: The Idea of Doctrinal Development* (Cambridge, 1957), 99–101.
7. *Ibid.*, 163.
8. J. H. Newman, *Apologia Pro Vita Sua* (London: Dent, 1949), 159, 162, 164.

rejection of historical Christianity; secondly, that Reformation is, in practice, a process of restoration by violence. To these two notions, explicit in the reviews, a third can be added, which is there at least implicitly, that there is another concept of reformation, a patristic one, which calls not only for restoration but for transformation as well, and that this concept, when applied in the area of doctrinal reform, provides the pattern for a theory of Development. These three notions deserve some attention in the context of the reviews and other early work of Newman.

I. The first of the three notions just now set forth, namely that ultra-Protestantism and the Christianity of history are incompatible, not only appears in the reviews but is the theme of the opening section—actually of the opening words—of Newman's *Essay on the Development of Christian Doctrine*: "Christianity has been long enough in the world to justify us in dealing with it as a fact in the world's history. . . . The hypothesis, indeed, has met with wide reception in these latter times, that Christianity does not fall within the province of history—that it is to each man what each man thinks it to be. . . . The Christianity of history is not Protestantism. . . . Protestantism, then, is not the Christianity of history. . . . To be deep in history is to cease to be a Protestant."[9] The position attested here is not new with the *Development*, and is definitely that of the writer of the reviews as is readily verified both from the titles of the books actually selected for review and by recurring statements made by the reviewer. Thus Le Bas's *Life of Archbishop Laud* is praised because it stimulates and even supplies the "thirst for ecclesiastical history," the want of which thirst being "one of the most deplorable evils of this time." The following passage from the same review is especially pertinent and significant:

> Writers now-a-days open the volumes of our old divinity, not to know their contents or gain instruction from them, but to see if there be anything there which will tell in favour of their own views. They turn over the pages, and, if any passage strikes them as apposite, down it goes in their notebook, and is forthwith published without any solicitude about its why or wherefore, its history, its parentage, its occasion, or its content.[10]

9. J. H. Newman, *An Essay on the Development of Christian Doctrine* (New York: Image Books, 1960), 31–36 *passim*.
10. Article VI, *British Critic*, XIX (1836), 355–356.

In "Taylor versus Ferrar" appears a clearly drawn and pointed statement which the Introduction to the *Development* but generalizes and expands:

Now if there is one thing more than another on which his opponents [i.e. Taylor's opponents, the Tractarians] have insisted it is this: that they did not rest their cause on individuals, however eminent, and had no need to do so; that Catholicism was an historical *fact*, like any other historical fact, not a creed such as the Lutheran or Calvinistic, originating in this or that teacher, or in any conspiracy of teachers.[11]

It is quite clear from these and other texts that the Newman of the *Development* was still the Newman of the *British Critic* 1836–1841 regarding Protestantism's alleged incompatibility with an historian's Christianity.

One must bear in mind that the foregoing excerpts from the reviews and the *Development* represent only one part of Newman the historian, the part which resisted the notion that the Church of Christ was so totally invisible, so completely spiritual, so isolated from the humane that it could not be the subject of historical study. They do not show how he also recognized that the process of dealing with the Church of history introduces a whole new set of problems equally challenging for the historian. One should read beside passages like the above Newman's important "Advertisement" and "Essay on Miracles" written but a short time after the reviews during the early months of 1842 at Littlemore and prefaced to the English versions of Fleury's *Ecclesiastical History*.[12] Here Newman carefully distinguishes between sacred and profane history, criticizing all historians who "put forward a theory, or write as apologists or controversialists," including specifically Mosheim, Milner, Gibbon, Neander, Milman and Döllinger. Even here Newman demonstrates, using among others the argument of antecedent probability, that although "the history of religion is necessarily of a theological cast, and is occupied with the supernatural," it must nevertheless be presented as "a minute and exact narrative of the course of ecclesiastical events, as they occurred."[13]

II. The second notion, that reformation is concerned with the

11. *British Critic*, XXVI (1839), 444.

12. *The Ecclesiastical History of M. l'Abbé Fleury*, trans. with notes and An Essay on the Miracles of the Period (Oxford, 1842).

13. *Ibid.*, v–xi.

process of restoration, is more difficult to deal with. Certainly Newman regarded the Reformer as a restorer, but primarily, it seems, as one for whom restoration is accompanied by some violence. Distasteful as he finds it to do so, he concedes that any Reformer, be it Knox reforming *with* his age or Laud *against* his age, must commit excesses *on principle*. This basic bias can be found in the defence of Laud in the review of Le Bas's *Life of Archbishop Laud*:

It is sad work noticing the failings of men to whom we are indebted, and it does good to no one. Who is surprised at reading of Knox's violence and extravagances, his exulting approval of Cardinal Beautoun's assassination, and his violence towards Mary? He was not simply betrayed into excesses, but committed them on principle; yet we are accustomed to take them as part of his whole character, we take him for what he is, as a fact in history, and we bear to mention his name without reviling it. We call him magnanimous, and so in charity veil his pride and insolence. In like manner we endure in Luther great liberties of language, because he was a great man; liberties which we should be shocked even in imagination to impute to Laud. Calvin, again, in burning Servetus, went very far beyond Laud; as did the mild and cautious Cranmer himself, when, not from warmth of temper, but actuated by the spirit of the age, he kindled the flames of Smithfield in behalf of the Anabaptists. Charges, then, of ill-temper, peevishness and the like, are unfair and invidious when urged against so considerable a man as Laud; they were failings certainly, and not to be explained away; but we may fairly ask for such persons as are not, in some respect or other, as faulty as he was, to cast the stone at him, and may allow his infirmities to pass sub silentio till we find a ruler or reformer of these last degenerate times less open to serious charges in life or manners. The real difference between him and the Reformers who preceded him seems to be this, that he was intemperate *against* his age, and they *with* their age; and, as treason never prospers, so strong measures, when unsuccessful, pass for rashness and tyranny. It is not a question between them of truth, but of good policy.[14]

Though the operation of the principle of violence is primary in Newman's concept of "Reformer," it remains true that the fundamental and positive principle is that the reformer is a restorer. Thus Laud was a Reformer because he tried while at the University to bring back the notion that the Church is *visible*; he was a Reformer as Dean of Gloucester because he tried to bring back "sanctity and a permanent form, to the externals of religion." In this sense the entire *via media*

14. *British Critic*, XIX (1836), 372.

can be called a thesis of reform because it seeks on principle to have the Church, located as it is between Popery and Puritanism, restore those things of which it has been despoiled by distortion or loss. Historians, too, are involved in this kind of reform: "For instance, at present we are evidently working out principles and events of three centuries old, elements of good and evil, which have to be sifted, separated, repressed, fostered, as the case may be, and have employed in this very work our great Divines and Churchmen ever since."[15]

There are senses, however, in which Newman finds restoration to be not true reform but "accommodation." To assert, for example, in expunging the accretions of Rome and bringing back the sanctity of the early Church, that theological doctrine is but secondary is to "accommodate the ancient theology to the habits of this day." To replace the word "Church" by "Covenant," or to call baptism a "token" rather than a "means" displays an unwillingness "to admit the received *language* of divinity" and is "an accommodation in the writer to the temper of the day."[16] Besides being open to distortion by accommodation, reform may also reveal, indeed create, deficiencies within the human or social order. The total removal of religious houses as part of the violent process of reform is so dealt with in the second part of "Taylor versus Ferrar" where Newman, or whoever with his knowledge wrote the second part of this review, comments in the words of Archbishop Leighton that the providing of "neither places of education nor retreat for men of mortified tempers" was "the great and fatal error of the Reformation."[17]

These instances taken from the reviews reveal a preoccupation on Newman's part with the idea of reform as restoration, an idea he no doubt accepted the more readily in that it was both traditional and patristic. The idea of reform as restoration was a common one among both Greek and Latin Fathers. It took over ancient ideas of renewal—cosmological like the World Year or the Golden Age, vitalistic like the Roman Renovatio, millenarian as Messianism and apocalyptic transcendence. Reform was with the Fathers a conscious and repeated attempt on the part of man to return to paradise, to recover the lost image and likeness of God, and to establish on earth the heavenly

15. *Ibid.*, 363, 355.
16. On Burton's *History of the Christian Church* in *British Critic*, XX (1836), 229–30.
17. *British Critic*, XXVI (1839), 455.

kingdom. In so far as the Reformers reflected attitudes of this kind, Newman could have no essential quarrel with them. They were but continuing the Church of the Fathers, always to him an acceptable and congenial function. The texts just dealt with are but a few of the many in which he is carefully sorting out the various phases of reform.

III. There is, however, a further aspect of the patristic idea of reform which Newman seems not to have found in the Reformers: the tendency of many Fathers to achieve a kind of balance between reformation as restoration and reformation as transformation and improvement.[18] Such a concept of reform still entails the increasing recovery by the individual of the image and likeness of God lost by Adam's sin, but it also envisages the achieving of something still more wonderful as expressed sometimes liturgically in the *felix culpa.* In this context reform frequently takes on the quality of constant and continuing perfectibility. Thus it is not enough for Tertullian merely to recognize the principle that reform is based on the tendency of things to return to their beginning, merely to say that its "universal condition is one of recurrence" (*universa conditio recedivo est*), he must also say that reform moves towards something better (*in melius reformare*).[19] This distinction within reform is not unique in Tertullian but is stated also in Ephraem, Ambrose, Augustine and others, and is a very real part of the patristic ideology of renewal.

Newman seems not to have been satisfied that this aspect of patristic reformation thinking was sufficiently characteristic of the Christianity of his own day. Many Anglican divines, including Newman, confined themselves more or less rigidly to the position of St. Vincent of Lérins. Vincent's *Commonitorium* was a useful work for anyone anxious to avoid heresy, and many theologians have leaned heavily upon it. Vincent, however, was not a typical Father of the Church. He regarded the great Augustine as an innovator on the doctrine of grace, and many of Vincent's formulations can be fairly described as ultra-conservative, his general conception of the truths of Christianity as static. Although he provides a criterion of orthodoxy, he does not reflect the full patristic thinking on renewal and reform. The moment Newman allowed himself to forget the cautions of Vincent

18. For an excellent treatment of this subject see G. B. Ladner, *The Idea of Reform: Its Impact on Christian Thought and Action in the Age of the Fathers* (Cambridge, Mass., 1959).

19. *Ibid.*, 133 ff.

(cautions heeded by Cranmer, Ridley, Jewel, Hooker, Laud, Usher, Hammond, Bull, Jebb, Kaye[20]), he immediately found himself in the freer atmosphere of Fathers less disposed to hamper truth in the service of custom, and more likely to provide a climate of thought in which "Development" could find expression.

The further question to arise concerns the extent to which the Fathers can be said to have had in mind real doctrinal development and not simply some progressive notion of reform. An answer to this cannot be attempted here partly because it would take us far beyond the reviews on which the present discussion focusses, partly because the question raises what appear at present to be insoluble problems as between development which is but a mere polishing up or filing down of the original deposit of faith, development which is a progressive clarification of dogma by passing from the implicit to the explicit, and development which consists in the discovery of "hitherto unrecognized aspects of inexhaustible revealed truth."[21] All that can be said here is that the reviews provide an insight into Newman's preoccupation with the idea of reform, an idea which he did not find satisfactorily present in the Reformers, but an idea known to many Fathers and treated by them in such a way as to provide him with the pattern of thinking which lies behind his *Essay on the Development of Christian Doctrine*.

20. See the English translation of the *Commonitorium* published in 1841: *Vincentius of Lirins against Heresy* (Oxford).

21. Ladner, *The Idea of Reform*, 412.

Ruskin, Hooker and "the Christian Theoria"

MALCOLM MACKENZIE ROSS

AN INQUIRY into the religious dimension of Ruskin's theory of art may seem now to be little more than an antiquarian exercise. We are nearly reconciled to the notion that art, once the handmaiden of religion, is, in these latter days, "the charwoman of science." Or else we exult in the illusion that art, freed from all need of objective reference and from commitment of any kind, creates, at her own sweet will, new heaven and new earth.

Yet it would be pointless to attempt a reading of Ruskin in terms of the prejudices accounted orthodox in the mid-twentieth century. I do not think that even "the best of Ruskin" can be assimilated by the art theory now current. I do think that in "the best of Ruskin" there can be found the makings of a counter-attack against current theory.

It will not be possible in these pages to consider Ruskin's theory of art in all its phases. Nor would it be desirable so to do. Surely Ruskin has suffered from having been presented *in toto*. In these matters the whole truth sometimes yields anything but the truth. Our scholarly fidelity to "the man" and his "system" deafens us often to instances of living ideas that cry out to be delivered from the body of their death. We have to be Platonists or Aristotelians, Hegelians or Marxists, Freudians or Jungians—never one-quarter Platonist, one-eighth Freudian, two-twelfths Hegelian, and so on. That is to be "eclectic." (Besides, it would take too much work.)

There are no Ruskinians. The species is extinct. Nor would anyone be so fond as again to father such a brood and breed. But a quarter-Ruskinian might be worth something, and I shall try to show that the perdurable "quarter" in Ruskin's theory of art is Christian. Not only is this specifically Christian element at cross-purposes with the dominant assumptions of recent aesthetics; it is also in contradiction to other and large elements in Ruskin's own thought—or perhaps one should say that within a framework broadly Christian, Ruskin occupies a series of positions incompatible with one another. It will therefore be necessary to specify the perdurable "quarter" of Ruskin's theory of art, extricate it from entanglements and contradictions, and relate it to a great and perennial order of ideas (the other "three-quarters").

The way in to the specifically Christian core of Ruskin's thought is by no means easy. Not only must we un-sophisticate ourselves to read Ruskin on art (after Croce and Collingwood and Sir Herbert Read); we must also un-read some of the conventional chapters in the history of ideas—especially the chapter which tucks Ruskin into "the romantic movement" at just the point where it is crossed by Victorian prudery, bolstered by evangelical piety and bedevilled by a pseudo-Gothic sensibility.

The Christian "quarter" of Ruskin's theory of art is to be found in the second volume of *Modern Painters*. This volume is not a pretty piece of romanticism—although romantic influences are not absent. In its religious dimension it does not constitute a merger of the Nature-God of romanticism with the God of Christianity.[1] Nor is it, in its piety, evangelical. In volume II, shaping his rapt naturalism to the image of Richard Hooker's Thomistic structure of Law (Law Eternal, Natural, Human, Divine), Ruskin manages, for a while at least, to hold in check both evangelical pietism and romantic pantheism. Thus he is able to propose a theory of art in its essentials consonant with a Christian sacramentalism.

That this sacramental theory of art is not maintained consistently in the final books and the later writing will be obvious enough. But even the strange shifts and deviations of the later work can be instructive; the process away from and around the core of Christian theory in volume II places Ruskin's perdurable "quarter" in sharp relief, and at

1. This view is urged by Francis G. Townsend, *Ruskin and the Landscape Feeling*, in *Illinois Studies in Language and Literature* XXXV, no. 3 (University of Illinois Press, 1951), 7–9.

the same time hints at the shape and texture of a radically different (and very modern) aesthetics.

The Christian implications of *Modern Painters*, volume II, have been obscured by the conventional image of young Ruskin as a Wordsworthian romantic who blurred together his evangelical God and the Nature-God of the poets, and for whom Turner was both Moses and Christ. Graham Hough has realized more clearly than most that the concern for religion in Ruskin (and in the Pre-Raphaelites and Pater) is different in kind from anything to be found in the earlier romantic writers. "Keats might be said to make a religion of beauty, but he makes no attempt to connect it with traditional religious attitudes: and the religious traditionalism at which both Wordsworth and Coleridge arrived has little connection with their more intense imaginative experiences." Nor would the early romantics "have sympathized with Ruskin's dictum that all art is worship, or with the story of Fra Angelico painting on his knees."[2]

In his recent (and superb) study of Ruskin, John D. Rosenberg draws a parallel between two "religious" experiences of nature—one Ruskin's, the other Wordsworth's. In the valley of Chamonix, Ruskin hears a crash of thunder:

> . . . and when I looked up, I saw the cloud cloven, as it were by the avalanche itself. . . . One by one, pyramid after pyramid, the mighty range of its companions shot off their shrouds. . . . Spires of ice—dome of snow—wedge of rock . . . a celestial city with walls of amethyst and gates of gold—filled with light and clothed with the peace of God. And then I learned . . . the real meaning of the word Beautiful. *With all that I had ever seen before . . . the image of self had not been effaced* . . . without sense even of existence . . . the immortal soul might be held forever . . . wrapt in the one contemplation of the Infinite God. It was then that I understood that all which is the type of God's attributes—which in any way or in any degree—*can turn the human soul from gazing upon itself . . . and fix the spirit—in all humility*—on the types of that which is to be its food for eternity; this and this only is in the pure and right sense of the word Beautiful. [Italics mine.][3]

2. *The Last Romantics* (London, 1947), 24–5.

3. *The Darkening Glass* (New York, 1961), 19. The passage is included in the Appendix, *The Works of John Ruskin*, Library ed., ed. E. T. Cook and A. Wedderburn (London, 1903–12), IV, 364–5. It is from the Allen MSS., unpublished in Ruskin's lifetime but composed in relation to the first draft of volume II. The Chamonix incident occurred before Ruskin began work on this volume. Volume and page references in the text of this article are to this edition of the *Works*.

For Wordsworth, in another Alpine valley, a crash of storm, "giddy prospect," "raving stream," "tumult and peace"

> Were all like workings of one mind, the features
> Of the same face, blossoms upon one tree,
> Characters of the great Apocalypse
> The types and symbols of Eternity,
> Of first and last, and midst, and without end.[4]

After remarking that Wordsworth's idiom no less than Ruskin's is "an adaptation of the language of faith to the experience of nature," Professor Rosenberg "begins to suspect that the Romantic esthetic, with its demand for submissiveness and loss of self, its ennobling of the peasant before the aristocrat . . . its mystical ecstasy before the beauty of God-in-nature, is an unconscious pilfering from modes of Christian experience."[5] This statement helps to put the horse back in front of the cart. And certainly the resemblance between the two Alpine experiences is startling and real. Yet there are differences between Ruskin and Wordsworth, perhaps only implicit here, but to become quite explicit in the elaborated treatment of the Beautiful in *Modern Painters*, volume II. Even here one scarcely can fail to recall that in Wordsworthian romanticism the "loss of self" which Professor Rosenberg speaks of is often complicated by surprising manifestations of self-assertion and self-concern.

What of "loss of self" in Ruskin's Chamonix vision?—"With all that I had ever seen before . . . the image of self had not been effaced in that of God." But self-assertion, self-concern?—"It was then that I understood that all which is the type of God's attributes—which in any way or in any degree—*can turn the human soul from gazing upon itself* . . . and fix the spirit—*in all humility*—on the types of that which is to be its food for eternity; this and this only is in the pure and right sense of the word Beautiful [italics mine]."

The self is not effaced. Nor does it face inward. Nor is the gaze fixed darkly as through a glass of apocalyptic types and symbols on the visible face of God. Not yet. The Beatific Vision in which "the immortal soul might be held forever," is anticipated and imagined analogically through and in the intensity of this single aesthetic moment. For there is a humility in this ecstasy at Chamonix. The self

4. Quoted by Rosenberg, 19. *The Prelude*, VI, 631–40.
5. Rosenberg, 20.

at once is and is not (St. Paul's "I, yet not I"), just as the spires of ice, the dome of snow, actually of this very time, this very place are analogically the shape and substance in eternity of the Celestial City. Even in the shock of vision, the flesh of the actual is no mere "vesture" of the ideal or the divine. I have stressed this Chamonix passage because it contains in germ the whole theory of art as Ruskin is to develop it in *Modern Painters*, volume II. It will become apparent enough that the divine attributes discernible in nature are not for Ruskin escape-hatches designed to let us out of the actual and into "the Real." The particularity, the "thisness" of things, is jealously guarded by the frame of thought in volume II. The mark of the divine is on the make of things. The Glory of God is declared not by things-as-windows but by things-as-themselves. In Ruskin's Alpine apocalypse, we remember, the "types" and "symbols" do not rush and converge to form "the features of one face," but rather, in this lightning moment, stand and show forth the substance and the relevance of the Beautiful.

The wonder is that Ruskin could sustain and deepen the wisdom of the Chamonix vision. Not the ecstasy—the wisdom. The air he breathed was kind enough to ecstasies and he might easily have been teased into raids on the transcendent and forays into the lost jungles of the self.

Perhaps, for a while, Ruskin's fundamentalism stood him in good stead. The God of Abraham, Isaac, and Jacob was not easily to be dissolved into the Spirit of the Universe or made over into a synonym for the creative imagination. By 1858, of course, Ruskin's simple evangelical faith was to lie in ruins. While Rosenberg is right in insisting that Ruskin never repudiated an "ultimate" belief in Christianity,[6] it is clear that Ruskin's religious views were to undergo a radical change after 1858. Indeed, as Rosenberg notes, his evangelical piety was threatened as early as the 1840's.[7]

We are concerned at this point with the 1840's—the period in which Ruskin made his distinctive contribution to art theory. *Modern Painters*, volume I, is, in a sense, an effortless book. God's in his heaven, all's right with nature, Turner proves it so. The religious

6. Ruskin's account of his "unconversion" at Turin is given in E. T. Cook, *Life of Ruskin* (London, 1911), I, 519. The religious doubts and reservations, apparent in the final volumes of *Modern Painters*, reached a climax in the incident at Turin.

7. *The Darkening Glass*, 30.

dimension is assumed but never examined as Ruskin talks about fidelity to nature and the "great ideas" that govern the works of art. Volume II is a strenuous and searching book. There is evident now an earnest even relentless effort to cut through habitual assumptions about God, nature, and art. There is not the slightest suggestion in the book that Ruskin has lost, or is losing, his faith. But there is the urgent need in it to think out the relevance of his faith both to art and to experience. He wants a structure of ideas to fit and hold the Chamonix vision. Simple evangelical piety will not serve. Richard Hooker will.

As a stylist, Richard Hooker always had a strong attraction for Ruskin. Very little attention has been given to the intellectual and theological influence of Hooker on Ruskin, although Henry Ladd, observing that Ruskin must have encountered a Christianized Aristotelianism at Oxford, lists Bishop Butler's concept of analogy and Richard Hooker's concept of law as among the early formative influences.[8]

Here, certainly, is a line of thought that could have no truck with either the romantic God-in-nature or the Calvinist God-out-of-nature. It is the line of thought which provides Ruskin with a context for his Chamonix vision, and thereby enables him to formulate a theory of art consonant with that vision.

Many years later, in *Praeterita,* Ruskin recalls his study of Hooker at the time when he was composing the second volume of *Modern Painters.* He emphasizes style—but style for the sake of argument (and there is more than a hint here of the strain and strenuousness of the argument he felt he had to make):

> The style of the book was formed on a new model, given me by Osborne Gordon. I was old enough now to feel that neither Johnsonian balance nor Byronic alliteration were ultimate virtues in English prose; and I had been reading with care . . . Richard Hooker's *Ecclesiastical Polity.* I had always a trick of imitating, more or less, the last book I had read with admiration; and it farther seemed to me that for the purpose of argument (and my own theme was, according to my notion, to be argued out invincibly), Hooker's English was the perfectest existing model. At all events, I did the best I then knew how, leaving no passage till I had put as much thought into it as it could be made to carry. (XXXV, 414)

Ruskin took detailed notes on the *Ecclesiastical Polity*, and much

8. *The Victorian Morality of Art* (New York, 1932), 157.

later, in his polemical *Notes on the Construction of Sheepfolds*, was to lean heavily on Hooker's curiously Protestant notion of "the invisible church."[9] But in *Modern Painters*, volume II, it is the Thomistic Hooker who is quoted, and quoted abundantly (and strategically) enough to make it evident that Ruskin is as much concerned with the matter as with the manner of the *Ecclesiastical Polity*. We hear from Hooker on law, on moderation, on nature, on the will. He is even brought into a discussion of ideal beauty and the contemplative fancy.[10] We shall look at pertinent details in a moment. It will also be apparent that the broad implications of Hooker's system of law have crucial importance for Ruskin's treatment, in volume II, of the relation of the natural order to the divine, and of the creative act of the imagination as it relates itself to both.

In locating the main line of Hooker's thought in the history of ideas, Peter Munz[11] outlines the three dominant views of the natural order and human reason that have been entertained by Christian theologians. Hooker, in the tradition of St. Thomas Aquinas, holds to the second of these views and, as we shall see, it is this view which gives structure to Ruskin's theory of beauty and art in *Modern Painters*, volume II.

The first view, characteristically Protestant and Puritan (and, one would have supposed, congenial to Ruskin's kind of piety), insists on the utter depravity of human nature and tends, according to Munz, to "a rejection of the natural order." In the second view, "human nature, though weakened, has not been entirely corrupted and can, therefore, within the order of nature itself, recognize through reason those rules of conduct which are known as natural law. . . . The all-permeating spirit here is one of love, a love for a world which is indirectly a creation of God, and as such good, as well as a love for God himself." In the third view, there is maintained "a rigid distinction between the order of nature and supernature. . . . The material, natural world . . . is one complete and self-contained order; and human life as it transcends this order is another order, purely spiritual and self-contained."

9. *Works*, XII, 523–58.

10. While there are scattered references to Hooker throughout the *Works*, significant use of and quotation from the *Ecclesiastical Polity* is confined almost entirely to *Modern Painters*, II (*Works*, IV). Of these the most important are: i.2.1–2 in IV, 138–9; i.5.3 in IV, 136; i.6.2 in IV, 57; i.8 in IV, 44; i.11.3 in IV, 98; v.1.2 in IV, 206.

11. *The Place of Hooker in the History of Thought* (London, 1952), 3–28.

Professor Munz observes that the first view "lays itself open to the charge of 'vilificatio naturae' . . . while the third pushes God far beyond the stage on which the scenes of human life are laid." It is the second view, celebrated by Hooker, which makes possible, in Christian terms, a working doctrine of analogy. For in this view of reality the natural order, the world of things (and, supremely, of persons) is known and loved in all its diversity, its scandalous particularity, its concreteness, its opaqueness, its temporality. And yet it is known—and loved—not only in itself and for itself but also in its *degree*—its degree of participation in the vast hierarchy of being which reaches to God.

As against the analogical character of this second view, Munz's first view (with its fixed and exclusive concentration on the divine) is univocal in tendency. The third view, which holds to a "rigid distinction between nature and supernature," is clearly equivocal. It is only in *Modern Painters* volume II, written under the tutelage of Hooker, that Ruskin is to sustain consistently the analogical mode of thought. In the later lapses, successively, into equivocity and univocity he is to anticipate the Collingwoods, the Reads, and the Hulmes of our day.

But when Ruskin began the second volume of *Modern Painters* he had behind him the Chamonix vision and there before him the *Ecclesiastical Polity*. With its magisterial insistence on Law (Law Eternal, Natural, Human, Divine), and its compelling proclamation of the analogical integrity of nature, reason, and the will (under Law Eternal), the *Ecclesiastical Polity* provided Ruskin with precisely the frame he needed.

It is the frame, at once firm and free, which is so important. Hooker, of course, had nothing to say about the imagination, the beautiful, art. Nor is Ruskin, in *Modern Painters*, volume II, intent on theology, the concept of law, or in defining the relation of nature to grace. Instead he goes about his proper business of unravelling the mystery of beauty and explaining its relevance; he tries to plumb the workings of the creative imagination and to appraise its product; he tries to "place" the work of art in its relation to the nature of man, the nature of things, the nature of God. Following closely the warp and woof of Hooker's argument (as he admits he does), Ruskin, by a kind of extrapolation, seeks in volume II to celebrate the truth of imagination as Hooker had celebrated the truth of reason, maintaining its integrity in its own degree, but denying to it an absolute autonomy, refusing it any presumption of hostility or indifference to either order, the natural or the divine.

At the very core of Ruskin's argument in volume II is a concern to establish the validity of man's imaginative response to the natural order. In *Modern Painters*, volume I, he had rejected the conventional idea of art as "copy," while, at the same time, insisting on the fidelity of all great art to nature. Volume II is, in part, an attempt to get to the roots of this seeming paradox. Can the imagination be "true" to nature without being subservient to it? But volume II is also, in part, an attempt to answer another (and related) question. Can the imagination create without aping the Creator, without becoming God?

As Hooker (and St. Thomas) attributed to human reason a status of creativity and freedom midway between the merely animal and the purely angelic, so Ruskin strove to articulate a theory of the imagination which would be at once faithful to the natural report of the senses and to the supernatural intimations of the divine.

Significantly enough, before treating of the creative imagination as such (and the making of the work of art) Ruskin proposes, as a kind of cradle for the imaginative life, the "theoretic faculty." This faculty, shared in some degree by all men, is apprehended by Ruskin in the light of a definite *credo* about the "use and function" of man himself:

> Man's use and function (and let him who will not grant me this follow me no further, for this I purpose always to assume) is, to be the witness of the glory of God and to advance that glory by his reasonable obedience and resultant happiness. Whatever enables us to fulfil this function, is in the first and pure sense of the word useful to us. Pre-eminently therefore whatever sets the glory of God more brightly before us. But things that only help us to exist, are in a secondary and mean sense useful, or rather if they be looked for alone, they are useless and worse, for it would be better that we should not exist, than that we should guiltily disappoint the purposes of existence. (IV, 28–9)

It follows for Ruskin that what the artist does is bound inextricably both to the conditions and to the purposes of human life. Art, therefore, must not restrict herself to the secondary and mean things that only help us to exist. Neither may she fly free of these into the proud heaven of her own autonomy. Nor need she. The theoretical faculty rests *on* the secondary and mean conditions but not *in* them. Art, albeit with roots in the sensuous life, must aspire beyond the order of the sensuous or its works will be nothing more than "ministers to morbid sensibilities, ticklers and fanners of the soul's sleep."[12]

With recourse to Hooker (*Ecclesiastical Polity*, i.8), Ruskin insists that true impressions of beauty are neither sensual nor intellectual, but moral. Following Hooker, Ruskin defines his idea of the moral in terms of the disciplinary power of the will. Man, under the dictate of reason, chooses among the pleasures offered to him by the senses. There are inferior pleasures and "the primal ground of inferiority in these pleasures is that which *proves* their indulgence to be contrary to reason." Of all the pleasures only those of hearing and sight rise above subservience to mere existence. They are "no means or instrument to life but an object of life. Now in whatever may be infinitely and for itself desired, we may be sure that there is something divine, for God will not make anything an object of life to his creatures which does not point to, or partake of, Himself."[13]

Here is no simple "moralism." Ruskin is trying to delineate a human as distinct from an animal mode of perception. He does so not by disparaging the senses but by recognizing the human need to make discrimination and to direct the swirling traffic of the senses. The will, schooled by reason to be wary, must stand alert on the very threshold of perception, if man's capacity for beauty is to be fulfilled. For it is in this fulfillment of his God-given capacity for beauty that man is able, from the distance of his creatureliness, to apprehend the marks and attributes of the Divine Beauty.

Beauty, therefore, is neither the apotheosis of the natural nor an alternative to the divine. Ruskin's theoretic faculty (like Hooker's reason) keeps its place and knows its function. For it is "necessary to the existence of an idea of beauty, that the sensual pleasure, which may be its basis, should be *accompanied* [my italics] first with joy, then with the love of the object, then with the perception of kindness in a superior intelligence, finally with thankfulness and veneration towards that intelligence itself" (IV, 48).

This entwined "love of the object" and love of God reaffirms the profound and pervasive humility of the Chamonix vision—a humility in which the identity of self is never lost, even while the self, in outward gaze, is rapt in contemplation of domes and spires, transfigured (but not transparent) in this high moment of thankfulness and

12. *Works*, IV, 36. 13. *Works*, IV, 44–6.

veneration. More clearly now, within the ordered hierarchy of being whose lawful boundaries have been drawn for Ruskin by Hooker, the theoretic faculty neither despises nor presumes. The limits are fixed. There will be no blurring of self and not-self—and no playing at God.

However it is not to be thought that the theoretic faculty ("Theoria") is concerned only with that surface of beauty in the natural order which we call "loveliness";

The Christian Theoria seeks not, though it accepts and touches with its own purity what the Epicurean sought, but finds its food and the objects of its love everywhere, in what is harsh and fearful as well as what is kind, nay, even in all that seems coarse and commonplace, seizing that which is good, and delighting more sometimes at finding the table spread in strange places, and in the presence of its enemies, and its honey coming out of the rock, than if all were harmonized into a less wondrous pleasure. (IV, 50)

The theoretic faculty is by no means blind to imperfection and to what is "harsh and fearful" in nature and in life. But this taking of the honey from the dread rock is not precisely the task of the creative imagination itself. In discussing the agreement and the difference between Theoria and Imagination, Ruskin says:

Both agree in this, that they reject nothing, and are thankful for all; but the Theoretic faculty takes out of everything that which is beautiful while the Imaginative faculty takes hold of the very imperfections which the Theoretic rejects, and by means of these angles and roughnesses, it joins and bolts the separate stones into a might temple, wherein the Theoretic faculty in its turn, does deepest homage. (IV, 241)

The imagination "takes hold of the very imperfections which theoria rejects," but shapes them anew to the pattern of divine attributes apprehended by Theoria and visible to her through all the confusions and imperfections of nature. Theoria, in first taking the honey from the rock, releases, and so reveals to contemplation "the seal or impress of divine character"[14] implicit in even the broken stones of fallen nature. The imagination, intent on the rock (but mindful of the honey), "joins and bolts" the separate stones, thus making explicit "the seal or impress" of the divine intention. The artist, in his way, assists in the economy of redemption. He raises his temple even out of the fragments of the Fall. He gives beauty back.

Ruskin will accord to the practising artist an astonishing—if always

14. *Works*, IV, 59.

responsible—freedom. One thinks of Turner, and one remembers that Ruskin is not specifying a formally "religious" art. Turner's landscapes are as much "temples" as are Angelico's and Tintoretto's Crucifixions. The point is that Ruskin, in his concept of Theoria, has sought to establish that, impressed on the Creation and accessible to the imagination, there are laws of beauty as demanding and as eternal as those other but analogous laws, accessible to reason, which Hooker had discerned through all the workings of nature. These laws of beauty are promulgated and conveyed in the divine attributes which are stamped and sealed into the particularities of the Creation, made "intra-real" not "extra-real," *in* the Creation, *of* the Creation, *from* the Creator.

The theoretic faculty, by a kind of connaturality with the created order, finds in the make of things the very "style" of God. Infinity, unity, repose, purity, moderation—these are the marks of that style. Woe betide the creature who seeks to create in defiance of such a great style-book as this! The laws of beauty, discerned by Theoria, are the laws by which the imagination does its work.

Ruskin has no compunction in bringing artists to trial in the court of these eternal laws. Turner, for instance, realizes "with singular consistency" the true impression of the divine attribute, Infinity. Raphael, in his later works, does not. The attribute of Moderation (or "the type of government by law") leads Ruskin into a rebuke of slapdash art and a demand for careful craft. Skilled and finished works are to be extolled for "their greater resemblance to the working of God, whose 'absolute exactness,' says Hooker, 'all things imitate by tending to that which is most exquisite in every particular.' "[15]

By another transposition to the imagination of an aspect of Hooker's Law of Reason, Ruskin urges upon the artist the moderation of a "self-restrained liberty." The human imagination should be schooled

> by the image of that acting of God with regard to all his creation, wherein, though free to operate in whatever arbitrary, sudden, violent, or inconstant ways he will, he yet . . . restrains in himself this his omnipotent liberty, and works always in consistent modes, called by us laws. And this restraint or moderation, according to the words of Hooker ("that which doth moderate the force and power, that which doth appoint the form and measure of working, the same we term a Law"), is in the Deity not

15. *Works*, IV, 90, 84–5, 136. Ruskin's later doctrine of the imperfection of good art is not a defence of the slap-dash but rather a recognition of man's limitation.

restraint, such as it is said of creatures, but, as again says Hooker, "the very being of God is a law to his working," so that every appearance of painfulness or want of power in material things is wrong and ugly; for the right restraint, the image of Divine operation is, both in them and in men, a willing and not painful stopping short of the utmost degree to which their power might reach, and the appearance of fettering or confinement is the cause of ugliness in the one, as the slightest painfulness or effort in restraint is a sign of sin in the other. (IV, 138–9)

But of even sharper significance for an understanding of Ruskin's conception of the working imagination is the chapter on the divine attribute of Unity, "or the type of the divine comprehensiveness." Again it is Hooker who gives Ruskin the key. "All things," says Hooker, "(God alone excepted) besides the nature which they have in themselves, receive externally some perfection from other things." Accordingly, Ruskin asserts that "the appearance of separation or isolation in anything, and of self-dependence, is an appearance of imperfection" while "all appearances of connection and brotherhood" are "typical of that unity which we attribute to God." However, the very complexity of Godhead-in-Unity gives Ruskin pause. It is better, he concludes, to speak of comprehensiveness rather than Unity, "because Unity is often understood in the sense of Oneness or Singleness, instead of Universality."[16] Thus it is that in his account of the creative act he stresses the comprehensiveness of the imagination as it grasps and refashions the clashing and seemingly ill-assorted contraries and imperfections of nature. The imagination shuns "onenesses." It cannot do its work upon them. "Likeness destroys unity, difference does not necessarily secure it, but only that particular imperfection in each of the harmonizing parts which can only be supplied by its fellow part.... Both must be faulty when separate, and each corrected by the presence of the other."[17]

The strange associative power of the imagination is indeed something that "looks as if man were made after the image of God." And Ruskin marvels:

... two ideas are chosen out of an infinite mass ... two ideas which are separately wrong, which together shall be right, and of whose unity, therefore, *the idea must be formed at the instant they are seized as it is only in that unity that either are good, and therefore only the conception of that unity can prompt the preference.* [Italics mine] (IV, 234–6)

16. *Works*, IV, 92.

17. *Works*, IV, 233.

The imagination, in a prophetic flash, seizes its objects in accordance with a pattern which is only revealed to it in the very instant of the flash. And, still marvelling, Ruskin observes that in a great work

not only certain couples or groups of parts must be separately imperfect; but all parts of a noble work must be separately imperfect; each must imply, and ask for all the rest, and the glory of every one of them must consist in its relation to the rest, neither while so much as one is wanting can any be right. (IV, 236)

A passage from a modern Roman Catholic comment on the nature of the analogical mode of thought will help to determine the significance of the position Ruskin has come to in the passage just quoted. Father Lynch is contrasting "the invariancy of the analogical idea of being over against the invariancy of a univocal idea":

As the latter [the univocal idea] descends in its shaping and organizing function, it must eliminate everything in the members of a class which makes them really many and diverse. Or else it must forfeit its invariancy, its sameness. . . . But existence, as it descends, is analogous. It is never the same act of existence. It is a completely new act, for it must adapt itself completely to the new materials it confronts, adapting itself in its bone and heart to the bone and heart of each new subject of being, each new part of the total organism. So too with an analogical idea, with our inward thinking about being. The work, the thinking of it, is never done. The process of adaptation is eternal. . . . Only the proportion is the same; but the two parts of the proposition are always changing. . . . [analogical] thinking is never done *until the last member is found.*[18] [Italics mine]

Ruskin's theory of the imagination is surely analogical in its rejection of the univocal principle of sameness; in its respect for the infinite and unpredictable variety of existence; in the sense that it has of the unity given to the work only in the prophetic but free and unpremeditated moment of discovery; and in its clear recognition that

18. William F. Lynch, S.J., *Christ and Apollo* (New York, 1963) 150–1. Father Lynch moves from the analogy of existence to analogical thought and thence to the analogical imagination. The analogical mode is not, of course, specifically Christian. Father Lynch indicates roots in both Platonic and Aristotelian thought and can point to the pressure of the analogical imagination in works as far apart in theological assumption as *Oedipus Rex* and *Riders to the Sea.* But the analogical mode is not possible in a one-storey universe, or to a one-dimensional view of reality. The idea of analogy is confirmed and sharpened by the doctrine of the Incarnation with its proclamation of the interpenetration of the natural and the divine. It is my contention, of course, that Ruskin's analogical treatment of the imaginative process itself rests upon the analogical view of existence which he took from the Thomistic elements in Hooker's thought.

the work of art, like the work of the analogical mind, is not complete "until the last member is found." It cannot be because all the members "ask for all the rest" and "neither while so much as one is wanting can any be right."

In the full imaginative act, subject and object, the "imager" and the "imaged," interpenetrate and are made known the one to the other. For in its shaping and prophetic flash of insight, the imagination not only unites, it also plunges deep into all that it has seized upon and into the self, into the deep wells of subjectivity.

The "penetrative" imagination "cuts down to the root and drinks the very vital sap of that it deals with: once there it is at liberty to throw up what new shoots it will, so always that the true juice and sap be in them." The imagination is free, for freedom can do no violence to truth. "That which has no truth, life, nor principle" is, by the free but necessary act of the imagination, "dissipated into its original smoke at a touch."[19]

But "the utmost truth," with its "awful under-current of meaning" drawn out of "the deep places" is revealed only in "that metropolis of the soul's dominion,"[20] the counter-depth of subjectivity itself. Ruskin detects "a reciprocal action" between what he calls "the intensity of moral feeling" and the penetrative power of the imagination

> . . . for, on the one hand, those who have keenest sympathy are those who look closest and pierce deepest, and hold securest; and on the other hand, those who have so pierced and seen the melancholy deeps of things, are filled with the most intense passion and gentleness of sympathy. Hence, I suppose that the power of the imagination may always be tested by accompanying tenderness of emotion, and thus . . . there is no tenderness like Dante's, neither any intensity or seriousness like his . . . (IV, 257)

Here Ruskin trembles on the edge of an insight into the connaturality of subject and object which Jacques Maritain finds at the core of the creative act of modern man, a phenomenon

> without parallel in logical reason, through which Things and the Self are grasped together by means of a kind of experience or knowledge which has no conceptual expression and is expressed only in the artist's work. Are we to think—how can this be possible?—that in such an experience, creative in nature, Things are grasped in the Self and the Self is grasped

19. *Works,* IV, 250–1.
20. *Works,* IV, 252.

in Things, and subjectivity becomes a means of catching obscurely the inner side of Things?[21]

One cannot but recall Ruskin's "awful under-current of meaning . . . the shadow upon it of the deep places out of which it has come . . . often obscure, half-told," and the "reciprocal action" between self and things at the very heart of the imaginative process.

Under Theoria, then, obedient to the laws she has discerned in the divine attributes, the imagination is at once faithful to the truth of things and the truth of self. Such truth as this has nothing to do with stated ideas or moral pronouncement. Its mark is on the thing made. The temple of stones joined and bolted (pierced and known) gives beauty back. For the "uttermost" truth of art is not truth of copy, truth of statement, truth of impression, truth of expression. Its truth is whole. Theoria herself, who knows the marks and attributes of the Divine, "does deepest homage." And she is not to be deceived.

Ruskin's "Christian Theoria" and his sure analogical grasp of the imaginative process were to last no longer than his absorption in the thought of Richard Hooker. By the time of volume III, all sense of the lively interpenetration of the natural and the divine had vanished from the page. In the first volume, before the encounter with Hooker, there had been evidences of a purely univocal way of thought. Was it not Ruskin's unexamined evangelical pietism that had led him into the embarrassing moralism of his appraisal of Landseer's faithful dog? (Here, with a vengeance, was art as moral statement, and Ruskin would not say it nay.) Similarly, the insistence throughout volume I that the greatest picture is the picture with the greatest number of great ideas, tended to univocity both of precept and of method. Everywhere in volume I there can be felt the rush and downsweep of the Idea as it seizes the flesh of things by beak and talon. How different this is from volume II (the Hooker volume), where the unifying idea only comes to birth in the unpremeditated moment of the imaginative encounter.

There is not room in these pages for an analysis of the change that comes over Ruskin's thought and method in the last books of *Modern*

21. *Creative Intuition in Art and Poetry* (New York, 1953), 33–4. Sister Mary Dorothea Goetz in her indispensable *A Study of Ruskin's Concept of the Imagination* (Washington, 1947), was the first to note a parallel between the thought of Ruskin and of Maritain. It is my belief that Ruskin's response to Thomistic elements in Hooker helps to explain this parallel.

Painters. Certainly, the analogical frame provided by Hooker is discarded. While it is too much to say that Ruskin has "lost his faith," it is obvious that with the intense (but uncharted) concern for the social and historical order, his way of thought veers towards the equivocal.[22] Increasingly, in volume III, a "rigid distinction" is made between the natural and supernatural orders. In Peter Munz's "third view," we recall, "the material, natural world . . . is one complete and self-contained order; and human life as it transcends this order is another order, purely spiritual and self-contained."[23] In volume III, the artist is "a God-made great man."[24] But God is off in his heaven, the artist here, and great art is the *expression* of the man.

With the dismissal of the analogical kind of truth proposed to the imagination by "the Christian theoria," the penetrative imagination does not always care about the object it penetrates. "If the imagination can be excited by this its peculiar work, it matters comparatively little what it is excited by. If the smoke had not cleared away, the glass roof might have pleased me as well as an Alp. . . . "[25]

Yet Ruskin is still obsessed with the facts of nature. He still talks of "truth." Remembering his earlier observation of a "reciprocal action between the intensity of moral emotion and the power of the imagination," contemplate, if you will, the dialectic of fact and truth in this statement: "Does a man die at your feet, your business is not to help him, but to note the colour of his lips; does a woman embrace her destruction before you, your business is not to save her, but to watch how she bends her arms."[26] Scarcely the tenderness of a Dante! In this surprising a-morality, this new "truth" of art for the sake of art, there is no longer an analogical interpenetration of subject and object, of "imager" and "imaged."

22. Peter Munz argues convincingly that Hooker himself, under the pressure of Tudor politics, was to slip from the "second" to the "third" view. There is no evidence that Ruskin is aware of the change in Hooker's thought. He is influenced by very different social and intellectual forces. I shall have to deal separately with this problem and with Ruskin's shift of interest from art theory to art history. I hope also to deal separately with Ruskin's treatment of the Gothic as it relates to Pre-Raphaelitism, the Catholic Revival, and the "Decadents."

23. Munz, *The Place of Hooker*, 4.

24. *Works*, V, 189.

25. *Works*, V, 178.

26. This passage is from "Notes on a Painter's Profession as Ending Irreligiously" given by Cook and Wedderburn in the Appendix to *Works*, IV, 388–9. These Notes as a whole, written much later than *Modern Painters* II, illustrate most strikingly Ruskin's rejection of "Christian theoria" and the analogical method of volume II.

True, in the later work, the spiritual order, if self-contained, aloof, is never quite denied. Belief in the supernatural may still be the final cause of what the artist makes. But the supernatural has no efficient part now in the purpose and effect of the work of art. Any sense of the *practical* interpenetration of the natural and the divine disappears: "The Assumption is a noble picture because Titian believed in the Madonna. But he did not paint it to make anyone else believe in her. He painted it because he enjoyed rich masses of red and blue, and faces flushed with sunshine."[27] (Even Whistler could have found little wrong with this pronouncement.)

We are startled, in volume V, to hear the prophet of Christian Theoria tell us that if God made man, man has only himself as book "to read about God in":

> The fleshbound volume is the only revelation that is, that was, that can be. . . . Therefore it is that all the power of nature depends on subjection to the human soul. Man is the sun of the world; more real than the sun. The fire of his wonderful heart is the only light and heat worth gauge and measure. (VII, 261–2)

This is the equivocal mind. The two orders are made to stand apart, self-sufficient, self-contained.

Years later, in 1874, before the darkness closed wholly in, Ruskin, in Assisi, dreaming that he was a tertiary of St. Francis, renounced his naturalism, his "religion of humanity," his doctrine of justification by works alone. Giotto, with his "purist" spirituality, was now seen to have more "in the make of him" that the mighty fleshly Titian.[28] Art, now, at its highest, must show forth the white radiance of the Eternal, spurning nature in a rage for transcendence. Ruskin had almost come full circle, from the equivocity of the naturalist ideal (and the practical autonomy of art), to the disincarnation of a univocal spirituality, to a conception of art as *exclusively* religious. From this last position, the line is straight to T. E. Hulme's plea for an abstract religious art. Hulme's geometricity would have appalled Ruskin.[29] Nevertheless, it is the logical terminus of the univocal illusion. Paradoxically,

27. *Works*, VII, 298.

28. *Fors Clavigera*, 76; *Works*, XXIX, 82.

29. And, of course, Hulme thought of Giotto as the begetter of Renaissance naturalism! There is a nice problem in relativity here: Giotto, looked back to from Titian, seems "purist" indeed, but perhaps not when looked forward to from the ante–(not anti-) naturalism of Byzantine art. Incidentally, Hulme failed to understand that Byzantine art, with Christ reigning from the Tree, was a victory over nature, not a withdrawal from it. Nor did he realize that to sail to Byzantium

Ruskin had been closer to a Catholic theory of art with Hooker than he was to be, with Giotto, in the monk's cell at Assisi.

There is something in Fr. Vincent Turner's contention that the ground of modern aesthetics is to be found in nineteenth-century German idealism. One remembers that idealism has always been "an alternative to the Christian religion; it is a philosophy that claims to be a philosophy of life . . . the occupant of a pulpit, and a pulpit alternative to the Christian pulpit.[30] The influence of Hegel persists among us despite the conscious rejection of idealist thought by art critics like Sir Herbert Read. That this idealist ground is denied or unrecognized by such people "may well be an element in the malaise of our aesthetic; if a child is unsure of himself it is all the worse if he does not know who his parents are."[31]

Certainly Croce's post-Hegelian metaphysics of spirit with its "heroic picture of mankind rising from light to light,"[32] provides the basis not only for an unashamed doctrine of self-expression, but also for that practical optimism of our day which justifies "innovation, originality, the revolutionary vision, as spiritual progress. For art, influenced by idealism, has become a kind of counter-religion:

A generation that has lost a belief in a Redemption and even in God the Creator has not lost the hope of salvation from the old Adam. At the moment the especial hope is put in the visual arts. . . . Not 'art' as technique, of course, or as didactic or as pleasurable, as representational, or enhancing the act of living . . . but 'art' as the preconceptual and unpresupposed self-expression of spirit, the greatest Liberator of them all![33]

---

is never to arrive. And while Ruskin still called Giotto's work a "human achievement," his "God-made great man" is no longer a law unto himself (as in volume III), or under the law of the Christian Theoria (as in volume II), but a God-speaker, presumably above all law. Perhaps one should say that Ruskin is tempted by this spiritual absolutism. He does not work out the implication for a theory of art.

30. "The Desolation of Aesthetics," *The Arts, Artists and Thinkers* (London, 1958), 291. Father Turner's strictures on contemporary theory and practice in the arts have helped to sharpen my awareness of the implications of Ruskin's thought for our own day, as they have also made me ponder Ruskin's practical precepts for the working artist in any day. I am not, however, convinced by Father Turner's apparent assumption that Jacques Maritain's recognition of the fact of subjectivity in modern art is of a piece with the "subjectivist" theories of the post-Hegelians.

31. *Ibid.*, 305.

32. Quoted by Turner, *ibid.*, 276.

33. *Ibid.*, 294, 291. This is not to say that there are no significant insights to be culled from contemporary art theory and practice. One assumes that Christian thought, a living organism, can assimilate all the virtue of non-Christian thought. But she assimilates to herself, to the shape and texture of her own flesh. She may not risk her identity.

Does it not seem that while the univocal imagination withdraws to the frozen empyrean of the *a priori*, the equivocal imagination, beginning in a rigid distinction between nature and supernature, fails at last to keep the distinction, smuggling into the natural order an idealism of "spirit" and "myth" (the ghosts of supernature)—finally naturalizing God Himself? Despite notable triumphs,[34] the drift, in practice, has surely been towards increasingly restless innovation (seen as "spiritual progress") and, in theory (paradoxically enough), towards a new determinism within which the movement of the imagination (and of whole cultures) can be plotted and predicted as confidently as one tells and foretells the cycles of weather and season.

For ultimately the equivocal mind is driven to a thoroughgoing monism, to another univocity. Behold, it is the Imagination that is God, the inbound God of the divinized self whose heaven is "expression"!

The Ruskin of *Modern Painters*, volume II, would not have been able to understand why the fact of the artist's subjectivity makes irrelevant the subject-matter of art, renders all representation "anti-art," puts forever asunder the artist's mimetic and expressive needs and impulses. He would have been stumped by the claim (a dogma in some quarters today) that art has nothing to do with craft but is rather an occult exercise in "expression" by which the artist discovers himself and his emotions to himself and for himself. In Ruskin's theory, a work of art is something *made*. It is out there, in that frame, on that wall—a thing-in-itself, yet, too, a thing-for-us, purposefully arousing feeling in us, communicating to us, teasing us into thought. What is more, the feelings aroused, the insights communicated in such a way as to lift us to the threshold of contemplation, can be placed and judged in accordance with a hierarchy of values to which art (like everything else made or done or said) must be prepared to

34. It is not merely that the great artist still builds better than he knows. Since Ruskin's day the very threshold of perception has been extended. The physicist, the astronaut, the depth psychologist have all had their part in the valid extension of the artist's perception. But our concern here is not with the item upon which the imagination may now seize. Our concern is not with the physics but the *metaphysics* of perception. The vast new wealth now made available on the threshold of perception is, in the absence of a ruling metaphysics, in danger of being squandered. The Christian Theoria might point, with equal alarm, at two tendencies in recent art: the pure interiorism of the abstract expressionist, and the pure exteriorism of the artist who pursues infinite novelty of surface effect, or who, alternately, is content to be the ingenious illustrator of the ultimate univocal superstition—scientism.

submit herself. For Ruskin a painting is a painting is a painting and "not another thing," yet other "things" and values there be to which paintings (and poems) stand in real relationship.

In volume II, Ruskin does not narrow his concern to "religious" art as such. His concern (and this is quite a different matter) is with the Beautiful and with Imagination as they can be interpreted and understood by the Christian mind. However, his conclusions in *Modern Painters*, volume II, manifestly oppose any conceivable claim for art as an alternative to or substitute for religion. The Christian Theoria stands against the whole drift of romantic idealism in any of its forms and reincarnations, against any tendency to monism. And the Christian Theoria stands against all theories of the autonomy of art. By the laws of the Christian Theoria, such an autonomy could only seem synonymous with the triviality of art.

For a brief space, then, Ruskin was able to put a dyke against romantic, idealist and naturalistic illusions. The perdurable "quarter" of his thought on the Beautiful, on Imagination, on art was given baptism at Chamonix. It was confirmed by the perennial wisdom—and authority—which Ruskin encountered, providentially, in the pages of Richard Hooker.

The Problem of Spiritual Authority in the Nineteenth Century*

NORTHROP FRYE

THE ASPECT OF VICTORIAN CULTURE represented by such names as Carlyle, Mill, Newman, Arnold, and Samuel Butler has always been one of the chief interests of the scholar and teacher to whose honour this book is dedicated. Although I have taught the corresponding undergraduate course at my own college for many years, Victorian thought is far from being what I hopefully think of, in my furtive non-administrative moments, as my "field." But there is one aspect of Victorian thought that interests me a good deal, and that is the extraordinary fertility and suggestiveness of its educational theories. I speak of the problem of spiritual authority, because all educational theory seems to me to be essentially an application of that problem.

The source of actual or "temporal" authority in society is seldom hard to locate. It is always in the near vicinity of whatever one pays one's taxes to. As long as it can be believed that might is right, and that the tax-collecting power is not to be questioned, there is no separate problem of spiritual authority. But the thesis that might is right, even when as carefully rationalized as it is in Hobbes, has seldom been regarded as much more than an irresponsible paradox. There has almost certainly never been a period in history when the taxpayer did not try to cheat the publican, and even the desire to cheat raises the question of what kinds of authority may be thought

*A slightly different version of this paper has appeared in *Literary Views: Critical and Historical Essays*, edited by Carroll Camden (Rice University, Houston, Texas; Semicentennial Publications).

of as overriding the actual one. For self-interest also has a separate authority.

Spiritual authority is usually connected, of course, with religion, God being normally thought of as a sovereign spirit. Our cultural tradition has inherited from the Old Testament a conception of the will of God which may often be in the sharpest possible opposition to the will of man, especially an Egyptian or Babylonian or Philistine will. But if a religion can find an accredited human representative, the two kinds of authority again tend to merge. The medieval theory of the Pope's right to temporal power and the post-Renaissance conception of the divine right of kings are examples of an effort to make the spiritual order a guarantee of the stability of the temporal one. As far as the normal workings of the human mind can go, the will of God differs in degree but not in kind from the will of man, and the metaphors applied to it, such as the metaphor of divine "sovereignty," are drawn from the more primitive forms of human society. When Greek philosophers began to frame ethical conceptions of justice and righteousness, they ran into similar problems. Their traditional gods, as they appear in Homer, still had all the arbitrary and whimsical quality of a human aristocracy, and submitting to a human conqueror would not be psychologically very different from praying to Poseidon the irascible earth-shaker. In Christianity the human product of spiritual authority is supposed to be charity, but Christian charity has usually been, down to quite recent times, supported by temporal power, and it may be significant that the word charity itself has come to mean chiefly a form of voluntary taxation.

Ordinary social consciousness usually begins in a sense of antithesis between what the ego wants and what society will allow it to have. Hence temporal authority comes to the individual first of all in the form of an external compulsion. In this stage freedom is identified with the ego's side of this antithesis. But education, and more particularly education of the reason, introduces us to a form of necessity or compulsion which is not opposed to freedom but seems to be rather another aspect of it. To assent to the truth of a geometrical demonstration is psychologically a contrast to assenting to the will of a social superior. Hence reason can do what faith, hope and even love by themselves cannot do: present us with the model or pattern of an authority which appeals to the mind rather than to the body, which compels but does not enforce. Such authority confers dignity on the person who accepts it, and such dignity has no context of hierarchy: there is nobody at whose expense the dignity is achieved.

The nineteenth-century social and political writers in Great Britain had inherited from Milton a conception of spiritual authority of this sort, and a singularly lucid and powerful one. For Milton the source of spiritual authority was revelation from God, more particularly the revelation of the gospel which had spiritualized the law, and delivered those under the gospel from the sense of external constraint. St. Paul tells us that where the spirit of the Lord is, there is liberty, and those under the gospel should do as they like, because what they like to do is the will of God, not the illusory pseudo-acts suggested by passion or selfishness. For Milton, again, the accredited human agent of spiritual authority is the church in the sense of the society of individuals who are under the gospel, among whom the one who has authority is the apostle or saint, which according to Milton is what the New Testament means by an *episcope* or overseer. Such authority clearly has no relevance to magistrates or penal codes. Revelation from God accommodates itself to man primarily in the form of reason. Reason manifests itself in the decisive acts of a free life ("Reason is but choosing," Milton says in *Areopagitica*, annexing Aristotle's conception of *proairesis* to the Christian *logos*), and as revelation is the opposite of mystery, there is no conflict between spiritual authority and reason. A revelation from an infinite mind may transcend the reason of a finite one, but does not contradict or humiliate it.

Human society, as Milton saw it, is conditioned by the inertia of original sin to seek the habitual and customary, to do things because they have been done before, to make an idol of tradition. The impact of revelation, coming through reason, is always subversive and revolutionary: it is bound to shake up the somnambulism of habit and confront it with the eternal opposition of God and fallen man. Such reason is also liberty, which man does not naturally want, but which God wants him to have. Purely social changes are, at best, gradual adjustments: genuine liberty is sudden and apocalyptic:

> In state many things at first are crude and hard to digest, which only time and deliberation can supple and concoct. But in religion, wherein is no immaturity, nothing out of season, it goes far otherwise. The door of grace turns upon smooth hinges, wide opening to send out, but soon shutting to recall the precious offers of mercy to a nation.

Temporal authority, however essential, is also provisional, the result of the permanent emergency in human affairs caused by the Fall. It can never be accepted as an end in itself: the reason why it is there is stated in scripture, and all nonscriptural ways of trying to justify it are suspect. There is no inherent authority, in other words, in tradition or custom or precedent, on which temporal authority may rest as a basis. Hence no church which bases its claim to authority on tradition can be a genuine embodiment of revelation. Milton's regicide pamphlet, *The Tenure of Kings and Magistrates*, is a work of extraordinary originality of thought, outlining an early theory of contract and being one of the earliest efforts to try to give some functional place to revolution in history. But even this involves an appeal to precedent, and Milton embarks on an appeal to precedent with the greatest unwillingness: "But because it is the vulgar folly of men to desert their own reason, and shutting their eyes, to think they see best with other men's, I shall show, by such examples as ought to have most weight with us, what has been done in this case heretofore."

We have, then, in Milton, a spiritual authority with its roots in revelation and manifesting itself largely in reason, and a temporal authority which is to be acknowledged and obeyed in its own sphere, but should not be rationalized by arguments drawn from precedent or custom. Temporal authority is primarily something that is there, whether we like it or not. If we don't like it, we turn to a conception of spiritual authority and subordinate the temporal power to it as far as possible, if only in our own minds. If we do like it or want to defend it, on the other hand, we tend to see in tradition, custom, habit, in short the process by which temporal authority came to be, some kind of inherent right. We may note in passing that if social revolution is not, for Milton, organically related to precedents, it is not organically related to the future either. The rebellions of the Jews against their overlords, as recorded in the Old Testament, had varying degrees of success, but none were permanently successful. Hence the significance of such a rebellion is typological, manifesting the power of the true God for and at the moment. The extent to which Milton was able to reconcile himself with the failure of the revolution of his own day is perhaps indicated in *Samson Agonistes*, where the temporary victory of Samson in destroying the Philistine temple has this kind of significance.

In the eighteenth century the conception of the natural society in

Bolingbroke and Rousseau brought a new kind of revolutionary dialectic into social argument. Rousseau thought of man in his context as a child of nature, and not, as Milton did, in his context as a child of God whose original state was civilized. It was reason and nature that were associated in his thought, not reason and revelation, and the original free and equal society of man was not something intended for man by God which man irrevocably lost, but something man still has the power to recapture. Rousseau's thought resembles Milton's only in associating reason and revolution, and in thinking of reason as essentially the vision in the light of which the free act is performed. It is with the counter-revolutionary thought that developed in Britain in opposition to Rousseau, particularly in Burke, that the problem of spiritual authority in the nineteenth century begins.

For Burke, in almost direct contrast to Milton, the first justification for temporal authority consists in the fact that it is there: the right underlying its might, therefore, is the process of tradition and precedent that has brought it into being. The social contract of any society "is collected from the form into which the particular society has been cast." Any developed society is found to consist of various classes, and the tendency of each class is to promote its own interest by acting "merely by their will." This creates tyranny, whether exerted by the king (who is historically a class in himself), by the nobility, or, as in France, by the "people," which means one class or group of people. The source of spiritual authority for Burke, therefore, is to be found, not so much in tradition as such, as in a kind of *telos*, a sense of belonging to a social organism whose health is preserved by maintaining a balance of power among the different organs. The health of the social structure is the end of all social action from any class, and the standard by which such action should be judged. Revolutionary action, which sets free an automatic and unconditioned will, is to society what the cancerous growth of tissue is in the individual. A social organism of this kind is the only genuine form of natural society, for nature is to be thought of as an order that preserves constancy in change by a process of continuous repair. "Thus, by preserving the method of nature in the conduct of the state, in what we improve, we are never wholly new; in what we retain, we are never wholly obsolete."

Two factors in Burke's thought are particularly relevant here. In Milton, the current of liberty, so to speak, normally flows in a deductive direction, from revelation to reason, and from reason to social action. For Burke, liberty can only be preserved by the inductive, empirical, even *ad hoc* procedures of the political action that operates on the basis of what is there: prudence is the greatest of political virtues, and prejudice the only valuable form of deductive thinking. It is the revolutionary action leading to tyranny which is deductive, like the "metaphysical" French Revolution which had begun with a set of major premises about the abstract rights of man, and had then attempted "a decomposition of the whole civil and political mass, for the purpose of originating a new civil order out of the first elements of society." Hence reason, given its full deductive and speculative head, is not an emancipating but a destructive and ultimately enslaving power in politics. Spiritual authority, at least, is something to which we owe loyalty, and loyalty is not primarily rational; hence society is held together by profounder forces than the reason can express or reach.

In the second place, most temporal authority is vested in the ascendant class: this class is faced with a strong revolutionary bid for power coming from further down in society: the maintenance of the health of the social organism, which means the maintenance of spiritual authority, is therefore bound up with preserving the existing rights and privileges of the ascendant class. "We must suppose [society] to be in that state of habitual social discipline, in which the wiser, the more expert, and the more opulent conduct, and by conducting enlighten and protect the weaker, the less knowing, and the less provided with the goods of fortune." Burke goes on to say that "the state of civil society, which necessarily generates this aristocracy, is a state of nature"—i.e., once again, the genuine form of natural society. The ascendant class includes the church, as for Burke the church is a continuous social institution, and its spiritual authority is inconceivable without that continuity. Hence Burke says, in what from our present point of view is a key statement of his thought:

> Nothing is more certain, than that our manners, our civilization, and all the good things which are connected with manners and with civilization, have, in this European world of ours, depended for ages upon two principles; and were indeed the result of both combined; I mean the spirit of a gentleman, and the spirit of religion.

The ascendant class, therefore, and more particularly the aristocracy, comes to represent an ideal authority, expressed in the term "gentleman," at the point in history at which its effective temporal authority had begun to decline (though of course its privileges and much of its prestige remained for another century). The social function of the aristocracy has always included the art of putting on a show, of dramatizing a way of life. It is natural that America, with no hereditary aristocracy as such, should have invented an *ad hoc* aristocracy out of its entertainers, who attract much the same kind of identification that royal figures do in British countries. In the thought of Carlyle, who has no interest in spiritual authority distinct from temporal authority, and wants only to identify the two, the reactivating of aristocracy naturally occupies a central place. For Carlyle the "holiness" or radiance of the indwelling divinity in man, which is perceptible in the hero, is the source of an undifferentiated authority which is spiritual and temporal at once.

Yet even Carlyle distinguished the *de jure* authority of the aristocracy from the *de facto* authority of captains of industry and self-made heroes of the Napoleon and Cromwell category. The basis of the distinction seems to be that as *de facto* or temporal authority is essentially active, so *de jure* or spiritual authority has something about it associated with the contemplative. In his chapter on symbolism in *Sartor Resartus* Carlyle sees the heroic personality as an "intrinsic" symbol (i.e., one that has value in itself, as distinct from the flag or the cross which are extrinsic and have value only as indicators). As a symbol, the hero is the focus of a community, and the purely *de jure* figure seems to have the most of it. Crowds gather to see the Queen in order to see their own unity as a society reflected in her. Here again there is a link between the recognition of spiritual authority and the dramatic function of an ascendant class.

Samuel Butler also associates spiritual authority with the aristocracy, in a more speculative and paradoxical way. He is, of course, particularly fascinated by the working of the evolutionary process in human society, and his conception of education, traditional as it is in itself, reflects this interest. He points out in *Life and Habit* that no skill is learned thoroughly until it passes through consciousness into the unconscious. It follows that the most profoundly educated people are those who have been born to wealth, leisure, and privilege, and have never been troubled by a conscious idea, which includes a good many of the aristocracy. Thus in *The Way of All Flesh* the hero, Ernest Pontifex, at that time engaged in social work in East London, meets an old classmate named Towneley who is large, handsome, simple-minded, well-to-do, and altogether admirable. Ernest asks Towneley effusively if he doesn't love the poor: Towneley says no, and gets away as quickly as possible. It could hardly be a briefer encounter, but it is an epiphany for Ernest: spiritual authority has spoken, as unmistakably as it spoke from the burning bush. Ernest considers this situation carefully, and finally decides:

I see it all now. The people like Towneley are the only ones who know anything that is worth knowing, and like that of course I can never be. But to make Towneleys possible there must be hewers of wood and drawers of water—men, in fact, through whom conscious knowledge must pass before it can reach those who can apply it gracefully and instinctively as the Towneleys can.

We are reminded of the respect paid in Erewhon to those who are handsome, healthy, and rich, and how Erewhon considers it a crime to be ill or unfortunate. In Huxley's terms, society's sympathies are with nature, rather than with ethics, even though society itself is an ethical creation. Yet Ernest's solution is still a trifle immature, and *Erewhon* brings us a little closer to Butler's real view of spiritual authority. Most of the Erewhonians, according to Butler, are unthinking, instinctive conservatives, whose values are determined entirely by habit and prejudice: worshippers, as he says, of the goddess Ydgrun. But there is also in Erewhon a small group of "high Ydgrunites," whom Butler describes as the best people he met in Erewhon. Of them he says: "They were gentlemen in the full sense of the word; and what has one not said in saying this?" The high Ydgrunite would be somebody like Montaigne, presumably: able to live in and with society, able to see not only the power but the real significance of convention and prejudice, yet remaining intellectually detached from them. Such gentlemen are not only the natural aristocracy but the genuine apostles of society, correcting instinct by reason and reason by instinct, and never allowing the two to make that fatal alliance which is the mark of all bigots, whether reactionary or revolutionary.

The problem of spiritual authority, we see, has as its crucial point the problem of defining the community of such an authority. The writers we have been quoting, all of whom are deeply conservative, associate this community with the ideal aristocracy which the term "gentleman" conveys. For a revolutionary thinker, such as William Morris, spiritual authority would be isolated from society, confined to the small conspiratorial group of those who repudiate its values and are shut out from its benefits. It is perhaps worth noting that Morris's revolutionary ideal, as outlined in the future Utopia depicted in *News from Nowhere*, is the assimilating of the conception of a natural aristocracy to the whole of society. In *News from Nowhere* everybody has the creative versatility and the *sprezzatura* that are the marks of the ideally educated courtier in Castiglione, except that, of course, there is no court and no prince, and no one to serve except one another. They are at once producers and consumers, and as consumers they have the sharply limited and defined quality of a privileged class. "We know what we want," says one of them, "so we make no more than we want." This applies even to the production of human beings: the population has become stabilized, apparently, because people are no longer rutting out of nervous instability, as they do in societies based on exploitation. The curiously childlike quality of Morris's ideal citizens is also significant, for of course the real natural aristocracy in all ages, the society of those who are genuinely entitled to leisure and privilege and consuming the goods produced for them by others, are the children.

II

We have just traced a parabola from the counter-revolutionary polemic of the later Burke to the revolutionary polemic of Morris. The former places spiritual authority in the middle of the ascendant class, or at least its centre of gravity is to be found there, and the *Appeal from the New to the Old Whigs* ends in contemptuous ridicule of John Ball, "that reverend patriarch of sedition," who could not find the conception of "gentleman" in the original producing society when Adam delved and Eve span. Morris, in contrast, places spiritual authority for his own time in the small alienated group who are possessed by the ambition of realizing the dream of John Ball. For Morris the Peasants' Revolt was the one brief moment when something like a proletariat appears in British history. In the thought of John Stuart Mill the problem of spiritual authority is located in a much less simplified view of society. For Mill, Burke's continuum of habit and prejudice is the way in which the majority of people live. Being a majority, they are not confined to a single class, and the progress of democracy involves making their will the source of *temporal* authority. As in Burke and Butler, their motivation is instinctive and empirical. Over against them are the smaller group of the liberal opposition, a much more highly individualized group, of whom Mill says that they initiate all wise and noble things.

Mill, somewhat unexpectedly, resembles Hegel in seeing the political opposition of Conservative and Liberal as the symbol of an ideal or intellectual opposition of conservative and liberal attitudes. As the liberal opposition is intellectually always a minority, it has the peculiar problem of getting enough mass support to be effective in a democratic election. Some of Mill's devices, such as a plurality of votes for the educated, are sufficiently desperate to indicate that this is a matter of some difficulty. To grasp the nature of the ideal opposition we have to grasp two principles. First, the majority is always right, for the majority is the source of temporal authority. Second, the majority is always wrong, for it is not the source of spiritual authority. The latter is to be found in the intellectual opposition, for "almost all the greatest men who ever lived have formed part of such an Opposition."

Authority in its two forms, therefore, rests on a paradoxical and illogical tension between majority rule and minority right. The minority are not a class but an élite, and no social epithet like "gentleman" will apply to them. In practice most of them may be gentlemen, but that is not why they belong there. The gentleman behaves according to a social convention, and for Mill the toleration of unconventional or eccentric behaviour is the mark of a mature society. What holds this élite together is something intellectual, though it is certainly not intellectual agreement. To put the question in another way, what gives a minority a right? Criminals are a minority, but clearly have no right to be criminals. In the *Essay on Liberty* the right appears to be the ability to contribute something to the area of free thought and discussion, of what for Mill is the real parliament of man, the ideological debate that is close to being the source of spiritual authority because it supplies the vision for temporal power. To permit freedom of thought is to direct freedom of action, as unrestricted speculation is the best check so far discovered on premature, spasmodic, or panic-stricken action. Here again we run into a Hegelian element in Mill's thought: no idea contributed to this social debate has any real effectiveness unless it contains its own opposite: unless, therefore, the possibility of refuting it is also present. Mill draws our attention to the peculiar importance of Rousseau in challenging the validity of the structure of society itself.

Burke's counter-revolutionary argument was based on a completely inductive conception of political action; Mill's argument attempts to associate his liberal opposition with a more deductive point of view. He remarks for example that "the non-existence of an acknowledged first principle has made ethics not so much a guide as a consecration of men's actual sentiments." The Utilitarian philosophy held his loyalty because it provided a major premise for majority behaviour. That people will seek what they consider pleasure and avoid what they consider pain is individually probable and statistically certain. But this purely descriptive principle supplies no standard or value, no way even of distinguishing reality from illusion in the conception of pleasure. In Milton, who in *Areopagitica* presents a similar conception of truth as something arrived at dynamically through the conflict of opinion, the major premises come from scripture. Milton never conceived the possibility of a free society trying to find truth without the aid of scripture. In Mill there is no clear source of the premises of debate of this kind, no set of standards and assumptions that can be taken as given. The absence of such a source may be one reason for his curious attraction toward the most uncongenial types of political dogmatists, including Carlyle and Comte (it would take us too far afield to apply this principle to Harriet Taylor), as though he felt that they held some missing piece he was looking for.

In Newman, on the other hand, the source of spiritual authority is the church catholic: his great strength as a nineteenth-century thinker lay in his unvarying acceptance of that view. At no time in his adult life was Newman ever anything that a Protestant would call a Protestant: his problem was only to decide whether the Anglican or the Roman communion was the genuinely catholic one. He takes our present argument a step further by finding the road to spiritual authority through education. Education for him is partly social, and retains the social aim of producing the "gentleman" which we met in Burke and Butler. Even its intellectual characteristic, a disinterested or liberal quality in it which is "its own end," has an analogy with the social ideal which is detachable from the necessity of earning a living. On its intellectual side, liberal education is essentially a discipline of reason, as in Milton, and, as in Mill, it seems to have something to do with a "master view of things," a deductive or synoptic sense of intellectual form which gets one's head above the habit of living:

> The principle of real dignity in Knowledge, it worth, its desirableness, considered irrespectively of its results, is this germ within it of a scientific or a philosophical process. This is how it comes to be an end in itself; this is why it admits of being called Liberal.

But the university turns out to be a function of the church, and the education it gives confronts the student with a dilemma: he must either attach himself along with his education to the church or keep his education as a private possession. Recurrently we have come to this crucial point of having to define the community of spiritual authority. The individual can readily be seen to be capable of understanding more than society in general, and hence of possessing standards and values, with an authority superior in kind if not in power. But the conception "gentleman," however interpreted, defines the superior individual rather than the superior group, even granted that one may recognize the individual as one of a group. For Newman only the church provides this community, and of the gentlemen who cannot commit themselves to it he says: "When they do wrong, they feel, not contrition, of which God is the object, but remorse, and a sense of degradation. . . . They are victims of an intense self-contemplation."

In Newman's view of the church there is no place, as there would have to be in Protestant thought, including Milton's, for a dialogue between scripture and church. The church for Newman is the definitive teacher of doctrine, hence it encloses scripture, and operates on ordinary society very much as the British constitution does in Burke. For Burke the conflict of classes and their interests, in a free society, is settled by a legal compromise which preserves the rights of both parties, and these compromises then form a series of precedents diffusing freedom through society, as the quarrels of king and barons produced Magna Carta and the quarrels of king and Parliament the Bill of Rights. Newman sees church doctrine as developing in a somewhat similar way, being evolved out of the crises of history, defining a dogma here, marking off a heresy there, in an endless pilgrimage toward the City of God. Thus spiritual authority in Newman is, as in Milton, a revelation, but a revelation that has no place for metamorphosis, for the revolutionary and apocalyptic transformation of society.

In Arnold, the conception "culture" is the basis from which we have to start. In using the phrase spiritual authority to describe a pervasive problem of nineteenth-century thought, I have been putting unfamiliar conceptions into the minds of some of my writers. For Mill, the problem is not exactly one of *spiritual* authority, and for Butler, it is not exactly a problem of authority. But Arnold is quite explicit about the authoritative nature of culture:

> If we look at the world outside us we find a disquieting absence of sure authority. We discover that only in right reason can we get a source of sure authority; and culture brings us towards right reason.

The traditional elements of gentleman and liberal education are both involved in Arnold's culture, but Arnold clears up a point about the social location of spiritual authority that has been confusing us thus far. We noticed that the more conservative a writer is, the more inclined he is to locate spiritual authority in the middle of actual society, in the place of greatest prestige and prominence. The more radical he is, the more inclined he is to locate it in an opposition, an alien or even excluded group. Something in Arnold—possibly the Romantic poet in him—realizes that the centre is the place of greatest isolation. The argument of *Culture and Anarchy* is to the effect that what is of greatest cultural value, such as a university or the established church, is central to society and demands to be placed at the centre, in the position of Carlyle's intrinsic symbol. Society itself presents a conflict of class interests, and culture for Arnold operates like law in Burke or doctrine in Newman, as a harmonizing principle creating a new kind of order out of this conflict. Those who support it have to begin by isolating themselves from class conflict, which means isolating themselves from the present structure of society: "Within each of these classes there are a certain number of *aliens*, if we may so call them,—persons who are mainly led, not by their class spirit, but by a general *humane* spirit, by the love of human perfection."

Culture represents an evaluation—the *best* that has been thought and said—and the conception of "best" is bound up with permanence. Class conflict deals with temporary issues, and its arguments are rationalizations based on a temporary situation. Temporal power is based on the ascendancy of one class—here we come back to Milton's conception of temporal power as an interim power. The class *qua* class is always anti-cultural: the aristocracy, considered purely as a class, are only barbarians, the middle class only Philistines, the lower class only a populace. Hence it would be the wildest paradox to think of creating a new society through the dictatorship of one class. It is culture that is the genuinely revolutionary force in society, for culture "seeks to do away with classes," and tends to create out of actual society an ideal order of liberty, equality, and fraternity. Culture for Arnold is a whole of which the church forms part, but as culture is not, like church, the name of a specific community, the problem of defining the community of spiritual authority is still with us.

The question of the origin of spiritual authority, and of whether that origin is purely human, partly human, or wholly superhuman has come up at various times in this inquiry. Anyone working out this question in Christian terms, whether Catholic or Protestant, would be likely to say that its origin is out of human reach, though the fact that Christ is at once God, Man, and Logos guarantees the validity of human reason as a means of receiving it, at least up to a point. For Burke and Butler, in different ways, spiritual authority, or whatever is homologous with it, comes to us as a process of nature, a datum or something given, which we may modify but must first of all accept. We have seen that spiritual authority begins in the recognition of truth, and truth usually has about it some quality of the objective, something presented to us. But for a liberal thinker, such as Mill, there can hardly be any real spiritual authority apart from what man himself creates. A revolutionary thinker would go a step farther and see in truth itself a human creation which, as man continues to create it, he may also recreate. Marx's second thesis on Feuerbach makes this quite clear:

The question whether objective truth can be attributed to human thinking is not a question of theory, but is a practical question. In practice man must prove the truth, that is, the reality and power, the this-sidedness of his thinking.

Arnold's "culture" unites these qualities of the datum and the continuous creation, being a human construct which, so far as it is rooted in the past, possesses an objective authority. This authority, we should note, is not exclusively intellectual, for "many things are not seen in their true nature and as they really are, unless they are seen as beautiful," and the imagination as well as the reason may recognize a monument of its own magnificence.

Wherever we turn in nineteenth-century thought we meet some version of a "drunken boat" construct, where the values of humanity, intelligence, or cultural and social tradition keep tossing precariously in a sort of Noah's ark on top of a menacing and potentially destructive force. This is the relation of the world as idea to the world as will in Schopenhauer, of ethics to evolution in Darwin and Huxley, of the ascendant class to the proletariat in Marx, and, later, of ego to libido and id in Freud. There are also many variants of a "saving remnant" theory, ranging from Coleridge's "clerisy" to various pleas for a new kind of monastic movement (one thinks of the symbolic function of the idealized monastery in the argument of Carlyle's *Past and Present*). Of other metaphors of spiritual authority, two are conspicuous. One is the metaphor of the human body, whose seat of intelligence and authority ought to be somewhere on top, as it is in the individual body. The other is the thermostat or feedback metaphor which has organized so much social thinking in the last two centuries. In a sense the search for spiritual authority is really the search for a "governor" in the mechanical sense, something that distributes the rhythm of a mechanism without being involved in the mechanism itself. This figure appears in Huxley's *Evolution and Ethics*: "To this extent the general cosmic process begins to be checked by a rudimentary ethical process, which is, strictly speaking, part of the former, just as the 'governor' in a steamengine is part of the mechanism of the engine."

The problem dealt with in this paper could of course be extended over a far wider area of nineteenth-century thought than I am here able to cover. So far as I know, the twentieth century has not added much to the question, which may be one reason why the political axioms and assumptions of the twentieth century are still rooted in the nineteenth. It seems to me, however, appropriate for the readers of a book in honour of a university scholar and teacher to consider whether the university itself may not have a peculiarly close relationship to the question. In particular, the university seems to me to come closer than any other human institution to defining the community of spiritual authority. Newman's view that the university is a function of the church, with theology occupying a central role as the queen of sciences, does not seem to be borne out by the development of universities in the last century. I have no doubt that religion indicates where the ultimate source of spiritual authority is, nor that the churches have an essential function as custodians and interpreters of its tradition. But in the present-day shape of society, so dominated by science and technology, they clearly have only a partial and peripheral role in embodying the spiritual authority of that society.

Arnold comes nearest to seeing the universities in this light, but universities in his day, and more particularly as he conceived them, made it necessary for him to distinguish them from "culture." A century later, we seem to be living our lives on two levels. One is the level of ordinary society, which is in so constant a state of revolution and metamorphosis that it cannot be accepted as the real form of human society at all, but only as the transient appearance of real society. Real society itself can only be the world revealed to us through the study of the arts and sciences, the total body of human achievement out of which the forces come that change ordinary society so rapidly. Of this world the universities are the social embodiment, and they represent what seems to me today the only visible direction in which our higher loyalties and obligations can go.

A. S. P. Woodhouse: Scholar, Critic, Humanist

DOUGLAS BUSH

WHEN IN MY TWENTIES I picked up a book dedicated by G. L. Kittredge to J. M. Manly, "my friend for almost thirty years," my involuntary thought was "What biblical patriarchs they both must be!" And now I can say "over forty years" about Arthur Woodhouse—if this were 1764, one would ejaculate *Eheu fugaces, Postume, Postume*. Though we were contemporaries at the University of Toronto, he was in Modern History at University College and I was in Classics at Victoria, so we did not meet until the spring of 1921, when we had both committed our destinies to the Harvard graduate school. In September we found ourselves in the queue of young men who had brief colloquies with Professor Kittredge as he sat on the porch steps of Warren House, immaculate and Olympian with white hair and beard and the invariable light-gray suit, boiled shirt, and cigar. I still remember the dampening of scholarly ardour that I felt when one young man in the queue asked another (later identified as Leslie Hotson and Thomas M. Raysor) if he was finishing that year and received the doleful answer "God willing." Arthur happened to follow me in the line and was later somewhat aggrieved because I had sped smoothly through St. Peter's wicket while he had been held up on account of having acknowledged that he read German with a dictionary; I could only say, in all candour, that it had never occurred to me that anyone read German without a dictionary.

At that time the doctoral programme of courses was a grim round of Gothic and kindred things, with bits of literature if they could be squeezed in. Those of us who were not philologically minded, the majority, led lives of quiet desperation relieved only on Saturday nights, when, like so many Typhons under Etna, we belched verbal lava, or sought escape in fifty-cent seats (or were they 25¢?) at a Boston repertory theatre. For those who craved more than dusty answers one positive and enduring relief was found in the courses of Irving Babbitt (I, unhappily, was then an ultra-romantic and would have none of him). Arthur recognized Babbitt's aesthetic and critical shortcomings and the degree of prejudice in his crusading zeal, but, like some other good minds, he, without being a blind disciple, valued such passionate concern with moral ideas that mattered.

In the 1920's the advanced study of literature, whether in doctoral theses or the most mature work, still meant chiefly "research" into sources, influences, literary backgrounds, a kind of study which had and has its solid virtues but, as commonly pursued, remained factual and external. Although the new historical study of ideas had been growing, it had not yet widely revitalized scholarship. Among thesis-writers at Harvard and doubtless elsewhere there was subterranean rumbling against such limited endeavours, and Arthur and some others faced toward the new light. (He has never at any time been torn, as he once said of a troubled scholar, "between two slogans, 'Back to Saintsbury!' and 'On to the Records Office!' ")

Woodhouse—shifting from reminiscence to impersonal biography seems to require a shift from Christian name to surname, since one can't say "Professor" a hundred times—was well prepared both to resist Babbitt's erratic dogmatism and to absorb all that was good in him. As an undergraduate in University College he had matured under the sage and stable as well as stimulating wisdom and insight of such teachers as he later commemorated—W. J. Alexander, Malcolm Wallace, W. S. Milner, and others.[1] The very full and substantial account of Alexander as critic and teacher was written in 1944 by one "who, in simple truth, owes him everything." Allowing for Woodhouse's own natural growth, we may perhaps modify a phrase inspired by generous devotion and gratitude without underestimating his debt to Alexander's finely incisive, well-balanced, aesthetic, ethical, and political mind. Woodhouse's concentrating in history indicated his early bent and foreshadowed his lifelong concern not merely with

1. "In Memoriam: William John Alexander . . . II, Critic and Teacher," *UTQ* XIV (1944–5), 8–32; "Staff, 1890–1953," *University College: A Portrait*, ed. C. T. Bissell (University of Toronto Press, 1953), 51–83.

religious and political thought but with the necessity of an historical approach to literature.

I embark on a short account of Woodhouse's studies in the history and interpretation of ideas with well-founded diffidence. When we were at Harvard together he was already showing his philosophical acumen and I was in the mental state represented by a remark of mine he did not allow me to forget—"I always knew that Locke was involved with innate ideas but I can never remember whether he was for them or against them"—an imbecility perhaps a little extenuated by struggles with Gothic and Middle English dialects but still not unrelated to congenital defects. So, as I say, I have misgivings. Besides, Woodhouse's expositions are so carefully thought out and so carefully worded that brief summaries are hazardous as well as inadequate; and, finally, I cannot take account of his many reviews, which are never perfunctory but are themselves contributions to the subject in hand.

Woodhouse's first major publication was the elaborate "Collins and the Creative Imagination."[2] Here he spoke of Babbitt's having first aroused his interest in Romantic and pre-Romantic views of the creative imagination, but whatever the general stimulus of Babbitt and other teachers and of new approaches to the eighteenth century in scholarship at large, this monograph was a fresh, illuminating, and wholly disinterested inquiry. In analysing and clarifying the pattern of eighteenth-century ideas and placing Collins' individual conception in that pattern, Woodhouse deployed much learning in the service of critical interpretation. The study showed what were to be characteristic qualities—clarity of thought and style and precise definition and discrimination, with nothing left loose or blurred.

Woodhouse's abiding interest in Romantic ideas—and in the whole philosophic pattern of the eighteenth and nineteenth centuries—has continued uninterruptedly in his teaching but has found public expression only in some reviews and in the paper, "Romanticism and the History of Ideas," read at the International Conference of University Professors of English held at Oxford in 1950.[3] This paper, printed in abridged form, was a further analysis of the role of the imagination

2. *Studies in English,* by Members of University College, Toronto, ed. Malcolm W. Wallace (University of Toronto Press, 1931), 59–131.

3. *English Studies Today,* ed. C. L. Wrenn and G. Bullough (Oxford, 1951), 120–40.

in aesthetic theory from Sidney to Coleridge. It was a logical sequel to, or enlargement of, the study focused on Collins, and its philosophic range and density might suggest that the author, in the nineteen years between the two, had been reading nothing but British philosophy and aesthetics. He had, however, much earlier moved his centre of gravity back to the seventeenth century, to its political and religious thought, and to the thought and poetry of Milton in particular. To this main line we may turn.

Woodhouse's shift coincided with early stirrings of modern inquiry in that troubled and exciting era. A number of scholars had been setting up "the new Milton" in opposition to the petrified image of the grim Puritan. In 1933–4 William Haller, Perry Miller, and a few others were bringing new documents and new light to the study of English and American Puritanism and were showing the complexity of a subject popularly assumed to be simple. (One remembers the classic capsule in *1066 and All That*: "The Royalists were wrong but romantic; the Roundheads were right but repulsive.") In a number of reviews and especially in the article "Milton, Puritanism, and Liberty,"[4] Woodhouse, already a master of the sources, set forth some seminal and more or less original ideas which he was to develop more fully in his later writings. One such idea was what he called the Puritan principle of segregation, the capacity, even of those who saw all life as enveloped by religion, to separate the secular from the religious—a principle at the centre of problems of freedom of conscience, toleration, and the relations of church and state.

Still more central and important and, when Woodhouse began to expound and emphasize it, more novel was the doctrine of "Christian liberty," which Luther and Calvin had carried on from St. Paul and which for some seventeenth-century Englishmen, notably Milton, could become dynamic and revolutionary individualism. In brief, this meant the abolition of the Mosaic law, an involuntary and partly ceremonial code suitable for the early Jews' degree of enlightenment, and the Christian acceptance of free grace, the full freedom given to the regenerate through faith in Christ and the inward law of love. Woodhouse sees Milton's exposition of inward Christian liberty as presented wholly in ethical terms and the Miltonic state of grace as an

4. *UTQ*, IV (1934–5), 483–518.

ethical condition rather than a spiritual experience; this is certainly true for much of Milton, perhaps for all, but one may be inclined to qualify the judgment when one thinks of the peculiar elevation and intensity of Milton's ethical passion, of his almost mystical phrases about God and light and order, of the exultant passage on Christian liberty near the end of *Paradise Lost* (all of which, of course, Milton's interpreter knew and had weighed). In the public sphere, Woodhouse's comparison of Milton and Roger Williams in this article and elsewhere—a comparison writers on Williams do not always seem to have assimilated—illuminates both men in showing how Milton's radicalism stopped short of the devoutly religious Williams' secular, egalitarian democracy; Milton the Renaissance humanist remained a classical republican, his "aristocratic" conception of the Platonic philosopher-king coalescing with the likewise "aristocratic" Puritan conception of "the saints."

Milton's was only one of many voices of the revolutionary era and Woodhouse's lecture of 1937 on "Puritanism and Democracy"[5] was a broader and fuller approximation to the introduction to *Puritanism and Liberty* and no less closely packed. In both, comprehensive and minute knowledge of the sources, controlled by discriminating insight, enabled Woodhouse to chart a sea of theory and opinion so complex and confusing in the variations of individuals and groups that a less strong-minded and stout-hearted explorer might well despair of achieving any intelligible order. But Woodhouse is so saturated in the pamphlets and ideas of the period, in the mentality of persons and parties, that he can in a way think like them and then interpret their thinking in the light of a philosophic modern historian's understanding. Naturally he brushes aside the facile formulas about Puritan "rationalizations" that find such ready acceptance among secular liberals who cannot comprehend religious motives. Instead, Woodhouse demonstrates how the central and constant vision of "the holy community" could inspire the most complex diversities in religious and political thought, and how logical apparent inconsistencies turn out to be. In this article there is further development of concepts that Woodhouse has made his own, Christian liberty, the principle of segregation, and—appearing perhaps for the first time—another version of the latter, "the dogma of the two orders," that is, nature and grace.

5. *Canadian Journal of Economics and Political Science*, IV (1938), 1–21.

This phrase, a larger and more suggestive formulation, is to furnish the key for later interpretations of poetry.

Puritanism and Liberty (1938; second edition, 1950) was recognized at once as a standard book, indispensable for anyone who would understand seventeenth-century Puritan thought, religious and political. While the texts reprinted are mainly those of the Army Debates of 1647–9 on the constitutional settlement, the twin questions of political democracy and religious liberty, the spectrum is filled out with supplementary extracts, carefully selected. In the controversial confusion after the civil war the large pattern of victorious Puritanism shows reactionary Presbyterianism on the right, liberal and progressive Independency in the centre, and miscellaneous radical sects and parties on the left; and, apart from all these, a loose group of secular Erastians. But within this general pattern and within parties, as we have noted already, there were endless variations; everyone who had the gift of utterance (and few men lacked it) had his own thoughts or visions to proclaim. In the 100-page introduction the main attitudes and ideas treated in Woodhouse's earlier articles naturally reappear, now further developed and set in a fuller context. All the general and some particular comments that were made on the articles may be emphasized and enlarged in their application to this work. The author's immediate task, a sufficiently difficult one, is to interpret the Army Debates and place them in their setting; but the introduction goes far beyond that and is, in fact, the most compendious, fully rounded, and closely discriminating analysis we have of mid-century Puritan beliefs, ideas, and modes of thought. In spite of the lucidity of the exposition, its specific gravity is so high that—to change metaphors—digestion requires more than one or two readings.

Woodhouse's chief later discussion of political thought has been "Religion and Some Foundations of English Democracy,"[6] in which the Puritans are overshadowed by Hooker—a figure in himself more congenial to Woodhouse's Anglican temper and strong sympathy with the tradition of Christian humanism. Apart from this, the paper on Romanticism already noticed, discussions of the humanities at large or in Canada, and several reviews, his writings in the last dozen years have been mainly Miltonic and mainly literary. One of these is of more scholarly than critical concern (though the distinction, in regard

6. *Philosophical Review*, LXI (1952), 503–31.

to Milton, is only relative). "Notes on Milton's Views on the Creation: The Initial Phases"[7] dealt with Milton's heretical view of the creation as *de Deo*, not *ex nihilo*, and with the striking religious and metaphysical implications of that doctrine. The very full "Notes on Milton's Early Development"[8] is also of mainly scholarly concern, although Woodhouse uses Milton's ideas and attitudes along with external evidence in his attempt to date and arrange in sequence a number of Milton's early poems and thus make coherent a partly cloudy phase of this poetic evolution. The weighing of imponderables and inferences drawn therefrom are necessarily tentative, but there are here, along with critical comments on Latin and English poems, some persuasive arguments which have somehow been neglected by scholars pursuing the same problems.

Discussing "practical criticism" with special reference to Milton,[9] Woodhouse laid down a simple and judicious principle: "The business of the critic of poetry is with the understanding and appreciation of individual poems and of a poet's total output as expressive of his mind." Understanding and appreciation "are mutually dependent," but the former stresses historical knowledge and relative objectivity, while the latter is inevitably more subjective. Woodhouse's approach to Milton's poetry is mainly historical, but it issues in the most substantial kind of appreciation. The first and probably the best-known and most discussed of his Miltonic critiques was "The Argument of Milton's *Comus*,"[10] which has been pronounced "within the limits of its defined purpose, the best study of the poem we know, the only commentary we could recommend as an indispensable aid to the reading of *Comus*,"[11] and "the most seminal influence on Milton criticism since Tillyard's *Milton* in 1930."[12] The essay is a cardinal example of the necessity and value of historical criticism, of setting forth a poet's

7. *PQ*, XXVIII (1949), 211–36.

8. *UTQ*, XIII (1942–3), 66–101.

9. "The Approach to Milton: A Note on Practical Criticism," *Transactions of the Royal Society of Canada*, Third Series, XXXVIII (1944), Section II, 201–13. A later extension was "The Historical Criticism of Milton," *PMLA* LXVI (1951), 1033–44.

10. *UTQ*, XI (1941–2), 46–71; supplemented by "*Comus* Once More," *UTQ*, XIX (1949–50), 218–23.

11. Cleanth Brooks and J. E. Hardy, *Poems of Mr. John Milton* (New York, 1951), 235–6.

12. W. G. Madsen, "The Idea of Nature in Milton's Poetry," *Three Studies in the Renaissance: Sidney, Jonson, Milton*, by R. B. Young, W. T. Furniss, and W. G. Madsen (Yale University Press, 1958), 214.

assumptions, his intellectual frame of reference, which in his own time he could take for granted but which must be rebuilt for modern readers. Here that frame of reference is what Woodhouse had already designated as "the dogma of the two orders" of nature and grace. These two orders had been a primary fact of consciousness throughout the Christian tradition; no educated person could be unaware of the gulf between the natural light of pagan reason and the illumination of Christian truth, a gulf which Christian humanists had always tried to bridge by making pagan reason and the rational pagan virtues stepping stones to Christian virtue and faith. But, however familiar this general tradition, Woodhouse was the first to formulate it in full, explicit, and usable terms and apply it directly to *Comus*. (Milton himself, in the *Apology for Smectymnuus* of 1642, was quite open in relating "the noblest morality" of the pagans, Plato above all, to Christian teaching.) Woodhouse sees in *Comus* a triple equation: temperance or continence, which belongs to the order of nature; chastity, which is grounded in nature but, in Platonic terms, approaches the level of grace; and virginity, the illustration and symbol of purely Christian grace. Some readers find this scheme more elaborate and specific than Milton's text seems to warrant and would ask if he makes a clear distinction between chastity and virginity. However, even with such a possible reservation the essay loses little of its enlightening quality. Since it is so well known, one need not attempt a summary—and, as I remarked before, it is hard to summarize Woodhouse's closely wrought expositions. Among other things, he completely extinguishes the not uncommon notion that Milton's conception of chastity, of virtue, was austerely negative; on the contrary, it was positive and glowing. A more special point is the first explicit interpretation of the difficult epilogue. Another special point was added in a later note, the idea that Sabrina is a symbol of grace. This is a brilliantly logical intuition and certainly what Milton should have meant, though one may not feel quite sure that he did mean that, since the chief local legend provided a graceful ending and since Sabrina is enveloped in mythological reference to a degree rather beyond even the large freedom of Christian poetry of the Renaissance. But perhaps such objections are not strong enough to stand against so persuasive a suggestion.

The theme of this article and references in it to Spenser invite us to digress from the Miltonic path and take in a Johns Hopkins lecture of 1949, "Nature and Grace in *The Faerie Queene*."[13] For Spenser, as for Milton and other men, the dual order was a central and all-embracing fact, and he himself had signalized both the difference and the measure of affinity by making Holiness and Temperance the themes of the partly parallel narratives of his first two books. In interpreting Spenser's conception and delineation of the Christian and classical orders and virtues, Woodhouse shows his usual concern for precise definition, since essential points may not be manifest to modern readers unversed in theology. Thus when Arthur rescues the Red Cross Knight from Orgoglio's dungeon, the act signifies the infusion of grace into the will of the sinner; when, however, Arthur protects the prostrate Guyon from enemies, he represents, not grace, but magnanimity (his normal role) and also the intervention of Providence in the natural order. One new, brilliant, and wholly convincing idea is that the diseased, grisly, and almost invincible Maleger, captain of the band attacking the house of Alma (mind and body), symbolizes original sin; his strength is renewed by contact with earth, and he is destroyed only when cast into the water (of baptism). Since all fresh and good criticism provokes queries, one may question Woodhouse's putting his thesis or hypothesis as a complete dichotomy: that grace operates only in book one, nature (sometimes with Providence as ally) everywhere else. His own interpretation of Maleger, a figure in the book of classical temperance, makes one admitted and striking exception, and there may be one or two other arguable cases, such as Britomart. But, even if one hesitates over a few particulars, the study has the great value of providing a point of view that clarifies and enriches our reading of Spenser and adds dimensions and subtleties that we might easily miss.

To return to Milton, in "Milton's Pastoral Monodies"[14] Woodhouse treated two poems in which Milton characteristically focused "upon the drama of his own existence," both representative of his double inheritance, classical and Christian. In the relatively impersonal *Lycidas* and the directly personal *Epitaphium Damonis*, as in *Comus* and indeed all Milton's major poems, experience poses a problem

13. *ELH*, XVI (1949), 194–228.

14. *Studies in Honour of Gilbert Norwood* (University of Toronto Press, 1952), 261–78.

"demanding to be either solved or transcended" and generating "an emotional tension requiring to be resolved." And in both elegies Milton employed what the pastoral tradition fully sanctioned, "a species of allegory which is midway between direct statement and dramatic projection." The account of *Lycidas*, though short, is one of the best-rounded discussions of that complex and much-discussed poem, notably of its mingled classical and Christian strains. But the explication of the *Epitaphium*, probably the fullest and freshest the poem has ever had, is more provocative. Woodhouse's analysis of structure, texture, and symbolism almost convinces me that the *Epitaphium* is a much better poem than I am able to think it is.

Woodhouse's central concern with theme and structure is in tacit opposition to the recent tendency to emphasize imagery at the cost of more basic elements. This concern governs his essays on the three late and long works. In "The Pattern of *Paradise Lost*"[15] he starts as usual from firm and familiar ground, in this case the premise that "Milton's principal models were Homer and Virgil, and that what he was attempting was a classical epic poem on a Christian subject." But Woodhouse does not take the commonplace road. He illustrates Milton's sense of design in two microcosmic passages—Eve's asseveration of her love for Adam (IV, 634–58) and the invocation to Light (III, 1–55)—and goes on to the design of the whole and to thematic and structural comparisons with the ancient epics. Here again the orders of nature and grace serve as a basis. Since Milton's theme is Christian, his poem is a divine comedy, though with "ample provision for tragic episodes." In his conception of Providence and in his structural pattern Milton is closer to Virgil than to Homer—and also in the prophetic pictures of human history in Books XI–XII, even if, as individual pictures, they resemble those on the shield of Achilles. *Paradise Lost* has two protagonists, the earthly Adam and the heavenly Christ, who redeems what Adam lost. As for Satan, Milton does not abandon "the pagan standard of the heroic"; "in Satan it is presented, judged, and condemned." The poem as a whole is true to its title in concentrating upon the fall of man, not his recovery, though it ends on the note of "peace with hope."

Coming to *Paradise Regained*,[16] Woodhouse aims as usual at the

15. *UTQ*, XXII (1952–3), 109–27.
16. "Theme and Pattern in *Paradise Regained*," *UTQ*, XXV (1955–6), 167–82.

centre of the target and his essay is a pretty complete guide to the reading of this shorter poem. He feels no need of defending a work that has been relatively disparaged ever since it was published, and his assumptions concerning its very Miltonic power are quietly borne out by fresh comment on theme, structure, and some significant details. One example of pregnant succinctness is his summary of the climactic temptation, which resolves the dramatic tension of the whole by revealing Christ's true identity to both Satan and himself:

> Satan's intention is that Christ shall fall and the result will answer his question. His injunction to stand is purely ironical: that it is possible, he never for a moment conceives. But if Satan can be ironical, so can Christ and the event. For the first and only time, he complies with Satan's suggestion; but it is not in surrender to Satan: it is in obedience to God—like Samson's going to the festival of Dagon. This is Christ's supreme act of obedience and trust, and it is also the long-awaited demonstration of divinity. The poem's two themes are finally and securely united; and "Tempt not the Lord thy God" carries a double meaning, for, in addition to its immediate application, it is Christ's first claim to participate in the Godhead. In an instant, and by the same event, Satan receives his answer and Christ achieves full knowledge of himself.

Two essays on *Samson Agonistes,* of 1949 and 1958, go together and their titles indicate their respective emphasis.[17] Woodhouse would date the tragedy in 1660–1, as against both the traditional 1667–70 and the recent (and surely quite untenable) arguments for 1646–8 or 1652–3. His reasons are that Milton's personal experience in 1660–1 would best explain the mood of *Samson,* which is out of key with the settled equanimity of his later years, and that that date would make acceptable what seem to be clear topical and personal allusions; Woodhouse concedes that the drama might have sprung from a later temporary depression and might therefore be what conventional opinion has made it, Milton's last work (which seems to me a somewhat preferable view). In any case the drama links itself with the two epics in its theme of "temptation, disobedience, repentance, obedience, restoration," though here "the whole series is run through in the person of the hero." All three works are assertions of eternal Providence, and when Milton composed *Samson* such an assertion

17. "*Samson Agonistes* and Milton's Experience," *Transactions of the Royal Society of Canada,* Third Series, XLIII (1949), Section II, 157–75; "Tragic Effect in *Samson Agonistes,*" *UTQ* XXVIII (1958–9), 205–22.

would test even his invincible faith. In the first essay on *Samson* Woodhouse considers the degree to which Milton's experience is projected and sublimated in the drama—not that he set out on dramatic autobiography but that his chosen theme kindled and was kindled by thoughts of his nation's and his own heroic past and of the ignoble Restoration. Woodhouse, with conscious temerity, suggests that Samson's sin and confession of sin reflect Milton's retrospective view of his own disastrous first marriage.

Remarks in the first essay on *Samson* as a Christian tragedy in Greek form are enlarged in the second. Some critics have denied the general possibility of a Christian tragedy because faith in Providence or in heaven would rule that out; but Woodhouse makes clear how such faith can accommodate what are, in a limited human view, tragic events. "If he [Samson] is an instrument of Providence, he does not cease to be an individual, fallible, though corrigible, heroic—and by his own action doomed." Milton works on the human level before invoking the providential, and in this Hebraic drama he does not invoke any hope of heaven. Samson and Hamlet alike perish at last in giving effect to the moral order. "They are on the side of the power—the overruling power—which destroys them." Milton "has made the way of repentance and restoration, the way back to God, also the way that leads inevitably to the catastrophe, and has thus achieved at a stroke the only kind of irony that is at once compatible with a Christian outlook and as potent as any to be found in tragedy anywhere."

Attitudes and ideas assumed or expounded throughout these Miltonic essays are drawn together in the first Sedgewick Memorial Lecture, "Milton the Poet," delivered at the University of British Columbia in 1955.[18] Perhaps the most basic premise of all Woodhouse's Miltonic criticism is the unity of Milton's personal, aesthetic, and religious experience. Some general facts and ideas summarized in this lecture are: Milton's "strong sense of literary tradition and of genre"; his originality, which recreates traditional forms; his feeling for aesthetic pattern and for what that is woven upon, "a firm structural framework" (and these are not static but dynamic and progressive). A more general principle, of a poem as the realization of experience, holds for any poet, but for Milton in a special way as

18. Published as a pamphlet by Dent (Toronto, 1955).

conditioned by the instincts and gifts already indicated: an "extra-aesthetic experience, problematic and productive of tension," is objectified in a poem but reviewed "in the light of the poet's profounder convictions, which likewise receive poetic utterance; and the result is the transcending of the problem. But both steps are taken under the impetus of an aesthetic pattern; and it is not enough to say that the problem is transcended: the emotional tension is also resolved." Woodhouse then goes on to analyse the various workings of such principles in Milton's poems. Ideas that we have met before are compressed into a compendious whole; they can be because they have developed so coherently in the critic's mind—a process brought home to one by the consecutive re-reading of the whole series of essays. The lecture is thus a "short view" of the results of Woodhouse's long and penetrating study of Milton and his age. It is also of special interest because its opening is a statement of his own position in respect to current critical fashions—a statement enlivened by the urbane and incisive wit that sprinkles Attic salt and pepper over his conversation.

It might be wished that these Miltonic essays had been collected long ago, and one may still hope; at any rate Woodhouse will be discussing and annotating all the minor poems in the Variorum Commentary that is in prospect. One volume that will doubtless soon appear, and will take in Spenser and Milton and much else, I can only refer to. That is the lectures on religion in English poetry, delivered in Cincinnati in 1962 as the inaugural series on the Weil foundation.

Woodhouse's long and large services, in action and in print, to the study of the humanities in Canada would demand another paper. This rapid and most inadequate survey of his writings on history and literature cannot begin to suggest how much he has taught students of all ages on several continents. He has been equally strong as an historical analyst of ideas and as a critic of poetry, and these two faculties, not often found together, have strengthened each other. His writings combine active learning, philosophic breadth and depth, and aesthetic insight—both "wit" and "judgment," in the old sense, in a rare and happy balance—and these virtues are all fructified and warmed by an understanding of Milton in particular that is at once profoundly sympathetic and wholly candid.

The qualities of mind and character that are the strength of Woodhouse's writing are no less, it may be assumed, the strength of his classroom teaching. In two general discourses on the humanities he started, characteristically, from history and worked up to the elements of both continuity and change in the modern study of literature.[19] Characteristic also was his refusal to leave the plane of sober fact and dispassionate thought for emotional and inspirational rhapsody. It is not, he affirms, the function of a humanist to indoctrinate, to try to spiritualize the community, but to expound his authors as best he can and let their art and wisdom do their own work. Among the major groups of disciplines only the humanities have as their "sole purpose the general cultivation of mind and sensibility which was the traditional end of liberal education." The writings of Arthur Woodhouse achieve that end.

19. "The Nature and Function of the Humanities," *Transactions of the Royal Society of Canada*, Third Series, XLVI (1952), Section II, 1–17; "The Place of Literature in the Humanities," *Man and Learning in Modern Society* (University of Washington Press, 1959), 111–25.

Publications of A. S. P. Woodhouse

M. H. M. MACKINNON

BOOKS

Puritanism and Liberty, being the Army Debates (1647–49) from the Clarke Manuscript, with Supplementary Documents, selected and edited with an introduction by A. S. P. Woodhouse. Foreword by A. D. Lindsay (London: J. M. Dent, 1938, reprinted 1951). Pp. 506.

The Humanities in Canada. Watson Kirkconnell and A. S. P. Woodhouse. (Ottawa: Humanities Research Council of Canada, 1947). Pp. 287.

Milton the Poet. Sedgewick Memorial Lecture at the University of British Columbia. (Toronto and Vancouver: University of British Columbia and J. M. Dent, 1955). Pp. 30.

*ARTICLES**

"Collins and Martin Martin." *TLS*, Dec. 20, 1928, p. 1011.

"Thomas Warton and the 'Ode to Horror.'" *TLS*, Jan. 24, 1929, p. 62; May 23, 1929, p. 420.

"Imitation of the 'Ode to Evening.'" *TLS*, May 30, 1929, p. 436.

**AHR*, American Historical Review; *CJEPS*, Canadian Journal of Economics and Political Science; *EHR*, English Historical Review; *ELH*, English Literary History; *JEGP*, Journal of English and Germanic Philology; *MLN*, Modern Language Notes; *MLR*, Modern Language Review; *PQ*, Philological Quarterly; *PR*, Philosophical Review; *QQ*, Queen's Quarterly; *RES*, Review of English Studies; *TLS*, Times Literary Supplement; *Trans. RSC*, Transactions of the Royal Society of Canada; *UTQ*, University of Toronto Quarterly.

"Collins in the Eighteenth Century." *TLS*, Oct. 16, 1930, p. 838.

"Collins and the Creative Imagination: A Study in the Critical Background of his Odes (1746)." In *Studies in English*, by members of University College, Toronto, ed. Malcolm W. Wallace. (Toronto: University of Toronto Press, 1931). Pp. 59–130.

"Milton, Puritanism and Liberty." *UTQ*, IV (1934–5), 483–513.

"Puritanism and Democracy." *CJEPS*, IV (1938), 1–21.

"The Argument of Milton's *Comus*." *UTQ*, XI (1941–2), 46–71.

"Notes on Milton's Early Development." *UTQ*, XIII (1942–3), 66–101.

"The Approach to Milton: A Note on Practical Criticism." *Trans. RSC*, Third Series, XXXVIII (1944), Section II, 201–13.

"In Memoriam, William John Alexander: Critic and Teacher." *UTQ*, XIV (1944–5), 8–32.

"Charles Norris Cochrane." *Trans. RSC*, Third Series, XL (1946), 83–7.

"Undergraduate and Graduate Studies." In *Report of the National Conference of Canadian Universities*, Toronto, May 27–29, 1946. (Toronto: 1946). Pp. 81–2.

"Research in the Humanities." In *The Humanities Research Council of Canada, 2nd Report* (for period 1947–9). 1949. Pp. 18–24.

"Nature and Grace in *The Faerie Queene*." *ELH*, XVI (1949), 194–228.

"Notes on Milton's Views on the Creation: The Initial Phases." *PQ*, XXVIII (1949), 211–36.

"*Comus* Once More." *UTQ*, XIX (1949–50), 218–23.

"*Samson Agonistes* and Milton's Experience." *Trans. RSC*, Third Series, XLIII (1949), Section II, 157–75.

"William Robert Taylor: 1882–1951." *Trans. RSC*, Third Series, XL (1951), 115–16.

"Romanticism and the History of Ideas." In *English Studies Today*, Papers read at the International Conference of University Professors of English, Oxford, 1950, ed. C. L. Wrenn and G. Bullough. (London: Oxford University Press, 1951). Pp. 120–40.

"The Historical Criticism of Milton," *PMLA*, LXVI (1951), 1033–44. Reprinted with minor revisions in *The Modern Critical Spec-*

trum, ed. Gerald J. and Nancy M. Goldberg. (Englewood Cliffs, N.J.: Prentice-Hall), 1962. Pp. 233–43.

"Religion and Some Foundations of English Democracy." *PR*, LXI (1952), 503–31.

"The Nature and Function of the Humanities." *Trans. RSC*, Third Series, XLVI (1952), Section II, 1–17.

"Milton's Pastoral Monodies." In *Studies in Honour of Gilbert Norwood*, ed. Mary E. White. (Toronto: University of Toronto Press, 1952). Pp. 261–78.

"Pattern in *Paradise Lost*." *UTQ*, XXII (1952–3), 109–27.

"Chairman's Report." *Humanities Research Council of Canada, 4th Report* (for period 1951–3). 1953. Pp. 3–4.

"The Humanities—Sixty Years." *QQ*, LX (1953), 538–50.

"Staff, 1890–1953." In *University College: A Portrait, 1853–1953*, ed. C. T. Bissell. (Toronto: University of Toronto Press, 1953). Pp. 51–83.

"Gilbert Norwood." *Trans. RSC*, Third Series, XLIX (1955), 117–21.

"Nature and Grace in Spenser: A Rejoinder." *RES*, VI (1955), 284–8.

"Theme and Pattern in *Paradise Regained*." *UTQ*, XXV (1955–6), 167–82.

"Humanities," *Encyclopaedia Britannica*, 1957.

"The Humanities." In *Canada's Crisis in Higher Education*, Proceedings of a Conference held by the National Conference of Canadian Universities, Ottawa, November 12–14, 1956, ed. C. T. Bissell. (Toronto: University of Toronto Press, 1957). Pp. 127–47.

"Human Values and the Evolution of Society." In *Our Debt to the Future*, Royal Society of Canada Symposium presented on the Seventy-Fifth Anniversary, 1957, ed. E. G. D. Murray. (Toronto: University of Toronto Press, 1958), 107–11.

"Some Reflections on How to Read Milton." *Seventeenth Century News*, XVI (1958), 8–9.

"Universities: Historical Development," *Encyclopaedia Canadiana*, 1958.

"English Study in the English-Language Universities" (with R. S. Harris), *Encyclopaedia Canadiana*, 1958.

"The Place of Literature in the Humanities." In *Man and Learning in Modern Society*, Papers and Addresses delivered at the Inauguration of Charles E. Odegaard as President of the University of Washington, November 6 and 7, 1958. (Seattle: University of Washington Press, 1959). Pp. 111–25.

"Chairman's Report." *Humanities Research Council of Canada, 6th Report* (for period 1957–9). 1959. Pp. 3–7.

"Tragic Effect in *Samson Agonistes*," *UTQ*, XXVIII (1958–9), 205–22.

"The Humanities in Canada, 1959." *Bulletin of the Humanities Association of Canada* (Oct., 1959), 10–17.

"Spenser, Nature and Grace: Mr. Gang's Mode of Argument Reviewed." *ELH*, XXVII (1960), 1–15.

REVIEWS AND REVIEW ARTICLES

A. S. Turberville, *Johnson's England*. *UTQ*, III (1933–4), 396–404.

William Haller, ed., *Tracts on Liberty in the Puritan Revolution, 1638–1647*. Review entitled "Puritanism and Liberty." *UTQ*, IV (1934–5), 395–404.

"Milton and His Age." *UTQ*, V (1935–6), 130–9. (Reviews books by J. H. Hanford, Arthur Sewell, Basil Willey, Perry Miller, P. E. More, V. de Sola Pinto.)

A. O. Lovejoy, *The Great Chain of Being*. *JEGP*, XXXVIII (1938), 109–14.

E. G. Ainsworth Jr., *Poor Collins, his Life, his Art, and Influence*. *JEGP*, XXVIII (1938), 116–18.

"Pope and the Tides of Taste." *UTQ*, VIII (1938–9), 461–67. (Reviews books by R. K. Root, G. Tillotson, B. S. Allen, H. N. Fairchild.)

W. Haller, *The Rise of Puritanism*. *AHR*, XLV (1939), 123–5.

A. Sewell, *A Study in Milton's "Christian Doctrine*." *MLR*, XXXIV (1939), 593–6.

J. W. Allen. *English Political Thought, 1603–1660*. *EHR* (1939), 731–4.

"The Plain Man and the War." *UTQ*, IX (1939–40), 231–8.

"Background for Milton." *UTQ*, X (1940–1), 499–505. (Reviews books by M. M. Knappen, W. K. Jordan, D. M. Wolfe, G. W. Whiting, F. A. Patterson.)

H. E. Fletcher, *The Complete Poetical Works of John Milton*. *JEGP*, XLI (1942), 99–102.

R. M. Davis, *The Good Lord Lyttelton*. *MLN*, LVII (1942), 298–9.

D. M. Wolfe, *Milton and the Puritan Revolution*. *JEGP*, XLI (1942), 102–5.

M. Kelley, *This Great Argument*. *PR*, LII (1943), 206–8.

"Milton Today." A review article, part of a section entitled "On Milton's Poetry." *UTQ*, XIII (1943–4), 462–7. (Reviews books by L. P. Smith, C. Williams, C. S. Lewis, E. M. W. Tillyard, R. Graves.)

"Seventeenth-Century Radicals." *UTQ*, XV (1945–46), 98–101. (Reviews books by W. Haller and G. Davies, D. M. Wolfe, Z. S. Fink.)

"Time and *Paradise Lost*." *UTQ*, XV (1945–6), 200–5. (Reviews books by D. M. Saurat, C. M. Bowra, D. Bush, G. R. Hamilton, E. E. Stoll.)

J. S. Diekhoff, *Milton's "Paradise Lost": A Commentary on the Argument*. Review entitled "The Argument of *Paradise Lost*." *UTQ*, XVI (1946–7), 433–5.

W. J. Bate, *From Classic to Romantic*. *UTQ*, XVI (1946–7), 94–8.

B. Rajan, *"Paradise Lost" and the Seventeenth-Century Reader*. Review entitled "Milton and his Readers." *UTQ*, XVIII (1948–9), 202–5.

A. O. Lovejoy, *Essays in the History of Ideas*. Review entitled "Professor Lovejoy and the History of Ideas." *UTQ*, XIX (1949–50), 190–4.

F. M. Krouse, *Milton's Samson and the Christian Tradition*. *MLN*, LXVI (1951), 116–18.

J. M. French, *The Life Records of John Milton*, vol. I. Review entitled "Milton Day-to-Day." *UTQ*, XXI (1951–2), 193–6.

F. R. Leavis, ed., *Mill on Bentham and Coleridge*. Review entitled "Brighton Pier." *UTQ*, XXI (1952), 318–20.

M. H. Abrams, *The Mirror and the Lamp*. *MLN*, LXX (1955), 374–7.

R. Wellek, *A History of Modern Criticism: 1750–1950*. Review entitled "History of Criticism for our Time." *UTQ*, XXV (1955–6), 507–10.

J. J. Cope, *Joseph Glanvil, Anglican Apologist. MLN*, LXXIII (1958), 436–9.

H. N. Brailsford, *The Levellers and the English Revolution. Church History*, XXXI, No. 4 (December, 1962), 467–8.

Robert Hoopes, *Right Reason in the English Renaissance. MLR*, LIX (1964), 102–3.

LETTERS IN CANADA

Professor Woodhouse served as general editor of this annual survey of Canadian writing from 1936 to 1942, from 1943 to 1947, and again in 1954. As editor he wrote each year the Introduction and also contributed, with some assistance from his colleagues, the section "Remaining Material."

The volume and page references of *UTQ* for "Letters in Canada" for the years in question are:

V (1935–6), 359–456.
VI (1936–7), 338–460; 558–600.
VII (1937–38), 339–450; 552–600.
VIII (1938–9, 293–384; 479–511.
IX (1939–40), 282–395.
X (1940–41), 283–399.
XI (1941–42), 287–388; 475–518.
XIII (1943–44), 306–365; 424–461.
XIV (1944–45), 261–328.
XV (1945–46), 269–332; 397–429.
XVI (1946–47), 246–340.
XXIV (1954–55), 247–340.

Acknowledgments

THE EDITORS are most grateful to the authors of these essays for their interest and co-operation in the making of this book, and we share with them our obligation to the Editor of the University of Toronto Press, Miss F. G. Halpenny, a former student of Professor Woodhouse, who has given us expert assistance in the preparation of the manuscripts for printing, and has overseen all stages of the production of the book.

We acknowledge also our indebtedness to the Publications Fund of the University of Toronto Press and the Alumni–Alumnae Giving Fund of University College for grants in aid of publication.

www.ingramcontent.com/pod-product-compliance
Lightning Source LLC
Chambersburg PA
CBHW060620100726
47907CB00006B/1701